REMEMBERING NICAEA

WRITINGS FROM THE GRECO-ROMAN WORLD

General Editors
John T. Fitzgerald and Clare K. Rothschild

Editorial Board
Theodore de Bruyn
Andrew Cain
Margaret M. Mitchell
Teresa Morgan
David T. Runia
Karin Schlapbach

Number 52
Volume Editor
William Adler

REMEMBERING NICAEA

The *Ecclesiastical History*
of Anonymous Cyzicenus

Introduction and translation by
Martin Shedd, Sean Tandy, and Jeremy M. Schott

Copyright © 2024 by SBL Press

All rights reserved. No part of this work may be reproduced or transmitted in any form or by any means, electronic or mechanical, including photocopying and recording, or by means of any information storage or retrieval system, except as may be expressly permitted by the 1976 Copyright Act or in writing from the publisher. Requests for permission should be addressed in writing to the Rights and Permissions Office, SBL Press, 825 Houston Mill Road, Atlanta, GA 30329 USA.

Library of Congress Control Number: 2024909366

Contents

Acknowledgments vii
Preface ix
Abbreviations and Sigla xiii

Introduction 1
   1. The Misattribution to "Gelasius of Cyzicus"   1
   2. Situating Anonymous Cyzicenus and the *Ecclesiastical History*   4
   3. The Contents and Structure of the *Ecclesiastical History*   7
   4. Defending Chalcedon, Memorializing Nicaea   12
   5. Cyzicenus's Theology   15
   6. Anonymous Cyzicenus and His Sources   25
   7. Text and Reception   41

Translators' Note 49

A Treatise on the Holy Council of Nicaea 53

The Second Treatise of the *Ecclesiastical History* 83

The Third Treatise of the *Ecclesiastical History* 211

Appendix 1. The Byzantine Epistolary Supplement 273

Appendix 2. The *Pinakes* for Book 3 291

Appendix 3. The Testimony of Photius 295

Appendix 4. The 1599 *Editio Princeps* and the Attribution
   to "Gelasius of Cyzicus" 301

Works Cited
    Works on The *Ecclesiastical History* 305
    General Bibliography 306

Scriptural Passages Index 313
People and Places Index 318

Acknowledgments

This project began as a Friday afternoon Byzantine Greek reading group, housed at the former Scholars Inn Bakehouse in Bloomington, Indiana. Much gratitude is owed to the initial members of the group, whose enthusiasm for the oddities of the text convinced us it was a project worth pursuing. Also critical to our continued motivation were the baristas of the Scholars Inn Bakehouse, Needmore Coffee, Soma Coffee Shop, The Inkwell, Hopscotch Coffee, Rainbow Bakery, Brilliant Coffee Company, Runcible Spoon, Sofra Café, The Campus Café (Wells Library), Round Mountain Coffee, and Blue Sail Coffee. Enough gratitude cannot be expressed to our partners and families, who supported us through this project and often served as sounding boards for perplexing problems.

We benefited greatly from the conversation, advice, and fellowship of many colleagues during our work on this project. John Walbridge was crucial for helping us formulate the project as we transitioned from a casual reading group to a team focused on a scholarly translation, with much good advice on how to approach the challenge. Bill Adler's keen editorial eye and critical questions vastly improved the quality of our final translation. David Maldonado Rívera provided especially helpful feedback on the introduction. Our research assistant through the final stretch, Katie Shy, masterfully combined the notes and directions from three (at times exacting) scholars and saved us from many an error. Any that remain are entirely of our own making.

Portions of the research for this project were supported by an Indiana University New Frontiers Exploratory Travel Fellowship. Some of the early research, particularly into the transmission and reception of the text, took place during Sean Tandy's tenure as a Rome Prize fellow at the American Academy in Rome. The time to think and work provided by the academy, as well as the thoughtful comments and suggestions of the other Rome Prize fellows (particularly Talia di Manno and Denis Robichaud), greatly contributed to the shaping of this volume. Parts of the final editing process were completed during Martin Shedd's tenure as the Society for Classical Studies fellow to the Thesaurus Linguae Latinae, funded by the National Endowment for the Humanities. Any views, findings, conclusions, or recommendations expressed in this volume do not necessarily reflect those of the National Endowment for the Humanities.

Preface

The text presented in this volume largely has been neglected by historians of early Christian thought and culture as well as scholars of late antiquity more generally. On the one hand, this disinterest is understandable. As a self-described compilation (*proem.* 24), the text offers little in the way of innovative theology or new historical insights. Much of the text summarizes or repeats verbatim other, better-known texts, such as the histories of Eusebius, Theodoret, and Socrates. On the other hand, the text merits study precisely as a compilation. To put it succinctly, the *Ecclesiastical History* attributed to "Gelasius of Cyzicus" is most important not as a factual source on the emperor Constantine or the Council of Nicaea but as a case study in the ways the council and Nicene orthodoxy were imagined and constructed during the theological controversies ongoing in the late fifth century.[1]

The present volume therefore seeks to rectify the neglect of the *Ecclesiastical History* by placing the text back into its late fifth-century context. Compilations in general are not neutral collections of past textual fragments but rather are motivated by contemporary ideological concerns. This particular compilation explicitly states these concerns. The author claims to have created the text in order to prove that the true heirs to the Council of Nicaea (325 CE) were those who supported the decisions of the Council of Chalcedon (451 CE), whom he labels orthodox, rather than the opponents of Chalcedon, the so-called Eutychians, whom he has been encountering (*proem.* 9–13). The author also suggests that his image of Constantine should serve as a model for Christian Roman emperors, their theology, and their interactions with the church (see, e.g., *proem.* 1; 1.10.10; 3.1.1–5). To fulfill these purposes, he takes excerpts from earlier

---

1. In seeing historical texts about Constantine less as sources for facts of his life than as windows into the authors' times, methods, and goals, we follow in the footsteps of Kazhdan 1987; Lieu 1996, 2012; and several excellent contributions in Bjornlie 2017.

writers—sometimes altering the words of the text—and juxtaposes them in order to create a new narrative that imagines Nicaea as an indisputable precursor to Chalcedon and portrays Constantine as an unwaveringly pious, orthodox emperor. In this way the *Ecclesiastical History* demonstrates the importance of the Christian past to a Christian present and the power of historical narratives in contemporary debates.

This does not mean that the *Ecclesiastical History* is valueless for historical studies of the Council of Nicaea. One of the letters that scholars use to understand the Arian controversy, the central theological debate at Nicaea, survives only in the *Ecclesiastical History* (3.15.1–5; *Urk.* 32). Other letters survive in few independent sources, making the versions preserved in this text essential for comparison.[2] The *Ecclesiastical History* also features the earliest Greek version of the canons of Nicaea (2.32). This document may have been transmitted through the *Ecclesiastical History* of Gelasius (2018, 13–21), the bishop of Caesarea, whose complete account has been lost but is known to us through the testimony of several Byzantine bibliophiles, including the patriarch Photius. Comparison to other historical texts shows that our text borrows heavily from a document-rich historical source that scholars generally identify as the Gelasius's (2018, xlv–l) history, making this *Ecclesiastical History* crucial for understanding the scope and purpose of its lost source.[3] The *Ecclesiastical History* thus furnishes evidence from earlier Christian historians who also fashioned their own versions of Nicaea's legacy. One of the more interesting examples of this is the Dispute with Phaedo, a long dialogue apparently taken from an unknown earlier source that dramatizes a debate between an Arian philosopher and the church fathers attending the Council of Nicaea. This document appears in no other surviving text, and neither do three other unique texts preserved in this account: a long speech at the start of the council attributed to Constantine, possibly derived from another lost historical text by Philip of Side (2.7.1–41; Hansen 1998; Heyden 2006), a

---

2. For example, *Urk.* 28 survives only in Athanasius's *De decretis* and the epistolary appendix to the *Ecclesiastical History* (see appendix 1); *Urk.* 4b, 25, 27, 31, 33, 34 survive in three sources, including the present text.

3. Van Nuffelen (2002) reopened debate on the *Ecclesiastical History* of Gelasius with an important rereading of the evidence, suggesting that the source shared by Anonymous Cyzicenus and the fifth-century ecclesiastical historians was actually a mid-fifth-century composition that drew from Rufinus and Socrates and was circulated pseudonymously under the name Gelasius of Caesarea. If Van Nuffelen is correct, then Anonymous Cyzicenus was drawing on this pseudonymous composition.

confession of faith purportedly spoken by Hosius of Cordoba (*Hist. eccl.* 2.12), and a list of regulations of the church supposedly ratified by the council (2.31).

Beyond its value as a repository of lost texts and as an example of the creative use of the past in post-Chalcedonian Christian controversies, the *Ecclesiastical History* is significant for its subsequent reception in Byzantium. In the ninth century, the patriarch Photius read a copy that presented the text as if it were the official minutes and proceedings, or *acta*, of the Council of Nicaea (Photius, *Bibl.* cod. 15). Later Byzantine authors paired the *Ecclesiastical History* with the genuine *acta* from the Council of Ephesus, and some authors even quoted from the Dispute with Phaedo with the citation formula "from the *acta* of the Council of Nicaea."[4] Three letters of Constantine concerning the Arian controversy and its aftermath were attached early on to the end of the second book of the history in order to compile these related documents together. In short, the *Ecclesiastical History* successfully reimagined the first ecumenical council in a way that continued to appeal to subsequent generations of Greek-speaking, pro-Nicene Christians and, eventually, when the text came to Western Europe in the fifteenth century, Catholics of the Counter-Reformation.

Our translation, the first published in English and only the second in a modern language,[5] includes the surviving portions of all three books of the *Ecclesiastical History* with explanatory footnotes analyzing the author's manipulation of sources, as well as points of theological and historical interest. In order to guide the reader through the patchwork of source material and highlight Cyzicenus's authorial voice, we mark passages borrowed from other sources by offsetting them from the framing narrative. This narrative describes, in order, how Constantine established a "peace of the church" (book 1), how the fathers at Nicaea debated with heretics and established "orthodoxy" (book 2), and how the machinations of Arius's supporters crumbled before the piety of Constantine as well as the efforts of Athanasius to support Nicene orthodoxy (book 3). Also included in this volume are four appendixes essential for understanding the text: three letters that Byzantine and early modern copies of the text always

---

4. For Byzantine authors quoting the text as "from the acts of the first council" (ἐκ τῶν πρακτικῶν τῆς πρώτης συνόδου), see Hansen 2002, x n. 1, and also the critical apparatus for the Dispute with Phaedo, 50–82. For the text being paired with the Acts of the Council of Ephesus, see xii–xiii.

5. The first was Hansen's (2008) German translation.

include (appendix 1); the Byzantine *pinakes*—content listings—for book 3, which include information crucial to reconstructing the lost ending of the *Ecclesiastical History* (appendix 2); selections from the *Bibliotheca* of the patriarch Photius, whose description of the text is the only independent testimony for our history and whose summary also provides details for reconstructing the lost ending (appendix 3); and a letter from publisher Fédéric Morel to translator Robert Balfour explaining why their forthcoming edition of the previously anonymous work would bear the name Gelasius (appendix 4). In the introduction that follows, we explain the critical questions surrounding the *Ecclesiastical History* attributed to "Gelasius of Cyzicus," including the background to the theological controversies of the late fifth century, the author's sources, and the overall structure and plan of the history. But first we begin with the shadowy figure of the author himself, explaining why we have placed scare quotes around the name "Gelasius of Cyzicus."

Abbreviations and Sigla

ACO	Schwartz, Eduard, and Johannes Straub. 1914–1984. *Acta Conciliorum Oecumenicorum*. 4 vols. Berlin: de Gruyter.
Alex.	Plutarch, *Alexander*
Anab.	Arrian, *Anabasis*
AnBoll	Analecta Bollandiana
Apol.	Plato, *Apologia*
Apol. Const.	Athanasius, *Apologia ad Constantium*
Apol. sec.	Athanasius, *Apologia secunda* (= *Apologia contra Arianos*)
As. Mos.	Assumption of Moses
BAI	*Bulletin of the Asia Institute*
BHG	*Bibliotheca Hagiographica Graeca*
BHG 185	Life of Athanasius
BHG 1279	Life of Metrophanes and Alexander
Bibl.	Photius, *Bibliotheca*
ByzF	*Byzantinische Forschungen*
ByzZ	*Byzantinische Zeitschrift*
C. Ar.	Athanasius, *Orationes contra Arianos*
C. Chalc.	Acts of the Council of Chalcedon
ca.	circa
Chron.	Jerome, *Chronicon Eusebii a Graeco Latine redditum et continuatum*
ClQ	*Classical Quarterly*
CNS	*Cristianesimo nella storia*
cod.	codex
Cod. justin.	Codex justinianus
Cod. theod.	Codex theodosianus
col(s).	column(s)
Cor.	Tertullian, *De corona militis*
CSCO	Chabot, Jean Baptiste, et al., eds. 1903. Corpus Scriptorum Christianorum Orientalium. Paris.

d.	died
Decr.	Athanasius, *De decretis*
Eccl. theol.	Eusebius, *De ecclesiastica theologia*
Ep.	*Epistula*
Ep. Aeg. Lib.	Athanasius, *Epistula ad episcopos Aegypti et Libyae*
Ep. Afr.	Athanasius, *Epistula ad Afros episcopos*
Ep. mort. Ar.	Athanasius, *Epistula ad Serapionem de morte Arii*
Eran.	Theodoret, *Eranistes*
Eunom.	Basil, *Adversus Eunomium*
flor.	floruit
FontChr	Fontes Christiani
GCS	Die griechischen christlichen Schriftsteller der ersten Jahrhunderte
GNO	*Gregorii Nysseni Opera*
GRBS	*Greek, Roman, and Byzantine Studies*
Haer.	Irenaeus, *Adversus haereses*
Hist. eccl.	*Historia ecclesiastica*
Hist. nov.	Zosimus, *Historia nova*
Hist. trip.	Cassiodorus, *Historia tripartita*
Hom.	*Homilia*
Il.	Homer, *Ilias*
Inc.	Athanasius, *De incarnatione*
Inst.	Lactantius, *Divinarum institutionum libri VII*
JEA	*Journal of Egyptian Archaeology*
JECS	*Journal of Early Christian Studies*
JLAnt	*Journal of Late Antiquity*
LXX	Septuagint
Mort.	Lactantius, *De mortibus persecutorum*
NPNF	Schaff, Philip, and Henry Wace, eds. 1886–1889. *A Select Library of Nicene and Post-Nicene Fathers of the Christian Church*. 28 vols. in 2 series.
Od.	Homer, *Odyssea*
ODCC	Louth, Andrew, ed. 2022. *The Oxford Dictionary of the Christian Church*. 4th ed. 2 vols. Oxford: Oxford University Press.
Or.	Gregory Nazianzen, *Oratio*
Or. sanct.	Constantine, *Oratio ad sanctos*
par(r).	parallel(s)
Pan.	Epiphanius, *Panarion*

Phaedr.	Plato, *Phaedrus*
Praep. ev.	Eusebius, *Praeparatio evangelica*
Princ.	Origen, *De principiis (Peri archōn)*
proem.	proemium
PG	Migne, Jacques-Paul, ed. 1857–1886. Patrologia Graeca [= Patrologiae Cursus Completus: Series Graeca]. 162 vols. Paris.
r.	reigned
REByz	*Revue des études byzantines*
RelArts	*Religion and the Arts*
Res gest.	Ammianus Marcellinus, *Res gestae*
RHE	*Revue d'histoire ecclésiastique*
RM	*Rheinischen Museum*
Sac.	John Chyrsostom, *De sacerdotio*
SC	Sources chrétiennes
SDAWB	Sitzungsberichte der Deutschen Akademie der Wissenschaften zu Berlin: Klasse für Sprachen, Literatur und Kunst
Sib. Or.	Sibylline Oracles
Spir.	Basil, *De Spiritu Sanctu*
SRom	*Spicilegium Romanum*
Syn.	Hilary of Poitiers, *De synodis*; Athanasius, *De synodis*
Syr. d.	Lucian, *De syria dea*
Tim.	Plato, *Timaeus*
TTH	Translated Texts for Historians
Urk.	Opitz, Hans-Georg, ed. 1934. *Urkunden zur Geschichte des arianischen Streites*. Vol. 3.1–2 of *Athanasius Werke*. Berlin: de Gruyter.
VC	*Vigiliae Christianae*
Vir. ill.	Jerome, *De viris illustribus*
Vit. Const.	Eusebius of Caesarea, *Vita Constantini*
Vit. Porph.	Mark the Deacon, *Vita Porphyrii*
ZAC	*Zeitschrift für Antikes Christentum*
ZKG	*Zeitschrift für Kirchengeschichte*

Sigla

< >	conjecture
<...>	conjectural lacuna

[ ]   added for clarity of translation

References to manuscripts of the text follow the sigla in Hansen's edition, reproduced below.

A	Ambrosianus gr. 534 (M 88 sup.), thirteenth century
R	Vaticanus gr. 1142, thirteenth century
H	Hierosolymitanus 111, 1588
a	Tradition common to A R (H)
V	Vaticanus gr. 830, 1446
E	Vaticanus gr. 1918 (Emmanuel Probatares), ca. 1546–1556
O	Vaticanus Ottobonianus gr. 261, ca. 1545–1560
p	Tradition common to E O
C	Cantabrigiensis Trinity College B.9.5, ca. 1546–1556
M	Matritensis 4672, ca. 1546–1556
b	Tradition common to V p CM
T	Taurinensis gr. 10 (B.I.1), fourteenth century (ca. 1370)
B	Athous Vatopedinus, cod. 31, fourteenth century
W	Vindobonensis hist. gr. 127, fourteenth century

Introduction

1. The Misattribution to "Gelasius of Cyzicus"

In a letter dated Christmas Eve 1598, Fédéric Morel II (1552–1630), noted French humanist and royal printer (*impremeur de roi*), conveyed news of an important discovery to his collaborator, Scottish Aristotelian philosopher Robert Balfour (ca. 1553–ca. 1621).[1] Balfour had been commissioned to edit and translate a history of the Council of Nicaea, which Morel would publish. But the work was anonymous or was thought to be until Morel received word from eminent jurist François Pithou (1543–1621). Pithou had found reference to the very text Morel and Balfour were working on in the Byzantine author Photius (ca. 810–after 893). Pithou informed Morel (and Morel informed Balfour in turn) that Photius had read the history of the Council of Nicaea and had attested that it was then attributed to a "Gelasius of Palestinian Caesarea." Photius had also noted that the author identifies his "fatherland" as Cyzicus (for a translation of the letter, see appendix 4). After relaying these findings to Balfour, Morel published the text one year later as the *Syntagma* ("collection") of "Gelasius of Cyzicus."[2]

Morel's interpretation of Pithou's reading of Photius soon gained wide currency, and "Gelasius of Cyzicus" became widely accepted as the name for the history of Nicaea first published by Morel in Paris in 1599. Early in the seventeenth century, for example, Greek-born Italian scholar Leo Allatius (1587/8–1669) added the ascription "of Gelasius of Cyzicus" into a fifteenth-century manuscript of the text in the Vatican Library on the authority of Morel and Balfour's *editio princeps* (Hansen 2002, ix).[3] In the late seventeenth century, influential German pietist historian Gottfried

---

1. All dates are CE unless otherwise stated.
2. For the date of publication, see the text included in Kecskeméti 2014, 128. The Latin version of the title was *Gelasii Cyziceni Commentarius Actorum Nicaeni Concilii*.
3. *Pace* Croke (2018), whose assertion that "an early editor" relied on a marginal note in a manuscript to attribute the work to "Gelasius of Cyzicus" is mistaken. Hansen attests Allatius's note as the only comment on authorship in the manuscripts. Allatius

Arnold (1666–1714) cited "Gelasius of Cyzicus" in his *Impartial History of Churches and Heresies*.[4] In 1860 Jacques-Paul Migne (1800–1875) reprinted Balfour's text and translation in his Patrologia Graeca series (PG 85:1179–1360) with the attribution "Gelasius of Cyzicus." In 1861 Antonio Ceriani (1828–1907) printed a recently discovered third book to the text, which Angelo Mai had uncovered in Milan twenty years previously, under the name "Gelasius of Cyzicus."[5] The first critical edition of the text by Gerhard Loeschke (1880–1912) and his student Margret Heinemann (1883–1968) was published in 1918 as *Gelasius Kirchengeschichte*.[6] By this point, Morel and Pithou's attribution was accepted as fact.

It was not until 2002, when Günther Christian Hansen (2002, ix–xi) revised Loeschke and Heinemann's century-old critical edition, that the attribution to Gelasius of Cyzicus was seriously challenged. Hansen revisited Morel and Pithou's original attribution, compared it with the manuscript history and Photius's testimony from the *Bibliotheca*, and found it fundamentally lacking. Hansen notes that, beside Allatius's after-the-fact attribution, no surviving manuscript includes an attribution to any author, let alone to "Gelasius of Cyzicus." Furthermore, Hansen points out that "Gelasius of Cyzicus" is a "phantom" that does not correspond to any known historic personage.[7] Photius had in fact found evidence for an attribution to "Gelasius, bishop of Palestinian Caesarea," an author attested in the historical record (ca. 335–ca. 395; see 6.2.3 below), not for a "Gelasius of Cyzicus."[8] Outside Morel and Pithou's attribution, there is, in fact, no evidence that such an author existed. Finally, Hansen posits that the manuscript in which Photius found the attribution had been compromised by an earlier scribe, who mistakenly carried over to the history of Nicaea the name of Gelasius of Caesarea.[9] Hansen therefore treats the text as a truly

---

would have been too young to add the note before the *editio princeps* was published, and it was the *editio princeps* that created the name "Gelasius of Cyzicus."

4. Arnold 1729, 182.

5. Ceriani 1861, 129–55; Mai 1841. See Hansen 2002, xxxviii–xli.

6. Heinemann completed the critical edition Loeschke had begun but left incomplete at his death. For the attribution, see Loeschke and Heinemann 1918, xxviii.

7. Hansen 2002, xi: "dieses von Pithou erdachte Phantom sollte aus den Handbüchern verschwinden."

8. Croke (2018) is incorrect on this point: Photius did not attribute the text to "Gelasius of Cyzicus" but to "Gelasius, bishop of Caesarea."

9. Treadgold (2007, 165 n. 201) suggests that, because Photius only ascribed the text to a "Gelasius" (without toponym) in an earlier report on the same work (cod.

anonymous work. He rechristened the text the "Anonymous Church History" and its author "Anonymous Cyzicenus."[10]

Hansen's arguments can be further strengthened by recourse to Photius's original testimony about the present history of the Council of Nicaea (for a translation, see appendix 3). Photius's monumental literary catalog, the *Bibliotheca*, contains summaries (of varying lengths) and assessments of works of Christian and non-Christian literature that the patriarch had read. The *Bibliotheca* is therefore essential for understanding lost and partially preserved works from antiquity, such as this anonymous history.[11] Photius's treatment of the authorship of the history of the Council of Nicaea is anything but straightforward. In the first place, it is worth emphasizing that the first manuscript of the text that Photius read was anonymous.[12] Furthermore, it was only after searching for another copy of the text that Photius found a manuscript that attributed the history to Gelasius, bishop of Caesarea in Palestine. A knowledgeable bibliophile, Photius was aware of two other works attributed to Gelasius of Caesarea: another ecclesiastical history and an apologetic treatise (see cod. 88–89). Photius was by no means sure of his tentative attribution to "Gelasius, bishop of Palestinian Caesarea," especially since he noticed chronological impossibilities in attributing all three works to the same Gelasius, bishop of Palestinian Caesarea. The patriarch also noticed great stylistic variations in the three works. In the end, Photius confesses that he is not sure whether he is dealing with one or three Gelasii, bishops of Palestinian Caesarea. He sums up his findings on a note of uncertainty: "Whoever this Gelasius is, I have not been able to learn with certitude."[13]

---

15), he may have inferred or misremembered the fuller name "Gelasius of Palestinian Caesarea" (cod. 88). While it is plausible Photius made such a mistake, this fact, if true, does not provide any positive evidence that the author's name was Gelasius or provide a basis for modern scholars to "reasonably call" the author "Gelasius of Cyzicus" as Treadgold (165) suggests.

10. The title in German is *Anonyme Kirchengeschichte*. Hansen (2008) later titled the work the "Ecclesiastical History of Anonymous Cyzicenus" (*Anonymous von Cyzicus: Historia Ecclesiastica Kirchengeschichte*) in his German translation. An Anglicized alternative, "Anonymous of Cyzicus," is sometimes used in modern English-language scholarship.

11. On Photius's *Bibliotheca* generally, see Treadgold 1980; Wilson 1996, 93–111.

12. As already noted by Hansen 2002, xi.

13. Photius, *Bibl.* cod. 88.35–36: Τίς ποτε δέ ἐστιν ὁ Γελάσιος οὗτος, οὐκ ἔχω σαφῶς ἐκμαθεῖν.

We accept, therefore, Hansen's position that the author's name is unknown and that we are dealing with an anonymous text. Throughout our introduction and translation we will refer to the author as "Anonymous Cyzicenus," or the briefer "Cyzicenus," or simply "the author," and the text as the *Ecclesiastical History* for reasons that are explained below in section 3. However, due to the widespread acceptance of Morell and Pithou's attribution, all scholarship from 1599 to 2002 refers to the author as Gelasius of Cyzicus.[14] Therefore, much of the scholarship quoted in the introduction and cited in the notes and bibliography refers to the author as "Gelasius of Cyzicus" or, alternatively (after 2002), as "Pseudo-Gelasius."[15] The reader should be aware that both of these names refer to the same unknown author of this ecclesiastical history, Anonymous Cyzicenus.

2. Situating Anonymous Cyzicenus and the *Ecclesiastical History*

While Photius includes a short biographical sketch of the author in his *Bibliotheca*, the details of that sketch derive from the *Ecclesiastical History*. Therefore, all that can be said about the author of the *Ecclesiastical History* emerges from the text itself, specifically from the *proemium*. In the *proemium* the author explains circumstances that led him to compose the *Ecclesiastical History* and in so doing provides incidental details about his life and times. We must exercise caution, however, since the author's narrative about his past experiences has been crafted to serve rhetorical purposes rather than provide prosopographical data. Nonetheless, we can surmise from the information in the *proemium* that the author was a partisan of the Council of Chalcedon, that he was probably a monk or priest living in Roman Bithynia, and that he composed his history in the reign of the Emperor Zeno or shortly thereafter.

---

14. Contemporary scholarship, especially reference works, sometimes includes the name "Gelasius of Cyzicus" as a principle of organization even when accepting Hansen's rejection of that name. See, e.g., Croke 2018 and, with less explicit rejection, Cross and Livingstone 2005.

15. The appellation "Pseudo-Gelasius" is also used by Van Nuffelen and followers of his thesis to refer to the Greek history other scholars attribute to Gelasius of Caesarea. Van Nuffelen (2002) argues that this attribution is pseudonymous and the work is a translation and expansion of Rufinus's and Socrates's *Ecclesiastical Histories* (hence Pseudo-Gelasius; see below, section 6.2.3). We point this out here to avoid any possible confusion.

To begin with the last point, Anonymous Cyzicenus provides us with one chronological indicator around which the rest of his biography must be built. Cyzicenus recalls, "After some time, I came to this place, I mean to the province of the Bithynians, by the goodwill of God, at the time when the greatest disturbance and dispute arose against the apostolic and universal church of God and against the apostolic faith that was practiced in it, during the rebellion of the unholy Basiliscus" (*proem.* 9). Basiliscus revolted against the emperor Zeno in 475 and ruled for a little over a year before he was deposed when Zeno reclaimed the throne. Cyzicenus provides another important piece of information connected with the revolt of Basiliscus. The author explains how, during Basiliscus's revolt of 475–476, he engaged in a theological debate with "Eutychian" heretics in the province of Bithynia. During their debate these "Eutychian" heretics claimed to be the true heirs of the Council of Nicaea, and this assertion spurred the author's historical investigation: "On account of these matters and many others that had been stirred up against our holy and orthodox faith" (*proem.* 12–13). While these details situate Anonymous Cyzicenus in the late fifth century, they provide neither a firm date for the composition of the *Ecclesiastical History* nor an indication of the life span of its author.

Though Basiliscus's revolt and the subsequent debate with "Eutychian" heretics spurred the composition of the *Ecclesiastical History*, it does not necessarily follow that the work was composed immediately after these events.[16] In the first place, the author states that these events "and many other things" spurred his research. We do not know which specific event the author refers to or when they took place in relation to Basiliscus's revolt. Further, Cyzicenus only tells us that these events spurred his historical investigations. We do not know how long it took him to find his sources and compose his history. Finally, the religious politics of the next several decades provided ample motivation for producing an anti-Eutychian treatise about the proper interpretation of the Council of Nicaea. Further challenges to the legitimacy of Chalcedon continued into the sixth century, until the nominal healing of the schism under Justin I (519 CE).[17] However, since Cyzicenus mentions no further shifts in imperial power after Basiliscus's usurpation, it seems safest to date the text within the reign

---

16. Despite the general assumptions the text was composed in or ca. 476 or 480. See, e.g., Hansen 2002, xi; Croke 2018; Graumann 2021, 18 n. 19.

17. For the ecclesiastical divisions during this period that emanated from the Council of Chalcedon, see Meyendorff 1989, 165–206.

of the emperor Zeno (d. 491 CE). This provides a chronological range of 476–491 for the composition of the *Ecclesiastical History*.

It is also worth noting that the details about "the unholy Basiliscus" and the "Eutychian heretics" serve a rhetorical rather than historical purpose in the *proemium*. By "Eutychians," the author presumably means followers of one-nature (miaphysite) Christology generally (see below, section 5). "The unholy Basiliscus," in Cyzicenus's telling, was the heretic emperor who helped these "Eutychians" increase their influence, necessitating the corrective to their heretical ideas provided by Cyzicenus's historical account. The accounts of Basiliscus's revolt and the author's debate with the "Eutychians" situate the author and his project: the author as an opponent of miaphysite Christology and the history as a record of Nicaea that justifies the theology and ideology of Chalcedon, where Eutyches was condemned as a heretic. Because these details are included for these rhetorical reasons, we should not assume they represent precise chronological markers for the *Ecclesiastical History*. Other events may have occurred that the author glosses over since they would not necessarily help situate his project.

The account of Basiliscus's revolt and the debate with Eutychian heretics is also of only limited help in situating the life span of the anonymous author of the *Ecclesiastical History*. Because he gave no indication of his age at the time of Basiliscus's revolt, it is unclear whether the author was an old, middle-aged, or young man at the time of composition. If an old man, he may have been born in the early fifth century and could have lived through the tumultuous events of the Councils of Ephesus and Chalcedon. If a young man, he may have lived into the sixth century. One possible clue is provided by the author's adoption of a religious vocation.

That the author was involved in a religious life as a priest or monk is perhaps the most secure aspect of his biography that can be pieced together from the information provided in the *proemium*. The author relates near the start of the *proemium* that he first read about the Council of Nicaea in the house of "my father according to the flesh," who served as a priest in the city of Cyzicus in Hellespontus under the bishop Dalmatius (*proem.* 2). Later in the *proemium*, the author relates, "After some time, I came to this place, I mean to the province of the Bithynians, by the goodwill of God" (*proem.* 9), around the time of Basiliscus's revolt. The phrasing "by the goodwill [*eudokia*] of God" likely refers to a religiously motivated lifestyle change, since the Greek term *eudokia* was also used in fifth-century documents to describe the adoption of a religious vocation (Tandy 2023, 112–13). The author's participation in public theological debates also suggests a religious calling of some kind. Warren Treadgold (2007, 166) suggests that the author may have been a priest like his father, and by the mid-fifth century there was an established tradition of sons following their fathers into an ecclesiastical career. More recently, Sean Tandy (2023, 110–14) suggests that the author was a monk, basing this argument on the large number of monasteries in Bithynia (where the author moved), the implication of the term *eudokia*, the prevalence of monks in theological debates after Chalcedon, and the use of the circumlocution "father according to the flesh." Late antique monastic sources use this expression to describe biological parents and to contrast biological parents with the new spiritual fathers, the abbots of monasteries. Though this is a very plausible interpretation, we prefer to keep open the possibility that Anonymous Cyzicenus held another type of religious vocation, such as a priest. Since no previous abandonment of a secular lifestyle is mentioned, it is perhaps more likely this religious vocation was taken up earlier in the author's life. If true, this suggests a birthdate for the author around the middle of the fifth century (ca. 450 CE).

Though much in addition to his real name remains uncertain about Anonymous Cyzicenus, the details provided in the *Ecclesiastical History* provide enough context to situate the author and his project. The author came from Cyzicus in Hellespontus and moved to an unknown location in Bithynia for religious purposes around the time of Basiliscus's revolt. He was either a priest or monk of pro-Chalcedonian, dyophysite leanings who composed his work sometime between 476 and 491 to combat miaphysite interpretations of the Council of Nicaea.[18]

3. The Contents and Structure of the *Ecclesiastical History*

The *Ecclesiastical History* comprises three books of radically unequal length that cover in turn the rise of Constantine (book 1), the Arian controversy and the Council of Nicaea (book 2), and the aftermath of the council and "the remaining zealous acts of piety" of the emperor Constantine (book 3). Book 2 is the longest of the three books by far, commanding 60 percent of the pages of the Greek text in Hansen's edition, which is fitting given that the very first words of the *Ecclesiastical History* promise the reader "an

---

18. Frend 1972 remains a useful overview of the controversies between dyophysites and miaphysites, although subsequent scholarship has rejected the term *monophysite* as a polemical term that misrepresents the miaphysite Christology. See Brock 2016 for a summation of the modern state of the terminology question.

account of the holy, great, and ecumenical council of bishops gathered in the city of the Nicaeans" (*proem.* 1). Rather than beginning with the council itself, however, the author states that he will "begin my account ... from the reign of the most pious and Christ-bearing emperor Constantine, who ordered the council of bishops to be gathered in the city of the Nicaeans" (*proem.* 25). Book 1 acts therefore as the necessary background to understanding the events of Nicaea. Though Cyzicenus began his account with Constantine's rise to power, he twice ended it in different places: originally with an account of the Nicene fathers promulgating the council's decisions and, after some revisions, with the death of Arius, whose theology was the cause of the council, and of Constantine, who convened the council.

Book 3 gives every indication that it was added at a later date and acts therefore as a supplement to the original two-book narrative. Cyzicenus announces at the end of book 2, "I ... shall cease my account here" (2.37.29) after describing the promulgation of the council's decisions. In the same passage the author states that he is "intending to arrange the remaining zealous acts of piety of the all-blessed and most faithful emperor" (2.37.30), a promise suggesting future fulfillment. Since Cyzicenus had also promised a work on Constantius and the early life of Constantine (*proem.* 25) that does not seem to have materialized, it could easily have been the case that he would have never finished writing the "remaining zealous acts of piety" of Constantine. When he did get around to composing book 3, Cyzicenus added a second prologue to this book and also clearly indicated that it was an addition to the previous two-book history. After a brief summary of what the first two books contained, the author ends his second prologue by indicating, "Now, I will proceed onward from there to a narrative" of the contents of book 3 (3.1.7). Finally, additional details indicate that book 3 was distinguished early on from the unit of the first and second books, particularly the numbering for the titles, which runs consecutively through the first two books but restarts for book 3.[19] The ending of book 3 is not preserved but can be reconstructed in part through recourse to a set of *pinakes* (tables of contents) that inform us of the topics covered later in book 3 and the summary of Photius in his *Bibliotheca*.

In its final three-book format, Anonymous Cyzicenus's *Ecclesiastical History* narrates the cooperation between the pious emperor Constantine

---

19. Loeschke and Heinemann (1918, xxv) argue that these titles could not be proven to belong or not to belong to Cyzicenus's original text.

and the "holy fathers" of Nicaea to overcome the diabolical challenge posed by Arius's teachings.

A sizeable *proemium* explains why this history was important to produce in a fifth-century context. The author relates how, as a boy living in his father's house in Cyzicus in the Roman province of Hellespontus, he spent a good deal of time reading a text that told the history of the Council of Nicaea. This text owed its creation to Dalmatius the bishop of Cyzicus, a signatory of the Council of Ephesus (431), in whose church the author's father served as a priest (*proem.* 1–8). Years later the author moved to an unknown location in the province of Bithynia where, during the revolt of Basiliscus in 475–476, "Eutychian" heretics were emboldened to declare in public debates, in which the author took part, that they were the true heirs of Nicaea (*proem.* 9–12). Our author's account, therefore, was meant to serve as a corrective to this mistaken view and to defend orthodox doctrine in his own age (*proem.* 24). The *proemium* also describes the author's research and indicates several of his major sources, including Eusebius, "Rufinus" (meaning the tradition associated with Gelasius of Caesarea), and an unknown "Presbyter John" (*proem.* 21–22; see §6 below for the sources of the *Ecclesiastical History*).

After the *proemium*, the narrative of the *Ecclesiastical History* covers a variety of topics both connected and tangential to the council itself, using different source types and narrative structures. Book 1 includes descriptions of battles in Constantine's rise to power, while book 3 includes numerous descriptions of church building and narratives of missionary activity outside the Roman Empire: in Ethiopia and the Caucasus. Book 2 includes speeches and debates as well as records of numerous letters and documents purportedly emanating from the council. Book 1 introduces Constantine, the principal character of the history, while Arius, the work's chief antagonist, is introduced at the start of book 2. The revised three-book version of the *Ecclesiastical History* sees these two chief characters die in close proximity to each other, the heretic dying in ignominy in a public latrine (*pinakes* 20; Photius, *Bibl.* 88) and the pious emperor being baptized by an Orthodox cleric on his deathbed (Photius, *Bibl.* 88). This overall unity can disguise the somewhat digressive nature of much of the *Ecclesiastical History*. A further subdivision of the major sections of the *Ecclesiastical History* is included in the table below.

Though Constantine looms large throughout the *Ecclesiastical History*, Pierre Nautin's argument that the text is actually a "Life of Constantine" masquerading as an ecclesiastical history overdetermines the work's genre.[20] Identifying the text as a life of Constantine contradicts Cyzicenus's own understanding of his work. Our historian says that he plans "in another writing, if it pleases God, [to] set out a description of [Constantine's] birth and the times of the reign of his father, the most God-beloved Constantius" (*proem.* 26). In other words, Cyzicenus is explaining that he is not going to provide all the details necessary for a life (*bios*) according to the criteria of the well-defined ancient genre.[21] Furthermore, though most Byzantine manuscripts identify the text as a "collection" (*syntagma*), this again reflects the perception of later readers, not the author. Cyzicenus clearly identifies his work as an *Ecclesiastical History*, referring to it by that label on at least eight separate occasions (1.5.7, 1.11.32, 2.1.12, 2.37.29, 3.1.1, 3.7.14, 3.10.26, 3.15.23) and expressly comparing his work with previous ecclesiastical historians: Eusebius, "Rufinus," and Theodoret (e.g., *proem.* 20–24, 1.1.8–11, 3.16.10; Tandy 2023, 110–11 with n. 18). Though an ecclesiastical history based on preexisting texts and one that focuses on the emperor Constantine, it is an ecclesiastical history none the less.

As will be discussed in more detail later in the introduction, though the *Ecclesiastical History* is a self-styled compilation (*proem.* 24, 1.5.3, 1.10.2, 3.16.10), the author played an active role in shaping the final work.[22] In addition to organizing the overall narrative, in many places the author alters his source text. Cyzicenus also includes narrative details not recounted in other sources, such as the baptism of Constantine by an unnamed orthodox cleric rather than Eusebius of Nicomedia (Photius, *Bibl.* 88). Cyzicenus is also the only author to give a name (Eutocius) to the Arian presbyter who helps Eusebius and his allies inveigle their way back into Constantine's good graces (*Hist. eccl.* 3.12.2). Cyzicenus's history also incorporates four documents not preserved elsewhere. These include a speech attributed to Constantine at the opening of the Council of Nicaea (2.7), a profession of faith by Hosius of Cordoba before the assembled council (2.13), a long dia-

---

20. Nautin (1983, 301): "On ne connaît de lui qu'un ouvrage, qui nous est parvenu mutilé de la fin sous le titre de *Syntagma du saint concile de Nicée*, mais qui est en réalité une Vie de Constantin." Nautin (1992, 179) reasserted his belief the text was a life of Constantine in a later article on Gelasius of Caesarea.

21. The popularity of Christian *bioi* in late antique Christianity also all but guarantees our author knew the general requirements for the genre. Cyzicenus was also himself aware of at least one *bios* of Constantine, Eusebius's *Life of Constantine*, though he only quotes it through intermediaries (see introduction, 6.2.2).

22. On the compiler as author, see Shedd 2022.

logic dispute between an Arian philosopher named Phaedo and the most important Nicene fathers (2.14–2.24), and a set of ecclesiastical "regulations" (*diatyposes*) supposedly adopted by the council (2.31). For more on the potential source of each of these documents, see section 6 below.

The following chart summarizes the principal contents of the *Ecclesiastical History*, highlighting events and texts that are unique to Cyzicenus's history (bold font) and giving a sense of the organization of the narrative:

Passage	Topic
Proemium 1–25	Preface to history; sources and inspiration for the work
1.1–1.7	Constantine's rise (battles with Maxentius)
1.8–2.1	Constantine's rise (battles with Maximinus and Licinius)
2.2–2.4	Arius and the origins of the Arian controversy
2.5–2.6	Preparations for the Council of Nicaea
2.7	Constantine's oration to the council
2.8	Early conciliar events (Constantine burns petitions of quarrelsome bishops)
2.9–2.11	Short lives of notable attendees (Paphnutius and Spyridon)
2.12	Hosius of Cordoba's profession of faith before the council
2.13	A humble confessor bests an Arian philosopher in debate
2.14–2.24	The Dispute with Phaedo: the Nicene fathers debate another Arian philosopher, named Phaedo
2.25–2.27	Decisions of the council on the faith (Nicene Creed at 2.27)
2.28–2.30	Signatories and reactions to the council's decisions
2.31	Some "regulations" (*diatyposes*) approved by the council
2.32–2.33	The Nicene canons

2.34–2.37	Promulgation of the decrees of Nicaea (including other matters dealt with at the council such as the Meletian schism and the date of Easter)
2.28; 2.38 (unique in this form)	List of signatories of the Council of Nicaea
3.1	Second prologue
3.2–3.5	Constantine's acts of piety after the council (church building in Constantinople and Jerusalem, commissioning copies of Scripture)
3.6–3.8	Helena in Jerusalem; discovery of the true cross
3.9–3.11	Emerging Christian communities in Ethiopia, Georgia, and Persia
3.12–3.13	Arius and the Arians inveigle their way back into Constantine's good graces
3.14–3.18	Arian plots against Athanasius
Pinakes	Further letters concerning Arius and the Arians
Pinakes and Photius, *Bibl.* 88	Death of Arius; Constantine gladdened at the news
Photius, *Bibl.* 88	Constantine baptized on deathbed by orthodox cleric

4. Defending Chalcedon, Memorializing Nicaea

It cannot be emphasized enough that the conciliar tradition was very much in the process of development and contestation in the fifth century. While opponents and supporters of the decisions reached at the Council of Chalcedon agreed that ecumenical councils were the proper venue for the articulation of dogma, exactly which councils counted as ecumenical and which decrees stood as dogma were contested. Pro- and anti-Chalcedonians did concur, though, that Nicaea and its statement of Christian creed were authoritative, and they conceptualized Nicaea as the archetypal ecumenical council (Price and Gaddis 2007, 56–59; Smith 2018). Consequently, *how* Nicaea was imagined and *who* could leverage control over that memorialization were of tremendous significance.

Hence Cyzicenus's preface to his work. Whether or not the "book of exceptional age" he recalls reading in his youth was a real codex or a fiction, the vignette he paints does important work to establish his credentials (*proem*. 2). First, the image of a young man diligently reading the history and *acta* of Nicaea embodies the notion that Nicaea is formative—it shapes the young churchman as it should shape the church. Implicit (though only just so) is that Cyzicenus's anti-Chalcedonian opponents are malformed and without an orthodox pedigree. The aged book itself is a metonym for Cyzicenus's orthodox lineage, and by extension that of his readers. The volume, he asserts, originated with Dalmatius, bishop of Cyzicus: "These pages had originated at the hand of the godly, renowned Dalmatius, who was at that time archbishop of the holy, universal church of the illustrious metropolis of the Cyzicans" (*proem*. 2). This reads, in fact, as though Cyzicenus is describing a colophon—a statement at the end of a manuscript describing the circumstances of its copying—and thus should probably be taken to mean that the book was copied by or commissioned by Dalmatius from an even more ancient copy.[23] The book thus represents Nicene orthodoxy embodied in an orthodox codex created by the hand of an orthodox bishop, whence it was conveyed to an orthodox presbyter, Cyzicenus's father, in whose library it became formative reading for our orthodox historian (*proem*. 2–3).

Cyzicenus admits that he was unable to keep the entire text in his memory, though he claims to have noted everything important (*proem*. 3). Here his language invokes the material practices of ancient reading. His verb for "taking note" (*episēmainō*) suggests not merely taking note of but, more literally, marking (or even copying) significant passages for later reference or use—like the abbreviation ΣH (for *sēmeiōsai*, "take note") that stands next to "noteworthy" passages in Byzantine manuscripts. In other words, the reader is to imagine that, even before the compilation of his history, Cyzicenus's mind was like a notebook containing all of the key information about Nicaea and Nicene dogma. In medical literature, the verb can also convey the idea of giving off signs, or rather "symptoms," and thus suggests that those raised on a diet of good orthodox fare show all the symptoms of Nicene orthodoxy. Barely implicit, again, is the notion that the anti-Chalcedonians have forgotten or never properly noted the

---

23. If Cyzicenus's description of the ancient book is pure fiction, it is a fiction that is believable in its details. Whether the book was real, however, has little bearing on the way the account functions as backstory to his own writing project.

true happenings of Nicaea and instead show the symptoms of an unhealthy teaching, as opposed to the healthy or "salutary" (*hygiainōn*) doctrine of orthodoxy (*proem*. 4). In his conflict with the Eutychians of his day, he thus portrays himself as returning to his carefully curated notes, while the heretics, though claiming to know Nicaea, spout "things worse than the blasphemies of Arius" (*proem*. 10–11). This competition over the memory of Nicaea is, according to Cyzicenus, the reason for his writing this text, which he describes as a reconstruction of the book of his youth. Though he has consulted a number of sources—he names Eusebius of Caesarea, Rufinus, and an otherwise-unknown presbyter, John (*proem*. 21–22)—he finds in none of them as complete an account as that in his remembered book (*proem*. 23). Thus, he must become a compiler himself, making selections from his sources to reconstruct an orthodox account of Nicaea (*proem*. 24).

Cyzicenus's text fills a gap that was and is quite apparent to any reader of fourth- and early fifth-century accounts of Nicaea: namely, a much-desired, complete narrative of events during the council, including *acta*, simply did not exist. That churchmen of Cyzicenus's day were able to consult the *acta* of the subsequent ecumenical councils of Ephesus and Chalcedon would have made this absence more acute. The written sources closest in time to the events of Nicaea, the most important of which were composed by Eusebius and Athanasius, are polemically selective, or even deliberately obfuscating, in their descriptions of the council. Cyzicenus signposts the edges of Eusebius's *Ecclesiastical History* when he notes that Eusebius's narrative ends before the events of the council (2.1.8). Later authors, including Rufinus and a Greek history reconstructed by similarities across later works, provided some details about events during the council, many of which are reiterated here by Cyzicenus. These include the accounts of confessors at Nicaea (2.9–11), a dispute with an unnamed Arian philosopher (2.13), and the canons of Nicaea (2.32), as well as, perhaps, the purported speech of Constantine (2.7).[24] He also includes a long theological dialogue, the Dispute with Phaedo (2.14–24), the source of which is unclear but which is generally considered another "found text" rather than Cyzicenus's own composition. Still, despite the pervasive notion that the councils at Ephesus and Chalcedon merely clarified Nicaea, there was nothing like a full

---

24. The identity of the Greek historian is contested, on which see section 6. Hansen (1998) attributes Constantine's speech to Philip of Side, an attribution also further discussed in section 6.

narrative, much less *acta* of the archetypal council.[25] Cyzicenus proffers his text as just such a narrative, with his selection and curation of sources serving to create a story of Nicaea as a definitive refutation of the Eutychians of his own day.

5. Cyzicenus's Theology

There is little theology written in Cyzicenus's own voice in the history, but from his selection and editing of his sources we can discern what theological issues mattered to him. The "Eutychianism" against which he says he is responding (*proem.* 10) was characterized by a specific variety of miaphysite (single-nature) doctrine associated with Eutyches and opposed to the dyophysite (dual-nature) understanding of Christ confirmed by the Council of Chalcedon. To better situate Cyzicenus's work as a response to Eutychianism, it will be helpful to review, if very briefly, the christological controversies that preceded Chalcedon. Theologians throughout the fourth century (and earlier) had grappled to account for both the divinity and humanity of Christ. In the late 420s CE, two dominant christological trajectories collided when Nestorius, the patriarch of Constantinople, challenged Cyril of Alexandria's description of Mary as *Theotokos*, or "God-bearer." Nestorius objected that the term implied that Christ's divinity had been "born," which he claimed was appropriate to say only of his humanity; it was acceptable, he argued, to term Mary *Christotokos*, or "Christ-bearer."[26] Behind their debate over the proper title for Mary lay two different ways of understanding the co-presence of the human and the divine in Christ.

Nestorius, often described as emerging from an Antiochene christological trajectory, distinguished between humanity and divinity as two hypostases and two natures (*physeis*) conjoined in one person (*Ep.* 5.6, Nestorius to Cyril). Nestorius's account emphasized the persistence of this distinction between human and divine natures in the incarnation. The emphasis is perhaps clearest in Nestorius's insistence that nothing

---

25. On Ephesus and Chalcedon clarifying Nicaea, see Gavrilyuk 2021. On the record-keeping protocols and surviving documents of the Council of Nicaea, see Graumman 2021, 18.

26. The most important of Cyril's letters in his conflict with Nestorius can be found in Wickham 1983. Nestorius's letters to Cyril are *Letters* 3 and 5 in the collection of Cyril's letters and can be found in English in Cyril 1987.

characteristic of Christ's human nature (e.g., suffering, birth, death) should be ascribed to his divine nature (*Ep.* 5.8, Nestorius to Cyril). Cyril, for his part, argued that Nestorius's Christology denied a true union of divine and human in the incarnation. While he maintained that neither the human nor the divine nature was mixed or changed in their union, he held that Nestorius's emphasis on the divine and human as two hypostases in effect posited two Christs (Cyril, *Ep.* 17.4–5; third letter to Nestorius). Cyril would go as far as to ascribe suffering to the Son, articulations that his opponents described as radically miaphysite (Cyril, *Ep.* 17, anathema 12; third letter to Nestorius).

In 431 CE, the Council of Ephesus was called to resolve the dispute between Cyril and Nestorius. Nestorius was deposed and his two-hypostasis articulation condemned. The council likewise rejected Cyril's more radical formulations. Cyril, though, was able to rehabilitate himself in a letter of 433 CE to John of Antioch. Cyril's articulation in this letter, often termed the Formula of Reunion, of Christology and the term *homoousios* ("of one being") would come to form much of the basis of the Chalcedonian definition. Here, Cyril affirmed a "union of two natures ... which involves no merging" and defined the incarnate Christ as "*homoousios* with the Father in respect of the godhead and *homoousios* with [humans] in respect of the humanity" (*Ep.* 39.3, our translation). Cyril also relented his more radical claims, acknowledging that while some scriptural statements are predicated of the single person Christ, others are rightly attributed to either the divinity or humanity. Debate continued in the years after Ephesus, though the terms set out by the council and in Cyril's conciliatory letter increasingly came to define the bounds of Christological speculation.

In the post-Ephesian milieu, Eutyches's Christology was a zealous response to what he perceived to be the radical dyophysitism of Nestorius. He held that, while Christ was "from two natures," these natures were united in a single nature in the person of Christ, and that his humanity was, to use a phrase leveled by his opponents, diluted like a drop of vinegar in the sea (C. Chalc. 1.513–514, 527).[27] In other words, he accepted that Christ came from two natures, but while he argued that the divine nature remained unchanged and immutable in the unity of Christ's hypostasis, he imagined the human nature to have been all but subsumed in the divine

---

27. See Flavian of Constantinople's summaries of Eutyches's Christology in his letters to Leo the Great (Leo, *Ep.* 22, 26).

nature. In arguing for a single nature after the hypostatic union, Eutyches's position followed closely the more staunchly miaphysite articulations found in Cyril of Alexandria (e.g., *Ep.* 44), who often used the articulation "one nature after the union." In the late 440s CE, Eutyches's teaching was enjoying enough currency to represent a threat to the tenuous christological détente established by Ephesus, and to the authority of Flavian, the patriarch of Constantinople. In 448 CE, Flavian called a synod of bishops subordinate to the Constantinopolitan See—often termed the "Home Synod" in historical accounts—where Eutyches was brought up on charges of heterodoxy. The key differences between his Christology and that which was to be affirmed at Chalcedon in 451 CE are evident in his responses to several questions posed by the synod. Eutyches was first asked to affirm the Formula of Reunion, the basis for the formula approved at Ephesus. The Formula of Reunion reads, in part:

> We therefore acknowledge our Lord Jesus Christ, the only-begotten Son of God, perfect God and perfect human ... the same *homoousios* with the Father in respect of the Godhead and *homoousios* with us in respect of the humanity. For there has occurred a union of two natures, and therefore we acknowledge one Christ, one Son, one Lord. By virtue of this understanding of the union which involves no merging, we acknowledge the holy Virgin to be *Theotokos*. (Cyril, *Ep.* 39 [to John of Antioch], quoted in C. Chalc. 1.246 [Price and Gaddis])

Eutyches was then pressed on whether he would accede that Christ is *homoousios* with human nature and whether he would acknowledge that Christ is "of two natures" after the incarnation (C. Chalc. 1.490). On the former point, he was willing to state that "the Holy Virgin is *homoousios* with us," and therefore in this specific sense recognized that "if one must say that he is from the Virgin [then he is] *homoousios* with us" (1.522). His articulation of the phrase "of two natures" was slightly but significantly different from the articulation found in the Formula of Reunion. The former permitted Eutyches to conceive of Christ as a union of two natures that were distinct and unchanged before the union, but allowed that the human nature had been changed in the union to such an extent that one should speak of "one nature after the union" (1.527). Eutyches was quoting a Cyrillian formulation, and like Cyril in his more miaphysite writings, he was most concerned to theologize in a way that preserved the immutability of the Son, or as Eutyches put it, "I do not say *homoousios* [i.e., with humanity] in such a way as to deny that he is the Son of God" (1.522). In other words, he feared that the co-presence of human and divine natures after the union dragged down Christ's divinity in such a way as to jeopardize the unified essence (*ousia*) of the Trinity. Two natures after the union, for Eutyches, meant positing a miscegenated or hybrid God-Human that could no longer be considered *homoousios* with the Father and Spirit. Eutyches's opponents argued that his position denied the reality of Christ's humanity. If Christ's humanity consisted only in the Son's having taken on and in effect subsuming the nature of flesh, then Christ's suffering, dying, and rising were mere appearances. Thus, the synod's anathematization equated Eutyches with the second-century gnostic Valentinus, who was described in heresiological texts as holding a docetic Christology, that is, holding that Christ's humanity was merely an appearance (1.551).[28]

After his condemnation at the Home Synod of 448 CE, Eutyches appealed to the emperor, Theodosius II, arguing that the acts of the synod had been falsified.[29] A second synod was called, in 449 CE, affirming the decision against Eutyches (Evagrius, *Hist. eccl.* 1.9). Eutyches then appealed to Leo, bishop of Rome, as did Flavian of Constantinople; Leo responded with the letter familiarly known as the Tome of Leo, which contended that Eutyches's error was the result of intellectual mediocrity and a pious desire to refute Nestorianism. The Tome also affirmed the Creed of Nicaea as a complete statement of faith concerning Christology, expounding that "the distinctive character of each nature [was] preserved and came together in one person" (C. Chalc. 2.22 [Price and Gaddis]). In an effort to resolve the growing friction among the patriarchs of Constantinople, Alexandria, and Rome, Emperor Theodosius II called a council at Ephesus, to be presided over by Dioscorus of Alexandria.[30] Both Dioscorus and Theodosius stood to benefit from Flavian's deposition, the patriarch by installing a fellow patriarch aligned with Alexandria, the emperor by removing a patriarch who, he felt, had been less than grateful to him when appointed (Evagrius, *Hist. eccl.* 1.9–10; Pseudo-Zachariah, *Hist. eccl.* 2.3). This Second Council

---

28. On Valentinus's docetism in proto-orthodox and orthodox heresiology see, e.g., Irenaeus, *Haer.* 1.6.1; Epiphanius, *Pan.* 31.7.3–5.

29. Theodosius II (r. 402–450) had previously supported Nestorius prior to the condemnation of his theology at the Council of Ephesus (431) and appears to have been sympathetic to Eutyches's cause. On the legacy of Theodosius II and his religious policies, see Watts 2013.

30. Dioscorus was the patriarch of Alexandria from 444–451, after Cyril. Because of his conduct at Ephesus II, he was deposed, and he died shortly thereafter.

of Ephesus affirmed a miaphysite understanding of the union of human and divine in Christ, restored Eutyches, and deposed Flavian of Constantinople, Theodoret of Cyrrhus, and Domnus of Antioch (Evagrius, *Hist. eccl.* 1.10).[31] Leo rejected the council, calling it a council of thieves, or *Latrocinium*. For the miaphysite churches of the East, however, Ephesus II was and still is regarded as an ecumenical council.

The political landscape shifted once again with the death of Theodosius II and the accession of Marcian in August of 450 CE, just one year after Ephesus II. Marcian called for another council, this time to be held at Nicaea. The choice of site was loaded with meaning, of course—this was to be an ecumenical council in the image of Nicaea. The location was shifted to Chalcedon, closer to Constantinople, to allow the emperor to respond with alacrity to any imminent threat on the Danubian frontier, where the Huns had been making incursions (Pseudo-Zachariah, *Hist. eccl.* 3.1d).[32] Chalcedon annulled Ephesus II: those who had been deposed were restored, and Eutyches's condemnation was confirmed once more. The Creed of Nicaea was again affirmed to be a complete and accurate statement of faith, with the council issuing a definition of Christology. This famous Chalcedonian Definition—*horos* in Greek ("boundary," "limit")—was intended to define the bounds of christological speculation. In language drawn in large part from Cyril's Formula of Reunion, the definition looked to set the ways in which the terms *nature, hypostasis,* and *person* should be used to refer to oneness and twoness in Christ:

> Following, therefore, the holy fathers, we all in harmony teach confession of one and same Son our Lord Jesus Christ, the same perfect in Godhead and same perfect in humanity, … *homoousios* with the Father in respect of the Godhead and *homoousios* with us in respect of humanity … one and the same Christ, Son, Lord, Only-begotten, acknowledged in two natures, without confusion, without change, without division, without separation; the difference of the natures being in no way destroyed by the union, but rather the properties of each are retained and united in one

---

31. Theodoret of Cyrrhus (ca. 393–ca. 466) had supported Nestorius against Cyril and remained a supporter of Nestorius long after the latter's deposition. On Theodoret's writings as a source for Cyzicenus's history, see introduction, 6.2.4. Domnus was patriarch of Antioch (442–449) and likewise a supporter of Nestorius.

32. Opponents of Chalcedon viewed the decision to move the council as a divine defense of the orthodoxy of Nicaea against the innovators of Chalcedon. See Gwynn 2009, 16.

single person and single *hypostasis*; he is neither separated nor divided in two persons. (C. Chalc. 5.34 [Price and Gaddis])[33]

To return for a moment to Eutyches: on a charitable reading, Eutyches's resistance to the notion of Christ having two natures after the union is more understandable if one recalls that, for many theologians of the mid-fifth century, including Cyril of Alexandria, *nature* was used in a way almost synonymous with *hypostasis*—that is, as though *nature* named the distinct subsistent entity that was the subject of Christ's statements, sufferings, and actions. For Eutyches, as for Cyril, to say that Christ was of two natures after the union was to suggest that the incarnate Christ was two beings or even two Christs. The definition, by contrast, understood *nature* as what endows a subject with characteristics (e.g., human nature, divine nature), and is nearly synonymous with *essence* (*ousia*). *Person* and *hypostasis*, for their part, refer to a distinctly existing being—they name the subject (e.g., the person and hypostasis Christ) which *has* a nature or natures. Indeed, despite the Chalcedonian Definition, confusion and contestation over christological terminology persisted.

This brings us at last to Cyzicenus's text and his theology. When he writes (*proem.* 10) that he was driven to compose this text as a response to "Eutychians," he is referring to a period during the reigns of Basiliscus and Zeno when the Definition of Chalcedon was at risk of being overturned. Shortly after Basiliscus usurped power in 475 CE, he was approached by an embassy of Egyptian monks who had come to argue for the restoration of Timothy Aelurus (i.e., Timothy "the Cat," a sobriquet perhaps referencing his political wiles), the miaphysite patriarch of Alexandria who had been living in exile. Serendipitously, the brother of one of the monks was now Basiliscus's *magister officiorum*, and thanks to his influence Basiliscus ordered Timothy back from exile (Pseudo-Zachariah, *Hist. eccl.* 5.1). Timothy then succeeded in petitioning Basiliscus to issue an encyclical declaring Chalcedon void.[34] The encyclical, yet again, affirmed the comprehensiveness of the faith of Nicaea, and characterized the Chalcedonian definition as a controversial "addition" (5.2b). According to some sources, partisans of Eutychian doctrine in Constantinople imagined they would have an ally in Timothy. Timothy and his anti-Chalcedonian allies, for their part, read-

---

33. Translation slightly modified.

34. The text of Basiliscus's encyclical, or *Encyclicon*, can be found in Evagrius, *Hist. eccl.* 3.4; Pseudo-Zachariah, *Hist. eccl.* 5.2.

ily condemned Eutyches alongside Nestorius as representatives of radical miaphysitism and dyophysitism, respectively (5.4). For pro-Chalcedonians such as Cyzicenus, though, "Eutychian" served as a polemical epithet, a way to libel all of their miaphysite, anti-Chalcedonian opponents.

Timothy, in fact, wanted Chalcedon overturned for political reasons as much as out of miaphysite conviction; Chalcedon had affirmed the primacy of the patriarchate of Constantinople in the East, and its nullification would restore more power to Alexandria.[35] Timothy then moved to depose the pro-Chalcedonian patriarch of Constantinople, Acacius, and install an ally, while Acacius roused the Constantinopolitan public to his side, accusing Basiliscus of heresy and organizing public processions that included the famous stylite ascetic Daniel (Pseudo-Zachariah, *Hist. eccl.* 5.5; Evagrius, *Hist. eccl.* 3.6–7). About to face Zeno, who was approaching Constantinople to contest the usurpation of his throne, Basiliscus felt pressed to issue a counterencyclical, withdrawing the earlier imperial order and explicitly reiterating the condemnation of Eutyches (and Nestorius).[36] Zeno, upon emerging as the victor, then issued his own imperial letter, the *Henoticon*, in 482 CE, which remained in force under his successor Anastasius I.[37] The letter was intended to cultivate unity by affirming the authority of the Nicene Creed, which the Councils of Constantinople and Ephesus I are characterized as "confirming." The *Henoticon* deliberately makes no mention of Chalcedon or its definition and instead uses the language of the Formula of Reunion.[38]

This forty-plus-year period of uneasy efforts at compromise is the theological environment to which Cyzicenus's *Ecclesiastical History* belongs. In the spirit of both Basilicus's and Zeno's imperial letters, the text studiously avoids any specific mention of Chalcedon and instead articulates orthodoxy in terms that could be construed according to the "Cyrillian" language affirmed in the *Henoticon*. In the *proemium*, he writes that he has

---

35. The privilege of the patriarch of Constantinople was affirmed by canon 28 of Chalcedon. On this issue and other political aspects of the Chalcedonian council, see Gaddis 2009.

36. For the text of the anti-encyclical, see Evagrius, *Hist. eccl.* 5.7.

37. The text of the *Henoticon* can be found in Evagrius, *Hist. eccl.* 3.14; Pseudo-Zachariah, *Hist. eccl.* 5.8. Anastasius I (r. 491–518) was accused of miaphysite sympathies and faced a rebellion led by Vitalian, who rallied pro-Chalcedonian Christians to his cause.

38. In particular, the formula "*homoousios* with the Father in respect of divinity and the same *homoousios* with us in respect of the humanity" (Evagrius, *Hist. eccl.* 3.14).

researched Nicaea, but his description of what was defined there (*proem.* 13–17) reads like a refutation of Eutychianism. Cyzicenus emphasizes, in particular, the necessity of hypostatic union. He adduces 1 Tim 3:16 ("He was revealed in the flesh and seen by the angels") to demonstrate the necessity of the divine *ousia*'s union with human nature: without it, the divine *ousia* is beyond the comprehension even of angels. Cyzicenus assiduously avoids using the terms *hypostasis*, *nature*, and *person* here, and describes Christ's humanity as "our kind" (*genos*) instead (*proem.* 15). He in turn cites the baptismal formula of Matt 28:19 and extends the passage with a brief *prosopopoieia*, or "speech in character," having Christ explain that the addition of the flesh does not add to the Trinity.[39] The last phrase has as its target Eutychian concerns about the threat of hypostatic union to the coessentiality of the Trinity. The reiteration of the word *horos*, "definition," is also noteworthy. Cyzicenus emphasizes that Nicaea investigated the *horos* of the faith (*proem.* 13), that the genuine suffering and resurrection of Christ's real flesh "confirmed through himself the divine and venerable *horos*" (*proem.* 15), and that this *horos* was preached apostolically (*proem.* 18). It is difficult not to hear these as allusive references to the *horos* of Chalcedon without explicitly naming the controversial council. Rhetorically and ecclesiologically, though, Cyzicenus is locating the *horos* not in the proceedings of the bishops at Chalcedon but as the core of the faith defined at Nicaea. Here, Nicaea and the subsequent councils that confirmed the Nicene faith are all merely affirmations of the truth manifested in the incarnation itself. For Cyzicenus, it is a faith that must be reaffirmed in the face of heretical challenges, whether of Arius or Eutyches, and in this sense the story of Nicaea and the story of Cyzicenus's present are the same story.

Once one is aware that Cyzicenus's narrative of Nicaea is always already an account of Chalcedonian orthodoxy, his theology is evident throughout the text. A few examples are illustrative. In Cyzicenus's account of Nicaea, the theological debates proper begin after a declaration of faith by Hosius of Cordoba. In this declaration, the central phrases ascribed to Hosius exhibit key elements of Chalcedonian Christology:

> Now then, it is necessary for us to confess that there is one will, one kingdom, one authority, one dominion over all created natures both visible and intelligible, one Godhead and the same *ousia* for the Father and the

---

39. Matt 28:19 reads, "Go forth and teach all nations, baptizing them in the name of the Father and of the Son and of the Holy Spirit."

Son and the Holy Spirit, since we do not proclaim a mixture or a division
of the hypostases of that ineffable and blessed Trinity. (2.12.5)

This statement could have been written in a theological context anytime circa the Council of Constantinople (381 CE) or later. All the elements can be found, for instance, in the Cappadocian fathers and other late fourth-century theologians. Variations on the list of that which the persons of the Trinity possess as a unity—will, kingdom, authority, and dominion—can be found, for instance, in Gregory of Nyssa.[40] A more precise context might be the mid- to late fourth-century debates over the divinity of the Holy Spirit, as indeed similar lists were deployed in that context.[41] Hosius's statement is obviously anachronistic in an early fourth-century context but would not have seemed so to Cyzicenus and other late fifth-century theologians, for whom it was axiomatic that all dogma had been defined in the Nicene Creed. In addition, the centrality of the denial of "mixture or division of the hypostases," while used here of the Trinity, would have echoed in the ears of a pro-Chalcedonian as confirming the terminology of the Chalcedonian Definition.[42]

In the narrative, Hosius's declaration is followed by Arian "murmur[ing]" (2.12.8). The Arians then put forward two philosophers to contend with the orthodox assembly. The first disputation scene (2.13.1–15) appears in another version in Rufinus (*Hist. eccl.* 10.3) and may derive from Gelasius (2018, 84–91). In both versions, the unnamed philosopher is countered by the simple, frank speech of an unlearned confessor. The differences between the version in Rufinus and that in Cyzicenus are worth examining together.

The version in Rufinus:

There is one God, who made the heaven and the earth, and who gave spirit to humankind, which he had formed from the mud of the earth, created all things that are seen and that are not seen by virtue of his Word

---

40. See, e.g., *Ad graecos ex communibus notionibus* (*GNO* 3.1:25,8–11): "For the persons of the Trinity are separate from each other neither in time, place, will, occupation, activity, nor experience, nor any of those [differences] that are conceptualized by humans."

41. See, e.g., Epiphanius, *Pan.* 74.13.5, 9: "The Spirit is not a servant, but of the same Godhead … understand one knowledge and foreknowledge in the Spirit, the Son and the Father": οὐ δοῦλον τυγχάνει τὸ Πνεῦμα, ἀλλὰ τῆς αὐτῆς θεότητος … οὕτω μοι καὶ περὶ Πνεύματος καὶ Υἱοῦ καὶ Πατρὸς τὴν μίαν γνῶσιν καὶ τὴν προγνωσίαν (Williams).

42. Compare, e.g., Basil, *Hom.* 16.4; *Spir.* 77; Gregory Nazianzen, *Or.* 20.7; John Chrysostom, *Sac.* 4.4.

and made them subsist by the sanctification of his Spirit. This Word and Wisdom, whom we call the Son, because he took pity on human waywardness, was born from a virgin, freed us from unending death through his suffering of death, and bestowed on us everlasting life by his resurrection. And he it is whom we await to come as the judge of all things that we have done. Do you believe these things are so, philosopher? (10.3)[43]

And in Cyzicenus:

And the holy man said to him, "There is one God, who has crafted the heaven and the earth and the sea and all things in them, who also formed humankind from earth and caused all things to subsist by his Word and Holy Spirit. We, knowing that this Word is the Son of God, philosopher, venerate him, believing that, in order to ransom us, <u>he has been made flesh</u> and been born and <u>been made man</u> from a virgin, and, through the suffering <u>of his flesh on the cross</u> and his death, he freed us from eternal condemnation, and through his resurrection he acquired for us eternal life. And we also await him, who has ascended into heaven, to come again and to be the judge of all the things that we have done. Do you believe these things, philosopher?" (2.13.9–10)[44]

Cyzicenus's version contains unique phrases—perhaps interpolations—that are pro-Chalcedonian and anti-Eutychian. The addition of "made flesh" and "made man" to the incarnation formula emphasizes the continuing reality of Christ's human nature in the incarnation and recalls the way in which Eutyches was pressed by the Home Synod to accept this based on

---

43. Our translation of: *deus unus est, qui caelum fecit et terram quique homini, quem de terrae limo formaverat, spiritum dedit, universa, quae videntur et quae non videntur, virtute verbi sui creavit et spiritus sui sanctificatione firmavit. hoc verbum ac sapientia, quem nos filium dicimus, humanos miseratus errores ex virgine nascitur et per passionem mortis a perpetua nos morte liberavit ac resurrectione sua aeternam nobis contulit vitam. quem et expectamus iudicem omnium, quae gerimus, esse venturum. credis haec ita esse, philosophe?*

44. καὶ ὁ ἅγιος πρὸς αὐτὸν »εἷς ἐστιν ὁ θεός« φησίν »ὁ τὸν οὐρανὸν καὶ τὴν γῆν καὶ τὴν θάλασσαν καὶ τὰ ἐν αὐτοῖς πάντα δημιουργήσας, ὃς καὶ τὸν ἄνθρωπον ἐκ γῆς διαπλάσας ὑπεστήσατο τὰ πάντα τῷ λόγῳ αὐτοῦ καὶ τῷ ἁγίῳ πνεύματι. τοῦτον τὸν λόγον, ὦ φιλόσοφε, θεοῦ υἱὸν ἡμεῖς εἰδότες προσκυνοῦμεν, πιστεύοντες διὰ τὴν ἡμετέραν ἀπολύτρωσιν ἐκ παρθένου αὐτὸν σεσαρκῶσθαι καὶ τετέχθαι καὶ ἐνηνθρωπηκέναι καὶ διὰ τοῦ τῆς σαρκὸς αὐτοῦ πάθους τοῦ ἐν τῷ σταυρῷ καὶ τοῦ θανάτου ἐλευθερωκέναι αὐτὸν ἡμᾶς ἐκ τῆς αἰωνίου κατακρίσεως διά τε τῆς ἀναστάσεως αὐτοῦ ζωὴν ἡμῖν αὐτὸν αἰώνιον περιποιεῖσθαι, ὃν καὶ εἰς οὐρανοὺς ἀνελθόντα ἐλπίζομεν πάλιν ἐλεύσεσθαι κριτήν τε ἔσεσθαι περὶ πάντων ὧν διεπραξάμεθα. πιστεύεις τούτοις, ὦ φιλόσοφε;«

his consent that Christ's flesh derived from Mary (C. Chalc. 1.516–522). The addition of "the suffering of his flesh" on the cross is also an anti-Eutychian accent. The holy man in Cyzicenus is further described as one "who knew nothing 'except Jesus Christ and him crucified' in the flesh, according to the Scriptures" (*Hist. eccl.* 2.13.7; citing 1 Cor 2:2). The qualification of "crucified" by "in the flesh, according to the Scriptures" would read to Cyzicenus and his allies as a rejoinder to Eutychian denials of the genuine humanity of Christ. The emphasis on the scriptural basis for the reality of Christ's human nature, moreover, contradicts Eutyches's insistence, recorded at the Home Synod, on the lack of scriptural authority for the vocabulary of hypostatic union, and his assertion that the scriptures take precedence over patristic authorities (C. Chalc. 1.359, 620). The confessor also opens his remarks with the phrase, "In the name of Jesus Christ, who always exists with the Father as the Word of God" (2.13.9), which would read as a rejoinder to the Eutychian concern that hypostatic union entailed a degradation or change in the Son's divine nature.

The differences between Rufinus's account of the simple confessor and that found in Cyzicenus leave uncertain whether Rufinus has abridged his source or whether Cyzicenus or one of his sources elaborated on the story, adding pro-Chalcedonian theology, but comparison to later, Greek accounts suggests the latter.[45] Similar differences, moreover, persist throughout the passages in Cyzicenus that derive from identifiable, extant sources or present closely parallel accounts to those in church histories of the early to mid-fifth century. As Nicaea was the focal point of contemporary theological debate, around which Cyzicenus constructs his account of the "pure and unblemished orthodox and apostolic faith" (*proem.* 8), the narrative of the council is instrumental in proving that Chalcedonian theology was prefigured and in many ways obviated by Nicaea.

6. Anonymous Cyzicenus and His Sources

6.1. Cyzicenus's Methods

In the preface to his history, Anonymous Cyzicenus outlines the compositional methods he plans to employ for his work, saying, "I found as much

---

45. For the comparison to other Greek accounts, see Wallraff, Stutz, and Marinides 2018, 85–91.

as was known to me and was proper to the truth, following the book that I had read previously, and, making selections from others, I thought it was necessary to write it in this book" (*proem.* 24). The author thereby states two occasionally contradictory goals for the work. First, he wants to offer a comprehensive account of the Council of Nicaea, predominantly through quotations of source material. Second, he makes his selections according to his perception of what is fitting with "the truth" of the council. The resulting product presents a complicated patchwork of borrowed passages from inconsistently cited sources, some identifiable and some not, that frequently diverges from other surviving versions.

Cyzicenus employs several tactics for arranging and reinterpreting his source materials. At his simplest, he uses extant narratives from prior historians such as Eusebius of Caesarea or Theodoret of Cyrrhus as the skeleton for his account, adding in supplementary sources where that narrative is cursory or omits a story he finds critical for his audience to know. At other times, he intertwines multiple accounts into a single, brief narrative and reorders his source material to create a sensible progression. His methods have been criticized as being uncritical and at times clumsy (e.g., Treadgold 2007, 166). Cyzicenus does not, however, transmit verbatim the majority of the passages to be found in the *Ecclesiastical History*.

Comparison between Cyzicenus's text and that of his sources, both those he himself cites and those we can identify through philological analysis, reveals a careful editorial hand at work throughout. In addition to the inclusion of pro-Chalcedonian language absent from the source material, discussed in the previous section, the three dominant patterns in the textual variants are

- reader aids, in the form of names, pronouns, prepositional phrases, and similar, which identify an agent or recipient of an action identified outside the excerpt or left unspecified in other versions (sometimes actually adding confusion to the sentence);
- additional characterization of the figures in the narrative, often with judgments on their morals or doctrinal beliefs such as "most pious" (*eusebestatos*) or the frequent epithet for Constantine, "most God-beloved" (*theophilestatos*); and
- reinforcement of the piety, sincerity, and divine authority of the champions of Nicene orthodoxy.

Constantine's treatment illustrates this last point. In Cyzicenus, he is never less than piously orthodox, even as he contemplates allowing Arius back into the church in book 3 (3.12–18). Nor does Cyzicenus's Constantine yield command to others, whether it be to his mother, Helena, whose actions are attributed regularly to the will of her son (e.g., 3.7.10), or to the bishops (2.8.3), although the parallel account by Rufinus (*Hist. eccl.* 10.2) depicts an emperor who subordinates himself to the church leaders. Thus, Cyzicenus does not merely quote sources but edits and delimits them in order to fit "as much as was known" into a framework "proper to the truth" (*proem.* 24). The boundaries are not necessarily imported from his sources.[46]

Cyzicenus's departure from his sources is perhaps clearest when treating the character of Eusebius of Caesarea, on whose *Ecclesiastical History* the present text relies heavily. In Cyzicenus's text, Eusebius serves as one of the key spokesmen for the consensus of the Nicene orthodox fathers in a lengthy debate against an Arian philosopher named Phaedo (2.14–24).[47] Historically, however, Eusebius had a complicated relationship with Arius and his supporters. Between the letter written by the patriarch Alexander of Alexandria condemning the theology of Arius and the debates over Arius's theology at the Council of Nicaea—assembled partly in response to that letter—a smaller council had assembled at Antioch in 325 CE, at which Eusebius was excommunicated for Arian sympathies.[48] Arius included Eusebius in a list of supporters describing broad agreement on his theological views throughout the churches of the East (*Urk.* 1, preserved in Theodoret, *Hist. eccl.* 1.5). Eusebius himself appears to have written a letter to Alexander of Alexandria accusing the bishop of misrepresenting Arius's theological arguments and expressing support for them (*Urk.* 7).[49] Cyzicenus has eliminated any suggestion of Eusebius's Arian sympathies from his own history. In order to avoid discussing Eusebius's involvement with a trial that targeted Athanasius, who by Cyzicenus's day was remembered as

---

46. For a more detailed discussion of Cyzicenus's editorial tendencies, see Shedd 2022.

47. Eusebius takes the role of primary speaker at 2.17–20.

48. Alexander's letter can be found in the collection of documents pertaining to the Arian controversy as *Urk.* 4b. A letter preserving the proceedings of the Council of Antioch survives in several Syriac manuscripts, included as *Urk.* 18.

49. This document is first attested in the acts of the second Council of Nicaea in 787. As other documents purporting to preserve earlier conciliar acts were invented to support particular theological arguments in the later councils, the lateness of this testimony may caution against accepting the authenticity of the document. On the matter of inventing conciliar documents, see MacMullen 2006, 104–6.

the foremost champion of Nicene theology, Cyzicenus moves the location of the council at which the trial occurred from Eusebius's home in Caesarea to Antioch (*Hist. eccl.* 3.16.27).[50] Twice, he mounts a direct defense of Eusebius's orthodoxy: once after the final citation of Eusebius's histories (2.1.8–12) and once when citing a passage in which his source had named Eusebius as an anti-Nicene conspirator (3.16.13). Cyzicenus clearly intends to rehabilitate the reputation of one of his best-regarded sources and modifies his other materials as necessary to preserve the "truth" of Eusebius's orthodoxy.

Cyzicenus is certainly not alone among his contemporary historians in viewing the truth as a matter separate from a simple narrative of doings and sayings.[51] Theodoret, whose work is among Cyzicenus's pastiche of sources, uses a similar documentary method with the overall aim of defending his brand of orthodoxy through the letters and conciliar testimony that make up over 40 percent of his history (Parmentier and Hansen 1998, 63–65). To support his claim that *homoousios* was a commonly accepted term, for instance, Theodoret (*Hist. eccl.* 1.13) employs two passages from Eusebius of Caesarea's *Life of Constantine* (3.13–14, 3.21–22) that profess the unanimity of the council. Neither passage, however, explicitly quotes the language of the creed or directly addresses the term *homoousios*. Theodoret merely uses the implications of unanimity to support his argument about the orthodoxy and tradition of his preferred terminology. Cyzicenus, for his part, borrows these same Eusebian passages, most likely known through Theodoret, and recontextualizes them as proof of Constantine's great piety and support of orthodox Christian doctrines (see *Hist. eccl.* 2.29.5–9, 2.37.26–27). The cited sources thus become a vehicle for a larger message that takes precedence over verbatim replication of the quoted materials. The reader of Cyzicenus's text should thus be wary of accepting the author's stance that the passages cited are unaltered and true reflections of preexisting source materials, particularly when those pas-

---

50. Details about the trials of Athanasius appear at 3.16.25–3.18.20. Cyzicenus's account does not hint that Constantine would eventually banish the bishop to Trier. Athanasius's own vast corpus of writing had little direct influence on the history by Cyzicenus.

51. Scott (2010) notes the frequency with which Byzantine chroniclers play with the boundary between direct citation and free composition, with particular focus on Theophanes. Humphries (2008) addresses how Rufinus also did not design his translation of Eusebius to be strictly in conformity with its model, attaching his own historical principles.

sages support Chalcedonian Christology or assert the irrefutable defeat of Arius's ideas at the Council of Nicaea.

6.2. The Sources of the *Ecclesiastical History*

True to Cyzicenus's initial statement (*proem.* 24), much of the *Ecclesiastical History* consists of excerpts from previous authors carefully rearranged to tell the story of Constantine's rise to power and role in the theological disputes of the early fourth century CE. Over the course of the three books, Cyzicenus explicitly names five different sources: the codex he read at his father's house (*proem.* 2–8), a set of books by a presbyter named John (*proem.* 21), and three writers of ecclesiastical histories: Eusebius of Caesarea (*proem.* 22), Theodoret of Cyrrhus (2.33.7), and a source he initially identifies as Rufinus of Aquileia (*proem.* 22) but later as "Rufinus, or rather Gelasius" (1.8.1). From patterns of similarity with the works of other historians, including Rufinus, it is evident that Cyzicenus, like others of his time, had at his disposal a Greek text that has not survived, which was at the time attributed variously to Rufinus and to Gelasius of Caesarea.[52] Eusebius, Theodoret, and the lost Greek history form much of the basis on which Cyzicenus builds his work but are supplemented by other sources, unnamed and more difficult to identify directly. Each of Cyzicenus's sources will be considered briefly here, including the extent to which their works appear in the *Ecclesiastical History*. The footnotes that accompany the translation give more detailed information about the passages cited and any major departures from the surviving texts for these sources.

6.2.1. The Codex of Dalmatius and Writings of John the Presbyter

The two sources to which Cyzicenus attributes the greatest authority over the matters that transpired during the Council of Nicaea have left no traces in any other surviving text. The miraculous codex that he read as a child in

---

52. Photius (cod. 88–89) erroneously states that Gelasius had translated Rufinus's text into Greek. On the confusion between the two authors and the scholarship that strongly suggests Gelasius was in fact one of Rufinus's sources, see Wallraff, Stutz, and Marinides 2018, xxiii–xxviii, xxxiii–xxxiv. Van Nuffelen (2002) argues that the confusion stemmed from the production of a work produced in the mid-fifth century, consisting in part of translation of Rufinus into Greek, that circulated pseudonymously under Gelasius's name. See also section 6.2.3.

his father's attic, commissioned or composed by Dalmatius and containing all the events of the council "in unbroken sequence" (*proem.* 2), never reappears as a cited source later in the text. It is nevertheless on the testimony purportedly found in this book that Cyzicenus rests his authority to refute the "Eutychians" and undertake an investigation on the true proceedings and meaning of the council. When describing the research that led to the production of the *Ecclesiastical History*, Cyzicenus reminds the reader that he "had learned about [the proceedings] beforehand, as [he] said above" (*proem.* 20). He establishes this book, no longer at hand for him and otherwise unknown to us, as the foundation for the greater truth he will reveal beyond that which could be read in other, more widely known sources. Indeed, Cyzicenus claims that the insufficiency of his sources, including Eusebius and "Rufinus," compels him to supplement their narratives in order to be "in accordance with that holy book" and to write a history that was "proper to the truth, following the book that I had read previously" (*proem.* 23–24). This book, conveniently for Cyzicenus, is inaccessible to his foes—and to modern scholars. We may reasonably question whether it existed.

The writings of John the Presbyter occupy a similar position among Cyzicenus's sources. This John, "a man who was a presbyter of old and especially skilled in the art of writing, who wrote in very ancient quaternions" (*proem.* 21), is otherwise unknown to modern scholarship and may well have never existed. Yet, much like the enigmatic codex of Dalmatius, John's writings are credited with greater authority than any writings by identifiable authors. It is to John that Cyzicenus attributes the "clear records of what had been debated and written there" (*proem.* 20). It is not entirely clear what type of text Cyzicenus is describing here. Perhaps he means a collection of curated documentary evidence, something like the *Synodical Collection* of Sabinus of Heraclea, or is imagining records of the proceedings, *acta*, as were preserved from later councils but which—much to the dismay of theologians of the preceding century and a half—never appear to have existed for Nicaea.[53] Alternatively, he could be describing a text like his own, combining a narrative account and documents. Whichever the case, this enigmatic text, too, is unavailable to us.

Cyzicenus thus rests his authority on the foundation of two unattested, unrecoverable sources, which he never cites again. In both cases,

---

53. Sabinus of Heraclea's compilation, though no longer extant, was an important source for the historians Socrates and Sozomen. On Sabinus see Hauschild 1970; Löhr 1987.

he emphasizes the immense age of the books, which has the dual effect of establishing the credibility of their narratives and implying the perishability of their texts.[54] It is on the basis of their credibility that he claims to write a more truthful and accurate account than the reader can find elsewhere. It is perhaps unsurprising, then, that the passages that Cyzicenus borrows from his sources, both acknowledged and uncited, frequently diverge from the texts preserved in the surviving manuscripts of those works and other authors' citations thereof. Cyzicenus's truth necessitates establishing that the sources generally available were insufficient and that he had unique access to corrective texts.

6.2.2. Eusebius of Caesarea, Ecclesiastical History and Life of Constantine

Cyzicenus constructs the first several chapters of his history using passages from the historical work of Constantine's contemporary, Eusebius of Caesarea, to structure his narrative. Eusebius, says Cyzicenus, was the only author who "kept to the unswerving highway of truth, from the advent of the Lord until the times of the great Constantine" (*proem.* 23). The first book then begins with an excerpt of Eusebius's own *Ecclesiastical History* (8.13.12–14), describing Constantine's elevation as emperor and the character of his father, Constantius.[55] From the elevation of Constantine, Cyzicenus continues by selecting the parts of Eusebius's account that recount Constantine's gradual conquest of the Roman Empire and his victories over the "tyrants" Maxentius, Maximinus, and Licinius. These excerpts are presented in the same sequence in which they appear in Eusebius, with some authorial passages and related insertions separating the quotations, as shown by the table below:

Cyzicenus	Eusebius
1.1.1–3	8.13.12–14
1.1.4–5	9.9.1–2

---

54. *Proem.* 2: "in a book of exceptional age" (ἐν βίβλῳ ἀρχαιοτάτῃ). *Proem.* 21: "a presbyter of old … who wrote in very ancient quaternions" (τινι πρεσβυτέρῳ ἀνδρὶ παλαιῷ…ἐν τετραδίοις παλαιοῖς λίαν).

55. The most recent English translation of Eusebius's *Ecclesiastical History* is Jeremy Schott's (see Eusebius 2019). The most recent critical edition is that of Bardy (Eusebius 1952–1958), which depends heavily on Schwartz (Eusebius 1903).

1.7.4–7	9.9.8–11
1.9.1–4	9.10.1–5
1.9.4–10.1	9.10.13–11.1
1.10.7–9	10.4.8–11
1.11.1–16	10.8.2–9.4
2.1.3–7	10.9.5–9

Although the compressed narrative of Cyzicenus's text follows the sequence found in Eusebius, substantial portions of Eusebius's books have been omitted that are inconsistent with Cyzicenus's goals. A brief examination of both the passages omitted from Eusebius's account and linking narratives in Cyzicenus show that the primary principle of inclusion was the activity of Constantine himself. Eusebius, however, contains little information about the Council of Nicaea, making him an unsuitable source for Cyzicenus's account of the council itself. His *Ecclesiastical History* thus provides historical background only through the beginning of book 2, where Cyzicenus begins his detailed narration about the council.

Cyzicenus occasionally cites passages of Eusebius's *Life of Constantine*, which he likely knows only through intermediary sources.[56] Four passages from the *Life of Constantine* appear in the second book of Cyzicenus's history, but in each instance the quotations are "cut" at exactly the same points as in other, prior texts, as shown below:

Cyzicenus, *Hist. eccl.*	Eusebius, *Vit. Const.*	Socrates, *Hist. eccl.*[57]	Theodoret, *Hist. eccl.*
2.3.22–4.13	2.63, 69–72	1.7.1–20[58]	
2.4.13–6.1	3.6–9	1.8.1, 4–12	

---

56. For an English translation of the *Life of Constantine*, see Eusebius 1999. The most recent critical edition is Eusebius 1975.

57. Socrates of Constantinople, or Socrates Scholasticus (ca. 380–439), wrote an *Ecclesiastical History* in seven books that depended heavily on Eusebius and the history attributed to Gelasius of Caesarea. It is uncertain whether Cyzicenus used Socrates's work directly or whether their similarities derive from their shared use of the Gelasian history. The most recent critical edition is Socrates Scholasticus 1995.

58. In this passage, Cyzicenus's text matches more closely a later text, the Life of Metrophanes and Alexander (BHG 1279). Socrates, for his part, contains slightly longer quotations from Eusebius's text. Thus, it is more likely that Cyzicenus found this

| 2.29.5–9 | 3.13–14 | 1.8.21–23 | 1.13.2 |
| 2.37.26–27 | 3.21.4–3.22 | | 1.13.3–4 |

The consistency with which Cyzicenus's excerpts match the selection made by other, earlier authors makes it unlikely that he independently read a copy of the *Life of Constantine* himself. Nonetheless, he relies on Eusebius as an authoritative voice, copying over even the citation formulas that are found in the earlier authors.[59]

6.2.3. "Rufinus, or Rather Gelasius"

Although Cyzicenus considers Eusebius his most authoritative source (behind John and the book from his youth, that is), it is the work that he identifies as that by "Rufinus … or rather Gelasius" (1.8.1) that appears to provide the most material for the *Ecclesiastical History*. This source can be identified with some certainty with a now-lost history employed by several church historians and hagiographers, whose treatment of various historical episodes point to the independent usage of a common source. Modern scholarship has tended to attribute this history to Gelasius of Caesarea (ca. 355–395 CE), who is credited with writing a continuation of Eusebius's *Ecclesiastical History*.[60] But the relationship of Gelasius's history to that of Rufinus remains contested, as does whether the Greek text that was transmitted with both names up to the time of Photius was written by Gelasius with Rufinus's name included through misattribution, a translation of Rufinus mixed with Gelasius's text, or an independent extension of both

---

passage in the Gelasian history than in Socrates. On this matter, see Wallraff, Stutz, and Marinides 2018, 65–71, as well as the notes to the passage in this translation.

59. See this text, 2.5.2, and the accompanying note for an example of Cyzicenus borrowing citation formulas.

60. The most comprehensive reconstruction of the lost history is Wallraff, Stutz, and Marinides 2018. The editors attribute it to Gelasius, following the work of Winkelmann (1964, 1966a, 1966b). It is important to acknowledge the significant alternative assessment of the evidence presented by Van Nuffelen (2002), who posits that what has been reconstructed as the *Ecclesiastical History* of Gelasius of Caesarea is better accounted for as a mid-fifth-century text based in part on a Greek translation of Rufinus and circulated pseudonymously under Gelasius's name. If Van Nuffelen is correct, then Anonymous Cyzicenus's source would be this mid-fifth-century text.

histories pseudonymously attributed to Gelasius.[61] Whichever the case, material from this source text, which we will often call "Gelasian" for simplicity's sake, appears across all three books of Cyzicenus's text.

The degree to which Cyzicenus depended on this text can only be inferred with limited certainty by convergences between the language and narratives of Cyzicenus with the historical works of Rufinus, Socrates, Theodoret, and several later writers of historical and hagiographical texts (Wallraff, Stutz, and Marinides 2018, xix–xxviii; Hansen 2002, xliv–xlviii). In the first book, where Cyzicenus most frequently cites his sources, the Gelasian passages can easily be identified where Rufinus's name appears, especially as Cyzicenus's Greek matches too closely the wording found in earlier Greek sources to have been independently translated from Rufinus's Latin. Once the citations disappear in books 2–3, further borrowings can be identified only where Cyzicenus's narration and text closely parallel one or ideally two of the other sources.

Even by the relatively conservative reconstruction in the recent edition of Gelasius of Caesarea's fragments, Cyzicenus preserves versions of no fewer than thirty-two identifiable fragments of the lost history, and it is probable that some of the uncited, uncorroborated material between these fragments likewise derives from it. In book 1 of the *Ecclesiastical History*, where Eusebius's work provides the narrative framework, Gelasian material appears in at least eight of the twelve chapters. Books 2–3 depend even more on the lost history for their narrative sequence, although Cyzicenus employs other sources to expand and embellish the account. It is through Gelasian excerpts that we learn about the tyrannical acts of Maximinus and Maxentius (1.2.2–1.7.4), the sequence of events that occurred at the Council of Nicaea (book 2), Helena's travels in the Holy Land (3.6.1–3.7.13), and several Christianizing missions that occurred after the end of the council (3.9.1–3.10.25). As Gelasius is said to have continued his history from the work of Eusebius, the possibility remains that even the small pieces of Eusebius's *Ecclesiastical History* quoted in Cyzicenus's first book are positioned following the chronology and narrative of Gelasius (Hansen 2002, xlii–iii). Socrates and Cyzicenus begin their own histories with the same Eusebian passage (*Hist. eccl.* 8.13), suggesting they may have been inspired by a common ancestor.

---

61. For a more complete explanation of the relationship between Rufinus and Gelasius, see Wallraff, Stutz, and Marinides 2018, xxx–xxxvii. See Van Nuffelen 2002 for an important contrasting view of the evidence.

In the translation, passages from this history have been cited following the fragment designations in the most recent edition handling Gelasius of Caesarea (2018). Additional discussions about possible fragments not confirmed by other sources appear in the footnotes throughout.

6.2.4. Theodoret of Cyrrhus

The final source expressly named by Cyzicenus is Theodoret of Cyrrhus (393–ca. 458 CE), whose own *Ecclesiastical History* covered the century from the beginning of the Arian controversy to the death of Theodore of Mopsuestia in 428 CE.[62] Unlike Eusebius and Rufinus—or rather Gelasius—Theodoret is not named in the prologue to Cyzicenus's text, receiving mention first near the end of book 2 as an expert source on the activities of Eusebius of Nicomedia and his associates in the later 320s CE (*Hist. eccl.* 2.33.7). Despite the fact that Theodoret is cited explicitly only a few times, passages of his history appear throughout Cyzicenus's text to corroborate the account and expand on some of the shorter stories drawn from other sources.

The first probable borrowing from Theodoret's work appears, unmarked, in book 1 (1.11.22–31), where Cyzicenus reproduces the same excerpt of a Constantinian letter as found in Theodoret (1.20.1–10). Beginning in the second book, where sources are rarely specified or set apart by quotation formulae, Theodoret becomes the co-dominant source (together with the lost history) around which Cyzicenus constructs his narrative. Transitional passages between the major documents of Cyzicenus's second book often have parallels in Theodoret, as at 2.7.41–44 (Theodoret, *Hist. eccl.* 1.7.11–14) and 2.34.1 (Theodoret, *Hist. eccl.* 1.9.1). In the third book, the text shifts between Gelasian passages and selections from Theodoret with increasing rapidity, making distinctions between the sources uncertain.

Part of the difficulty in separating Gelasian material from Theodoret's stems from Theodoret's own evasive citation habits and the uncertain relationship between his *Ecclesiastical History* and the history attributed to Gelasius of Caesarea. The most recent edition of Gelasius (2018, xli–xliv)

---

62. Theodoret depicts his fellow bishop Theodore as one of the critical champions of the Nicene faith against rampant Arianism (*Hist. eccl.* 5.39). Other writers, particularly Cyril of Alexandria, classify Theodore as a Nestorian heretic, and he is one of the major heretical figures in Theodore of Raithu's *Preparation*.

identifies only one narrative (F15b and c) that has enough external, supporting evidence to name Theodoret as a primary witness to the Gelasian text. Cyzicenus's version of the same narrative includes the text covered by Theodoret but includes significantly more information as well (3.7.8–13; see Theodoret, *Hist. eccl.* 1.18.5–9). In this case and others like it, it remains unclear whether Cyzicenus preserves a text closer to the lost history, has expanded the text using yet another source, or has added original material. At other points of the third book (e.g., 3.7.2–7), the interweaving of material known only from Theodoret with Gelasian fragments suggests that more of Theodoret's text may derive from the lost history than a conservative reckoning of the fragments would count. Cyzicenus's relation to both texts in these moments is unclear. Indeed, a detailed reassessment of the relationship between the Gelasian history, Theodoret, and Cyzicenus, though beyond the purview of this brief introduction, is warranted.

6.2.5. Socrates Scholasticus

The *Ecclesiastical History* of Socrates Scholasticus is never cited directly in Cyzicenus, but it contains several passages that parallel Cyzicenus's text.[63] One reason for this could be both authors' reliance on the lost Gelasian history (see above, §6.2.3). In many instances where Cyzicenus and Socrates present the same information, comparison with a third text such as Rufinus or the Life of Metrophanes and Alexander (BHG 1279) suggests such a shared reliance.[64] In a few select instances, however, Socrates presents the only passage comparable to Cyzicenus among the surviving sources for the Council of Nicaea. The transitional material surrounding the enigmatic *Diatyposes* and the canons of the council parallels Socrates's text, suggesting that Cyzicenus borrowed it directly.[65] As in the case of Theodoret, however, Socrates rarely cites the source of his information, meaning that even

---

63. The best critical edition for Socrates is Socrates Scholasticus 1995. The best English translation remains that in *NPNF* 2/2.

64. The Life of Metrophanes and Alexander (BHG 1279) is an anonymous source from the mid-seventh to mid-ninth century that preserves many passages mirrored in other histories. On the nature of the text and its independence from Cyzicenus, see Wallraff, Stutz, and Marinides 2018, xlv–l, lvii–lxi. Van Nuffelen (2002) argues instead that Socrates is a source for the history discussed in 6.2.3, which in turn served as the source for Cyzicenus and BHG 1279.

65. Cyzicenus, *Hist. eccl.* 2.30.1–5 parallels Socrates, *Hist. eccl.* 1.10.1–4; Cyzicenus, *Hist. eccl.* 2.32.22–2.33.4 parallels Socrates, *Hist. eccl.* 1.11.3–7.

when he is the only parallel source to Cyzicenus, there is no guarantee that the material is not originally Gelasian (Wallraff, Stutz, and Marinides 2018, xlix–l). Nonetheless, in these cases we have cited Socrates in the footnotes as the relevant source for comparison to Cyzicenus's text.

6.2.6. Documents from the Council of Nicaea

Cyzicenus includes a series of letters from or addressed to participants in the Council of Nicaea in his *Ecclesiastical History* that are not always drawn from the identifiable sources employed in the surrounding narrative. Authors including Athanasius, Eusebius, Socrates, Theodoret, and the Gelasian history included selections of these documents, giving Cyzicenus a wide variety of potential sources. He borrowed the useful parts of each, rearranging the documents to structure his narrative and incorporating them in a unique sequence.

The table below shows the major letters and other, discrete documents that appear throughout the *Ecclesiastical History*. As it shows, the order in which Cyzicenus presents the excerpts does not correspond directly to their order in any of the other known sources. Where relevant, the chart also includes the numberings used in Hans-Georg Opitz's edition of the documents on the early Arian controversy, for easier comparison.[66]

Cyzicenus	Socrates	Theodoret	Athanasius, *De decretis*[67]	*Urkunden*
1.11.22–31		1.20.1–10	41	27
2.3.1–21	1.6.4–30		35	4b
2.4.1–13	1.7.2–10			17

---

66. *Athanasius Werke*, vol. 3.1–2, *Urkunden zur Geschichte des arianischen Streites*, established a standardized numbering system still in frequent use for the documents relating to the Arian controversy.

67. Athanasius's *On the Decrees of the Council of Nicaea* ends with a series of documents without additional commentary, excerpted in many later sources. There is no evidence that Cyzicenus employed Athanasius's work directly, although later scribes appended three letters to Cyzicenus's narrative that likely derive directly from Athanasius's account. See appendix 1.

2.27.1–6			37	24
2.34.2–14	1.9.1–14	1.9.2–13	36	23
2.35.1–18	1.8.35–54	1.12	33	22
2.36.1–2	1.9.30–31		39	33
2.37.1–9	1.9.17–25		38	25
2.37.10–22	1.9.32–46	1.10		26
3.3.1–6	1.9.46–50	1.15.1–2		
3.4.1–5	1.9.50–55	1.16.1–4		
3.5.1–8	1.9.55–63	1.17.1–8		
3.11.1–11		1.25.1–11		
3.13.1–5	1.14.2–6			
3.14	1.27.4			
3.15.1–5				32
3.17.1–7		1.29.1–6		

Cyzicenus frequently presents prefatory and transitional text that parallels one source before diverging from its sequencing. Surrounding the chain of five letters at the end of book 2 (2.34–37), the introduction and conclusion resemble passages from Theodoret. Cyzicenus's *Hist. eccl.* 2.34.1 corresponds to Theodoret's 1.9.1, and both passages lead into the letter to Alexander and the churches of northern Africa, while Cyzicenus's 2.37.23–25 corresponds to Theodoret's 1.10. Between them, however, Cyzicenus includes a letter from a later point in Theodoret as well as two that do not appear in the text of Theodoret whatsoever. If we presume that Cyzicenus went searching for additional information in a closely parallel source such as Socrates or Athanasius, this hypothesis does not explain why the letters at 2.36 and 2.37 should appear in reverse order from their arrangement in those sources.

Even when the arrangements in Cyzicenus, Socrates, and Theodoret do align with one another, questions remain about Cyzicenus's true source. Exactly the same sequence of three letters at 3.3–3.5 in Cyzicenus appears likewise in Socrates and Theodoret. However, the relationship between these two authors is as uncertain as that between Theodoret and the Gelasian history, as Theodoret often uses the same documents found in Socrates, but to different narrative ends (Parmentier et al. 2006, 82–87). This sequence of three letters may originate with a common source to Socrates, Theodoret, and Cyzicenus. For many of these documents, therefore, it is impossible to say for certain which historian provided Cyzicenus with his copies or whether he was using several different sources. Only notable divergences from all other surviving copies are marked in the footnotes to each letter.

6.2.7. Philip of Side

Günther Hansen (1998) raised the hypothesis that several of the unattributed passages in Cyzicenus's work derive from a fifth-century clergyman and historian called Philip of Side. To summarize his argument briefly, several passages of Cyzicenus appear to be rhetorically reworked and elaborated compared to their comparative passages in Socrates and Theodoret. In particular, the inventive speech attributed to Constantine (2.7) adopts a florid, "Asiatic" rhetorical style marked with accented clausulae, in a manner unsuited to the contemporary rhetoric of Constantine's day. Employing the testimony of Socrates (*Hist. eccl.* 7.26–27) and Photius (*Bibl.* 35), Hansen identifies the author behind this style of rhetoric as Philip of Side, disparaged by both Photius and Socrates for his overwrought and excessively repetitious narrative.

Hansen (1998, 198) admits that his work is speculative and leaves largely unaddressed the complex relationship between his identified Philip of Side passages and the fragments identified as Gelasian. In book 1 (1.4.2–5), he identifies as a possible fragment from Philip a passage of historical narrative for which there is no surviving parallel. This fragment, however, stands between two passages of Gelasian material (F6) that appear consecutive to one another in the Life of Metrophanes and Alexander (BHG 1279 289b–290a, 290a–290b). Furthermore, the attested Gelasian passage in 1.4.6 appears to refer to the narrative from 1.4.2–5, although the latter passage was not included in the Life. These details may point to a Gelasian origin for the whole section rather than an intruding passage of expansion by Philip of Side. This same pattern of seamless integration with Gelasian fragments reappears for many of the passages tentatively identified as belonging to Philip, as in 1.12.1–4, 2.13, and 3.12.1–14.5. Without further information or confirmed fragments of Philip of Side, it is impossible to know whether Philip incorporated extensive passages of the Gelasian history into his work, later cited by Cyzicenus through Philip, or whether these transitions between Gelasian fragments indicate simply that Cyzicenus copied more material from the lost history than the other known witnesses. In many cases of postulated origin from Philip, there is only one witness outside Cyzicenus to the adjacent Gelasian fragments.[68]

In the specific case of the pseudo-Constantinian speech, however, Philip of Side appears to be a reasonable candidate for authorship. The speech occurs shortly after Constantine arrives at the council, whereupon Socrates, Theodoret, the Life of Metrophanes and Alexander, and Cyzicenus all claim that he waited for the permission of the bishops before sitting. The Life proceeds with no mention of a speech (12.2–12.3). Socrates summarizes the emperor's opening address as a general call to unity (*Hist. eccl.* 1.8.18). Theodoret provides a few lines of a speech that calls for recourse to Scripture to reach unanimity on the theological disputes (*Hist. eccl.* 1.7.11–12). These lines reappear at the tail end of the long speech in Cyzicenus, but their complete absence in the other two sources suggests that either they originated with Theodoret and were expanded afterward, as Hansen suggests, or that Theodoret himself had a copy of the same speech that Cyzicenus did. In either case, Philip of Side remains a possible source for the full version of Constantine's welcoming speech.[69] Without further corroboration, a definitive answer remains elusive.

6.2.8. Unknown Sources

Despite the best efforts of recent scholars, the original contexts of many of the most interesting documents of Cyzicenus's *Ecclesiastical History* remain a mystery. While Constantine's speech has received some attention, particularly by scholars interested in its authenticity, three other sections of

---

68. Hansen's identifications of the fragments of Philip of Side are accepted by Heyden (2006, 225–27), with a note of caution that even if securely derived from Philip, they may be reworked to suit Cyzicenus's purposes.

69. If Theodoret relied on Philip of Side for his fragment of the speech, that would resolve the difficulty Hansen (1998, 193) acknowledges for explaining how Socrates could have been familiar with Philip's writing despite the claim that Theodoret's later history influenced Philip's work.

the second book are likewise unparalleled in the surviving literature.[70] The definition and defense of the divine hypostasis by Hosius of Cordoba (2.12), the lengthy theological dispute with the Arian philosopher Phaedo that occupies the central position of book 2 (2.14–2.24), and the *diatyposeis*— "regulations"—of the council (2.31) all exist only in Cyzicenus. These four documents present the key theological arguments of the history, making the definitions and decrees of the Council of Nicaea most relevant to the post-Chalcedonian church. Although the common opinion at present is that Cyzicenus has repurposed these documents from another, unknown context, there remains the possibility that he himself composed some portions of these, disguising personal contributions through his self-proclaimed reliance on previous sources and substantiated documentary habits.

7. Text and Reception

The textual tradition of the *Ecclesiastical History* presents several complications that bear on the understanding of the text. First of all, book 3 of the *Ecclesiastical History* is preserved in only one manuscript: Milan, Bibliotheca Ambrosiana, Greek 534 (M 88 sup.), dating to the thirteenth century. The text of the third book was actually copied *before* the first and second books in the Ambrosiana manuscript, demonstrating that the surviving text of book 3 derived from a separate, now-lost textual tradition. The general loss of the third book also suggests that most Byzantine readers after Photius (who attests to reading a three-book work [*Bibl.* 15, 88]) read the *Ecclesiastical History* in a two-book format (see appendix 3). A second complication is that book 2 in every copy of the *Ecclesiastical History*, including Ambrosiana gr. 534 (M 88 sup.), is followed by three letters of Constantine on topics relating to the Arian controversy, all of which seem to derive from Athanasius's *De decretis*.[71] The letters were later included in the first printed editions of the text. Because they formed an integral part of the Byzantine and early modern reception of

---

70. Other than Hansen (1998), the most recent contributor to the debate of the authenticity of the speech has been Ehrhardt (1980), who provides an overview of previous scholarship.

71. Documents 1–3 in the Byzantine Epistolary Supplement correspond to Athanasius, *Decr.* 40–42. The first of these three letters was originally included in book 3 of the *Ecclesiastical History*, but the medieval scribes who first copied the letters were unlikely to know this since the third book had already been lost when these texts were added as an appendix to books 1–2.

the text, we have included a translation of the three letters in appendix 1, "The Byzantine Epistolary Supplement." A third complication involves the date at which the chapter headings that appear regularly in the manuscripts were added to the tradition. Though later copyists often added running titles to the texts they copied in order to make certain passages easier to find, late antique authors also sometimes added titles to their own texts, especially when the text was a compilation.[72] We agree, therefore, with the estimation of Gerhard Loeschke and Margret Heinemann (1918, xxv), the editors of the first modern critical edition of the text, that it is impossible to tell whether the titles are original to Anonymous Cyzicenus or not. Moreover, since the chapter titles were also an important way later readers maneuvered through the text, we have chosen to include them in the text of our translation.

Using the evidence of the textual tradition, we can also begin to see some of the contours of the later reception of the *Ecclesiastical History*. The third book had been set apart from the first two, which formed a coherent set by themselves, by an independent set of *pinakes* and a separate title: "The Efforts Taken by the Pious Emperor Constantine after the Great Council in Nicaea." Formally an addition, the third book was easily removed from the first two by later readers. Hansen posits that this occurred because later Byzantine readers considered other sources more authoritative for the events after Nicaea but valued the detailed account of the council itself as presented in the *Ecclesiastical History*. Copyists preserved the first two books as a nominally accurate record of the Council of Nicaea but stopped copying book 3 (Hansen 2002, xii; see discussion in §6). Later users of the *Ecclesiastical History* clearly believed it contained genuine conciliar material, as suggested by the fact that later scribes often copied it alongside the Acts of the Council of Ephesus.[73] In fact, several medieval Greek authors quote from one section of the text, the Dispute with Phaedo (2.14–24), citing the text as if it were a record of an authentic Nicene dispute.[74] Several Byzantine authors even cite the dispute with the

---

72. For a parallel example nearly contemporaneous with Anonymous Cyzicenus, see Cassiodorus, *Hist. trip., praef.* 5.

73. For a summary of the texts found alongside the *Ecclesiastical History* and their place in the transmission of the text, see Hansen 2002, xii–xxiii.

74. Hansen's list includes the following authors: Niketas Stethatos (ca. 1005–ca. 1090); Nikephoros Blemmydes (1197–ca. 1269); Ioannes Bekkos (between 1230/40–1297), patriarch of Constantinople (1275–1282); Ioannes Kyparissiotes (ca. 1310–1378/9); Markos Eugenikos (ca. 1394–1445), metropolitan of Ephesus (1437–1445);

formula "from the acts of the first council."⁷⁵ At other times, the *Ecclesiastical History* was copied alongside heresiological works such as Theodore of Raithu's *Preparation* (*Praeparatio in incarnationem*), the text of which was included in the 1599 *editio princeps* of the *Ecclesiastical History*.⁷⁶ Other copies of the *Ecclesiastical History* appear alongside two anti-Arian epistles of Athanasius, *On the Opinion of Dionysus* and the *Epistle to the Bishops of Egypt and Libya*. In these latter instances, the *Ecclesiastical History* acts as a corollary heresiological treatise, treating the first and archetypal heresy, that of Arius. In both the heresiological and conciliar readings of the *Ecclesiastical History*, one can see a reason for including the epistolary appendix after the history: to include in one place a large number of the documents relevant for understanding the Arian controversy and supporting subsequent doctrinal stances.

The manuscript evidence also suggests that Anonymous Cyzicenus's work had only a limited circulation. Only eight manuscripts survive from before the sixteenth century, and most of those circulated in few monastic centers. One fragment of the *Ecclesiastical History*, again the Dispute with Phaedo, comes from the monastic enclaves of Mount Athos, and a subscription on another manuscript notes that it was copied "from an old parchment codex in the Chora monastery."⁷⁷ Moreover, outside Photius's two notices in his *Bibliotheca*, no author again refers to the *Ecclesiastical History* until the sixteenth century, confining themselves merely to quoting portions of it thought to stem from the Council of Nicaea.⁷⁸ We know that Photius (*Hom.* 15–16) also made use of the *Ecclesiastical History* in

---

and Gennadios Scholarios (between 1400/1405–ca. 1472), patriarch of Constantinople (1454–1456, 1463, and 1464–1465). See Hansen's (2002, 163–64) list of *Benutzer* with keys to the Greek text.

75. See Hansen (2002, x n. 1) and his comments on the various anonymous excerpters who copy from the Dispute with Phaedo under the rubric, "From the proceedings of the first council" (ἐκ τῶν πρακτικῶν τῆς πρώτης συνόδου), on xxiii.

76. Theodore of Raithu (flor. early sixth century CE) included in the *Preparation* a catalog of heresies and an examination of theological vocabulary and concepts.

77. Athous Vatopedinus, cod. 34 (B), dating from the fourteenth century. The Vatican manuscript, Greek 830 (V), dated to 1446, includes the subscription, "from an old parchment book of the Chora monastery" (μετεγράφη ... ἀπὸ βιβλίου παλαιοῦ μεμβράνου τοῦ μοναστηρίου τῆς χώρας). See Hansen 2002, xiii–xiv, xix–xx.

78. Hansen (2008, 48–49) addresses the reception directly, while the lengthier discussion of manuscripts and editions (2002, xii–xli) indirectly treats the reception of the text in this period.

two of his sermons on Arianism, and it is possible that later Byzantine historians, such as George the Monk (d. after 842) and Nicephorus Callistus Xanthopulus (*ante* 1256–ca. 1335) used the text.[79] Since both George and Xanthopulus were monks, their use of the text would be entirely consistent with what we know about its dissemination based on manuscript evidence. Thus, the *Ecclesiastical History* seems to have enjoyed a circulation largely limited to monastic centers, occasionally reaching a wider group of churchmen, but not widely known by a larger segment of literate Byzantine society. Engagement with the text was also largely limited to one portion of the text, the Dispute with Phaedo. The larger historical enterprise of the *Ecclesiastical History* seems to have been paid only minor attention.

By contrast, when the *Ecclesiastical History* came to Western Europe, the text became something of a hit among Catholic intelligentsia. It arrived in Western Europe sometime in the fifteenth century. Many manuscripts are attested in Italy early on, and perhaps the text first arrived here. A hypothetical entry point for the text into the intellectual world of Western Europe may have been during the Councils of Basel, Ferrara, and Florence (1431–1445), when Greek churchmen came to Italy to discuss the possibility of the reunion of the Western and Eastern churches.[80] To judge by manuscript copies alone, the sixteenth century was the high point for the popularity of the text. Almost 73 percent of surviving manuscripts of the *Ecclesiastical History* date to this century.[81] These manuscripts were

---

79. For Photius's dependence on Cyzicenus, see Photius 1958, 236–37, 245 n. 4, 255 n. 39, 261 n. 2. For George the Monk's possible dependence on Anonymous Cyzicenus, see Scott 2015, and De Boor's apparatus in his Teubner edition of George 1904, 489, line 23–490, line 6 (see *Hist. eccl.* 1.7); 505, lines 17–18 (see *Hist. eccl.* 2.8.1—this section is almost a quote); 505, line 18–507, line 15 (= *Hist. eccl.* 2.13). For Xanthopulus's possible use of Anonymous Cyzicenus, see Gentz and Winkelmann 1966, 82 n. 2; Wallraff 2015, 105 with n. 18.

80. Cardinal Isidore of Kiev (1385–1463), a proponent of reunion during the Council of Florence who died in Rome, had made a collection of council acts dated to 1446, including the *Ecclesiastical History*, which found its way into Pope Paul II's library. The modern shelf number is Vatican Greek 830. See Hansen 2002, xix–xx.

81. Twenty-four of the thirty-three manuscripts (72.7 percent) Hansen collated for his edition, besides excerpts, date to the sixteenth century. To be sure, many authors from antiquity experienced an increase in manuscript production in the fifteenth and sixteenth century, a process that can be at least in part attributed to the humanist movement in Western Europe. But, in Anonymous Cyzicenus's case, given the scale of

also owned by important patrons and scholars, such as Johannes Sambucus (1531–1584) and Cardinal Domenico Grimani (1461–1523), as well as by powerful Catholic bishops throughout Western Europe including Pope Paul II (1464–1471), Pope Paul III (1468–1549), Charles de Bourbon (1523–1590), Cardinal Richelieu (1585–1642), and Pope Alexander VIII (1689–1691; see Hansen 2002, xiii–xxiii). In 1599 the text was translated into Latin by Scottish philosopher and philologist Robert Balfour and first printed, increasing the reach of the text to those churchmen without Greek and those without access to the major libraries of Europe.[82] The popularity of this text during the sixteenth and seventeenth centuries is no doubt due at least partially to the conflict between Protestants and Catholics in the aftermath of the Reformation. Counter-Reformation thinkers were profoundly invested in investigating early Christian history, especially the conciliar tradition.[83] This cultural context was heavily favorable to a rediscovered text purporting to relate the doings of an event as important to Christian history as the Council of Nicaea.

Subsequent reception history has been less kind to the *Ecclesiastical History*. One manuscript is known to have been produced in the seventeenth century, after the text appeared in print (Hansen 2002, xxvi). In 1604, Balfour's text and translation were reprinted, attesting to a continued popularity. Then, a lull that lasted for more than two centuries. Migne reprinted Balfour's text and translation in PG 85 (1860), columns 1179–1360, including only books 1–2 with the three associated letters of Constantine at the end of book 2. An edition of the third book was produced the next year by Antonio Ceriani (1861, 129–55), twenty years after Angelo Mai (1841, 603–10) had

---

difference between the level of copying before and after the fifteenth century, it is most likely that the work gained significantly in popularity.

82. For more on this first edition's role in shaping subsequent reception of the *Ecclesiastical History*, see part 1 of the introduction. Before 1599, sections of the *Ecclesiastical History* were excerpted and translated into Latin. For example, the 1572 *Acta et canones sacrosancti primi oecumenici concilii Nicaeni* quoted from the *Diatyposeis* (*Hist. eccl.* 2.31), citing them as authentic records from the council: "Among the fragments of the acts of Nicaea which are in the Vatican" (*in fragmentis actorum Nicaenorum quae sunt in Vaticano*). See Hansen 2002, xxxviii.

83. Introductions to the use of the late ancient, Christian past can be found in Vessey 2009; Fruchtman 2018. For Christian history in the Reformation and Counter-Reformation, see Van Liere, Ditchfield, and Louthan 2012; Backus 1997. See Stinger 1985 for the politics of the papacy in Renaissance Rome. For the conciliar tradition, see Oakley 2003. For the threat of "Arianism" reborn, see Wiles 2001.

discovered the third book in Milan.[84] Some forty years later, the first critical edition of the text was undertaken by Gerhard Loeschke, who died six years before its publication. The edition was completed by his student Margret Heinemann and published in 1918 as *Gelasius Kirchengeschichte*. The Loeschke-Heinemann edition remained the most sustained scholarly foray into the *Ecclesiastical History* until Günther Christian Hansen produced his edition in 2002 and German translation in 2008. At least partially because it is no longer considered to be an accurate historical source for the Council of Nicaea or the reign of Constantine, little has been written about the *Ecclesiastical History* beyond textual and source criticism. We hope that this translation and introduction will open up a wider discussion of this often-overlooked reimagining of the Christian past.

For our translation we have relied on the more recent edition of Hansen while still consulting the older Loeschke-Heinemann edition in certain, limited instances. Hansen's edition collates far more manuscripts than Loeschke and Heinemann's, partially because some had not yet come to light or were too difficult to view when the earlier edition was made. Furthermore, Hansen presents a convincing, detailed manuscript history. Hansen (2002, xxiii–xxxviii) argues, in short, that while one line of transmission seems to present better readings, all manuscripts of the history have been heavily contaminated by errors, corruptions, corrections, and additions. Hansen therefore cautions that each individual reading needs to be evaluated independently on its own merits. Such evaluations are, of course, to some degree subjective. When we have disagreed with a reading presented in Hansen's text, we have noted this in the footnotes, giving the source of the reading we prefer and a translation of the alternative presented by Hansen in order to allow the reader to see all possibilities. Hansen's edition, however, does not include the Greek text of some of the material that we have translated in this volume. The chapter headings, which Loeschke and Heinemann (1918, xxv) argued could not be proven to belong or not to belong to Cyzicenus's original text, are excluded from Hansen's edition. The Byzantine epistolary appendix is also not included in Hansen's edition of the text, since it does not properly belong to the archetype of the *Ecclesiastical History* that Hansen reconstructs. We therefore follow Hansen in the case of the text itself but Loeschke and Heine-

---

84. This paragraph's history of the printed editions mostly follows Hansen 2002, xxxviii–xli.

mann for the chapter headings and appendixes, in order to present as much of the material that has accrued around the *Ecclesiastical History* as possible. We hope thereby to represent some semblance of the text's entire tradition as variously encountered by ancient, Byzantine, and early modern readers.

Translators' Note

In this translation, several key Greek theological terms—*ousia*, *hypostasis*, and *homoousios*—have been transliterated. Though perhaps not ideal, we have adopted this practice because these terms are difficult to render without overdetermining the meaning of the ancient theological debates and because the precise meanings of these terms were debated and refined during the period from Nicaea to the time of Anonymous Cyzicenus's writing.

Ousia is often translated by the English *substance*, which ultimately derives from the usual Latin translation of the term, *substantia*. In common English usage, however, *substance* suggests physical "stuff" or "material," which is not implied by early Christian theological usage. In meaning, *ousia* is closer to the word *essence*, since both this English word and the Greek term are nouns related to the verb "to be," and *ousia* refers to the "is-ness" or ontological nature of something. *Hypostasis*, for its part, designates something subsisting as a real, distinct entity. It came to be translated by the Latin *subsistentia*, whence the English *subsistent*; "subsistent entity" probably best captures the sense as used by early Christian theologians. *Homoousios* ("of the same *ousia*") is the famous term included in the Nicene Creed. It has traditionally been rendered in English as *consubstantial*, which is derived from *consubstantialis* in the Latin version of the creed, but poses the same issues as translating *ousia* as "substance." Its meaning can be understood as "same-essenced" or "co-essential."

Writing in the late fifth century, Anonymous Cyzicenus was familiar with what by that time had become the orthodox definitions of these terms. *Ousia* referred to what was one in the Trinity, while *hypostasis* signified what was three. As Theodoret put it in the earlier part of the fifth century: "According to the doctrine of the fathers there is the same difference between *ousia* and *hypostasis* as between the common and the particular, and the species and the individual" (Theodoret, *Eran.* 1.7 [*NPNF* 2/3]). Orthodox theologians describe the Trinity as three distinct *hypostases* that are equally God, or that have a single "Godhead," which in this volume translates the Greek word *theotēs*. In the debates preceding, during, and in the years immediately following Nicaea, however, *ousia* and *hypostasis* were used less precisely. Thus, in some of the Nicene-era texts that Cyzicenus quotes, the two terms are used as synonyms or near synonyms, for instance in the council's anathematization of the notion that the Son "is of a different *hypostasis* or *ousia*" (2.27.6), Eusebius's letter to Caesarea (2.35.13), and Constantine's letter to Arius and the Arians (appendix 1, 3.19.14). Readers should bear in mind, too, that at the time of the Council of Nicaea, there was real reticence on the part of some theologians to the term *homoousios* as a strange neologism or jargon, as Eusebius of Caesarea's efforts to find palatable ways to construe the term (quoted in this work at 2.35.1–18) show. Anonymous Cyzicenus, of course, takes the triumph of *homoousios* to be natural and inevitable, to the extent that one wonders whether he was able to hear the ambivalences in his Nicene-era sources.

For in-depth discussions of these terms and the history of usage in early Christian theology, interested readers should consult any of a number of excellent studies (e.g., Young and Teal 2010; Hanson 1988; Ayres 2004).

Another problematic Greek term for this translation is *pistis*. From its root meaning of "trust" or "confidence" in something, *pistis* took on the specifically Christian connotation of "faith." Sometimes the word refers to a specific textualization of the tenets of faith and in those instances can be translated "creed." Another common term for "creed," *symbolon*, literally meaning "a token" and so used for written documents that stand as a "token" for something, is also used. It is sometimes difficult to determine when a given passage in the *Ecclesiastical History* refers to a broader faith or means a specific formulation of a faith in a creed. As a principle, we have translated *pistis* with the more general term *faith*, to preserve the sense that even the statement formulated at Nicaea was simply an expression of proper belief. We have used *creed* only in specific instances where issues of textualization are prevalent, such as at 2.27.7 and 2.35.3. When there is a question or a play on these terms, it has been noted in footnotes.

Finally, we have taken special care to accurately render Anonymous Cyzicenus's unusually precise book terminology. From the beginning of the text, Cyzicenus describes his reading and writing procedures with great specificity while describing Dalmatius's book (*proem.* 2–3). Cyzicenus uses the verb *episēmainō* to suggest marking important passages (see above, introduction, §4) and noting specifically that the book was written on parchment leaves (*membranais*). Such specificity continues throughout the book when describing other historians' work (for example Eusebius's, at 2.1.8) and his own anthologizing procedures (for example, at 3.15.23–24) as well as in many other instances. Because this is a peculiar feature of Cyzicenus not shared (at least not to the same degree) with other ecclesiastical historians, we have tried to render the author's specific terminology in our translation. When this was not possible without creating a stilted or confusing translation, we have indicated the specifics of Cyzicenus's book terminology in the footnotes.

A Treatise on the Holy Council of Nicaea: Concerning the Disputes That the Heretics Brought against the Holy Fathers and a Proclamation of the Triumphant Orthodox Teaching

An Introduction about the Proceedings at the Holy Council of Nicaea

Proem. 1. An account of the holy, great, and ecumenical[1] council of bishops gathered in the city of the Nicaeans from practically all the provinces of the Roman world and from Persia; gathered both by the grace of God and by the decree of our God-loving, pious emperor Constantine on behalf of the apostolic and orthodox faith and against the wicked and impious teachings of the God-battling Arius.[2] 2. All these things that were said and done in that virtuous and holy council and were enacted long ago—even very long ago—I had read while still living in my father's house, having found these very matters written in a book of exceptional age on parchment pages that contained them all in unbroken sequence.[3] These pages had originated at the hand of the godly, renowned Dalmatius,

---

1. The Greek term οἰκουμενικός, which is sometimes translated "global" or "worldwide," specifically means "of the οἰκουμένη," that is, of the inhabited, civilized regions of the world, generally imagined to be the Roman Empire and sometimes including Persia or other neighboring civilizations. The term is thus narrower than *global* but wider than and with a different valence from *Roman*. We have thus opted to translate the term "ecumenical," though not intending to imply any of the confessional ideas that have grown around the word in certain Christian traditions.

2. Nearly this entire paragraph is one excessively subordinated sentence in the original Greek. We have broken up some of the clauses into separate sentences in order to make the text readable in English. Major breaks correspond to the breaks between major clauses in the Greek text.

3. This book is otherwise unknown and may be fictitious. Cyzicenus (*proem.* 23–24) later mentions his own knowledge and notes about the book when compiling his account but gives no indication as to its later whereabouts. No other account corroborates the existence of such an account of the Council of Nicaea.

who was at that time archbishop of the holy universal church of the illustrious metropolis of the Cyzicans, and they had ended up in the hands of the master of my former house (I mean, of course, my father according to the flesh),[4] who was counted worthy of the priesthood of that same most holy church.[5] 3. And since, when I had read this sacred book and had studied it a good deal, I was not able to keep it all in my memory—for no human being will be able to keep that ineffable sea of things contained in it memorized by rote—I took note[6] of as many things as pertained to 4. the beliefs of our holy fathers and bishops on the instruction of the salutary message; to their rebuttals against the Ariomaniacs and the refutations written in opposition to the blasphemy of those men, that blasphemy that the foul Ariomaniacs blasphemed against the Son of God, and not just that but even against the Holy Spirit;[7] 5. to the counterarguments of Arius's hireling philosophers against the bishops; to the clear explanations of our own bishops against them through written instruction against those very sophisms; 6. about the one Godhead, without beginning and pre-

---

4. Tandy (2023, 111–12) suggests that the author was a monk, in part based on this expression, which is used in fifth- and sixth-century monastic sources. The implication is that the author also has a "father according to the spirit," the abbot of the monastery.

5. It is unclear whether Cyzicenus intends to ascribe authorship to Dalmatius or whether Dalmatius is to be understood as the commissioner of the work. Dalmatius was ordained bishop of Cyzicus by Sissinius ca. 427 CE (Socrates, *Hist. eccl.* 7.28). He signed the *acta* of the Council of Ephesus (*ACO* 1:1.2, p. 62, no. 171). See Constas 2003, 43–44. Cyzicus was the administrative center and metropolitan see (seat of the leading bishop) for the province Hellespontus, in the northwest of modern-day Turkey. Its neighboring see to the east, in the province of Bithynia, was led at different times by the bishops in Nicomedia and Nicaea itself. At the time of the events of the Council of Nicaea, the metropolitan bishop for the see was Eusebius of Nicomedia, presented in this text as one of the lead villains of the Arian side.

6. The verb for "taking note" (ἐπισημαίνω) connotes not merely taking note of but, more literally, marking (or even copying) significant passages for later reference or use—like the abbreviation ΣΗ (for σημείωσαι, "take note") that stands next to noteworthy passages in Byzantine manuscripts. Cyzicenus means that, although he was not able to memorize the entire book, he had recorded the material he found important and useful.

7. The derogatory term rendered in English as "Ariomaniac" is truly the same portmanteau in Greek (Ἀρειομανίτης). The term seems to have been coined by Athanasius, and it gained wide currency in Orthodox circles, due in part to a popular link between heresy and insanity. Cyzicenus employs this term throughout his history both in quoted documents and in his own voice.

eternal, always coexisting with God and Father, of his Son and the Holy Spirit—one, eternal Godhead;[8] about the ineffable incarnation from the God-bearer,[9] the Virgin Mary, of the Son of God, the Word of God, for our salvation in the last days, and about the apostolic regulations of the church. And, in short, after examining in the aforementioned sacred book the whole matter that happened there, 7. and above all the divine and truly apostolic understanding of the most faithful emperor Constantine, who also took part in the council, I took so much joy in the contents of that holy book that I said to the Lord, 8. "How sweet are thy utterances to my throat, more than honey to my mouth."[10] Thus I was exceedingly glad in the things written there about the pure and unblemished orthodox and apostolic faith.

Proem. 9. After some time, I came to this place, I mean to the province of the Bithynians, by the goodwill of God, at the time when the greatest disturbance and dispute arose against the apostolic and universal church of God and against the apostolic faith that was practiced in it, during the rebellion of the unholy Basiliscus.[11] 10. And while those who allied themselves with the faction of the heretic Eutyches were then greatly enflaming and disturbing the imperial court,[12] they put forward to us, unsoundly, that they were, as they assert, the true champions of the faith received from the fathers in Nicaea.[13] And they were refuted by us, because they were enemies of that faith, 11. for they did not know what they were saying or

---

8. The Greek term is θεότης, signifying the divine essence of God. For pro-Nicene theologians, such as Anonymous Cyzicenus, this essence belongs in common to God as Father, Son, and Holy Spirit. The Arians are portrayed in this work as arguing that the Godhead belonged solely to God the Father (see 2.22.1).

9. The Greek term used here is θεοτόκος, the theological term that initiated the controversy that resulted in the Council of Ephesus. See introduction, section 4.

10. Ps 119 (118):103.

11. Flavius Basiliscus was Augustus from 475–476. A prominent military officer and brother-in-law to the emperor Zeno, Basiliscus revolted, then reigned for a little over a year and a half until Zeno reclaimed the throne.

12. On the archimandrite Eutyches (flor. 430s–450s) as well as Cyzicenus's association of the ascendency of anti-Chalcedonianism during Basiliscus's reign with his miaphysite Christology, see the introduction.

13. Textual corruption makes this sentence difficult to recover. The present translation attempts to incorporate the context of the remaining paragraph to fill in the sense of the argument. We have taken the disjointed expression κρατεῖν πίστιν ("faith prevailed" or "prevailed over the faith") that follows the lacuna to refer to the Eutychians' assertion of the dominance of their interpretation.

what they were affirming.[14] But whenever I put forth the things promulgated in that holy chorus of the orthodox priests of God—promulgated through these men in the Holy Spirit by the Lord—the wretched men kept turning away from us, using their tongue to utter things worse than the blasphemies of Arius against what had been defined there and hurling curses against those who thought thus. 12. On account of these matters and many others that had been stirred up against our holy and orthodox faith, the faith that comes from the holy apostles and our aforementioned holy fathers who gathered together in Nicaea, the faith that has been practiced from the beginning in the church of God, our mother—13. I made the greatest possible inquiry in "every way and in every place,"[15] trying with all diligence, as it is said, to investigate the things that had been done in that holy council concerning the definition of the same holy and apostolic faith, which the church of God received "not from men nor by men"[16] but instead from the Savior and God of us all himself, Jesus Christ, the Son of the living God. 14. And, after his divinely planned incarnate advent, the truly "great mystery of piety," just as it is written, "that he was revealed in the flesh" and "was seen by the angels"[17] 15. (for the Only-begotten would not have been visible to the angels according to the *ousia* of his Godhead, had he not been made flesh), he fulfilled all things according to his divine plan: the voluntary suffering on our behalf, and the burial, and the resurrection, by submitting in that holy and blameless flesh of his, through which he rendered our kind immortal. And by ascending into heaven he confirmed through himself the divine and venerable definition of this holy and undefiled faith. And he thundered greatly, as it is written, "the Lord went up into heaven and thundered,"[18] 16. and in another place, "the Lord thundered from heaven and the Most High put forward his declaration."[19] And why did he thunder? What sort of declaration did the Most High put forth? When addressing his disciples, he said: "'Go forth and teach all nations, baptizing them in the name of the Father and of the Son and of the Holy Spirit.'"[20] 17. For even if I assumed your flesh, animate and rational,

---

14. See 1 Tim 1:7.
15. Acts 24:3.
16. Gal 1:1.
17. 1 Tim 3:16.
18. 1 Sam (1 Kgs) 2:10.
19. 2 Sam (2 Kgs) 22:14.
20. Matt 28:19.

from the revered and holy Virgin Mary because of my love for humankind, even so the assumption of the flesh did not make any addition to the Trinity of the Father and myself and the Holy Spirit; rather, the Trinity remains a trinity. 'Therefore, go forth into and teach all nations, baptizing them in the name of the Father and of the Son and of the Holy Spirit.'"[21]

Proem. 18. The holy apostles, receiving this holy and venerable definition of the correct and blameless faith from the Lord, preached it to every church of God under heaven, with the result that at that time the prophetic utterance was fulfilled that states, "Their voice has gone out to the whole earth and their words unto the ends of the civilized world."[22] 19. After a great deal of time, when the persecution against the church of God had ceased, the enemy of our salvation again, through Arius, armed himself against the holy and blameless faith, this definition and this venerable gift, handed down to us through the godly apostles by the Son of God. And he introduced foreign notions by his blasphemous words against the Savior, through which he disturbed the church of the Lord throughout the entire civilized world.[23]

Proem. 20. For this reason,[24] the most faithful emperor Constantine gathered that famed, well-attended council in the city of the Nicaeans, all the proceedings of which I had learned about beforehand, as I said above. And in my investigations, it was only with difficulty that I was able to find clear records of what had been debated and written there in a few differ-

---

21. Matt 28:19. This section, from *proem.* 16–17, is an example of the rhetorical device prosopopoeia, speech in character. Here, "Jesus" explains the passage in pro-Chalcedonian and anti-Eutychian terms; Eutyches was led toward denying the persistence of Christ's human nature after the incarnation in part because he felt that this would entail the addition of something to the immutable *ousia* of the Trinity.

22. Ps 19:4 (18:5).

23. Cyzicenus here elides the figures of the "enemy of our salvation" (the devil) and Arius, as he will continue to do in the next paragraph, saying only that Constantine called the council on account of "him," without specifying which recently introduced figure is meant.

24. The Greek phrase used in this transition, Οὗ χάριν, can be taken in three ways. Most neutrally, it could mean "for this reason," referring to the preceding clause(s). More narrowly, οὗ could be taken as referencing the antecedent Arius, implying that the council occurred "on account of Arius." The οὗ could also be taken as referring to the noun ὅρος, "definition" (of the faith), a key idea in this passage repeated in *proem.* 13, 18–19. This would establish further that the same faith delivered by Jesus and spread by the apostles was attacked by Arius and defended by the fathers and Constantine at Nicaea.

ent lovers of learning, 21. chiefly in John, a man who was a presbyter of old and especially skilled in the art of writing, who wrote in very ancient quaternions,[25] though not a full account, and from a variety of other writers, 22. including Eusebius Pamphili, bishop of Caesarea, and Rufinus, the presbyter of Rome, who even participated in that holy council, and many other such writers.[26] 23. But I did not find the sequence of the whole arrangement to be in accordance with that holy book, which I had found, as I said above (for only the marvelous Eusebius Pamphili kept to the unswerving highway of truth, from the advent of the Lord until the times of the great Constantine), nor was I able to find full accounts.[27] 24. But I found as much as was known to me and was proper to the truth, following the book that I had read previously, and, making selections from others, I thought it was necessary to write it in this book for the common benefit and support of those who read this writing.[28]

Proem. 25. And so it remains for me to begin my account, with the ever-living Word of God leading and guiding me, from the reign of the most pious and Christ-bearing emperor Constantine, who ordered the council of bishops to be gathered in the city of the Nicaeans. 26. For in another writing, if it pleases God, I will set out a description of his birth and the times of the reign of his father, the most God-beloved Constantius.[29]

---

25. The phrase ἄγαν γραφικῷ ("especially skilled in the art of writing") describing John leaves some ambiguity about what elements of writing are meant. In codex books, the "quaternion" (τετράδιον) was the basic section of writing material to be bound, which (usually) consisted of four folded sheets, which formed eight leaves (or sixteen pages).

26. Rufinus was not an attendee at the Council of Nicaea; however, the text that Cyzicenus attributes to Rufinus (see introduction, 6.2.3) contained many documents related to it. It is possible that the author of that text claimed personal witness to the council or, more likely, that Cyzicenus has made the assumption because of the text's details.

27. Eusebius's *Ecclesiastical History* provides the historical outline of book 1 but does not give a detailed account of the Council of Nicaea itself. It is unlikely that Cyzicenus ever directly consulted Rufinus but rather knew the Greek text that circulated under his name (see introduction, 6.2.3).

28. On the complex question of Cyzicenus's books and his description of his own project, see the introduction.

29. If this work was ever written, it does not survive.

Concerning the Beginning of the Reign of Constantine

1.1. Not long after the tyrants Diocletian and Maximian set aside the imperial purple and resumed their private life, just as Eusebius says:[30]

> Emperor Constantius, who had been most mild through his entire life, most kindly to his subjects, and most amiably disposed to the divine Word, leaving behind his own legitimate son Constantine as *imperator* and Augustus in his place, ended his life by the common law of nature.[31] After his death, he was deemed worthy of every honor, as much as anyone owes to an emperor, since he had been a most virtuous and gentle emperor. 2. Indeed, he alone of the emperors of our time, since he conducted the entire duration of his rule in a manner worthy of his authority and showed himself to be most righteous and most beneficent to all people in other respects, received an honorable and thrice-blessed end to his life. He alone during his reign accomplished all things graciously and gloriously for the sake of his successor, his own legitimate son, who was wise in all ways and most pious. 3. This man's son, Constantine, immediately, from the beginning, was proclaimed most perfect emperor and Augustus by the legions, and even long before them by God himself, the King of all, and he made himself an adherent of his father's piety concerning our doctrine.

1.4. And after other things:[32]

---

30. Eusebius, *Hist. eccl.* 8.13.12–14, omitting the divinization of Constantius I as well as the list of atrocities Christians suffered during the Great Persecution.

31. The Greek term αὐτοκράτορος translates the Latin *imperator*. In the republican era of Roman history, the *imperator* was a military commander, which office became intrinsic to the titles and functions of the Roman emperor. Although *emperor* derives directly from *imperator*, αὐτοκράτορος is infrequently used as a term in Cyzicenus's text in comparison to βασιλεύς, which is generally translated "emperor" or, in other political contexts outside Rome, "king." Here, both terms appear in close succession.

32. Eusebius, *Hist. eccl.* 9.9.1–2. Note that (1) Cyzicenus's quotation applies the phrase "honored both for his understanding and piety" to Constantine, where in some key manuscripts of the *Historia ecclesiastica* it is applied to Licinius; and (2) it includes the additional detail that Licinius was sent by Constantine, possibly derived from another source; see 1.8.1 below.

Thus indeed when Constantine, who was, as we have said, an emperor born of an emperor and a pious man born of a man most pious and wise, honored both for his understanding and piety, was roused by God, the King of all the universe and Savior, against the most impious tyrants and had prepared himself for a lawful war, with God fighting alongside him most miraculously, Maxentius fell at Rome at the hands of Constantine, and the ruler of the East, who did not outlast that most shameful man very long, ended his life with death at the hands of Licinius, who was not yet raving at that time and had been sent against him by Constantine the most God-beloved emperor.[33] 5. And indeed even earlier, Constantine, the first in the station and rank of emperor to take mercy on those who attempted usurpation over Rome, who called on God, the heavenly one, and his Word, the Savior of all himself, Jesus Christ, as an ally through prayers, advanced the cause of ancestral freedom with the whole army, winning the Romans over.

So says Eusebius.

Concerning the Emperors Contemporary to Constantine: Maxentius and Maximinus

2.1. Now even if Rufinus did not set down the sequence in order and in truthful consonance with the history of Eusebius Pamphili, nevertheless, I will collect whatever I find in the said Rufinus and other writers that is akin to Eusebius's treatment and include them in this little book,[34] as I said above. And Rufinus says:[35]

---

33. Constantine defeated Maxentius at the Battle of the Milvian Bridge in October 312, and Licinius defeated Maximinus Daia ("the ruler of the East") in April 313. Maximinus died in August.

34. βιβλίδιον, the diminutive of βιβλίον, "book." Cyzicenus is describing his work as shorter than the histories he is drawing on (insofar as it is a selection of excerpts), but this gesture of deference is also intended to suggest that his account is authoritative because it derives from and harmonizes reliable accounts.

35. Cyzicenus here cites "Rufinus," but the quoted passage does not come from Rufinus's *Ecclesiastical History*. Instead it appears in the Greek text ascribed to Gelasius of Caesarea. See Wallraff, Stutz, and Marinides 2018, F5, as well as the introduction, 6.2.3, and the testimony about the confusion of the authors in Photius in appendix 3.

2.2. At any rate, after the abdication of Diocletian and Maximian and the death of Constantius, these emperors were left to rule the Romans simultaneously: Constantine, who had assumed his father's portion of the empire—this portion started in the land called Europa and stretched to both the Ister and to either Scythia,[36] to all the Celts and the Illyrians and Sarmatians and to the River Rhine that borders the land of the barbarians and to Macedonia and to both Thessaly and Achaia on the same sea and however many lands the Ionian Sea divides back toward the setting sun—3. and Maximinus, the son of Diocletian,[37] dealt with all the peoples in the East, *just as Eusebius reports*, and Maxentius [ruled] Rome and the lands from Italy to what borders on the ocean itself.[38]

Concerning the Tyranny of Maxentius

3.1.[39] Therefore Constantine, after the prescribed period of mourning for his father and the customary honors, considered his period of rest a blow to the Romans' poor circumstances. 2. For he heard that the city of the Romans was wearied by the evils of Maxentius, for the character of his rule was changing into that of a savage tyrant. For he was handing many of those who held office over to death without a trial, and decreed fines and banishments and land redistributions and inflicted further penalties without any investigation, and he was already corrupting other men's wives

---

36. Meaning the provinces of Moesia Secunda and Scythia Minor.

37. Putative kinship was a key element of tetrarchic ideology; like Galerius before him, Maximinus Daia took the nomen Valerius to signal kinship with Diocletian.

38. The passage aims to describe the state of the tetrarchy in ca. mid-311–mid-312, though it notably omits the death of Galerius (May 311) and that Licinius was governing the Balkans, Thrace, and Greece (and was technically Augustus of the West). The messiness here is due in part to the way Cyzicenus blends his sources in this quotation, harmonizing a Gelasian passage (F6) with Eusebius, *Hist. eccl.* 9.9.12.

39. Sections 1.3.1–7.4 appear to continue with Gelasian material (F6; Wallraff, Stutz, and Marinides 2018, 35–43). Cyzicenus's narrative, however, includes substantial sections not found in the other major witness (BHG 1279). Sections 1.4.2–5 and 1.5.2–7 appear only in Cyzicenus. While both Hansen (2002, 7–9) and Wallraff, Stutz, and Marinides (2018, 39–40) accept the second passage as Gelasian because the authorial voice identifies himself as a contemporary of Constantius II, Hansen suggests that the first belongs to the lost history of Philip of Side.

with flattery or forcing his way by direct orders, and ultimately it was unsafe to have an attractive wife,[40] and there was bloodthirsty desire throughout the city for the protection of modesty. 3. The most God-beloved Constantine was provoked when he heard these and many other things that are not fitting for the present work, for the injustice of others' deeds causes personal distress for pious men.

Concerning the Emperor Constantine: How He Encamped against the Tyrant Maxentius

4.1. Indeed, in the end it seemed necessary to him to take up arms and go to the defense of the Romans who were suffering these things, for delivering those men from their troubles was equivalent to saving all humankind as well, so to speak.

4.2. He then embarked on a plan to call back those cities that had previously fallen away from the Romans' dominion—some with words, some with weapons, and others with the beneficence of his love for humankind. For he both made their taxes less burdensome and granted them commercial equality, and he calmed their revolutionary spirit and madness sagaciously, saying nothing rather than threatening them, since he recognized that these were the revolution-prone peoples of the Sauri, Franks, and Germans and that they held a fickle inclination in regard to rebellions against emperors, and their opinion at any moment often served as their law.[41] 3. And he also brought under his command the Spaniards and Britons and the islands there and the remaining peoples

---

40. In Lactantius, *Mort.* 38, it is Maximinus Daia who is described as corrupting women.

41. Constantine's fiscal policies are described as more successful than those of his tetrarchic predecessors. For a detailed analysis of the available evidence, see Corcoran 1996, 205–33. The regions of the empire in modern France, Belgium, the Netherlands, and Germany had gained a reputation for rebelliousness, following numerous attempts at self-governance and promoting alternative candidates for emperor, most notably in the late third century under Postumus and, later, Carausius and Allectus, who claimed the title Augustus and controlled Gaul and Britain from 286–296, when the territory was recovered by Constantius I.

The inclusion of Sarmatians (Sauri) in this list causes geographical issues, as Sarmatians are generally located along the lower Danube and farther east, near regions of

and all those who are witness to the sun's settings, who, they say, know whether it truly sinks down into the ocean or whether, upon going around the water, it circles its way back to us again along another route. And he also won over the barbarian tribes there by force of arms, availing himself of a workaround for the task instead of battle. 4. For by subjecting some of them, and paying off others and so causing them to be friends instead of foes, partners instead of ancient enemies, he led them forth all as allies, giving no one cause for grief, nor besieging any, eager for the salvation of other men. 5. For where God fights as an ally, he guides all things for his own purpose and surpasses the reckoning of mortals. And with such God-loving intention, Constantine, most faithful in all ways, crossed the Rhine on the right, passed over many hills and many nameless streams with a small army, subdued many barbarian peoples, rallied ten bands of Gauls, Franks, and Spaniards, and in the end led his army to the hills of Italy.[42]

4.6. This was unexpected trouble for Maxentius when he heard about it, for he was not expecting anyone would ever cross so much territory that was blockaded by hills and rivers and various barbarians and the natural difficulties of the wilderness; for the desolation of its regions often becomes the greatest defense for an empire. 7. And indeed, he thought it best to slip away from Rome with great haste, lead his army out, and somehow keep him away from Italy. But when they took the field opposite one another and looked on each other's battle standards, from that point on the battle was holding forth unequal cause for hope. For those who had set forth from Rome and were pouring forth in phalanxes, coming off of a long vacation and rest, seemed to be clearly a match for the opposing army and bore themselves with equal confidence as was worthy of the city. 8. But those who were drawing up their ranks with Constantine had already covered much ground and were fatigued after transporting much plunder and many spoils of war, and since they had been on a race toward victory rather

---

the empire not under Constantine's control in 312. Hansen (2008) conjectures that we should instead read Saxons here and again in 1.4.5.

42. Hansen (2008) humorously notes that Constantine's diplomatic skills would have been taxed trying to rally Spaniards on the banks of the Rhine. As with the geographical issue at 1.4.2, he suggests an emendation to "Saxons."

than enjoying the reward of the things they had taken, they were already succumbing to their toil and giving in to the frequency of their hardships.

Concerning the Cross That Appeared to the Emperor Constantine in Heaven

5.1. But when the battle had not yet been decided and the two sides were evenly balanced, God from heaven armed Constantine by showing him the saving sign of the cross brilliantly in heaven; and writing revealed the force of this vision, which said, "By this, conquer."

5.2. This story, on the one hand, seems to be a fable to the faithless and a counterfeit made to suit our tenets, but to those in the habit of believing what is true, the proof of the deed is manifest. For after these events, this symbol's painter, God, displayed by deed that the favor of this writing spoke truthfully.[43] 3. But even if we are not yet persuasive with what we are writing about—for we are excerpting from earlier histories in order to collect the useful aspects of the life he lived—nevertheless one cannot disbelieve what happened subsequently, which those of our generation who served alongside Constantius, the son of Constantine, and who had themselves seen the disbelief of days gone by attended with fresh eyes.[44] 4. For if the ones speaking out against these things are Hebrews, what is believed in their books is less credible than these by far: that the sea was walked across and water formed a wall and the deeps were traversed by a path,[45] and God spoke out of a thorn bush[46] and as a flame set down the laws,[47]

---

43. I.e., the text seen in Constantine's vision, "By this, conquer."
44. This may be a reference to the appearance of a vision of the cross in Jerusalem in 351 CE and reported by Cyril of Jerusalem in his *Letter to Constantius II* (see also Philostorgius, *Hist. eccl.* 3.26; Sozomen, *Hist. eccl.* 4.5). Cyril reports that the vision terrified Jews and led to the conversion of many gentiles. Cyril's nephew, Gelasius, is a viable candidate for being the source of this section. The reference to making excerpts may originate with either Cyzicenus or his source material; his habit of adopting his source's citations makes the determination impossible.
45. Exod 14:29.
46. Exod 3:4.
47. Exod 19:18.

and a trumpet sounded in the wilderness without an instrument,[48] and angels were drawn up in ranks, and "the commanders of the Lord's might"[49] fought on behalf of their ranks, and "hailstones"[50] and shafts of flame[51] were cast in place of their usual spears; and nevertheless we who think correctly agree to these things unquestioningly, for nothing is impossible, if God so wills. 5. Or if the Greeks be the ones not acknowledging the wonder, we could say many things that we do not want to say: how many things the soothsayers proclaimed to Alexander when he was about to cross [the Hellespont] about the fight at Grancius and about the pitched battle against Darius—and indeed their fabrications do not have clear proof[52]—how a spirit forewarned the philosopher Socrates through a voice as to the outcome of things that should not be done;[53] and what was compiled about Pythagoras the Samian by his disciples.[54] 6. I leave off telling as well the fabrications of the poets and how some of the well-reputed among them say that some of those they consider gods even fought alongside them <…> in order that no one should think that I am comparing the domain of fable to true events and things that never happened to things that have. 7. For those who have experienced the grace of Christ with its many powers, from the time when it blossomed unto humankind, in heaven and on earth and in the sea and in the plants and in the trees and in the cloths <…> and in sickness and in health and in meats and in drinks, know the remedy of healing

---

48. Exod 19:16.
49. See Josh 5:14.
50. Josh 10:11.
51. 2 Sam 22:15.
52. Arrian (*Anab.* 1.11.2) reports a prodigy seen during poetic competitions Alexander held, at which a statue of Orpheus sweated. This was interpreted as an omen that Alexander's future labors would be the source of future epics. See also Plutarch, *Alex.* 27.
53. Plato, *Apol.* 31d. Socrates in his defense against the charge of corrupting the youth of Athens spoke of a spirit (δαίμων) that warned him against taking certain actions throughout his life.
54. Well-known lives of Pythagoras include those composed by Diogenes Laertius, Porphyry of Tyre, and Iamblichus of Chalcis.

that was and is and is to come, but we also will expound on it in due time as our history progresses.[55]

Concerning the Standard That the Emperor Constantine Made as a Copy of the Cross That Appeared to Him in Heaven

6.1. Constantine then converted what he had seen in the miracle into the form of a trophy and fitted it with stones inlaid in gold, attaching it to the front side of a very long spear, and he gave it to his first rank of cavalry to carry, seeking further through his actions what the writing promised.[56] 2. And he did not fail in his hope, for the more quickly he trusted in the things that he had seen, the more swiftly he received the victory of faith.

Concerning the Victory of the Pious Emperor Constantine against the Impious Maxentius

7.1. Then Constantine cut short the great toil of war by means of his faith and, not eying warily the army from Rome, nobly drew up his ranks in opposition. But Maxentius, because he still feared Constantine's prowess and moreover suspected the Romans' hatred for him (for he had brought reproach on himself in the eyes of the majority of them on account of his profligacy), looked to pursue his plot by trickery. His trick was a bridge in the form of a booby trap pieced together under the following principles. 2. The part that could be seen above looked like a crossing that would support Constantine, but what lay hidden was a deceitful snare contrived for his approach. For one but had to begin to cross and the mechanism was triggered, and his enemy was caught receiving an unexpected tomb as a place of destruction.[57] 3. And

---

55. A promise not fulfilled in Cyzicenus's text and thus evidence that the first-person voice here is that of his source.

56. The letters seen in the vision promised victory. This is a description of the labarum, a military standard bearing the *chi-rho* (the first two letters of the name "Christ" in Greek), superimposed to create a cross. For the earliest description of the labarum, see Eusebius, *Vit. Const.* 1.31.

57. According to Lactantius (*Mort.* 44), the bridge had been cut before the battle by Maxentius, in order to forestall Constantine's advance; he does not mention a contrivance or booby trap.

so Maxentius prepared his trap for Constantine's approach, but divine grace entrapped the contriver of evils with his own tricks. For before Constantine was caught, the tyrant himself first fell into his own devices. And thereupon since he had become his own tyrannicide and had prepared an effective plot against himself, on the approach to Rome at the bridge that is called Milvian, the aforementioned Maxentius himself sank into the river, asphyxiated, and died. 4. As a result, the entire population of Romans cried out, saying,

just as Eusebius Pamphili reports:[58]

"Let us sing praise to the Lord, for gloriously he has glorified himself; horse and rider he threw into the sea. He has become my helper and protector, for my salvation,"[59] and "Who is like you among the gods, Lord? Who is like you: glorified among holy ones, marvelous in glory, and working wonders?"[60]

7.5. To these things the same author adds:[61]

And after he had sung these praises and others akin and similar to them by his very deeds, to God the ruler of all and cause of his victory, as well as to his Only-begotten Son, Jesus Christ, Constantine pressed on to Rome with songs of victory. And everyone in one body along with all their children and wives, both men of

---

58. Both the Gelasian source and Eusebius appear to have reported at least part of these acclamations, derived from the book of Exodus. BHG 1279, following the Gelasian source, ends the first Exodus citation before Cyzicenus does and adds a second from Ps 7:16, not present in Cyzicenus. Eusebius, however, presents the acclamations as found here. Cyzicenus appears to have used these shared quotations as a method of transition between sources, picking up the narrative from Eusebius as the citation formula suggests. This also demonstrates the ways in which legends of the Milvian Bridge were combined and conflated as the memory of Constantine and the civil wars of the tetrarchy were retold and reframed over time. See Van Dam 2014.

59. Exod 15:1–2.

60. Exod 15:11.

61. Continuing from the previous set of quotations from Exodus, Cyzicenus picks up with Eusebius's narrative from *Hist. eccl.* 9.9.8–11, with the additional phrase "and his only begotten Son, Jesus Christ" as the object of Constantine's praise.

senatorial rank and those who were highly distinguished in other ways, together with the entire populace of Romans, eyes beaming with their very souls, received him as a deliverer and savior and benefactor, with acclamations and boundless joy. 6. But Constantine, because he was possessed of an innate piety toward God, was in no way stirred by their cries, nor inflated by their praises, and recognizing very well the help that came from God, immediately ordered that the trophy of the salvific passion be set up beneath the hand of his own statue, and indeed that they should place him holding the symbol of the cross in his right hand in the most prominent place in Rome. And he commanded further that this notice be inscribed with these very words, in the Roman tongue: 7. "By this salvation-bearing sign, by this veritable proof of courage, I saved your city and freed it from the yoke of the tyrant. And furthermore, by freeing it, I restored both the senate and the people of Rome to their ancient fame and splendor."

Thus writes Eusebius.

Concerning Licinius, Who Was Sent by the Pious Constantine against the Tyrant in the East

8.1. Rufinus, though, or rather Gelasius, tells these events as follows:[62]

After these events, the Roman senate requested that Licinius (who was the God-beloved Constantine's brother-in-law through his sister, Constantia) reign alongside Constantine. Constantine sent him back again out to the East against the tyrant there since he was concerned about rescuing the Christians there. For pious Constantine, because he had enjoyed such great benefactions from God, was eager to give thank-offerings to his benefactor. 2. And these thank-offerings were the freeing of the Christians from being persecuted, the recall of those who were in exile, the release

---

62. On the confusion of Rufinus with Gelasius of Caesarea, see section 6.2.3 of the introduction and appendix 3. Of the three witnesses to this Gelasian fragment (F7), Cyzicenus is the only one to report that the Roman senate influenced the elevation of Licinius. Cyzicenus also includes more language about Constantine's piety, particularly the phrase "since he was Christian in all ways."

of those in prisons, for those who had been subject to confiscation, the restoration of their former property, and the rebuilding of the churches. And he was doing all these things with great zeal, keeping in mind Christ's work. Since he was Christian in all ways, he was doing everything like a Christian: building up God's churches and honoring them with costly votive offerings and furthermore ordering the temples of the Greeks to be set ablaze and destroyed by fire.[63]

Concerning the Madness of the Tyrant in the East, Maximinus

9.1. Meanwhile, the tyrant in the East was ravaging the churches of God. But the cause that pressured him into this course of action was what follows.[64] Since Maximinus was unable to bear the magnitude of the authority unduly entrusted to him, but rather, due to his inexperience with prudent reasoning befitting an emperor, was trying his hand at matters ignobly and above all had unreasonably plumed his soul with boastful arrogance, he pushed himself to try to be bold in the face of the companions of the emperor and in the face of Constantine himself—who differed from him in every possible way: in stock, upbringing, and

---

63. The cancellation of the Diocletianic persecution was reiterated and the return of confiscated Christian property ordered in the Edict of Milan of 313 CE. From the 310s through the end of his reign, Constantine supported the building and restoration of church buildings by supplying land and resources (e.g., the Lateran Basilica in Rome and the Church of the Holy Sepulcher in Jerusalem). He did not, however, pursue an organized program against temples. Only four specific instances of Constantinian temple destruction are attested, all by Eusebius (*Vit. Const.* 3.54–58): a temple of Aphrodite on the site of the Holy Sepulcher in Jerusalem, two other Aphrodite complexes (at Aphaca and Heliopolis), and a temple of Asclepius at Aigai in Cilicia. Cyzicenus includes these same stories at 3.4.7 (Aphrodite in Aelia) and 3.10.24–25 (Aphrodite at Heliopolis and Aphaca; Asclepius at Aigai).

64. Beginning with "But the cause," Cyzicenus transitions back to Eusebius (*Hist. eccl.* 9.10.1–5; 9.10.13–11.1), whom he quotes through 1.10.1. Although Cyzicenus does not alert the reader to this transition here, he does cite Eusebius at the end of the quoted material. He follows the text of Eusebius closely, although additional clarifications about the actors and a few colorful descriptors appear. Omitted is the decree of Maximinus (*Hist. eccl.* 9.10.7–11) that extended protections to the Christians, as well as Eusebius's claim that Maximinus's gruesome death was still lessened in its potential severity because of this late act of contrition (*Hist. eccl.* 9.10.13).

education, in dignity and intelligence, and (the most important trait of all) in the illustriousness of his moderation and reverence toward the true God—and to publicly proclaim himself first in honor.[65] 2. And rising to the peak of insanity, he violated the agreements he had made with Licinius and opted for war with no quarter given. Then, in short, when he had stirred everything up and thrown the whole city into confusion and gathered the entire army many thousands strong, he set course toward Licinius for battle, both against him and against Constantine, who had sent him. And indeed, once he brought things to blows, he found himself bereft of God's oversight, since the one God of all had awarded victory over him to Constantine, who then held sway. 3. The transgressor first lost the heavy-armed troops on which he had been relying, and after he had been stripped of the bodyguards around him and everyone had abandoned him all alone and fled to the one who then held sway, the coward slipped out of his unsuitable imperial regalia as quickly as possible, slipped it off in cowardly, mean, and unmanly fashion, slipped into the multitude and then escaped. And, hiding himself in the fields and villages, he barely eluded the hands of his enemies, having to beg for what would bring him safety.[66] 4. Thus, by these very actions, it is possible to demonstrate that the divine prophecies are especially trustworthy and true in which it is said, "A king is not protected by great power, and a giant will not be protected by the abundance of his strength. A horse gives false security; he will not be protected by the abundance of its power. Behold! The eyes of the Lord are upon those who fear him, those who place their

---

65. As the first appointed member of the surviving imperial college consisting of Constantine, Licinius, and himself, Maximinus attempted to assert his rank as senior Augustus over the other two rulers. However, Licinius had been advanced to the rank of Augustus in 308 by Galerius, whereas Maximinus had not received any official recognition from a senior colleague. Maximinus and Licinius had an agreement to share the eastern provinces between them, but once Licinius and Constantine began to ally themselves more closely, Maximinus began to support Maxentius, the self-styled Augustus in Rome. See the parallel account in Lactantius, *Mort.* 43.

66. According to Lactantius (*Mort.* 47, 49), after defeat at the Battle of Tzirallum in April 313, Maximinus fled into Cappadocia, where he rallied troops to try to forestall Licinius's advance. Defeated there as well, he fled to Tarsus, where he died in August, whether by suicide or from disease is unclear.

hope in his mercy, so as to snatch their souls from death."[67] And so the impious man, struck by the sudden scourge of God, ended his life in the second encounter of the war. 5. And the events of his downfall are not of the same sort as those that befall commanding generals manly enough to face their celebrated end in battle many times with good courage in defense of their virtue and their companions. But in fact, since he was at once impious and God-battling, although his company was arrayed in position in one place before the battlefield, he himself was staying home and kept hidden. He received a suitable punishment, struck suddenly by the scourge of God to the point that he fell facedown, beset by terrible sufferings and great pains, and he was wracked with hunger, and all his flesh melted away due to an invisible, God-sent fever. The result was that, when he had wasted away, he became unrecognizable compared to his entire previous appearance and soon became nothing but desiccated bones, like a skeletal phantom left lingering by the length of time. Consequently, those present could think nothing other than that his body in its deadened and completely decaying form had become the tomb where his soul was buried. 6. And on account of the heat all the more violently consuming him from the depth of his marrows, his eyes popped out and, falling from their natural place, rendered him blind. And in these moments as he drew breath, and was giving thanks to the Lord and beseeching him for death and at his last moment, once he had confessed that he had suffered these things justly on account of his insobriety toward Christ, he gave up his soul.

Concerning the Rebuilding of the Churches

10.1. And so, with Maximinus out of the way, who was the only one of the enemies of piety remaining and showed himself the worst of all, by the grace of the almighty God the task of rebuilding the churches from their very foundations was taken up, and the word of Christ, which shone for the glory of the God of the universe, was spoken even more openly than before.

---

67. Ps 33 (32):16–19.

10.2. Eusebius Pamphili, best in all ways, included these things in the ninth book of the *Ecclesiastical History*. For, as I mentioned above, I am writing and compiling this little book by making a selection from his works and the works of others and shortening them,[68] and, with the greatest zeal, charting the path of our discourse toward the high and resplendent, holy and godly mountain of the apostolic and virtuous council of the priests of God at Nicaea, looking especially to the prophet who takes control of my hand and urges me on, saying, 3. "Come, let us climb to the mountain of the Lord and to the house of the God of Jacob, and he will announce his way to us and we will journey on it. For the law and the word of the Lord will come forth from Zion, from Jerusalem."[69] 4. For truly Zion and Jerusalem and the highest mountain of the Lord and the house of the God of Jacob is that divine company of the orthodox priests of God. They by the Holy Spirit investigated and proved "concerning the Word of life,"[70] that is to say, the Son of God, through the writings of the prophets and the evangelists and the apostles, that truly he was uncreated in the nature of his Godhead and not a created thing (which is exactly what the God-battling and most impious Arius blasphemed against him) and that he is of the same *ousia* as the Father is, who begat him before all ages, and of the same property.[71] And likewise they also proved most clearly that the Holy Spirit is of the same Godhead and *ousia* as the Father and the Son.[72] 5. And truly, the "high mountain of God," which was just mentioned, is this venerable and holy definition of the immaculate faith, which was granted to us from on high by the Lord himself through the apostles, and which has now been

---

68. See above, *proem*. 24; 1.2.1.
69. Isa 2:3.
70. 1 John 1:1.
71. The Greek term χρῆμα has a range of meanings, several of which are financial: "stuff," "property," or "money." Thus, another translation might be "'of the same coinage," in the sense that the persons of the Trinity are of the same *ousia* in the way that three gold coins are of the same *ousia*.
72. The divinity of the Holy Spirit was not vigorously debated before or defined at Nicaea, where the creed produced by the council included only the phrase "and in the Holy Spirit." The divinity of the Holy Spirit became a topic of debate in the later fourth century, during the period preceding the Council of Constantinople, which elaborated, "And in the Holy Spirit, the Lord and giver-of-life, who proceeds from the Father, who is co-worshipped and co-glorified with the Father and the Son, who spoke through the prophets."

elucidated through his priests at Nicaea with written testimonies.[73] As the treatise progresses, it will provide clearer proof on this matter for us, with the assistance of the grace of God.

10.6. But let us return to the subject before us in our ecclesiastical history, resuming with matters relating to the help brought by God the king to his people and to the destruction of the tyrants through his servant the God-beloved emperor Constantine. And through him he granted peace to his churches throughout the civilized world, he who alone is 7.[74] "the great Lord,[75] who alone works great wonders[76] and inscrutable things of which there is no number,[77] who changes the times and seasons, deposes and appoints kings,[78] raises the poor from the ground, and elevates the impoverished from the dung heap.[79] He knocks the powerful from their thrones and elevates the humble. He has filled the poor with good things and has cast the wealthy out destitute." [80] And "he has broken the arms of the arrogant,"[81] he who is wonderworker, doer of great things, master of the world, maker of the entire world, the Almighty, the all-good, the one and only God, to whom we send up the "new song,"[82] responding "to the one who alone does great miracles, because his mercy is everlasting; to he who smites great kings and kills mighty kings, because his mercy is everlasting, because in our humiliation the Lord remembered us."[83] 8. For all these reasons, let us not cease from singing the praise of the God of the universe and his Only-begotten Son, Jesus Christ our Lord, who with the Father is the cause of all good things for us, who is the one who initiates us into the divine knowledge of him, the teacher of piety toward him, the destroyer of impious men, the tyrant slayer, life's right guide, the Savior

---

73. The Greek text features a play on words: τὸ ὄρος means "mountain," while ὁ ὅρος means "boundary line" or "definition." Therefore, the ὄρος (mountain) to which the historian is leading us is the ὅρος (definition) of the faith.

74. The passage from 1.10.7–9 presents a compressed, edited, and rearranged version of Eusebius, *Hist. eccl.* 10.4.8–11, although the quotations are not signaled.

75. Ps 48 (47):1.
76. Ps 72 (71):18.
77. Job 9:10.
78. Dan 2:21.
79. Ps 113 (112):7.
80. Luke 1:52–53.
81. Job 38:15.
82. Ps 98 (97):1.
83. Ps 136 (135):4, 17–18, 23.

of those who despair; let us all praise Jesus with one mouth and with one heart, 9. because indeed he alone, being as he is <the one and only all-good Son> of the all-good Father, by the philanthropic will of the Father, of him himself, and of the Holy Spirit,[84] taking forethought for our salvation when we were abiding down here in corruption, right well put on our nature, just as a most noble physician who by taking on our sufferings and bearing our ailments both then and forever effected salvation and life for humankind.[85]

10.10. Indeed, this King of kings, ever mindful of his people, by equipping his own dear servant Constantine against the irreverent tyrants, Maxentius in Rome and Maximinus in the East, with the armaments of devoutness to him and faith, had raised him up, and upon destroying those tyrants through Constantine, he delivered a joyous and deep-rooted peace for his own people.[86]

Concerning the Wicked Ways of Licinius

11.1. And thus, says Eusebius Pamphili,[87]

> The sight of everything he witnessed was intolerable to the jealous hater of good and evil-loving demon, even as what befell the tyrants as shown above was not enough to bring Licinius to sound reason once he had turned away. He, although his rule was gladly celebrated, and although he was second in honor to the great emperor Constantine, and thus deserving to marry into the family and become kin, was failing in the imitation of Constantine's good deeds, and in addition was starting to exhibit the malice of the impious tyrants' reprobacy, and although he saw the disastrous end of their lives with his own eyes, he was more willing to follow their view than the better man's love and affection.

---

84. Cyzicenus has inserted statements emphasizing the activity of all persons of the Trinity in the divine economy where the Eusebian passage was only concerned with God, in the singular. The words in the lacuna are supplied from the text in Eusebius.

85. This final statement on the saving mission of Jesus is unique to Cyzicenus but bears resemblance to Isa 53:4, Matt 8:17.

86. I.e., the people of God, the church.

87. From 1.11.1–16, Cyzicenus quotes *Hist. eccl.* 10.8.2–9.4, omitting several of the longer rhetorical passages on the evil nature of Licinius and his actions against the inhabitants of the eastern half of the empire.

2. Therefore, out of envy of his universal benefactor, he carried out an unholy and most terrible war against him, disregarding the laws of nature, keeping in mind no memory of oaths, nor of blood, nor of pacts. 3. For the all-good emperor, extending such tokens of true goodwill to him, did not begrudge Licinius kinship with him and did not deny him the fellowship of joyous wedding celebrations with his sister.[88]

11.4. And after other matters:

But Licinius was acting in ways contrary to these, God-hater that he was, devising manifold schemes daily against the better man, considering all manner of plot, in order to repay his benefactor with evils.

11.5. To which Eusebius adds:

But God was beloved protector and guardian for him (I mean for Constantine), and exposed to him the plans devised by the tyrant in secret and darkness by driving them into the light.[89] So much does virtue, the great armament of the God-fearing,[90] prevail as a defense against enemies and as a guardian of his people's deliverance. And defended thus, our most God-beloved emperor Constantine escaped from the labyrinthine plots of the unspeakable man with help from God. 6. But the tyrant noticed that his secret plot was not at all turning out according to his plan, since God was rendering every trick and fraud manifest to the God-beloved one, and since he was no longer able to keep things secret, he finally opted for open warfare. 7. Indeed, resolved to make war on Constantine face-to-face, he presently both started to marshal his forces against the God of the universe on the grounds that he was Constantine's guardian, whom he understood Constantine to worship, and then oppressed the God-fearing people in his power.

---

88. Licinius married Constantine's sister, Flavia Julia Constantia, to solidify their alliance in 313.
89. See Eph 5:11–13.
90. Perhaps an allusion to the "armor of God" (Eph 6:11).

11.8. And after other matters:

> And his envy against them was of a strange sort, such as has never been heard of before.[91] For he ordered the cities in the vicinity of Amasya and the rest of those in Pontus to be oppressed with such great evils that he outdid every excess of savagery. There some of the churches of God were torn down from roof to foundation once again, and he ordered that others be closed down, so that nobody who was accustomed to could assemble there or offer the prayers and worship owed to God. 9. For he did not think that these prayers were given on his behalf, as he reckoned it in his wicked conscience—for how could the God-hater have thought that—but was convinced that we did this and were propitiating God on behalf of Constantine the God-beloved emperor. Hence, incited by this, he brought his rage down on us.

11.10. And a little later on:

> Many of the bishops were taken away and were punished without justification, as though they were murderers, although they had done no wrong. They also endured an unprecedented form of execution: their bodies were chopped to bits with a sword, and after this cruel and most abominable spectacle, they were thrown into the depths of the sea to become food for the fish. 11. And again all the God-fearing fled, together one and all, men and women, with children in tow. And again fields and deserts, forests and mountains received the servants of Christ because this impious one had stirred up war against all.

11.12. And a little later on:

---

91. Hansen's text follows the Eusebian original, in which the beginning of this passage refers to the "murder" (φόνου) of the Christian bishops in the East. The manuscripts of Anonymous Cyzicenus all present the word φθόνου, which would then refer instead to Licinius's "ill-will" or "envy." It is certainly plausible that the manuscripts have simply added a letter into an easily confused word. However, it is also plausible that Cyzicenus altered the word to preserve logical flow in his excerpts, disguising the original connection of the passage to attacks against the bishops that he had not included.

Had not God in his infinite goodness most swiftly taken forethought for what the future would be and, as if in a deep darkness and the gloomiest night, had he not suddenly shone forth a great light, the savior for all, guiding his servant Constantine by his mighty arm and his noblest hand...[92] 13. Therefore, the God of Constantine and of us all provided to Constantine from heaven above the fruit that his piety had earned, trophies of victory over the impious, and he cast the wicked one and all his advisers and dear ones down beneath the feet of Constantine. 14. For, since Licinius had driven all affairs under his direction to the heights of insanity, the emperor Constantine, the friend of God, having reckoned this situation to be unbearable, since he combined innate self-control with pious reasoning and mixed the firm character of a righteous man with clemency, decided therefore to bring aid to those who were enduring hardship under the tyrant and set himself to restoring humankind in its broadest extent once he had gotten a few of the corrupters out of the way. 15. For although the most clement emperor Constantine had always employed his singular clemency with the impious one prior to this and showed mercy to one who was not worthy of sympathy, nothing more happened on Licinius's part, who did not leave off his evil, but rather increased his rage against the peoples under his command, and there was no hope of salvation for those suffering these evils, oppressed by a terrible beast.

11.16. Therefore indeed, the orchestrator of good deeds, combining his hatred of evil with his clemency, set forth together with his son, the most clement emperor Crispus, away from the greatest Rome, that of the West,[93] toward the East against the tyrant, extending the right hand of salvation to all of those who were being destroyed. Having as guide and ally God the king of all and

---

92. In the source text, Eusebius says that Licinius would have succeeded in his war, "had not God" intervened, but the apodosis to the conditional clause is omitted in Cyzicenus.

93. By Cyzicenus's day, Constantinople, as the home of the court of many emperors ruling over the eastern provinces of the empire, came to be known as Nea Rhoma, "New Rome," in contrast to "old" Rome (i.e., Rome in Italy). This is, however, a fifth-century development, and Cyzicenus's reference to it is doubly proleptic since Constantinople was only renamed as such in 330, *after* Constantine defeated Licinius and after the death of Crispus.

Christ the Son, Christ the Savior, the emperor Constantine, the father, together with the emperor Crispus, his son, separated their force to encircle the army of the God-haters and won an easy victory, since everything had been made simple for them throughout the encounter according to the will of God the king of all, as well,

just as the most truth-loving Eusebius, the successor of the all-praiseworthy Pamphilus, relates.

11.17. And Rufinus says (even though he mentions nothing in full about the things that happened under Licinius, I will nevertheless excerpt these brief passages from him and insert them in the text)—he says:[94]

Therefore Licinius, co-emperor with him (that is to say, with the God-beloved Constantine), since he espoused Hellenic beliefs, hated Christians, and while he refrained from setting in motion an obvious persecution against them out of fear of the emperor Constantine, he still secretly conspired against many men. 18. But later on, he began stirring up persecution against them all openly in the regions of the East, resulting in many men in various places showing themselves to be martyrs for Christ. Indeed, with this act he spurred the emperor Constantine to utmost hatred against him, and they became mutual enemies.

11.19. So says Rufinus. But the rest, who agree with the truth as told by Eusebius Pamphili, say:[95]

Dividing the army between them, Emperor Constantine, the father, and his son, Emperor Crispus, hastened against the impious tyrant. The son, Crispus, therefore, made his journey to the regions throughout Asia with his army with him, but the father, Constan-

---

94. As before, the name Rufinus points to the Gelasian history (F8). The only differences between the text here in Cyzicenus and a parallel passage in Socrates (*Hist. eccl.* 1.3.1) are small, extra details about characters and locations.

95. The exact source of the following passage is uncertain. Hansen (1998, 193) conjectures that the phrase οἱ δὲ λοιποί ὅσοι ("but the rest, who") in this citation formula is a corruption of ὁ δὲ Φίλιππος ὁ ("but Philip, who"), a conjecture he prints in his 2008 text and translation, interpreting the passage as a segment of the lost ecclesiastical history of Philip of Side. See 6.2.7 in the introduction for further discussion.

tine, traveled his way through Europe with his bodyguards around him. 20. But the God-hating man, utterly full of impiety and bloodlust, coming from the East, took the field against them with as large an army as possible and carried on boasting. And upon arriving in the city of the Nicomedians, recognizing and understanding that the God-beloved Constantine revered the priests of God in his very soul and that he could lead with complete authority, Licinius paid off the bishop of the city of the Nicomedians, Eusebius, who was his longstanding client, and had him oppose the pious emperor Constantine. He did this supposing that through Eusebius and his party he could kill Constantine, even though he was protected by the unconquerable armaments of God. 21. Therefore, that "wonderful" Eusebius took his side, since he was entreated by promises of reward by Licinius, who was equally impious as him.

And that this is so can be confirmed by the very letter of the Christ-loving emperor that he sent to the Nicomedians, saying as follows, near the end of the letter:[96]

11.22. "Who is it who thus has taught the innocent crowd these things? Eusebius, obviously, the fellow initiate in this tyrannical savagery. For since he has become the usurper's protector

---

96. Cyzicenus here presents a portion of a letter against Eusebius and Theognius preserved also by Athanasius, Theodoret, and in the epistolary appendix transmitted with copies of this text (see appendix 1). The portion of the letter inserted into the text matches the segment attested in Theodoret (*Hist. eccl.* 1.20.1–10), although Cyzicenus often agrees with other traditions of the letter against Theodoret, and in 11.25 provides a plausible reading where all other traditions have serious textual issues. This may suggest that both Theodoret and Cyzicenus adopted this segment of the letter from a shared intermediary source, for which the Gelasian history stands as a plausible candidate. By strict chronology, this material ought to appear in book 3 of Cyzicenus's work, as it deals with Constantine's efforts to unite the church after the Council of Nicaea, but as inserted here it instead highlights a connection between Eusebius of Nicomedia and Licinius as enemies of the peace of the church.

The manuscripts of Cyzicenus's *Ecclesiastical History* also transmit the complete version of the letter along with several other letters, which we include as appendix 1. The translation of this letter provided there has been annotated in detail to serve as a case study on Cyzicenus's documentary and quotation practices.

on all sides, it is possible to see him from every quarter.⁹⁷ The murders of the bishops testify to this—of those truly bishops, at any rate—and the harshest persecution of Christians expressly cries out to this fact. 23. For I will at present say nothing of what has happened to me on his account, through which, when the onslaughts of the opposing factions were engaged most strongly against us, he also used to send spying eyes against me and did all but contribute armed assistance to the usurper out of gratitude to him.⁹⁸ 24. And let no one think that I am unprepared to prove these claims. For there is definitive proof, namely that it is publicly known that I have caught the presbyters and deacons who were sent out by Eusebius. But we are bringing these things up now not out of wrath but in order to shame them. This alone have I feared; this alone do I ponder: that I see you have been called into association with this charge. For through the lifestyle and perversion of Eusebius, you have acquired a conscience devoid of truth. 25. But the treatment is not too late, at least if you now take a faithful and inviolate bishop and look to God. And indeed, this is in your hands at present, and this would necessarily have depended on your judgment even long before, had not the aforementioned Eusebius arrived here by the cunning plot of those who then supported him and shamelessly obstructed the rightness of your situation.⁹⁹ 26. But since occasion has come to say a few things to your affection concerning this same Eusebius, listen patiently. Your forbearance will recall that a council of bishops took place at the city of the Nicaeans, where I myself was also fittingly present in service to my own conscience, since I desired nothing other than to bring about a general concord for all and to reprove and shake off in the presence of all that affair that had its beginning through the frenzy of Arius of Alexandria, and then immediately became

---

97. The manuscripts for Cyzicenus give the word προσφύλαξ, "guardian," whereas Athanasius (*Decr.* 41.9) and Theodoret (*Hist. eccl.* 1.20.1) preserve instead πρόσφυξ, "client" or "suppliant."

98. Here Constantine refers to Eusebius of Nicomedia's support for Licinius and portrays Eusebius as complicit in the persecution of Christian clergy.

99. An allusion to Eusebius of Nicomedia's leaving the episcopacy in Beirut to assume the See of Nicomedia.

entrenched through the absurd and deadly zeal of Eusebius. 27. But this very Eusebius, most dear and honored ones, supported his false doctrine, which has been refuted on every front—you know well with what a crowd, since he succumbed to his very own conscience, and with how great dishonor—sending various men secretly to me who made a case on his behalf and requesting some manner of alliance from me, in order that he might not, once proven guilty in so great an offense, fall from the office belonging to him. 28. My witness to these matters is God himself, and may he remain beneficent to me and you, because that Eusebius himself turned even me around and unfittingly misled me; but divine providence led me down its truest path, which you yourselves also recognized and will come to understand. For at that time all things were accomplished by him—I mean the unholy Eusebius—just as he himself desired, since he was then concealing all such evil in his own mind. 29. But first, in order that I might leave unmentioned the rest of this man's perversity, hear, I beseech you, in particular what he has plotted with Theognius, whom he holds as an associate in his unholy intent. He had commanded that certain Alexandrians who had withdrawn from our faith be sent here, since a fire of discord was being stoked through their ministry. 30. But these noble and good bishops, whom the truth of the council had once kept penitent, not only welcomed those men and ensured their safety at their own residences but even shared with them in the malice of their ways. On account of this, I have decided to do the following concerning those ingrates: I have ordered that those who have been caught be banished as far away as possible. 31. Now it is up to you to look to God with that faith by which it is established you have come to be and exist, and act in such a way that we may rejoice that we have holy, orthodox, and beneficent bishops. But if anyone should dare without due consideration to be all on fire for remembering or praising those destroyers, he shall immediately be restrained from his own daring through the action of the servant of God, that is, me. God will preserve you, beloved brethren."

11.32. These and similar things did the letter of the God-beloved emperor Constantine evidence most clearly concerning the impious Eusebius of

Nicomedia, who had become not only the protector of the God-hating Licinius but also his fellow initiate and minister of his tyranny and impiety.[100] But I shall continue with the subject of ecclesiastical history at hand.

Concerning the Victory of the God-Beloved Emperor Constantine against the Wicked Licinius

12.1.[101] Now then, when Licinius had set out from Nicomedia with his army with him heading toward Byzantium against the God-beloved emperor Constantine, who was there at that time, and once the military phalanxes on each side were protecting the Christ-bearing emperor within their defensive perimeter, the transgressor, seeing that he was deserted also by his own army, looked for the protection of the stronger men who had fled. He hastened at first to hide himself in Chrysopolis in Bithynia—that is, the port of Chalcedon—but since he was unable and he saw that he already lay prone before the feet of the emperor Constantine, he handed himself over. 2. Therefore, the most reasonable and most pious emperor, capturing him alive, showed his benevolence and did not by any means kill him but ordered him to live quietly in Thessaloniki. 3. And he, for a short time, thought it good to remain quiet. But after that, summoning some foreigners and making plans with them, he was eager to reverse his defeat. 4. When the most faithful emperor became aware of this, he ordered that the God-hater be done away with, and he was done away with, that usurper against both Christ and his servant.

---

100. The Greek term we translate "fellow initiate," συμμύστης, suggests that Eusebius of Nicomedia has joined Licinius as an initiate of "pagan" mysteries; i.e., that he is part of a Hellene conspiracy (see 1.11.17 above).

101. The source of what follows is unclear. BHG 1279 and Socrates, the two other witnesses to parts of this passage, both position a similar, shortened narrative of Licinius's final defeat immediately following the notice of persecutions that Cyzicenus includes at 1.11.17–18, suggesting its inclusion in the Gelasian history (F9). The relative complexity of the narrative in Cyzicenus compared to the similar but simplified version contained in the other two sources may suggest, however, that Cyzicenus drew his narrative from an embellished version of the mutual source or has taken personal liberties. Hansen (1998, 194), reading the final line of 1.11.32 as a resumption of the previous source rather than a resumption of the main narrative after the digression as we read it, postulates that the beginning of this section derives from Philip of Side and then transitions into material from Gelasius. He does acknowledge the possibility that the entire passage could be originally Gelasian (Hansen 1998, 194–95 n. 49).

The Second Treatise of the *Ecclesiastical History*: Concerning the Affairs after the Death of the Impious Licinius, the Sole Rule of the Emperor Constantine, and the Peace of the Churches of God

1.1.[1] Now Constantine, since he had become master of all things through the assistance given him by God and had been proclaimed the sole ruling emperor, was zealous to strengthen the Christians' causes still more and more. He did this by various means, because he had a burning faith and a most loyal inborn devotion toward the God of the universe. And the entire church under heaven was deeply at peace.

1.2. Let us hear then what Eusebius, the successor of the famous Pamphilus and most excellent, most truth-loving plowman of the ecclesiastical field, also says next.[2] He says:

1.3. Licinius, then, following the same path of impiety as the godless tyrants, justly wandered into the same abyss as them. 4. But while that man lay in the place where he had been struck down, the greatest conqueror, outstanding in every virtue of godly devotion, Constantine Augustus, together with his son Crispus, a most God-beloved emperor in every way most similar to his father, recovered the East as his own and brought about one united rule for the Romans as it was formerly, extending their entire rule around the globe from the rising sun, throughout each part of

---

1. Book 2 begins with a Gelasian fragment (F10) found in more compact form in both Socrates and BHG 1279. Cyzicenus's version more strongly asserts Constantine's connection to God, reminding the reader that Constantine only won "through the assistance given him by God" and specifying Constantine's pious motivations for the actions he took. Where Cyzicenus says that the "entire church under heaven" was at peace, the other two sources say simply "the affairs of Christianity."

2. 2.1.3–7 presents the concluding statements of Eusebius, *Hist. eccl.* 10.9.5–9, as the starting point for the discussion of the Council of Nicaea.

the inhabited world, both north and south together, to the ends of the dwindling day, leading it under their peace. 5. And thereupon every fear of their oppressors was removed from mankind and they observed splendid, festive days of celebration, and all things were full of light, and those who had been downcast before looked on one another with smiling faces and shining eyes, and hymns were sung by them through city and fields alike. They were first of all honoring God the king and his genuine Son Christ,[3] since indeed they had been taught this, and next they were acclaiming the pious emperor together with his God-loving children,[4] 6. and old ills passed from memory, and every impiety was forgotten, and they enjoyed their good fortune and looked forward to the things to come. Thereupon there spread to every place decrees full of the conquering emperor's benevolence and laws bearing the marks of magnanimity and true piety. 7. Thus truly, after all tyranny had been cleansed away, the steadfast and irreproachable powers of the rightful empire were preserved by Constantine and his children alone.

1.8. So great were the events of ecclesiastical history that the most rightly faithful of the old ecclesiastical writers, Eusebius Pamphili, left behind for us with no distortion, setting down and investigating the many great struggles in ten complete tomes, taking a selection from plain-spoken writers, 9. beginning from the advent of our Lord and bringing it to completion with these times, and not without difficulty (for how was he able to take on responsibility for so great a charge of preserving the harmony of such a collection?) but, as I just said, bringing to bear great effort and putting on himself an unspeakable wealth of toil.[5] 10. But let no one consider the man based on the accusations leveled against him, that he was ever at any time inclined toward the wickedness of the blasphemer Arius, but let them be persuaded that if ever he spoke of or wrote in some small way anything suspected to be part of Arius's doctrines, it was not by any means done in

---

3. The phrase "and his genuine Son, Christ" is unique to Cyzicenus.

4. The children of Constantine included not only Crispus (300–326 CE) but also the future Augusti Constantine II (316–340, r. 337–340), Constantius II (317–361 CE, r. 337–361), and Constans (320–350 CE, r. 337–350).

5. Compare Eusebius's description of his own project at *Hist. eccl.* 1.1.2–5, with which the preceding sentence shares some parallels in vocabulary and phrasing.

accordance the with impious ideas of that man but out of guileless sincerity, just as he himself also gave assurance of when giving testimony to these matters in his apologetic treatise, which he sent to the general assembly of orthodox bishops.[6] 11. And let every sensible person understand that the man was speaking the truth, since it is possible to be persuaded from that text that not then nor ever would he have heeded Arius's doctrines. And what was debated in the council in Nicaea against the impiety of Arius on behalf of the apostolic and orthodox faith will prove it.[7] 12. But let us return to the sequence of events of our ecclesiastical history.

Now then, the church of Christ, our Savior, was experiencing a profound peace throughout the inhabited world, and this peace had been granted to it by God, the king of all, through his servant Constantine and his children. 13.[8] But after the martyrdom of the godly Peter, who had been bishop of the church of the Alexandrians, since he had died in the very act of martyrdom and had donned the incorruptible crown for the fight, the church there was leaderless for one year. 14. But after a year, Achillas was appointed to fill the seat of the same holy martyr Peter. Achillas was a sturdy and noble man, reverent in his fear of the Lord as well as notable for being as wise as can be—just as the ancient and unerring texts

---

6. Anonymous Cyzicenus's defense of Eusebius's orthodoxy in some respects follows Socrates Scholasticus, *Hist. eccl.* 2.21. In that passage, Socrates quotes from Eusebius's *Against Marcellus* to prove his orthodoxy. It is uncertain whether this work is the "apologetic treatise" (ἀπολογητικῷ ... λόγῳ) referenced by Anonymous Cyzicenus in this passage or whether he instead has in mind Eusebius's letter to his own congregation after Nicaea (which Cyzicenus includes later in his history, at 2.35). In any event, Cyzicenus was not able to persuade all his readers of Eusebius's orthodoxy. One *scholion* to this passage, attributed to Hierotheus, metropolitan of Monemvasia in the Peloponnese, reads: "He says that he of Pamphilus is not of the Arian persuasion, but in many of his writings, he appears to be thinking the ideas of Arius." For Greek text, see Loeschke and Heinemann 1918, xiii–xiv; Hansen 2002, xxvii.

7. A reference to the Dispute with Phaedo, in which "Eusebius" plays a prominent part. See below, 2.17–20.

8. The lengthy segment from 2.1.13–2.6.1 derives in some manner from the Gelasian history (F11), although the sources that parallel Cyzicenus here (Rufinus, *Hist. eccl.* 10.1; Socrates, *Hist. eccl.* 1.4.5–1.8.12; BHG 1279, 291a) each provide different levels of detail. Consequently, it is difficult to say whether Cyzicenus emended the text, preserved different portions of the Gelasian history, or had an intermediary source. Hansen (1998, 195) proposes Philip of Side as an intermediary, noting that Cyzicenus contains specific information, such as the one-year vacancy in the Alexandrian bishopric, not mentioned in the other three sources' chronologies.

tell us—who, because he had been implored so much, accepted Arius into the diaconate. 15. But since that man lived only five more months after this, Alexander assumed leadership as high priest there over the church of the Alexandrians, a man well respected in all regards by the entire clergy and lay populace, modest, generous, well spoken, courteous, God-loving, benevolent, caring of the poor, dutiful, and kindly to all if ever anyone has been, who himself also appointed Arius as the presbyter next after himself [in rank].[9] 16. Under his leadership, while the peace over the churches shone ever brighter day by day and stood in solid unanimity and was being magnified by the trophies of the holy martyrs throughout the whole world, the devil, because he was unable to endure so great an increase in the church's faithful populace gathering for the heavenly worship of God, once more secretly stirred up trouble, motivated by some quarrelsomeness against those in the church.

Concerning the Heresy Invented by the God-Battling Arius

2.1. For that presbyter, whom we mentioned was deemed worthy of such great honor by Alexander the bishop of Alexandria, Arius by name, a man very pious in appearance but in all other respects an ardent lover of personal glory and subversive innovation,[10] began to introduce certain foreign teachings regarding the faith in Christ, which previously nobody had ever considered or introduced. 2. He tried to pry our only begotten Lord, Jesus Christ, apart from the ineffable and eternal divinity of the Father, and became an accessory to much tumult throughout the church. 3. But indeed Alexander, due to the mildness of his nature, was desiring to change Arius for the better through suitable exhortations, and for a while yet he did not deem it necessary to make a public judgment against him. For this reason, it so happened that the baneful pestilence of heresy spread to many others, as when a great fire blazes up from a tiny spark. 4. And the evil that began in the church of Alexandria flew through other cities and provinces. 5. At last, when he saw the evil was getting worse and worse,

---

9. I.e., Arius was most senior among the presbyters and the favored candidate for the episcopacy.

10. The manuscripts read "glory and vainglory." However, the Greek words for "vainglory" (κενότητος) and "subversive innovation" (καινότητος) would have had the same pronunciation in late antiquity and could easily be confused. In a parallel passage, Rufinus has *novitas*, "subversive innovation" (*Hist. eccl.* 10.1).

Alexander convened a council of the bishops under him, and, having condemned Arius, he explained the case thoroughly to his fellow clergy. And when he had laid out the charges against Arius more fully and instilled an eagerness for rejecting the heresy, he advised them to make preparations to carry out their decision, writing to them as follows:

> The Decree of Condemnation against Arius and Those with Him Disseminated by Alexander the Bishop to the Bishops Everywhere

> 3.1.[11] To his beloved and most honored fellow ministers of the universal church everywhere, Alexander greets you in the name of the Lord.
> 3.2. Since there is one body of the universal church and since there is a command in the Holy Scriptures to preserve the bond of its unanimity and peace, it is appropriate that we write to and notify one another about what has happened to each of us, so that, if one member is either suffering or rejoicing, we may suffer or rejoice with one another.[12] 3. Now then, in our community there recently emerged lawless and Christ-fighting men, teaching apostasy, which one could reasonably suspect of being a forerunner of the antichrist and call it so. 4. And I was planning to pass over such issues in silence, to see whether the evil, contained to the apostates alone, would dissipate and not befoul the ears of any innocents by spreading to other places. But since Eusebius, the one now in Nicomedia, who thinks that the affairs of the church are in his control because the penalties against him were not meted out after he abandoned Beirut and set his jealous eyes on the church at Nicomedia,[13] is the ringleader of these apostates and has tried to send letters everywhere in support of them, in order to rope some

---

11. The following letter (*Urk.* 4b) is preserved, without subscriptions, in both Socrates and BHG 1279, suggesting that the Gelasian history included a copy of the text. Athanasius's own version (*Decr.* 35) differs enough from the other three witnesses to constitute a separate transmission tradition. See Wallraff, Stutz, and Marinides 2018, 53 n. 4. Cyzicenus's text does not differ substantially from that of Socrates.

12. Compare Eph 4:3; 1 Cor 12:26.

13. Eusebius was first elevated to the episcopacy in Beirut, a coastal city in Phoenicia famous as a center for the study of Roman law. He became bishop of Nicomedia under Licinius, when the city served as the emperor's headquarters and an imperial capital. The issue of bishops changing sees was addressed at the Council of Nicaea;

unsuspecting people into this final, Christ-fighting heresy, I had a need, because I know what has been written in the law,[14] to remain silent no longer and to make a disclosure to you all at last, in order that you recognize both those who have become apostates and the wretched slogans of their heresy, and so you will not pay any heed, should Eusebius write to you.[15] 5. For he wishes through these men to reinvigorate now his old malevolence, which had been silenced for a time. Therefore, he is posturing as if he is writing on their behalf, but in fact it is obvious that he is zealously doing this on his own behalf.

3.6. Those who have become apostates, then, are Arius, Achilles, Thales, Carpones, another Arius, Sarmates, Euzoïus, Lucius, Julius, Menas, Helladius, and Gaius, and along with them Secundus and Theonas, who at one time were chosen as bishops. 7. What they have invented contrary to the Scriptures and blather about is as follows: "God was not always Father, but there was a time when God was not Father. The Word of God did not always exist but came into being out of nonbeing. For the God who exists has made the one who did not exist out of the nonexistent. For this reason, there was also a time when he was not. For the Son is a created and made thing. And he is neither like the Father according to *ousia*, nor is he the true Word of the Father by nature, nor is he his true Wisdom, but he is one of the created and generated things, and he is called 'Word' and 'Wisdom' by catachresis,[16] 8. and even

---

according to the canons of the council as preserved in Rufinus and in this text, this practice was forbidden (see below, 2.32.15).

14. Alexander claims scriptural authority for his public condemnation of Arius; he may have in mind passages such as Matt 18:17, Acts 18:9, Rom 16:17.

15. Upon Arius's excommunication, he sought support among other bishops in the East (for examples of Arius's correspondence, see *Urk*. 1, 2, 6). Eusebius of Nicomedia was among those who wrote letters in efforts to convince Alexander to readmit Arius (for an example of these letters, see *Urk*. 8). The letter quoted here, commonly known by its first words, *Of One Body* (Ἑνὸς σώματος), was sent by Alexander in direct response to this epistolary campaign; compare, too, Alexander's contemporary letter, *The Ambitious* (Ἡ φίλαρχος; *Urk*. 14), to his namesake in Thessaloniki.

16. "By catachresis" (καταχρηστικῶς): catachresis is a figure of speech in which a word is strained beyond its normal usage to convey a concept that would otherwise be difficult to convey. Alexander, by contrast, holds that these terms are applied "properly" (κυρίως) and not in a metaphorical, analogical, or other nonliteral manner.

he came into being by God's own word and the wisdom that is in God, in which wisdom God has made all things, including the Son. And for this reason, he is by nature mutable and subject to change, as all rational beings are. 9. The Word is alien, other and separated from the *ousia* of God. And for the Son, the Father is inexpressible. For the Word neither perfectly nor accurately knows the Father, nor is he able to view him perfectly. For, in fact, the Son does not know his own *ousia*, the manner in which he exists. For he had been made for our sake, so that God might create us through him as with a tool, and he would not exist had God not wanted to create us."

3.10. Someone then asked them whether the Word of God is able to change as the devil is changed, and they were not afraid to say, "Yes, he can, for he is of a mutable nature, being one having come into being and created." We, together with about a hundred bishops of Egypt and Libya, came together and condemned those in Arius's circle who were saying these things as well as those who were acting shamefully in these matters and their followers. 11. But Eusebius's faction welcomed them, hastily mixing falsehood with truth and impiety with piety. But they will not prevail, for truth triumphs; there is no "fellowship between light and dark," nor "concord between Christ and Belial."[17] 12. For who has ever heard of such things? Or who now hearing them is not shocked and does not plug their ears to prevent it lest the filth of these words touch their ears? For who, when he hears John saying, "In the beginning was the word,"[18] does not condemn those who say, "There was a time when it was not"? Or who, when hearing in the gospel "only begotten Son"[19] and "through him everything came into being,"[20] will not hate those spouting that he is one of the things that was made? For how is it possible for him to be one of the things that came into being through him? Or how can the only begotten be numbered together with all things, as those men say? And how could he come from nonbeing when the Father says,

---

17. 2 Cor 6:14–15.
18. John 1:1.
19. John 3:16.
20. John 1:3.

"My heart spilled forth a good word"[21] and "I birthed you from the womb before the morning star"?[22] 13. Or how could he who is the perfect likeness[23] and reflection of the Father[24] and who says, "He who has looked upon me has looked upon the Father,"[25] be unlike the essence of the Father? And how, if the Son of God is Word and Wisdom, was there ever a time when he was not? For that is the same as them saying that God was once without Word and without Wisdom. 14. And how can he who says in his own person, "I am in the Father and the Father is in me"[26] and "I and the Father are one,"[27] be changeable and mutable, when speaking through the prophet he says, "Behold me, that I am and change not"?[28] For even if one were able to apply the passage to the Father himself, nevertheless it would now be more fittingly said about the Word, that even after becoming human it has not been changed, but, as the apostle said, "Jesus Christ is the same yesterday and today and forever more."[29] But what persuaded them to say that he came to be on our account, even though Paul says, "By whom and through whom all things came to be"?[30] 15. For there is no need to be astonished at those who blaspheme, saying that the Son does not know the Father perfectly. For, once determined to fight against Christ, they reject even his own words when he says, "Just as the Father knows me, I also know the Father."[31] Therefore, if the Father only partially knows the Son, it is clear that the Son also does not perfectly know the Father. But if it is improper to say this, and the Father knows the Son perfectly, it is clear that just as the Father knows his own Word, so the Word also knows its Father, whose it is. 16. And by saying these things and unfolding the Holy Scriptures, we often put them to shame, and again they changed

---

21. Ps 45 (44):2.
22. Ps 110 (109):3.
23. Col 1:15.
24. Heb 1:3.
25. John 14:9.
26. John 14:11.
27. John 10:30.
28. Mal 3:6.
29. Heb 13:8.
30. 1 Cor 8:6, Col 1:16, Heb 2:10.
31. John 10:15.

like chameleons, bringing down on themselves the following passage, in their love of contentiousness: "Whenever an ungodly man comes into the abyss of evils, he regards it with contempt."[32] Now certainly many heresies have come into being before these men that, because they dared more than they ought, have fallen into senselessness. But these men, in trying to destroy the divinity of the Word with all their little slogans, have vindicated those heresies through their own actions, since they themselves have drawn nearer to the antichrist. On that account, they have been publicly condemned and anathematized by the church.

3.17. Therefore, while we are aggrieved at their destruction—and all the more so because they who once also themselves learned the ways of the church have now turned away from it—we are not amazed. For this happened to Hymenaeus and Philetus before them, and before them Judas, the follower of the Savior, later became a traitor and apostate.[33] 18. And we have not remained uninformed about these very things, but indeed the Lord has foretold, "Keep watch, lest anyone lead you astray; for many will come in my name saying 'I am he and the time is near,' and they will lead many astray. Do not follow them."[34] And Paul, having learned these things from the Savior, wrote "that in later times certain men will turn away from the sound faith, heeding spirits of deception and the teachings of demons who repudiate the truth."[35] 19. Therefore, as our Lord and Savior, Jesus Christ, both announced in his own person and signified through the apostle about such men as these, accordingly we who ourselves heard their impiety anathematized these men, just as we previously stated, having demonstrated that they are foreign to the universal church and faith. 20. We therefore reported this also to your piety, beloved and most estimable fellow ministers, in order that neither would you receive any of them if they should be so rash as to come to you, nor would you believe Eusebius or anyone writing about them. For it is fitting that we who are Christians repudiate as God-battlers and

---

32. Prov 18:3.
33. Hymenaeus and Philetus: 2 Tim 2:17; Judas: Mark 14:18–21.
34. Matt 24:4–5, 23; see Mark 13:6, Luke 21:8.
35. 1 Tim 4:1, with an interpolation of the last phrase, "who repudiate the truth," from Titus 1:14.

corrupters of souls all those men who say and think such things against Christ and that we not even speak a greeting to them, so that we never become complicit in their sins, as the blessed John enjoined.[36] Greet the brothers who are among you. The brothers with me send their greeting to you all.

The Presbyters of Alexandria[37]

3.21. I, Colluthus, the presbyter, am of the same opinion with the things herein written and with the condemnation of Arius and of the men working in impiety with him.

Alexander the presbyter likewise	Dioscorus the presbyter likewise
Dionysius the presbyter likewise	Eusebius the presbyter likewise
Alexander the presbyter likewise	Silas the presbyter likewise
Harpocration the presbyter likewise	Agathon the presbyter likewise
Nemesius the presbyter likewise	Longus the presbyter likewise
Silvanus the presbyter likewise	Piroüs the presbyter likewise
Apis the presbyter likewise	Proterius the presbyter likewise
Paul the presbyter likewise	Cyrus the presbyter likewise

Deacons

Ammonius the deacon likewise	Macarius the deacon likewise
Pistus the deacon likewise	Athanasius the deacon likewise[38]
Eumenes the deacon likewise	Apollonius the deacon likewise
Olympius the deacon likewise	Aphthonius the deacon likewise
Athanasius the deacon likewise	Macarius the deacon likewise
Paul the deacon likewise	Peter the deacon likewise
Amyntianus the deacon likewise	Gaius the deacon likewise

---

36. 2 John 10–11.

37. The following subscriptions mostly agree with those found in Athanasius, with discrepancies of substitution (e.g., where Cyzicenus has Silas the presbyter, Athanasius preserves Neilaras) and of omission. Neither Socrates nor BHG 1279 preserves a list of the signatories to the letter, but Wallraff, Stutz, and Marinides identify Gelasius (2018, 63 n. 8) as the probable source for Cyzicenus's version of the subscriptions as well as for the letter.

38. Either this Athanasius or the one listed three lines below was Athanasius (ca. 295–373), future bishop of Alexandria from 328 to 373.

The Presbyters of Mareotis

Apollos the presbyter likewise
Ammonas the presbyter likewise
Sostras the presbyter likewise
Tyrannus the presbyter likewise
Ammonas the presbyter likewise
Serenus the presbyter likewise
Heracles the presbyter likewise
Agathon the presbyter likewise

Ingenius the presbyter likewise
Dioscorus the presbyter likewise
Theon the presbyter likewise
Copres the presbyter likewise
Orion the presbyter likewise
Didymus the presbyter likewise
Boccon the presbyter likewise
Achillas the presbyter likewise

Deacons

Serapion the deacon likewise
Didymus the deacon likewise
Maurus the deacon likewise
Comon the deacon likewise
Tryphon the deacon likewise
Didymus the deacon likewise
Seras the deacon likewise
Hierax the deacon likewise

Justus the deacon likewise
Demetrius the deacon likewise
Marcus the deacon likewise
Alexander the deacon likewise
Ammonius the deacon likewise
Ptollarion the deacon likewise
Gaius the deacon likewise
Marcus the deacon likewise

3.22.[39] Although Alexander was writing such things to those in each city everywhere, the evil grew worse. After the emperor Constantine learned of these matters, he was heavily aggrieved in his spirit, and he considered the affair a personal disaster. Hastening to quench immediately the evil that had been kindled, he sent missives to Alexander and Arius through a trustworthy man: a bishop of one of the Spanish cities, Cordoba, since the emperor was fond of him and held him in honor.[40]

---

39. On the basis of the closer textual relationship Cyzicenus presents to BHG 1279 than to the similar paragraph with which Eusebius introduces the letter that follows in *Vit. Const.* 2.63, this transitional paragraph appears to originate with the Gelasian history (F11). Socrates's narrative presents a much more detailed narrative than Cyzicenus at this point (*Hist. eccl.* 1.6.31–1.7.1), describing the contention that followed the letter and repeating information about the succession in the Alexandrian bishopric, situating the growth of support for Arius and Meletius into the larger history of Alexandrian ecclesiastical matters. All of the material in Cyzicenus appears in full in Socrates, although divided by Socrates's additional information.

40. Hosius of Cordoba acted as a kind of liaison between Constantine's court and the Eastern bishops during the period leading up to the Council of Nicaea. He presided

The Letter of Constantine the Emperor to Alexander and Arius, Which Was Delivered by Hosius the Bishop of Cordoba

4.1. The victor Constantine Maximus Augustus to Alexander and Arius.[41]

I have learned that the foundation of the present controversy was laid when you yourself, father Alexander, were asking of the presbyters what each of them actually thought about a certain point written in the law,[42] or rather, he inquired about a part of some vain controversy; and you, Arius, without foresight retorted with the very thing you either should not have considered in the first place or that, once you had considered it, you ought to have consigned to silence. 2. Whereupon, since the disagreement had sprung up between you, your council came to naught and the most holy people was split into two parties and was severed from the harmony of a common body.[43] Therefore, let each of you, having presented your position on equal terms, accept what your fellow servant justly advises. 3. And what is that? It was neither appropriate from the first to ask such things nor, having been asked, to give an answer. For no necessity of any law prescribes any such investigations, but the quibbling of useless idleness prompts them. And if it were to arise in the course of some routine exercise, nevertheless we ought to contain it in our minds, and not rashly bring it out into public

---

over the Council of Antioch in 325 CE, which elected Eustathius. Aside from Caecilian of Carthage, he was the most senior Western bishop present at Nicaea.

41. Cyzicenus presents a truncated version of Constantine's letter to Alexander and Arius (*Urk.* 17 [= *Vit. Const.* 2.64–72]), which he probably found already abridged in the Gelasian history (Wallraff, Stutz, and Marinides 2018, 65–71). Socrates and BHG 1279 both begin their quotation of the letter at the same place as Cyzicenus, omitting a large portion of the beginning of the letter (i.e., *Vit. Const.* 2.64–68). Three similar abridgements appear in both Cyzicenus and BHG 1279, suggesting that their shared source cut the quoted material in this manner. Wallraff, Stutz, and Marinides (2018, 67–69 nn. 12, 14) suggest that Gelasius edited out problematic materials, such as Constantine's denial of difference between the two clergymen, denial of Arius's danger, and characterization of the dispute as trivial. Cyzicenus largely agrees with the text of BHG 1279 and, occasionally, Socrates.

42. I.e., in Scripture. *Law* is used in this sense in many Constantinian letters of this period.

43. Constantine is referring to a council of Egyptian bishops in 322 that failed to quell the Arian controversy.

assemblies, and not thoughtlessly entrust it to the ears of all people. For is each of you so great that he is able to understand precisely or worthily interpret matters so great and exceedingly difficult?

4.4. And after a bit:

Therefore, we must flee excessive bantering in such matters, given our inability, due to the weakness of our nature, to interpret what is put forward, lest the slower understanding of the listeners whom we teach not admit accurate comprehension of what has been said, and lest, in turn, the people come to grief on account of either of these, whether blasphemy or schism.

And after other matters:

It is a truism that discord is neither proper, nor is it appropriate in any way. 5. But in order that I may goad your reasoning by a small example: you surely know the philosophers themselves, how they all come together in one doctrine, but often, whenever they disagree in some part of their opinions, even though they also are divided in the excellence of their knowledge, they nevertheless inspire one another once again to unity of doctrine. And if this is so, how is it not much more correct for you who are established as the servants of the great God to be of like opinion in so great a principle of worship? 6. Indeed, let us examine with greater scrutiny and consider what was said with more judgment,[44] if indeed it is right on account of some love of quarreling among yourselves with vain words for brother to be set against brother and children against their father and for the honor of the assembly to be cleft by impious discord because of you two.[45] 7. Let us willingly shrink from diabolical temptations. Our great God, the Savior of all, extended a light common to all. And in accordance with his

---

44. Probably referring to the biblical passage that prompted Arius's and Alexander's dissension (see 2.4.1 above).

45. No other version of the letter casts the dispute as one of "children against their father," which may have been added to emphasize the subordinate rank of Arius to Alexander within the church. There is a possible allusion to the words of Jesus as recorded in Mark 13:12, Matt 10:21.

providence, grant to me, the servant of the Almighty, that I maintain this zeal to the end in order that I may lead you his people to the holy fellowship of the assembly by my address and service and constancy in counsel.[46]

4.8. And after other things:

And concerning the divine Providence,[47] let there then be a single faith between you, a single understanding, a single agreement about the Almighty. And whatever you should discuss in detail among one another during these trivial inquiries, even if you do not converge to a single opinion, it is fitting that these things, which remain within our thoughts, are protected by the secrecy of our mind. Indeed, let the excellence of your common affection and faith in the truth and the worship and honor of God and the law remain unshaken for you. 9. Indeed, return to one another's friendship and good grace, restore to the entire people their customary bonds of affection, and you yourselves acknowledge each other again as if you were purifying your own souls. For affection often becomes sweet after enmity has been put away and it restores you to reconciliation again. 10. Therefore, give me back calm days and worry-free nights, in order to preserve for me some enjoyment of the day's pure light and a gladness in life, at ease from now on. 11. But if not, I will have to groan and be utterly afflicted by tears, and I will not be able to endure the rest of my life calmly. For indeed, ultimately, how is it possible for me to stay sane any longer when the peoples of God, I mean my fellow servants, have been split apart in this way by an unjust and harmful love of quarreling with one another? 12. But listen, in order that you understand the extraordinary nature of my pain

---

46. It is not clear whether the word translated "assembly" (σύνοδος) refers to the "corporate body" of the church or to a specific council. Hall (1998, 86–104) argues for the latter, contending that the reference must be to the Council of Antioch held in early 325, while Parvis (2006, 77 n. 172) holds that the letter is addressed generally to the bishops of the East.

47. Constantinian documents often use the expression "divine Providence" as a periphrasis for God, in a manner somewhat analogous to using "your honor" or "your majesty" to refer to an individual instead of their name or official title.

on this matter. Recently, when I was near the city of Nicomedia, I was of eager mind to go immediately to the East. But when I was hurrying to you and a large part of my presence was already there,[48] the announcement of this affair reined in my plans, so that I might not be forced to see with my own eyes what I considered impossible to accept with my ears. 13. Open for me hereafter the road of the East through your unity with one another, which you barred for me by your love of quarreling with one another, and quickly make it possible for me to look with pleasure on you and on the other congregations, and in pleasing terms to express to the Almighty my debt of thanks for the general concord and liberation of all.

4.14. Such advice, wonderous and full of wisdom, did the emperor's letter urge, but the evil was yet mightier than the emperor's zeal and the trustworthiness of the one who administered to the missives.[49]

The Most God-Beloved Emperor Constantine Orders the Gathering of Bishops to Occur at the City of the Nicaeans

5.1. Therefore, because the emperor saw that the church had been thrown into confusion, he organized an ecumenical council, summoning in writing the bishops from everywhere to meet at Nicaea in Bithynia. It was the sixteenth year and sixth month of his *imperium* when he made these efforts for the sake of the peace of the church.[50] 2. And bishops were present from

---

48. In other words, Constantine was about to arrive, and a large portion of the imperial retinue (*comitatus*) had already arrived.

49. The emissary entrusted with the letters was Hosius of Cordoba, mentioned by name at 2.3.22 above. In the earliest testimony to this letter (Eusebius, *Vit. Const.* 2.64–72), Hosius in not referenced by name, but Eusebius's description of the emissary as a respected bishop in the imperial retinue is usually taken as a paraphrastic reference to Hosius (2.63).

50. Cyzicenus uniquely among surviving sources attempts a chronology of the council at this point. How Cyzicenus reckons the sixteen years and six months is uncertain, as it matches neither Constantine's proclamation by the army in 306 nor his defeat of Maxentius in 312. The most relevant historical event fitting in this chronology would be the meeting of the current and former tetrarchs at Carnutum in late 308, at which Licinius was promoted to Augustus in the West over Constantine, who refused to acknowledge his authority and continued to style himself Augustus. Constantine

many provinces and cities, about whom Eusebius Pamphili says this verbatim in his third book on the life of Constantine:[51]

> Therefore the foremost from the ministers of God from all the churches that fill all Europa, Libya, and Asia had been gathered at the same place and 3. one house of prayer, as if it had been widened out by God's doing, held within the same space Syrians together with Cilicians, Phoenicians and Arabians and Palestinians, and with these Egyptians, Thebans, Libyans, and those hailing from Mesopotamia; and actually even a Persian bishop was present at the council, nor was a Scythian absent from the company, and Pontus and Asia, Phrygia and Pamphylia sent men selected from among them.[52] And further, Thracians and Macedonians, Achaeans and Epirotes, and those who live further away still were there. And Hosius himself, that most celebrated Spaniard, was present, taking the place of bishop Sylvester of the greatest city, Rome,

---

was acknowledged as consul in the East in 309, but he himself did not acknowledge this in his imperial titles.

51. See Eusebius, *Vit. Const.* 3.7–9. Although the following narrative largely follows that of Eusebius, it does not transmit the surviving text of Eusebius precisely. The phrase translated "verbatim" (κατὰ λέξιν) also appears in Socrates, suggesting that the formula derives from the Gelasian history (F11). In comparison with the version in Eusebius (and as quoted in Socrates, *Hist. eccl.* 1.8), Cyzicenus explicitly names Hosius where Eusebius does not, and adds Vito and Vicentius. Moreover, Eusebius mentions the "city that is queen" (i.e., Rome) and its absent leader (i.e., Sylvester). Cyzicenus instead identifies the city as the "new" Rome (Constantinople) and Metrophanes, bishop of Byzantium (soon renamed Constantinople), as its leader. Below, at 2.38.13, Cyzicenus includes a list of attendees that includes Alexander, future bishop of Constantinople, attending as a presbyter representing the Cyclades islands. In the era in which Gelasius of Caesarea would have written, Rome was still a dominant city for the western empire, leading Wallraff, Stutz, and Marinides to suggest that Cyzicenus made this emendation at the eclipse of Rome's power in the late fifth century CE (see Wallraff, Stutz, and Marinides 2018, 73 n. 18).

52. Compare Acts 2:9–11, where a similar list of regions and peoples appears in the Pentecost narrative. The parallelism is deliberate; in the Acts narrative, each member of the multiethnic audience hears the apostles, who have just been endowed with the Holy Spirit, speaking in their own native language. The Acts narrative emphasizes and intertwines the notions of apostolic authority and the putative universality of the gospel; the council is thus described as mirroring and embodying this apostolic authority and universality.

and assembling with the presbyters of Rome, Vito and Vicentius, together with many others. 4. And the leader of the city that is now queen,[53] Metrophanes by name, was missing on account of his old age, but the presbyters in his community were performing his role, one of whom, Alexander, would become bishop of that city after him. 5. Alone throughout the ages, one emperor, Constantine, joining together with a bond of peace such a crown for Christ, offered it to his Savior as a thank-offering worthy of God for his victory over enemy combatants, when he gathered us in an image of the apostolic chorus. 6. Then, too, did the passage apply to them, which says that there were gathered "devout men from every people of those under heaven"[54] just as in the Acts of the Apostles, in which there were "Parthians and Medes and Elamites."[55] Only, these latter men were wanting in that not all were composed of the ministers of God, but in this present assembly the number of bishops was in excess of three hundred, and the number of presbyters and deacons and however many others followed them was inestimable.[56] 7. And among the servants of God, some were renowned for their wise speech, others for their constancy of life and patient endurance, and others were adorned with moderation. And some were honored for the length of their days, others were illustrious for their youth and the bloom of their life, and others had but recently come to the course of their service. 8. And the emperor arranged that copious provisions be arranged for these men each day.

Such does Eusebius Pamphili relate about those gathered there.[57]

---

53. I.e., Constantinople, the "New Rome."
54. Acts 2:5.
55. Acts 2:9.
56. Eusebius (*Vit. Const.* 3.8) gives the number as 250; however, the later tradition reflected in Socrates (*Hist. eccl.* 1.8.9) and Theodoret (*Hist. eccl.* 1.7.3) places the number of attendees over 300. The canonical number of bishops, 318, only appeared decades after the council in the works of Hilary of Poitiers (*Syn.* 86) and Athanasius (*Ep. Afr.* 2). The number 318 was chosen to correspond with the number of Abraham's servants at Gen 14:14. See Aubineau 1966.
57. This closing statement through 2.6.1 echoes the narrative of Socrates and BHG 1279, ending this particular Gelasian passage (F11) that began around 2.1.13.

The Emperor Assembles the Bishops

6.1. And the emperor, after he brought the victory festival over Licinius to a close, arrived in Nicaea himself.[58] And there on the next day all the bishops together assembled in one location. And the emperor also entered after them and, when he arrived, he stood in their midst and did not choose to sit until the bishops assented; such veneration and respect for the men restrained the emperor. 2.[59] And to these men the all-praiseworthy emperor delivered a hortatory and instructive speech as a hymn, doxology, and thanksgiving to the God of all, who showed such great favor to him, speaking as follows.

The Public Oration of Constantine Augustus to the Holy Council

7.1.[60] The sustaining justice of the all-powerful God has spread out many most glorious paths for the benefit of the human race, and not least this splendid and most illuminating path, which he, beyond all wonder, prepared for us all at the head of the most holy law of the universal church: the lordly dwelling place of faith. 2. And we see that its summit approaches as far as to the light of the stars, and we recognize that the foundations, although the work is still just beginning, have been rooted so deeply and faithfully by divine assent that the senses of the entire inhabited world perceive

---

58. There is a play on words in the Greek, juxtaposing the city of Nicaea (Νίκαιαν), whose name comes from the Greek word for victory (νίκη), with Constantine's victory over Licinius, expressed by the adjective describing the "victory" festival (ἐπινίκιον).

59. Socrates's narrative moves quickly from the summoning of the council to the formation of the Nicene Creed, bypassing most of the action of the council. The narrative in Cyzicenus closely follows that in Theodoret (*Hist. eccl.* 1.7.11–14), where the two authors share the phrase "the most blessed emperor" in the introduction to the speeches. The exact relationship between Theodoret and the Gelasian history is still uncertain. See Wallraff, Stutz, and Marinides 2018, xli–xliv.

60. The source of this speech is uncertain. Theodoret (*Hist. eccl.* 1.7.11) and Socrates (*Hist. eccl.* 1.8.18) mention that Constantine delivered a speech at the opening of the Council of Nicaea but relate little about its contents, while Sozomen (*Hist. eccl.* 1.19.3–4) presents a very short speech of Constantine. Eusebius (*Vit. Const.* 2.12) presents Constantine delivering opening remarks very different from this speech. Hansen (1998) conjectures, based on the un-Constantinian presence of metrical clausulae, that the speech was contrived in the fifth century and posits Philip of Side as its author.

it. 3. Now then, from the aforementioned summit, which wholly transcends all else, all the way to the end of the road there can be seen a level and even pathway furnished with the brilliance of the light. Its façade, adorned with a star-like seal, is supported by pillars twelve in number, shining whiter than snow, immoveable in the firmness of faith, strengthened eternally by the power of our Savior's Godhead.[61] 4. Now then, the architect of this great work has placed reverence in our minds, we who with all our spirit maintain the just faith of his immortal law. And he who wishes to approach its gates with only the confidence of a pure mind does so in no other way than with a holy and reverent desire impelling him. 5. And in this work, the reckoning of salvation furnished a certain marvelous, brilliant adornment.[62] I mean that within,[63] the faith of humankind, honored throughout the entire enclosure of the Lord's house with blossoming crowns, and which gathers the fruit of immortality, bringing the hallowed products[64] of human life into plain view, stands resplendent. Then, in turn, the heavenly glory, wreathing the outside, marks out prizes for the contest that is ever productive, or rather ever budding forth, and thus marked, it adorns the full realization of this work with fitting praise.[65] 6. And

---

61. The speaker blends a description of the faith of the church with a description of a physical building, suggesting that the original context of this speech may have been the dedication of a new church. The figurative interpretation of church architecture here can be compared with that of Eusebius of Caesarea's dedicatory oration for a basilica in Tyre (preserved in Eusebius, *Hist. eccl.* 10.4).

62. This sentence plays on the polyvalence of κόσμος, as the "universe" and that which is rationally ordered and therefore genuinely beautiful.

63. I.e., within the interior of the church.

64. Following Hansen's conjecture, τόκους ("product"), instead of the manuscript reading, τόνους ("tone/pitch"). Heinemann conjectures νόμους ("law").

65. The complexity of this sentence has prompted Hansen to conjecture several emendations, which we have adopted in our translation. In place of αἰῶνος ("age" or "era"), he suggests ἀγῶνος ("contest"), and instead of τραφέντα ("fostered") he puts γραφέντα ("inscribed" or "marked"). Accepting Hansen's conjectures, the passage contains an extended discussion of inscription, with the term ὑπογράφει: "inscribes" or "marks out." It may indeed refer to literal inscriptions on the church building being described.

In Hansen's version the rewards are tied to the idea of a constant struggle between Christians and the forces of evil, an idea that is otherwise absent from the speech. Reading with the manuscripts, τραφέντα ("fostered") would continue the growth and blossoming language begun in section 2 with the verb ἐρριζῶσθαι ("to become rooted")

this, the house of the Lord, is watched over by only two guards: the fear of God is there as corrective for the thinking of some,[66] while for those of sound mind the praise of the divine, too, is always present as the reward for understanding. For since each of these lies before the forecourts of this most holy place, the doors, when thrown open, welcome justice, and justice remains unsullied, housed within. And injustice is not permitted to approach the doors, but it is shut out and banished from this place. 7. O most honorable brethren, worthy of all praise, these matters led me toward the brilliance of the everlasting and undying light so clearly that, whichever way faith within my soul wavers, it does not make me stand far from harmony with the truth.[67]

7.8. But what shall I affirm first? Perhaps the impression of good fortune, such as lies hidden, carried close within my breast, or the divine favors done on my behalf by the all-powerful God?[68] From these examples, the number of these many deeds should already appear sufficient, then, to say that our very God, Father of all things, has fittingly pressed my modest ability into his own service. 9. Trust in the things being said, most honorable brethren, since you are receiving an honest faith. If also my intellect, sated on divine benefactions, seems especially fortunate, and if, from this state of affairs, it appears to have the capacity to bring outstanding praise to fruition, nevertheless, neither voice nor tongue satisfy the mandate of the intellect in rendering service to the degree of truth the faith clearly demonstrates, and quite rightly so! 10. For since the magnitude of his favors is immeasurable, the intellect, since it is a lofty thing, attains a plane higher than the

---

and the rewards belonging to the cosmological age. Translating with the manuscripts would read "the heavenly glory, wreathing the outside, marks out prizes for the age that is ever being born, or rather ever budding forth, and fostered thus, it adorns the full realization of this work with fitting praise."

66. More literally "as a house of correction" (σωφρονιστήριον), a very rare word.

67. Hansen (2008, 154) suggests that a portion of the text has fallen out at this point, in which Constantine states his intention to offer public thanks for these reasons.

68. Hansen (2002, 35) conjectures that a participle has been omitted by accident that would provide more information about the divine favors. A literal rendering of the extant text would say, "the divine favors, those on my behalf by the all-powerful God." This is potentially sufficient information for an ancient Greek speaker, but we have elected to insert the neutral verb *done* to make the sentence more sensible in English.

body, but since the tongue's movement is strictly confined to a quite narrow place and is nearly worthless, it keeps silence on all matters whatsoever. For who among us is so reckless of mind as to spew a speech of such great self-assurance, with which he might all too easily dare to assert that he has spoken glorious and deserved praises perfectly to the God who is all-powerful and the craftsman of all that is fairest? 11. If ever anyone should merely consider the magnificence of the one who ordained that he be begotten, once he realized this, he would keep in mind that he can find nothing to say that is worthy of God. 12. What, then, must the devotion of my humble self mention if not what the divine word of truth reveals? And let the greatest veneration wisely contemplate his greatness,[69] if it will be possible to arrive at it in the very things we say about him, and no error cause one to falter.

7.13. And would that I your fellow servant had abundantly sufficient facility at speaking, so that I could praise those things that are worthy of being proclaimed, namely what our divine Savior and protector of all our affairs revealed with a gentle nod of his Godhead at the very beginning of his advent when he, for the sake of our benefit, thought it fitting to take habitation of a sacred body, born from a virgin, making clear to all people the teaching of the compassion he held. 14. Where then should I begin? With his teaching and dignity? Or from the sacred instructions that he himself revealed in his own person as sole instructor, with no one instructing him? Or how so many people that it is not possible to enumerate them enjoyed respite by his providence, from a small bit of food, scantiest grain, and only two fish?[70] 15. Through his divine providence, after the death of Lazarus, he also made him rise again with a short stick and led him up once more into the brilliance of the light.[71] 16. How could I speak of his holy

---

69. I.e., the Word's.

70. The miracle of the loaves and fish feeding five thousand (Matt 14:13–21, Mark 6:31–44, Luke 9:12–17, John 6:1–14); the miracle of seven loaves and a few fish feeding four thousand (Matt 15:32–39, Mark 8:1–9).

71. The story of Jesus raising Lazarus from the dead appears at John 11:1–46. In early Christian iconography, Jesus is often depicted performing certain miracles, such as the raising of Lazarus from the dead, with a short wooden stick held in his right hand. See Jefferson 2010.

Godhead, through which, when he had caught sight of a certain woman who was suffering unspeakably and deemed her worthy merely of his teaching, he immediately rendered her healthy again and free from every illness?[72] 17. And who could tell in worthy fashion of his deed of immortal fame, through which a certain man, consumed by the relentless and lengthy wasting of an illness and lying with all his limbs torn and bleeding, upon suddenly being strengthened by divine healing, hoisted the very stretcher on which he lay on his shoulders and ran throughout his hometown and the country pouring forth praises of thanksgiving?[73] 18. Or further of his divine and steadfast stride, such that stepping onto the wild sea and treading it down, he walked on it, made firm the deepest sea's fluidity by his hallowed footsteps, and made his path through the middle of a sea the depth of which could not be determined by any measure, as if it were land?[74] 19. Or further still of his gentle forbearance, by which, since he is the victor in all things, he overpowered the arrogance of the senseless peoples and, having banished their conquered arrogance far away, subjugated their savagery to the law?[75] 20. Or even further of those brilliant and greatest deeds of his Godhead, by which we have life, by which we whosoever take joy in the hope of the happiness to come do not just await it but after a certain fashion already possess it? 21. What more dare I say, and with so little practice in speaking, if not just precisely that which is necessary for the purity of my devoted soul to understand: of what sort, then, is the all-powerful God who dwells in heaven, yes in regard to the entire human race, but most especially and in particular regarding his justice, which is the

---

72. Healing the woman with the issue of blood; Matt 9:18–36, Mark 5: 21–34, Luke 8:40–56.

73. The healing of the paralytic; Matt 9:1–8, Mark 2:1–2, Luke 5:17–26.

74. Jesus walking on the water; Matt 14: 22–33, Mark 6:45–52, John 6:16–21.

75. The trope of Christ as a bringer of civilization and law is common in early Christian literature; significant examples include, e.g., Eusebius, *Hist. eccl.* 1.2.23, where the advent of Christ and the beginning of the Roman Empire mark an axial point in a progress narrative of human civilization; Athanasius, *Inc.* 37.5–6, where Christ's defeat of idolatry civilizes stereotypically "barbarous" peoples; Constantine's *Or. Sanct.* 11.6, on the effects of Christ's teaching, carried on by the apostles: "This is the august victory, the true power, the great dead: virtuous moderation holding sway over all peoples." See also Schott 2008.

noblest and greater than any praise, when he counted it worthy to take the holiest body, according to worth, for his own holy spirit, to dwell in it,[76] and thus be the salvation for human bodies.

7.22. Therefore, because the boundless rage of the enemies—confounded, as it were, by a mist—does not hesitate to produce an interpretation of pernicious perversity concerning God's most holy and salvific dispensation (which is all-powerful), I shall attempt to describe in a few words how much my soul's faith and devotion for declaring its prosperity abounds. 23. For the perversities of these men, <just like those> of the gentiles, are introducing such an awful kind of shamelessness that with an impious mouth they do not fear to say that God, who is able to do all things, has not done or wanted to do everything that is revealed in the divine law.[77] 24. Oh, such an impious pronouncement, that deservedly calls down every punishment on itself! How madly and rashly it desires to oppose the glory of this divine benefaction, which no human can comprehend, since it is invisible. 25. For what is more worthy of God than purity? And purity indeed has proceeded from the most holy instruction from the font of justice and has flooded through every byway of the inhabited world and has displayed to humankind the powers of the holiest virtues.[78] But from the first considering these very virtues hateful to themselves, they suffered the [fate of] the Assyrians, whose poor example the rest of the gentiles were persuaded to follow.[79] 26. Yet among those people, as we can prove through our own inspection, we see that the divine compassion

---

76. Compare Luke 1:35.

77. Our reading here follows the text of the oldest and most complete manuscript (A), which calls the opponents mentioned "gentiles" (ἐθνῶν), as opposed to the other major manuscripts (H and T), which names them "enemies" (ἐχθρῶν). Hansen's conjectural additions have Constantine comparing the opposition to gentiles instead of directly calling them such. Without further evidence for the original context of this speech, however, both readings are equally probable.

78. "Instruction" translates ὁμιλία ("instructive conversation"), and refers to the instruction received in baptism, to the teaching of the incarnate Christ among humanity, or to both.

79. This seems to be an allusion to the story of Sennacherib's army, in which an angel of the Lord wipes out the Assyrian commander's army while they are sleeping to prevent him from trying to take Jerusalem. See 2 Chr 32:1–23, 2 Kgs 19:8–37, Isa 37:1–38.

of our Savior God assists when, day by day and year after year, he called many of those who were driven by the sting of their fiery madness to come back to the forbearance of his saving remedy. And not even thus was the greatness of such a benefaction able to benefit the rest, on account of the ignorance among humankind concerning the divine sovereignty's ability to raise up every people and magnify them on high, but also to bring them back down and ruin them. 27. But it would have turned out otherwise for human affairs if the God who is capable of all things did not set out to do all things by the silent nod of his holy Godhead. Instead the madness of humankind would have become widespread, and human presumption, having no limits, would have ravaged all souls, nor would other things as numerous as they are, those that perform their own duty in the revolutions of the universe, have been able to shine forth, 28. but all things together would swiftly have perished in ignorance of God. And the injustice of envy and malice would not have remained confined to a few people, and no one would be discovered a stranger to this malice, since cults would have spread so greatly and so widely in the souls of humanity that the light of this, our splendor, would be unjustly overshadowed by them, thanks to their shamefulness, and they would always be deprived of it.[80] 29. Therefore, not one word of what they say will be able to drive my faith from my soul, for a perfect power attends to it to which nothing base is an impediment: the living Word of truth, the one capable of all things, the protector of all endeavors, the guardian of our salvation. Thus, he seems in some way to bestow association with his most holy Word, to protect <...> of the liberator, and offer us the brilliance of the light.

7.30. Why, then, do the peoples of all the nations even now look not on the heavenly light and think little of the holiness that is most glorious, seeking for what is earthly, which has no basis in truth, nor brilliance of pure splendor, nor the power of the heavenly Godhead? 31. Oh, how worthless an act! Still even now when abandoning none of their impiousness and not looking away toward what is necessary, they do not see that they are sinking under their wretched error, and

---

80. The manuscripts say the light of faith would be overshadowed "justly" (ἀξίως), which Hansen amends to "unjustly" (ἀναξίως). We read with Hansen.

they do not cease defiling this splendor with those sordid works of worldly adornment, namely, consecrating wood and stone and bronze and silver and gold and such worldly <materials>[81] in order to fall down before them. And they promise that the hope of life comes from these things, erecting temples to them with renowned adornment and thereby thus increasing the accoutrements of their veneration to them, since indeed the magnitude of the edifices that they brought into existence presents a marvel worthy for them to look at. 32. Now then, because they think it right to do these things, it is clearly understandable that, although they are completely unaware of it and in their arrogance they do not see, they are caught thinking that it is proper to boast in their own works. Now then, how great and of what magnitude is the God who is ruler of all though not visible, who is likewise the master and judge of all, whom some men deride surreptitiously out of overconfidence in their own—as they think it—virtue?[82] 33. For even the shape of our body derives its appointed figure from his own full and perfect configuration. And he himself bound together the bond of all the limbs with the strongest of sinews, in order that in every action that we will, we might tirelessly achieve the peak of our proper harmony.[83] Now then, after these things had been perfected through his salvific configuration, he also breathed spirit into us, so that all these parts might have motion and flourish, and granted sight to our eyes and furthermore placed understanding in our head and within this space enclosed the reasoning capacity of all our intellect. 34. Accordingly, if anyone, provided he is of sound mind, should examine the rationale behind this configuration and should cease examining the rest, which can be comprehended neither by reason

---

81. A feminine noun has dropped out of the text. The general Greek term for "material," particularly materials such as were listed immediately prior, is ὕλη, which Loeschcke and Heinemann (1918) conjecture and Hansen follows.

82. We follow Hansen's conjecture, adding an appropriate participle to correspond to the active form of λανθάνω, "to elude the notice." Without a participle, the sentence would oddly suggest that these men escape the notice of God.

83. The manuscripts include a nearly identically doubled phrase at the start and end of this sentence that translates to "in order that we might achieve the fullness of harmony" (καὶ ἵνα σχῶμεν τῆς ἁρμονίας τὴν ἀκμήν). As the first variant would create an unusual sentence for Cyzicenus, conjoining unlike subjects with a simple "and" (καί), we follow Hansen in deleting it, preferring to keep the second statement of the clause.

nor by reckoning, with only a brief consideration he will be able both to see and to understand the eternal and saving power of the immortal God. And no human will be able to entrap that man with the snares of any deceit, since it is possible for him also to see clearly that all things that have come to be do exist by the power of God, in the ways God himself has willed them all to exist.

7.35. And in order that one may see that it was a lawless form of worldly governance that caused ignorance of God among humankind, when the first failure of reason in the wretched souls of foolish humans was born of the error of the enemy, we can make a clear demonstration of this from the divine law. 36. For from that very moment when the divine and holy command was not observed with due diligence by those two who were made in the beginning, thereupon bloomed the flower of this term—error.[84] And it has become continual and furthermore increased also from the time when the aforementioned two were thrown out by divine fiat. 37. Yet this very element of error has been propelled along with the foolishness of humankind for such a long time that it has condemned the East and the foundations of the West. And this excess of adversarial power itself has laid hold of and dimmed the intellects of humankind. 38. And yet even in this circumstance, holy and undying is the tireless compassion of the God who is all-powerful.[85] For in all the days and years that have gone by, God has set free countless enslaved masses of the people from this weight through me, his servant, and he will lead them out into the endless splendor of eternal light. Accordingly, from these considerations, my most beloved brethren, by a certain, more personal providence and by the glorious benefactions of our immortal God, I myself am convinced that I will be hereafter more notable for my purest faith toward him.

7.39. Accordingly, let this purest council of your holiness receive me, and let it not permit that this most prudent church

---

84. The Greek for "error" (πλάνη) can also mean "wander, stray." The allusion is to the expulsion of Adam and Eve from paradise and their subsequent wandering (Gen 3:23–24).

85. On the basis of 2.7.7, Hansen (2002) conjectures "eternal" (ἀίδιος) instead of "holy" (ἅγιος), which he adopts into the text of his 2008 translation, but we have not adopted here.

and even the doors of the mother holy and common to us all be set against me. Although above all even now the reasoning of my soul, though seeking the perfect purity of the universal faith, does not reckon itself worthy for this to occur easily, nevertheless it urges me onward and reminds me, and it has made my countenance a signal of my own reverence for all the most noble virtues. And it has begun to grasp onto the gates of immortality and knock at them, in order that you yourselves also may think it right to gather straightaway the affection of your brotherhood, looking toward a single unanimity and peace of the universal faith. 40. For this is suitable to God and concordant with the faith of the universal church and profitable for the common good, in order that we might all in common return a response worthy of the most honored peace furnished to us from God to the one who has graced us with this peace.

7.41.[86] For it would be terrible, were it true, indeed too terrible, that with our enemies destroyed and no one still venturing to resist, we strike at one another and grant pleasure and laughter to our enemies, especially when we are discussing divine matters and have at our disposal the written teaching of the All-Holy Spirit. For the evangelical and apostolic books and oracular utterances of the ancient prophets teach us clearly what we must think concerning the divine.[87] Therefore, driving away warmongering strife, let us find the solution to our questions from the divinely inspired words.

7.42.[88] These and similar things was the all-wise emperor offering like a child who loves his father to the priests as if they were his fathers, concerning

---

86. The speech concludes with a passage parallel to Theodoret's summary of the speech's contents at *Hist. eccl.* 1.7.11–12, adding only the phrase "were it true" concerning the internal strife of the church.

87. "Evangelical books" refers to the gospels; "apostolic books" to other New Testament texts, especially the Pauline corpus; and "oracular utterances of the ancient prophets" to the Hebrew Bible, especially the prophetic books.

88. Cyzicenus continues to parallel Theodoret (*Hist. eccl.* 1.7.13) closely through 2.7.42, with additional emphasis on the exact numbers of bishops at the council and on each side of the debate. At 2.7.43 he begins to diverge more clearly from Theodoret, substituting similar phrases at the beginning, before starting to parallel the accounts of Socrates (*Hist. eccl.* 1.8.13) and BHG 1279. Cyzicenus gives the longest list of Arian supporters of any surviving source, combining Eusebius, Theognius, and Maris mentioned

himself with the total harmony of the apostolic doctrines. And of the bishops of the council who had gathered into that place (and there were 318), about three hundred were obeying what was being said and were embracing unanimity toward one another and the soundness of the doctrines, 43. but the rest, just as we already said a while ago, were battling against the apostolic doctrines. And these men were striving overzealously to bolster the reputation of Arius, and they were seventeen in number: Eusebius of Nicomedia, as was said before as well; Theognius of Nicaea; Maris of Chalcedon; Theodorus of Thracian Heracleia; Menophantus of Ephesus; Patrophilus of Scythopolis; Narcissus of Neronias in Cilicia Secunda, which we now call Irenopolis; Theonas of Marmarica; Secundus of Egyptian Ptolemais; and eight others with them, who, mixing themselves in among the chorus of three hundred holy men, as if they were indeed orthodox, were working against the apostolic doctrines, advocating for Arius. 44.[89] But our fathers among the holy men nobly kept fighting them, the fathers being Alexander, then a presbyter of Constantinople, and Athanasius, the archdeacon of the church of the Alexandrians. And on this account envy readied itself against them, as we will say later. But our holy bishops called Arius into the council, by the will of the emperor victorious in all things (since, as we have recently said, he too sat in on the council), leaving it to Arius to support his own doctrines.

In Which the Emperor Receives the Petitions of the Bishops

8.1.[90] But it would be unworthy to consign to silence the marvelous event that occurred during the council on the part of the all-conquering

---

in Socrates and BHG 1279 with the list from Theodoret (beginning at Menophantes of Ephesus). Wallraff, Stutz, and Marinides (2018) identify portions of this passage as Gelasian in origin (F12a), following the witness of Cyzicenus and BHG 1279, but not incorporating the parallels between Theodoret and Cyzicenus. It is possible that Cyzicenus blends multiple sources for this short passage, but it is also possible that he presents a fuller version of the Gelasian history than other dependent sources.

89. From parallels with BHG 1279, Socrates, and George the Monk, the conclusion of the paragraph derives almost entirely from the Gelasian history. See Wallraff, Stutz, and Marinides 2018, 76–77. Cyzicenus differs from BHG 1279 and Socrates in identifying Athanasius as an archdeacon, rather than simply a deacon, and in attesting Constantine's personal desire for Arius to be summoned.

90. The passage from 2.8.1 to 2.8.4 bears strong resemblance to Rufinus, *Hist. eccl.* 10.2, with the addition of certain details corroborated by Theodoret (*Hist. eccl.* 1.11.4–

emperor. For after all the bishops had been gathered together and, as is customary, inquiries and judgments were raised among some of the bishops for the sake of quarrels among one another, and some petitions and written complaints had been collected by the pious emperor, he received them, sealed them with his own ring, and ordered that they be guarded.[91] 2. Noticing such noble bishops locked in battle with one another, he said that it was necessary for them all to come together at the same place on a certain day and deliberate on these matters. And when the previously appointed day was upon them, the emperor took his seat in their midst. And when there was quiet that suited the moment, he commanded that the petitions of all be brought in and indeed accepted them and set them in his own lap. And since he did not wish to examine the documents that were being brought in, he said, 3. "Since God has chosen you as priests and leaders to judge and render decisions on the multitudes and to be gods—inasmuch as he has set you as those who have authority over of all humankind in accordance with the passage 'I said, you are gods and all sons of the Most High'[92] and the passage 'God stood in the assembly of gods'[93]—you must disregard mundane matters, but dedicate all your effort to divine matters." 4. And after ordering that fire be brought in, he commanded that the petitions be set aflame. For he fervently desired that none of those outside should learn of the unusual strife of bishops of such stature.[94] So great was the reverence of the emperor toward the priests of God, which I wish everyone with sense would admire.

---

5) and the parallel account in Socrates (*Hist. eccl.* 1.8.18), which have Gelasian origin (F12b). In Rufinus's version of Constantine's remarks, the emperor explicitly gives the bishops the right to pass judgment over him, which Cyzicenus's Constantine does not. The honorific title "all-conquering" only appears in Cyzicenus.

91. The term translated as "petitions" here is λίβελλοι, a loanword from Latin (*libellus*), literally meaning "little book." The word essentially had two senses: a small, often controversial tract or pamphlet or, as here, a legal document registering an official complaint or accusation.

92. Ps 82 (81):6.

93. Ps 82 (81):1.

94. "Those outside" (οἱ ἔξω) here refers probably to those outside the council (i.e., the laity and general public), though in other contexts the same phrase often means "non-Christians" or "those outside the church."

8.5.[95] Nor do I think it right to consign to silence something similar that he did. For quarrelsome and abusive laymen wrote accusations against some of the bishops and delivered the written charges to the emperor. And this took place prior to the establishment of unanimity. 6. But he, accepting these charges as well, wrapped a band around them, marked them with his ring, and ordered that these, too, be guarded. Then, when he had effected the agreement for unanimity, he ordered that these documents be retrieved, and while all the bishops were present he burned these too with fire, having sworn that he had not read anything that had been written in them. 7. For he denied that there was any need for the offenses of the priests to become evident to the masses, so that they might not afterwards take this as a pretext for scandalous behavior and sin with abandon. And they say that he further added this: that, if he were to become an eyewitness of a bishop undermining another's marriage, he would cover the illegality with his purple robe, so that the sight of those doing the act might not harm those who saw. Such was the God-loving and admirable sagacity of the emperor.

8.8.[96] And for many days on end, and not just days but even seasons, meeting with the bishops, the emperor discussed with them matters of the faith and collected their differing opinions. For there were among them, just as we have said many times, certain men who agreed with the unlawful doctrines of Arius, battling against the multitude of the holy bishops who were fighting for the truth. But our fathers, best and most hallowed in all ways, fortified with the armament of truth, kept proclaiming the radiant and blameless faith with frankness of speech. And with them was a great

---

95. From 2.8.5–7 Cyzicenus repeats the narrative of the petition burning, this time adhering to the narrative and concluding moral found in Theodoret (*Hist. eccl.* 1.11.4–6). In Theodoret's account, the tale comes as a coda to the brief account of the Council of Nicaea, possibly suggesting two such scenes to Cyzicenus. To account for the doubling, Cyzicenus appears to have inserted phrases to distinguish this petition burning from the first and added the detail about the complaints of laymen. Possibly a further sign of Cyzicenus's uncertainty surrounding the chronology, the clause that specifies that this action took place "prior to the establishment of unanimity" appears in the following sentence in Theodoret, where Constantine accepted the charges "for the sake of establishing unanimity."

96. Parallels between 2.8.8 and Rufinus, *Hist. eccl.* 10.2, again suggest a Gelasian origin for this passage (F12c). In Cyzicenus's version, there is far more emphasis on the righteousness and holiness of the anti-Arian bishops.

number of confessors, who stood against those who wished to support the reprobate doctrines of Arius.

Concerning the Holy Paphnutius

9.1.[97] And there was among them also the great and holy Paphnutius, a man adorning the chorus of confessors and bishops, an Egyptian man, and a man of God from that assembly, whose right eye the emperor Maximian had gouged out and whose left leg he had hamstrung, handing down the order that he be imprisoned in the mines.[98] 2. In him the grace of God was so great that he himself worked signs no lesser than those brought about long ago by the apostles. For by speech alone he was putting demons to flight and was healing through prayer various people who were sick and, by asking God, he was giving sight to the blind and he was restoring the paralyzed to the full bloom of their nature, making their limbs work in good health. 3. The emperor treated him with great honor and was continually summoning him to the palace, and he kissed him on his gouged-out eye. So great a faith resided in the pious emperor toward holy men.[99]

Concerning the Holy Spyridon

10.1. And indeed Spyridon also, a Cypriot, famous in the Lord, who had dedicated his experience as a shepherd boy to the flock of Christ and lived a prophetic life,[100] was well known, as he, even when serving as a bishop,

---

97. 2.9.1–2.11.11 relates a series of stories about the notable figures at the Council of Nicaea derived from the Gelasian history (F12e). Rufinus and BHG 1279 relate the same stories in the same order, with similar phrasing. Compared to the other versions, Cyzicenus has more language that reminds the reader of his subjects' piety, holiness, and reverence for God.

98. In both BHG 1279 and Rufinus, the authors refer to Paphnutius as one among a group of confessors, all of whom had their eyes gouged out and legs hamstrung. The name Maximian probably refers to Galerius, who had taken the name Maximian when elevated to Caesar by Diocletian (see, e.g., Lactantius, *Mort*. 18), rather than Diocletian's Western imperial colleague, Maximian. Both Galerius and his junior colleague Maximinus Daia condemned Christians to the mines and ordered the mutilation of eyes and/or legs.

99. Neither BHG 1279 nor Rufinus specifies the object of Constantine's piety.

100. Here, the "prophetic life" is synonymous with "ascetic life," as ascetics (espe-

did not cease shepherding his personal flocks.[101] 2. And so kindly and patient in the face of evils was he that when robbers assaulted his flock by a deceitful attack and were overpowered by invisible fetters and could not move until morning, after he arrived, the blessed man by his prayer caused them to be released from their imprisonment. And not only this, but furthermore he gave them the strongest of his rams as they were departing, saying, "Take this and make use of it, young men, so that you will not leave without gain, and make me to blame for your trouble this evening." 3. And so we have heard also many other marvelous things concerning this holy man, but we will include just one of the many.

In Which He Raises His Deceased Daughter on Account of a Merchant

11.1. This blessed and well-renowned man of God had a daughter named Irene, who had ministered to the old man as was fitting and departed her mortal life in virginity.[102] 2. After the death of this girl, a certain merchant, returning from a voyage, demanded of the old man a deposit that he had left with his daughter, the virgin.[103] 3. But the blessed Spyridon was entirely unaware of the situation. But as the man was urgently entreating him, the old man searched up and down the house and was very distressed that he did not find it and said to the man that he did not know and that there was nothing in the house. 4. But the merchant, wailing and beset with tears and lamenting, kept begging for the deposit, saying that he would kill himself over the loss if he could not take what he had entrusted as a deposit, asserting that he had preserved this as a consolation for his old age by depositing it with her, the virgin.[104] 5. Now then, the old man, that holy man, was compelled to go to the tomb of his daughter together with the merchant in

---

cially anchorites) were imagined to live in the austere manner of prophets; John the Baptist was often taken as a model of the anchoritic life.

101. Spyridon is thus a shepherd of his church while continuing to make a living as a literal shepherd.

102. Cyzicenus specifies "mortal life," where the version in Rufinus simply reads "life," suggesting a distinction between a true death and a transition to the eternal life with God. Cyzicenus makes a similar distinction at 3.9.7, where the parallel passage in Rufinus does not, and again at 3.12.10.

103. Neither Rufinus nor BHG 1279 specifies the occupation of the stranger.

104. The narrative in Cyzicenus draws out the scene of lamentation, doubling the number of verbs describing the merchant's mournful actions compared to BHG 1279 or Rufinus.

order to investigate the matter. And when he arrived, he called his daughter by name and said to her, "My child, Irene." And she, responding from the grave, said to him, "What do you wish, Father?" And the old man said to her, "Where did you stow this man's deposit, Daughter?" And she said to him, "It lies in this certain place, Father," marking out the place clearly for her father. And he said to her, "Go in peace, my child Irene."[105] 6. Therefore, the old man, turning homeward and finding the deposit exactly where the virgin said it lay, gave it back to the man. 7. And many of the man's other marvels are praised in song and many deeds beyond belief, which even to this day are pointed out by the locals to those who are there for the confirmation of our true faith in Christ.[106] Up until those times, then, the church was noted for holy men such as these, many of whom were present throughout the council in Nicaea.

11.8. And furthermore Athanasius also, about whom we also spoke previously,[107] who was a deacon at that time, is agreed by all to have had a share in the chorus of those holy men; he was there with Alexander, bishop of the church of the Alexandrians, as his foremost aide. 9. At any rate, day by day our holy bishops were stirring up a great number of discussions over the faith for such a long time, being of the opinion that it was necessary to do nothing reckless or rash when it concerned a controversy of such magnitude. 10. And they often summoned Arius and, analyzing his propositions through repeated questioning, they pulled them to pieces, and there was the greatest exertion and attention on their part as to how necessary it was to make a decision on overturning his lawless doctrines and to present opposing definitions.[108] 11. Therefore, with great consideration and supplication to God, they made these decisions.[109]

---

105. This closing statement does not appear in Rufinus or BHG 1279, which both end the conversation after Irene describes the location of the deposit. Cyzicenus includes a pun on the name Irene, meaning "peace," with her father's closing words, perhaps adding this statement to lend finality to the conversation and Irene's lingering presence on the earth after he had specified that she was departing only her mortal life.

106. I.e., pilgrims or religious visitors to this region are given proofs of Spyridon's holiness.

107. See 2.7.44.

108. Cyzicenus is more emphatic about the defeat of Arius's doctrines than BHG 1279 or Rufinus.

109. Cyzicenus's version alone specifies that the bishops at Nicaea "supplicated God" as part of their decision-making process.

For that reason,[110] with surpassing wisdom and utmost harmony they countered with refutations against the lawless doctrines of Arius and those with him, tearing up their abominable blasphemies against the Son of God by the roots and destroying them utterly. 12. And to their saying that his Son was "not from God," our [bishops] countered with the statement "God from God"; and to their "not a true God," our bishops wrote in opposition the phrase "true God from true God"; and to their saying that he was a "created being," our bishops raised the counterdefinition "begotten, not made," and to the phrase *heteroousios* propounded by those men, our bishops countered with the statement, "the Son is *homoousios* with the Father, that is, begotten of the *ousia* of the Father"; and they proclaimed him creator and maker of things visible and invisible, in accordance with the apostolic faith handed down to his church from the beginning, announcing their proofs in written testimonials, as the following account will show. 13. Counteracting the deadly poisons with this antidote, at the same time they more clearly and in unison put the apostolic faith down in writing, from then on and forever.

Concerning That It Is Necessary to Understand and Believe That There Exist Inseparably Three Hypostases in the One, Ineffable Godhead of the Father and the Son and the Holy Spirit

12.1.[111] The holy, great, and ecumenical council of our holy fathers gathered in Nicaea, through the blessed and holy bishop Hosius of the city of Cordoba in the province of Hispania, who was also acting in the stead of the bishop of the church of Rome along with those presbyters previously designated from the bishop's throne, with another man translating for him, said, 2. "The Godhead is not one person, as is the assumption of the Jews, but three persons according to veritable hypostasis, not in mere name, and this is proclaimed by many testimonies from both the Old and the

---

110. The remainder of chapter 11 presents a brief synopsis of the Nicene Creed in opposition to the beliefs of Arius. Although this passage is not directly paralleled in BHG 1279 or Rufinus, both do recount that the result of the inquiries was a statement on the term *homoousios*. Other versions of the creed appear at 2.27.1–6 and in the letter of Eusebius of Caesarea at 2.35.8.

111. Although the text from 2.12.1–8 may well derive from another source that preserved a statement by Hosius, bishop of Cordoba, Cyzicenus does not identify any source, nor have any parallel passages yet been found. The theology of the statement is conventionally Trinitarian, echoing similar statements in fourth-century writers from Epiphanius to Athanasius to Gregory of Nyssa.

New Testament. 3. For the Old, although discoursing still in a more bodily manner, presented the Word as something spoken, but the New revealed the Word as God—with the phrase 'In the beginning was the Word, and the Word was with God, and the Word was God'[112]—and as perfect person from perfect. For the Son is God not as a part, but perfectly, just as the Father, since he is of the same *ousia* as the Father, who begat him ineffably. 4. And the Holy Spirit coexists in just the same manner, along with the Son and the Father, being of the same *ousia* and the same property as that of the Father and the Son. 5. Now then, it is necessary for us to confess that there is one will, one kingdom, one authority, one dominion over all created natures both visible and intelligible, one Godhead and the same *ousia* for the Father and the Son and the Holy Spirit, since we do not proclaim a mixture or a division of the hypostases of that ineffable and blessed Trinity. 6. And we believe that the Father always is and subsists truly as Father of a veritable Son, and that the Son always is and subsists truly as the Son of a veritable Father, and that the Holy Spirit always is and subsists truly as the Holy Spirit—a Trinity inseparable, ineffable, and truly incomprehensible and inexpressible, a single Godhead and its shared *ousia*. 7. And we also confess the perfect accuracy of the doctrines of this faith handed down to us from the beginning by the Lord through his holy apostles and through our holy fathers of old who faultlessly preserved their holy faith, since we readily are able, by the goodwill of the Holy Spirit, to show through many such witnesses from the divine Scriptures that these things are so."

12.8.[113] When these things had been proclaimed by them[114]—or rather through them by the Holy Spirit—those of the impious persuasion

---

112. John 1:1.

113. 2.12.8–2.13.15 gives a florid and dramatic account of the debates before the Council of Nicaea with parallels to the abbreviated accounts of BHG 1279 (12.13–13.28) and Rufinus (*Hist. eccl.* 10.3). Cyzicenus's version gives the most detail about the Arian dialectician, describing his specific argumentative points and tactics, and only in Cyzicenus does the Arian seem defeated before the simple churchman speaks up. Both Rufinus and BHG 1279 say that he managed to elude and twist the arguments of the bishops and other orthodox, whereas Cyzicenus says that the philosopher only "supposed" himself clever (13.4). Similarly, Cyzicenus alone suggests that the philosopher's own arguments confuted themselves (13.4) and were truly the work of a demon (13.6). The brevity with which both BHG 1279 and Rufinus tell this story suggests that Cyzicenus has either elaborated on the event himself or found an expanded version outside the Gelasian history (F12d). All parallel accounts place these debates before the narratives about Paphnutius and Spyridon. In Cyzicenus, they serve as a bridge between the

of Arius who were fighting against them began to murmur, since they were excessively afflicted (and these were the partisans of Eusebius of Nicomedia and Theognius of Nicaea, whom we already pointed out above),[115] but even so they all looked toward Arius's hirelings, certain philosophers, eloquent to a fault, whom Arius had paid as advocates for his own depravity and had come with them to that holy and ecumenical council. 9. For there were so very many philosophers present, in whom, as we have just now said, the enemies of truth had placed their hope, and who had deservedly been caught together with the very teacher of the blasphemy. By him and by them the Holy Scripture was fulfilled that says: "Every man is accursed who places his hope in humankind and whose heart withdraws from the Lord."[116] 10. For truly the blasphemous hearts of the God-battling Arius and the companions in his impiousness withdrew from the Lord, since they dared to call the Son of God, the creator and craftsman of all created natures, seen and unseen, a "creation" and "something made."

One of the Philosophers Declares the Greatest Number of Things on Behalf of Arius against That Holy Council of the Apostolic Priests of God

13.1. But a certain philosopher from among Arius's hirelings, who was particularly awe-inspiring compared to all the others, put forward many—indeed, excessively many—arguments to our bishops on behalf of Arius for as many days as possible, such that on each day a large audience assembled for the battle of words. A crowd of those who had gathered all streamed in together,[117] while the philosopher was propounding the impious blasphemies of Arius against what was being said by the holy council, saying about the Son of God that "there was a time when he was not" and that "he is a creation and something made out of what does not exist" and "he is of

---

description of the holy fathers attending the council and the lengthy debate between another philosopher, named Phaedo, and the council, which occupies the central part of the second book of his *Ecclesiastical History* (2.14–2.24). Hansen (1998, 195) postulates that this passage also derives from Philip of Side.

114. Grammatically, "they" could be Hosius and his interpreter, or alternatively the collective of the Nicene fathers speaking through Hosius.

115. See 2.7.43.

116. Jer 17:5.

117. Reading ἐπισυγχέοντος ("flowed together") with the manuscripts rather than Hansen's ἐπισυνθέοντος ("were added"), which he has inserted based on comparison of a parallel version of this story.

different *ousia* and hypostasis." 2. And great were his exertions on behalf of the abominable doctrines of Arius, as were the blizzards of words as he raged against the Son of God and inveighed against the chorus of those holy priests, because the enemy of the salvation of humankind spoke in him and through him. 3. But those fighting on behalf of the truth, our bishops, calmly brought forth before the philosopher the necessary and fitting counterarguments on behalf of the apostolic doctrines, resembling that great prophet and king David when he said, "I was prepared and was not disturbed."[118] For they were consuming all the philosopher's tangled, twisted propositions with the divine Word like flaxen rope with a fire. 4. But even so, the philosopher, confident in his devilish skill at words, began to fire back at the truth being proclaimed through the bishops, quite easily, as he supposed, meeting everything that was brought up to him. And he struggled to resolve the issues that were raised, contorting himself like an eel. For he seemed to himself to stand firm amid these debates, since he was writhing out of the powerful ideas being brought against him, but he was tripped up by his own statements and fell.[119] 5. But even so, raving like a Corybant,[120] he boastfully bore himself up against that most peaceful council, hoping to conquer the unassailable power of the insuperable Spirit of Christ within them. 6. But in order that God, who "catches the wise in their cleverness,"[121] might show that "his kingdom exists not in word but in power,"[122] through one of his servants there he not only mightily put to silence the wicked demon speaking in the philosopher but also cast it out. 7. For a certain man among the holy confessors present in the council, simple in nature, if ever any holy man was, and a man who knew nothing "except Jesus Christ and him crucified"[123] in the flesh, according to the Scriptures, who was present with the bishops and was watching the philosopher disparage our holy bishops and acting boastful in his depraved disputation, asked of the bishops, the priests of God, that they give him

---

118. Ps 119 (118):60.

119. Following the variant reading ἐπικρατεστέρων ("powerful," an adjective modifying "ideas") rather than Hansen's ἐπικρατεστέρως ("powerfully," an adverb modifying the participle "writhing out").

120. Corybants were priests of the Phrygian goddess Cybele who performed ecstatic dances.

121. 1 Cor 3:19, where Paul paraphrases Job 5:13. Cyzicenus's version alone includes this particular quotation.

122. 1 Cor 4:20.

123. 1 Cor 2:2.

leave to discourse with the philosopher.[124] 8. Then those on our side, the holy bishops, perceiving the simplicity of the man and that he was inexperienced with letters,[125] were prevailing on him not to put himself in the middle of things, so that there be no occasion for laughter on the side of the reprobates and enemies of the truth. 9. But he would not be held back and went before the philosopher and said to him, "In the name of Jesus Christ, who always exists with the Father as the Word of God,[126] hear the doctrines of truth, philosopher." And the philosopher said to him, "If you tell it to me." And the holy man said to him, "There is one God, who has crafted the heaven and the earth and the sea and all things in them,[127] who also formed humankind from earth and caused all things to subsist by his Word and Holy Spirit. 10. We, knowing that this Word is the Son of God, philosopher, venerate him, believing that, in order to ransom us, he has been made flesh and been born and been made man from a virgin, and, through the suffering of his flesh on the cross and his death, he freed us from eternal condemnation, and through his resurrection he acquired for us eternal life.[128] And we also await him, who has ascended into heaven, to come again and to be the judge of all the things that we have done. Do you believe these things, philosopher?" 11. And the philosopher, as though he had never had any experience reasoning through a counterargument, could not speak and, as if he were mute or speechless, thus kept his silence,

---

124. In later hagiographic tradition, the simple confessor came to be identified with Spyridon (see above, 2.10.1–11.7), e.g., BHG 1647, The Life of Spyridon. Cyzicenus's version of the story expands the confessor's doctrinal explanations. Cyzicenus, or his intermediary source, has elaborated on 1 Cor 2:2, specifying that the crucifixion was truly experienced in Christ's flesh. This elaboration fits well within Cyzicenus's aim of producing this history to confute "Eutychians" (*proem.* 10), who were accused of a radical monophysitism that denied the persistence of genuine humanity in the incarnate Christ.

125. "Inexperience with letters" (τὸ ἄπειρον αὐτὸν εἶναι γραμμάτων) does not imply that the old man was unable to read or write but rather that he did not possess a sophisticated, elite "education" (παιδεία/*paideia*) in grammar and rhetoric and other advanced subjects, such as the dialectic at which this philosopher was adept. The role of *paideia* in late antiquity has been studied extensively. See especially Kaster 1988; Brown 1992.

126. The key theological clauses in this statement are unique to Cyzicenus.

127. Cyzicenus preserves the longest form of this quotation, which appears both at Exod 20:11 and Ps 146 (145):6. BHG 1279 and Rufinus end after "the heaven and the earth."

128. Neither BHG 1279 nor Rufinus contains any of the explicit mentions of Jesus's corporeality and humanity that conclude the confessor's speech in Cyzicenus. Again, the emphasis on the reality of Christ's flesh supports Cyzicenus's anti-Eutychian agenda.

saying only this in an exceedingly pitiable voice in response to him, "I, too, think that these things are so and nothing is other than everything just as you have proclaimed." 12. And the old man said to him, "If you believe that these things are so, philosopher, rise up and follow me and let us hasten to the church, in which you will receive the sign of this faith."[129] 13. And the philosopher, turning himself completely toward the true piety toward the God of all things, stood up and followed the old man and turned around and spoke to his students and all those gathered in the audience. "Listen, men," he said, "as long as I acted in the pursuit of speechmaking, I pitted speeches against speeches and turned propositions upside down by my skill at speaking. 14. But when a certain divine power instead of words came from the mouth of this disputant, my speeches no longer had the force to marshal against that power; for a human being is not able to stand against God. For this reason, then, if any of you has the power to understand, just as I for my part have come to acknowledge, he will believe in Christ. And let him follow this old man, in whom God has spoken."

13.15. Adopting this manner of life, the philosopher was both enlightened and became Christian, and he rejoiced at being bested by the old man. And when this philosopher had been baptized and joined the church of God and was refreshed and rejoicing exceedingly at the great deeds of God, the council was joyful.[130]

The Refutation of Another Philosopher, Named Phaedo, Who Argued on Behalf of the God-Battling Arius and the Blasphemy Invented by Him[131]

14.1. *The philosopher's proposition to the holy council on the phrase "Let us make humankind":*

---

129. The old man refers to the sign of the cross performed during baptism. In other words, this is a direct invitation to convert and be baptized. The philosopher accepts baptism below at 2.13.15.

130. This coda (2.13.15) appears only in Cyzicenus.

131. The name of this second "Arian" philosopher derives from the title of one of Plato's famous dialogue, *Phaedo*. In the *Phaedo* a disciple of Socrates named Phaedo of Elis recounts how Socrates discoursed with his friends from his deathbed about the immortality of the soul. The name Phaedo in our text nods to the genre of this section (a dialogue) and also to the several Platonic resonances that are found in the dialogue (see notes at 2.15.7 and 2.19.4). It also suggests the advancement of Christianity over earlier Greco-Roman schools of philosophy, a recurring theme of the middle section of book 2.

"And God said, 'Let us make humankind in our image, according to our likeness.'"[132] Therefore, if the true meaning is the same as its ostensible meaning, then one who has been led astray would say that God is of human form. But we know that God is uncompounded and without form. Tell me, then, what are the meanings of these terms? Not, surely, that the divine is of human form?

14.2. *The response of the holy fathers given by Eustathius, bishop of Antioch:*

Of course not, philosopher, but rather God's saying, "Let them subdue all the earth" and "Let them have dominion over it and all the things in it," is the proper meaning of "making humankind according to the image of God"; that is, ruling over all the earth. 3. Since, as God rules all the earth and all those in it, so too he set humankind as a secondary ruler of all the earth and the things in it. I say that this is what humankind being "in the image" of God and "according to our likeness" means.

14.4. *A further response of the holy fathers given by the same Eustathius on the same matter:*

"Then God said, 'Let us make humankind in our image, according to our likeness.'" But let us ask to whom he spoke, philosopher. For the fact that it says, "Then God said, 'Let us make humankind in our image, according to our likeness,'" forces us to consider the question: To whom did God say, "Let us make"? For, after saying "And God said, 'Let us make humankind,'" it goes on to say, "So God created humankind in his image, in the image of God he created it; male and female he created them."[133] 5. Therefore, the meaning of the "Let us make" implies and introduces a person as a fellow creator, addressed simultaneously and equally.[134] For as God the Father is the one saying "Let us make humankind," so also is the one to whom he

---

132. Gen 1:26.
133. Gen 1:27.
134. "Person" translates πρόσωπον. By the time of the Council of Constantinople (381), this term had become the orthodox theological term designating what is different in the Trinity, that is, the persons of the Father, Son, and Spirit. The first-person plural of Gen 1:26–27 was interpreted by "Arians" and orthodox alike as indicative of this distinction of persons, but orthodox theology came to insist that the phrase also indicates that the Godhead of the speaker and addressee is identical.

said "Let us make" God, because the Godhead of both persons is one, both of the one saying, "Let us make humankind in our image, according to our likeness," and of the one who made humankind. 6. For the passage establishes that the phrase "Let us make" is the firm[135] and unchanging "Let us make" of the Godhead of the Father and the Son. For the image of God is simple and uncompounded, since it is fire in nature.[136]

14.7. *The unified response of the holy fathers:*

The *ousia* of the Holy Trinity is "light inaccessible"[137] and nature "unendurable."[138] This is the deeper meaning of the phrase "Let us make."

15.1. *The philosopher's rebuttal on behalf of Arius:*

Once again, I will say that God is simple, without form, and uncompounded. How then is one to understand the phrase "in our image, according to our likeness" and hold that the one speaking does not preexist the one to whom he said "Let us make humankind" and so on?[139] Explain to us clearly your proof for these matters, if you can.

15.2. *The holy bishops through Hosius the bishop of the city Cordoba, speaking through an interpreter, said:*

If the Father, as you say, preexisted the Son and the Son, born later, was created after some period of time by God and was proclaimed as his Son afterwards by the Father himself, just as you impiously say, blaspheming that he was created beforehand by God for the making of created natures, then, according to your impiety the uncreated God would have said to the created god, as you would have it, "Make for me a human being according

---

135. Some manuscripts (a, H, b, T) have πανάγιον, which would translate to "the all-holy and unchanging 'let us make.'"

136. The image of God as a fire recurs later in the dialogue in an explanation of the Trinity, perceived as fire, radiance, and light (see 2.22.8–16).

137. 1 Tim 6:16.

138. Hansen suggests that this is a reference to the apocryphal Odes of Solomon (12.5).

139. A concise summary of the argument against coessentiality, which holds that God's uncompounded essence precludes the essential identity of the Father and Son and, rather, entails the Son's ontological subordination.

to my image and likeness." 3. But since indeed God is always the Father, as we previously demonstrated, the Son also always coexists with the Father, not later born in time, nor lesser in power, nor circumscribed by place, but always and likewise eternally coexisting with the Father, begotten of him incomprehensibly and inexpressibly, just as we have previously said, true God who is eternal from the true God and Father who is eternal, without beginning together with the Father, coeternal with the Father, ruling eternally with the Father, *homoousios* with the Father, equal in power to the Father, and co-creator with the Father. 4. For if the divine voice of the gospels says both that all things came into being through the Son[140] and that "without him not one thing came into being which has come into being."[141] Nevertheless he did not create apart from the Father, since indeed the Father and the Son and the Holy Spirit have one Godhead and one will, as the Father always exists inseparably from the Son and the Son from the Father. 5. Therefore, one must understand, philosopher, that, regarding the *ousia* of their Godhead, the Father and the Son are one, just as also in the gospels the same Son to whom he said, "Let us make humankind in our image, according to our likeness," proclaims, "I and the Father are one."[142]

15.6. *The philosopher's rebuttal:*

Even in the earlier interrogations we already said that God was not anthropomorphic.[143] Then tell us, what is the meaning of this expression: "in our image, according to our likeness."[144] For the wording presents no small difficulty for us. We must speak about this first.

15.7. *The response of the holy council through the same bishop, Hosius of the city of Cordoba:*

The phrase "in our image," philosopher, must be understood not in reference to the composition of the bodies, but the word of truth demonstrates

---

140. John 1:3.
141. John 1:3.
142. John 10:30.
143. See 2.14.2–3.
144. Gen 1:26.

that the image was molded in reference to what is intelligible.[145] Listen, therefore, and understand. 8. Since God is good by nature, he implanted in the intellectual *ousia* of humankind the fact of existing "in his image" and "likeness," as respects, for example, goodness, sincerity, holiness, purity, liberality, kindness, happiness, and characteristics similar to these, so that, what God is by nature, humankind, created by him, would also be able to have by his grace, that is, his intelligible characteristics.[146] 9. And just as those who are skilled in painting, when painting likenesses of images on panels, invariably paint the images with different hues, not one color, so God granted that humankind, created by him, holds in the intellectual treasury of the soul, that is in the mind, the "image" and "likeness" through the virtues, 10. since the image is found without exception in humankind through the aforementioned divine qualities that God set within it, saying, "Let us make humankind in our image, according to our likeness."

16.1. *The rebuttal of the philosopher:*

Allow me to set these things aside for the present and let us instead inquire further about the one through whom God made humankind and all things visible and invisible. For it does not seem that what you have said is right, that the Father and the Son were eternally together, one and the same, and that the Son was always preexisting with the Father, as God. 2. But I would say that he was brought forth by God among the created beings as a helper.[147] For God needed a helper for the fashioning of humankind and the world. On that account, God the maker, intending to create the created natures, brought into being a tool for himself through which to create all natures. 3. For just as the carpenter preexists the tools for fabricating what

---

145. The ontological distinction between the sensible and corporeal and the incorporeal and intelligible was common to all participants in the theological controversies of the fourth and fifth centuries; the language has Platonic origins (see, e.g., *Tim.* 27d–28a).

146. In other words, human beings are made like God in the sense that they have the capacity for "deification" or "becoming godlike" (θέωσις), insofar as humans can be by participation what God is by nature (e.g., "good"), through the cultivation of the virtues.

147. "Helper" translates ὑπουργός; this term was applied to the Son by Eusebius of Caesarea to describe the cooperation of the Father and Son in creation (see, e.g., *Praep. ev.* 5.1, 5; *Hist. eccl.* 1.2.3), but it was rejected as implying the Son's subordination, for example by Athanasius, *Decr.* 7, 8.

he is going to make, so it is to be understood also concerning God, that after he had brought the Son into being as a tool for himself, he created the world through him. 4. For as to what was said by the apostles, that "all things came into being through him,"[148] those natures that exist through him were created through him as through a tool, and as to God saying "according to our image and likeness," God meant that humankind was created through the tool, that is, through the Son, according to his own image and likeness.

16.5. *The response of the holy fathers through Leontius, bishop of Cappadocian Caesarea, and Eupsychius, bishop of Tyana:*

If then, as you say, the Son was created by the Father as a tool for the making of created natures, you are falling away from your own arguments, philosopher. For the wording of the gospel says, as you yourself just recalled, "All things came into being through him," and continues, "and without him, not one thing came into being which has come into being."[149] 6. Therefore, if every created thing came into being through him and without him not one thing came into being, then the Son also created himself—a created being, as you say—and not the Father.

16.7. *The rebuttal of the philosopher:*

I said once that God made all things through him as through a tool, creating him for this very task before all creation, preparing him as a tool for the making of created natures.

16.8. *The response of the holy fathers through the same bishops, Leontius and Eupsychius:*

Say, best of men,[150] where did anyone proclaim to you that the Son of God or his Holy Spirit are tools? Show us the evidence for your hypotheses. Do you have written examples from someone inspired by the Spirit who claims that the Son of God, the creator of all the ages and all the heavenly hosts and all those on the earth, is a tool? 9. Well then, pay attention to the

---

148. John 1:3.
149. John 1:3.
150. A common ironic expression in ancient debates.

testimonies expounded in the holy writings, philosopher, that the Son of the Father is God coeternal with the Father, both creator and maker of all created natures. 10. Indeed, in the book of creation[151] you have Moses the prophet, who explained that the Son is the co-creator with God the Father. For, as we have previously told you, you best of men, in saying, "God said, 'Let us make humankind in our image, according to our likeness,'" he was naturally addressing the person who is co-maker, <the son>,[152] but not at all as a tool. For the phrase, "And God created humankind, in the image of God he created it; male and female he created them," signifies the authority of the persons. 11. For in the phrase "Let us make humankind" he does away with the thought of tools. Take the clearer testimony that sets forth the authority of just the Son's person, which shows that he is the maker of all begotten natures, as it is written in the book of Baruch, in the mouth of Jeremiah the prophet when he says: 12.

> The one that created the earth for all eternity, he filled it with four-footed animals. He called forth the light and it proceeds on its way. He called it and with trembling, it obeyed him. The stars shone out in their posts and rejoiced. He called them, and they said, "We are present." They shone with joy for the one who made them. This is our God. No other can be compared to him. He discovered every road of knowledge and he gave it to his child Jacob and to his beloved Israel. After these things he was seen on the earth and he associated with humankind.[153]

16.13. And Isaiah says to Israel: "Even now do you not know, or have you otherwise not heard? The God who has created the ends of the earth, he is eternally God."[154] Who then is this everlasting God, philosopher, who created the ends of the earth, who was even seen on the earth and associated with humankind? Do you say that the Son associated with humankind or the Father?

---

151. I.e., the book of Genesis.
152. Hansen conjectures this explanatory phrase. The manuscripts do not indicate who the "co-maker" is.
153. Bar 3:32–38.
154. Isa 40:28.

16.14. *The response of the philosopher:*

He said:[155] The Son associated with humankind, just as the divine writings have said, and I accept this, having been persuaded by them. But I still have an exceptionally strong and unanswerable refutation on this point, that God created him before all creation, in order to make all things through him, and I will demonstrate these things in the upcoming parts of the debates.

16.15. *The response of the holy fathers through the same most holy bishops, Leontius and Eupsychius:*

Not so, philosopher. It is not possible for you to prove the things you are saying. For he is begotten of God, not a made thing, just as we have proven in many ways. For, philosopher, who among men rich in godliness and wisdom is not amazed at so many acts of the natures divinely constructed by him as by God—that is, created by him—as Scripture proclaims, "God made humankind"[156] and "God saw everything that he had made, and indeed, it was very good"?[157] 16. But John the Evangelist most clearly says that he always coexisted eternally with the Father and is without beginning together with the Father. For he says, "In the beginning was the Word, and the Word was with God, and the Word was God. He was in the beginning with God. All things came into being through him, and without him not one thing came into being that has come into being."[158] 17. Look, it has been proven quite clearly, philosopher, that the Son is the maker of every begotten nature. Therefore, if he is the maker of every single creature, as he in fact is, of things seen and intelligible,[159] it is clear that he is truly God by nature and not a tool, as you say, and not a created or made thing, nor later-born than the Father. 18. For the phrase "he was," said four times by the evangelist, contains no implication of [the Father's] existing prior. But in

---

155. The Dispute with Phaedo in the Greek text is largely presented as a dialogue with one name representing the speaker followed by their words in several back-and-forth discussions. In a few places, as here, the author has also inserted minimal stage directions, noting some events happening concurrently with the dialogue.

156. Gen 1:27.

157. Gen 1:31.

158. John 1:1–3.

159. That is, of absolutely all created things, whether sensible and corporeal or intellectual and incorporeal.

order that you may understand most perfectly that he is not subordinate[160] but possessed of his own authority, just as the Father is also, receive another most unambiguous witness. 19. Indeed, listen to the godly Isaiah proclaiming. "And they shall be willing, if they have become burned by fire," he says, prophesying to the Jews. "A child is born and a son has been given to us whose authority is upon his shoulder and his name shall be called the messenger of great counsel, wonderful adviser, mighty God, and one having authority."[161] Notice, philosopher, that he is prophesied as having his own authority and not subordinate to the authority of another, as you all say. 20. But let us once more resume our reading: "mighty God, one having authority, Prince of Peace, Father of the coming age."[162] But in one of his benefactions—the healing of the man blind from birth—the only begotten Son of God himself showed that he is under his own authority and the creator of humankind in the restoration of the man blind from birth brought about by the son of God himself.[163] 21. For he is the coeternal "reflection" of the Father "and the exact imprint," unchanging, of his entire hypostasis,[164] just as the apostle Paul says, the "instrument of choice."[165] 22. You see, philosopher, so many testimonies prove that the Son of God is without beginning, since he is uncreated like the Father and the creator of all created natures, just as we have said so often, and of all things seen and intelligible. 23. But tell us where your evidence for "tools" exists, if you can. For perhaps you have believed and been baptized in tools, if indeed, as you assert, you really have faith in God.

17.1. *The rebuttal of the philosopher concerning the phrase "The Lord created me as the first of his ways for his works" from the Proverbs of Solomon:*[166]

He says: Since you commit so much violence against the truth, what should

---

160. Literally, "under another's power" (ὑπεξούσιος) as opposed to "under one's own power" (αὐτεξούσιος).
161. Isa 9:6 with variants.
162. Isa 9:6.
163. The reference is to the story in John 9, where Jesus heals a blind man and afterwards, when the Pharisees criticize Jesus for performing the miracle on the Sabbath, Christ asserts to them that he is the Son of God (9:35–37) and accepts the worship of the blind man, who believes Christ's profession (9:38).
164. Heb 1:3.
165. Acts 9:15.
166. Prov 8:22.

we say about this obvious text: "The Lord created me as the first of his ways for his works"?

17.2. The response of the holy fathers through Eusebius Pamphili, bishop of Palestinian Caesarea:

How can you, as you suppose, plausibly and easily escape the depths? Philosopher, do not pile up unmanly pretexts for yourself. Be careful that you do not fall headlong as you attempt to climb up dangerous cliffs. But we shall speak now about the phrase "The Lord created me." 3. Those before us have expounded many other things concerning this phrase "The Lord created me" as well as on the divine economy of our Lord Jesus Christ's appearance in the flesh, and you know well how they handled the exegeses.[167] 4. But now we will also give an explanation along other lines of inquiry, with our Lord Jesus Christ's help. And if you so desire, philosopher, let us set out the entire passage together with its beginning as well. 5. For the beginning of the passage says, "If I should proclaim to you what has happened day by day, I would mention all that has been reckoned throughout time." Next it goes on to say, "The Lord created me as the first of his ways for his works; before the ages he established me in the beginning. Before the creation of the earth, before the first appearances of the springs of waters, before the establishment of the mountains, before all the hills he begot me." Building on the statement "The Lord created me," it goes on to say, "The Lord made the habitable lands and those uninhabited."

17.6. Let us then seek for the Lord, the one who himself created and made the habitable lands and those uninhabited. For Solomon, inspired by the one who said to Job, "Where were you during my making of the earth?" thus said, "The Lord made the habitable lands and those uninhabited." 7. In the book of Baruch, from the mouth of the prophet Jeremiah, just as

---

167. The Greek term used (οἰκονομία) refers to the balanced management of a household. In early Christian theology it referred to God's balancing the accounts of his "household," the world, a system in which the incarnation was a reasoned transaction required in order to set humanity's ledger with God right. "Eusebius" refers here to pro-Nicene exegeses of Prov 8:22 that differentiated between the humanity and divinity of Christ, and ascribed Prov 8:22 to the humanity. Early examples of this exegesis include Eustathius of Antioch (see Theodoret, *Eran.* 3.12) and Athanasius, *Decr.* 3.13. It was not an exegesis employed by Eusebius of Caesarea in his extant works. The exegesis that follows is rather nonstandard, as the next sentence indicates.

we explained before, it says concerning the one who created the habitable lands and those uninhabited, "The sons of Hagar seeking understanding upon the earth, the merchants and the seekers of understanding; they do not know the road to wisdom, nor have they remembered her pathways."[168] 8. And shortly thereafter, "But he who knows all things knows her; he discovered her by his understanding."[169] Speaking about the one who discovered wisdom by his understanding, it continues, saying about his activities, "The one that created the earth for all eternity, he filled it with four-footed creatures. He sends out the light and it proceeds on its way."[170] 9. For it must not be overlooked, philosopher, that it declares the same things again with a view toward a clear explanation of the present subject. It says, "He sends out the light and it proceeds on its way. He called it and with trembling it obeyed him. The stars shone out in their posts and rejoiced. He called them, and they said, 'We are present.' They shone with joy for the one who made them. This is our God. No other can be compared to him. He discovered the whole road of knowledge and showed her to his child Jacob and to his beloved Israel. After this, he was seen on the earth and he associated with humankind."[171] 10. If, as is proper, we connect these two statements about the one who created the habitable lands and those uninhabited, which Solomon and Baruch—or rather Jeremiah—say (for after he says, "The Lord created me,"[172] he continues on with his activities, saying, "The Lord created the habitable lands and those uninhabited")[173] let us, best of men, consider this: Who is this lord who created the habitable lands and those uninhabited? 11. We shall think that it is none other at all than "the one who created the earth for all time" (for "creating the earth" is equivalent to "creating the habitable lands and those uninhabited"), the one who "filled it with four-footed creatures," the one who also called the light "and with trembling it obeyed him," and the rest, concerning whom it says that "he appeared on the earth and associated with humankind." 12. Therefore, one must understand that this refers to the Lord who created the

---

168. Bar 3:23.
169. Bar 3:32.
170. Bar 3:32–33.
171. Bar 3:32–38.
172. Prov 8:22, the passage that the philosopher has just adduced in his question. "Eusebius" is arguing that the meaning of the passage in Proverbs is complemented by the passage from Baruch.
173. Prov 8:26.

rational wisdom[174] as "the beginning of his ways," the one who created "the habitable lands and those uninhabited," who "created the earth for all time" prepared for a humanity "in his image."[175]

17.13. Let us again look at the beginning of the passage. He says, "If I should proclaim to you what has happened day by day" (but he did not say "what is to come") and furthermore he says, "I will remember to enumerate the things from eternity," but not "the things before eternity." 14. It was made known to us that the Son of God is the one who created the rational wisdom, "who created the earth for all time," who created "the habitable lands and those uninhabited," who said to Job, "When the stars came into being, all my angels praised me."[176] And Moses says concerning the one who created the light, "And God said 'Let there be light,'" and continues by saying, "And God made the two great lights and the stars" and so forth.[177] 15. What I have said seems to me sufficient and establishes the proofs, philosopher: that the Son of God is the one who created the rational wisdom in Solomon and all created things, and he is no tool.

17.16. But in order for us to make the true explanation of affairs more clear to you and to come more swiftly to the true meaning of the matter and the contemplation of it, let us read what comes from the Scriptures. 17. For when the prophet Moses was about to depart this life, as is written in the book of the Assumption of Moses, and when he had called Joshua son of Nun and was speaking with him, he said, "And the Lord foresaw me before the foundation of the world, that I would be the mediator of his covenant,"[178] and in the book of mystical sayings of Moses, Moses himself foretold of David and Solomon. 18. And concerning this Solomon he foretold thus: "God shall pour forth wisdom upon him and justice and full

---

174. In this section, *wisdom* is rendered in the lowercase whenever "Eusebius" is taking the word to refer to the rational wisdom provided to human souls, which in this exegesis is argued to have been created and provided to human souls by the Son, who is also the Word or Wisdom (uppercase).

175. A collocation of verses recently under discussion: Prov 8:22, Bar 3:32, Gen 1:27.

176. Bar 3:32, Prov 8:26, Job 38:7.

177. Gen 1:3, 16.

178. As. Mos. 1:6. The "mystical sayings of Moses" referenced below refers to the same text, known as the Assumption of Moses. The work survives only in full in a sixth-century Latin manuscript, though the Greek tradition is much older, being referenced by Origen, *Princ.* 3.2.1. Jude 9–10 also refers to a conflict between the archangel Michael and Satan over Moses's body, similarly recounted in the Assumption of Moses.

understanding; he shall build the house of the Lord," and so forth.[179] 19. But in order that what I am saying may be as clear as possible, let us thus consider the notion: Does humankind exist because of the world or the world because of humankind?

The philosopher:

Obviously, the world because of humankind.

17.20. *Our holy bishops through the same bishop, Eusebius Pamphili, said:*[180]

And if the world exists for the sake of humankind, since humankind was came before the world in God's plan, and the world came after humankind and the rational wisdom in God's plan, then humankind came before the world, as did wisdom. Therefore, coming beforehand, it preexists even the world's natures, such as heaven and earth, day, night, clouds, winds, deeps, springs, mountains, and hills. 21. Wisdom and humankind, on account of which the world exists, came before all these things in God's plan. Therefore, humankind and wisdom, being older even than the world's natures in the plan of God, indeed preexist the world. 22. But [humankind], then, coming later when it was created, was brought forth in the sequence of creation, while what came later than humankind in God's plan was pushed forward and came earlier in the sequence of creation. 23. But wisdom too, which the Son of God "found by his understanding"[181] and which he had given to humankind created "in his image,"[182] even she preexisted the world and its natures in the plan of God. 24. Therefore, Solomon knew in his own right, because he had been taught, by the wisdom of God granted to him, that humankind and wisdom preexisted the world and its natural elements

---

179. As. Mos. 1:14.
180. "Eusebius's" complicated speech at 2.17.20–36 continues the differentiation between rational, human wisdom and the wisdom of God, established in the previous speech (2.17.12–18). Asserting that the world was created for the sake of humankind, he argues that humankind was therefore conceived first. Since the main trait of humankind is its rational wisdom (see 2.15.7–10), wisdom also had to be created before the world, at the conception of humanity. This allows the phrase "The Lord created me as the first of his ways for his works" (Prov 8:22) to apply not to godly Wisdom but to human wisdom, denying the idea that the Son (equated with the Wisdom of God) was created.
181. Bar 3:32.
182. Gen 1:27.

in God's plan, when he proved…[183] that what had already preexisted the world in the plan of God "before the foundation of the world," and what the Lord "found by his understanding,"[184] those very things the Lord himself had already created, although they came later than the world and its natures. 25. Therefore Solomon says, as if in the persona of the wisdom that is in humankind, which preexisted the world in the plan of God, "The Lord created me as the beginning of his ways for his works."[185] 26. So then, what he was impelled to proclaim through the rational wisdom in humankind, which was prepared for humankind begotten "in the image" of God—this phrase "The Lord created"—refers to that which preexisted the world in the plan of God. But the phrase "He begat me," considered once more, he spoke given in reference to procreations according to nature, subsequent to this. Understand, then, philosopher, that the phrase "He begat me" is about the same nature as it ages and renews, right up until the end. 27. Therefore the phrase "The Lord created me as the beginning of his ways for his works"[186] must be treated with regard to the rational wisdom granted to humankind, whereas the phrase "begat me" applies to the begetting, according to God's foreknowledge, of that same nature (i.e., from the same, from the images, like a wheel that turns back to its beginning as it reaches its end) of the firstborn human who was created "according to the image" of God, in whom God placed created, rational wisdom and imprinted his pure love. 28. And effecting a renewal of this in himself,[187] the Savior spoke to the Father in a manner indicative of the divine plan: "because you loved me," he says, "before the foundation of the world."[188]

Now Solomon, by recounting the phrase "Before the ages he established me in the beginning,"[189] provided insight that the ages in this world have their basis in the passage of day and night, but observing in the course of these inquiries that to preexist day and night is to preexist these ages, Solomon expounded it in a way befitting humankind and wisdom. 29. Therefore he cried out in the persona of wisdom and spoke the phrase,

---

183. Lietzmann (see Loeschcke and Heinemann 1918) proposed a lacuna in the text, accepted by Hansen (2002).
184. Prov 8:22, Bar 3:32.
185. Prov 8:22.
186. Prov 8:22.
187. I.e., a renewal of the phrase uttered in Prov 8:22.
188. John 17:24.
189. Prov 8:23.

"The Lord created me as the beginning of his ways for his works; before the ages he established me in the beginning,"[190] understanding once more in his own right that, when God was going to bring into being those natures that were to come sooner in the world, namely, of humankind and wisdom, it was necessary that what came before be present. But once the natures were produced, it was necessary to narrate the natures in the order they were produced, and that humankind and wisdom were established to have precedence over the works. 30. Therefore, the rational and critical wisdom bestowed on humankind by God and poured out on Solomon, just as the great Moses says,[191] speaks in Solomon: "The Lord created me as the first of his ways for his works," and so forth.[192] 31. And in the persona of this wisdom, which together with humankind is earlier than the world, the same Solomon, when explaining the activities of God when he produced the natures in the world, says: "The Lord created the habitable lands and those uninhabited, the inhabited end of the world below heaven. When he established heaven, I was there with him, when he marked out his throne upon the winds. When he made firm the clouds above and set as secure the springs of the world below heaven—in establishing his command for the sea even waters shall not disregard the word of his mouth—and when he made firm the foundations of the earth, I was together with him acting in harmony, I was the one in whom he rejoiced."[193] 32. These things he spoke in the persona of wisdom, and he unmistakably demonstrated that it is clear that what preexisted the world in the plan of God, on account of which even the world was prepared, also preexisted the natures of the world. 33. Thus, the one who became knowledgeable of the sequence of the natures, the one who came before them, enumerates their order—wisdom, which "he found in his understanding" and which he supplied to humankind. 34. Who, then, is the one who prepared this wisdom beforehand and gave it to humankind, which guides their actions? None at all other than "the one who prepared the earth for all time" and the one who "filled it with four-footed creatures," who called the light "and it answered him trembling," who was seen "upon the earth" and associated with "humankind."[194] 35. The actual production of the natures has been allotted to him. All of

---

190. Prov 8:22–23.
191. See above, 2.17.17–18.
192. Prov 8:22–30.
193. Prov 8:26–30.
194. Bar 3:32–38.

this has demonstrated most clearly that "the Lord created me"[195] was said in the persona of the wisdom that is not the Son of God, but rather the rational wisdom prepared by the Lord himself and bestowed on humankind, on whose account the world was created, 36. and that it was spoken in the person of rational wisdom. And the Lord confirms what has been said in the gospel when he says, "The Sabbath was made for humankind, not humankind for the Sabbath,"[196] personifying the world in the guise of the Sabbath, instead of saying, "the world for humankind, but not humankind for the world."

18.1. *A different opposing argument from the philosopher:*

But, *he said*, the wisdom in Solomon is the Son of God, that is, the Wisdom of God, the one who said, "The Lord created me" and so on.

18.2. *The response of the holy bishops against the philosopher through the bishop Eusebius Pamphili:*

Tell us, philosopher, is the wisdom in Solomon, as you say, the Wisdom of God?

The philosopher:

Yes, *he said*, it is so.

The bishop:

Tell us, does the Wisdom of God have foreknowledge or not?

The philosopher:

Yes, it does.

The bishop:

Is the Wisdom of God, which you say is in Solomon, the Son of God?

---

195. Prov 8:22.
196. Mark 2:27.

The philosopher:

Yes, *he said.*

The bishop:

How does the one who judges judge? According to foreknowledge, no?

The philosopher:

Yes, *he said*, but how?

The bishop:

The one, then, who judges according to foreknowledge also judges according to deeds, as one who has knowledge beforehand?

The philosopher:

Yes, I said.

18.3. *The bishop:*

How, then, does the wisdom in Solomon say, "There are three things that are impossible for me to understand, and the fourth I do not understand?" And once she has mentioned the three things that she was unable to understand, the wisdom in Solomon said about the fourth that she did not know, "Even the paths of a man in his youth."[197] 4. Therefore, if the Wisdom of God is the wisdom in Solomon, how does it "judge the world"[198] if it does not know "the ways of a man in his youth"? And how can this be true that the one who created humankind according to the image of God—that is, the Son of God, just as Moses the prophet says,[199] but also John the Evangelist as well ("Everything," he says, "came to be through him"[200])—does not know "the ways of a man in his youth"—5. the same one "who fashioned

---

197. Prov 30:18–19.
198. Rom 3:6.
199. See Gen 1:26–27.
200. John 1:3.

the hearts of them individually, who has comprehended all their deeds,"[201] who "tests their hearts and minds"[202] according to the prophet who says, "You know my sitting and my rising; you perceive all my thoughts," he says, "from far away. You searched out my track and my miles and foresaw all my paths"?[203] 6. And again, in another place—"The one who educates the nations, will he not test them? He who teaches humankind knowledge? The Lord knows the thoughts of humankind, because they are futile."[204] 7. Therefore, does the one who understands these things and foresees all things not know "the ways of a man in his youth"? And it is possible to find many things in the Scriptures that prove the folly of those who interpret this passage poorly. 8. For how can "he who teaches humankind knowledge" himself not know "the ways of a man in his youth"? Therefore, know well, philosopher, that Solomon received critical wisdom, which the Son of God "found by his understanding,"[205] the syllogistic wisdom that he prepared for humankind created "according to his image."[206] 9. But, of course, the Lord offers further proof in what is said in the gospels. For when he says the phrase, "Behold, one greater than Solomon is here,"[207] he overturned those who say that he is the wisdom in Solomon. For even though "wisdom" is pronounced the same in the sound of the phrase,[208] yet the Wisdom of God, the Son of God, is one with foreknowledge, and he judges according to foreknowledge and according to deeds, indeed as creator and maker of all things, just as also Paul the "vessel of choice,"[209] 10. when writing thus to the Hebrews, speaks to the following effect about him, "For the Word of God is living and active and sharper than every double-edged sword and penetrates as far as the division of soul and spirit and discerns the thoughts and intentions of the heart, and there is no creature that is

---

201. Prov 33:15.
202. Ps 7:9.
203. Ps 139 (138):2–3.
204. Ps 94 (93):10–11.
205. Bar 3:32.
206. Gen 1:26.
207. Matt 12:42, Luke 11:31.
208. "Eusebius" asserts that this is an instance of Aristotelian homonymy, where an identical word has multiple distinct ideas to which it applies. "Wisdom" is said both in reference to the wisdom in Solomon and the Wisdom of God, and sounds the same when referring to either. The two different referents, however, have "definitions of essence" (λόγοι τῆς οὐσίας) that are distinct.
209. Acts 9:15.

invisible before him, but all things are naked and laid open to the eyes of the one to whom we must render an account."[210] 11. And the same man also writes to the Romans, saying, "whose are the patriarchs and from whom comes the Christ, according to the flesh, being God above all, praised unto the ages, amen."[211] 12. And thus these passages show that the Wisdom of God the Father is truly God from God himself, eternal from eternal and veritable from veritable, being the Son of the eternal God, the Father, by nature, eternally.

19.1. *The rebuttal of the philosopher:*

What about the passage, then, that says, "They did not know the way of wisdom nor recall its paths" and so forth?

19.2. *The response of the holy bishops through the same Eusebius Pamphili:*

Often when focusing on the sayings of Wisdom, philosopher, you marveled at the power of Wisdom, because indeed it is possible to find the greatest truth of understanding in the shortest of her sayings. 3. And perhaps someone could rightly compare the sayings of Scripture to the gospel parable that states clearly that the kingdom of heaven is like "a mustard seed," which is, on the one hand, smaller "than all the seeds on the earth," but grows and when it has reached its full size yields suitable shelter for the winged.[212] 4. Accordingly, let us look at the force of the divine sayings scattered in brief passages, and once the deeper meanings are brought to their full force and thoroughly extended like branches for the intellect of the winged, that is to say, humankind, such a force is discovered that it provides suitable shelter not only for the farmers but also for the winged that stand close by.[213] 5. Whence, therefore, was I moved toward this deeper understanding? Or whence was I moved from the exposition by the word of the Holy Scripture of the holy psalmist David toward the proof and confirmation not of the rational wisdom, such as you yourself have supposed,

---

210. Heb 4:12–13.
211. Rom 9:5.
212. Matt 13:31–32, Mark 4:30–32.
213. The term πετεινά normally translates to "birds," but here "Eusebius" takes the reference to winged creatures to be a figurative representation of humans, as beings with "winged" souls (see, e.g., Plato, *Phaedr.* 246a–249d).

but of the incomprehensible Wisdom, uncreated and without beginning, that gave the first impulse to that wisdom and everything that has come into being? That is to say, the Wisdom of Christ, 6. since Christ, the power of God and the Wisdom of God according to the manner of his ineffable and incomprehensible Godhead, is the true Word of God.[214] For he says, "The heavens were established by the Word of the Lord, and all their power was established by the Spirit from his mouth."[215] 7. You heard "the Word of the Lord"; you heard "the Spirit from his mouth." Hear then yet once more concerning the confirmation of the true faith understood and proclaimed piously by the pious, since indeed, I think, you have not at all received understanding of what was proclaimed to you previously by so great a spiritual choir of holy high priests. 8. Listen piously, then, and do not try to examine ineffable things by human reasoning.

He who is perfect neither diminishes nor increases. God the Father, unbegotten, is one. One also is the one begotten of him, the only begotten Son, God the Word. 9. Now, just as there is not another God co-unbegotten with God the Father, so, too, there is not another Son of God, co-begotten, previously begotten, or afterwards begotten along with the only begotten Son, God the Word. Truly one is God the Father; truly one is the Son, God the Word, inexpressibly begotten of him. 10. Therefore, just as God is not the Father only by expression, thus neither is he the Son only by expression but truly the Son. The Father is genuinely Father; the Son genuinely Son.[216] The Father is God, and the Son begotten of him is God. The Father is perfect, and his Son is perfect. The Father is incorporeal, and the Son is incorporeal. For the form and figure of an incorporeal being is clearly incorporeal. 11. Do you believe this, philosopher, that the only begotten

---

214. I.e., the philosopher's question assumes that Bar 3:23 is spoken in the person of the rational wisdom in individual human souls, as "Eusebius" has just claimed of Prov 8:22, but "Eusebius" claims that Bar 3:23 is spoken in the person of the Son, the Wisdom of God. That "wisdom" and "word" refer to the same hypostasis is clearer in the Greek, since the term λόγος ("Word") connotes the reason and rationality associated with wisdom. Most manuscripts include an extra word, θεός ("God"), at the end of the phrase, which would render the phrase "is the true Word of God as God." We have followed manuscript T in eliminating the word as a scribal mistake.

215. Ps 33 (32):6.

216. "Genuinely" translates γνήσιος, which, like the adverb "truly" (ἀληθῶς) in the previous statement, indicates that the names "Father" and "Son" describe the persons of the Trinity essentially, not accidentally. Used of human procreation, γνήσιος would also connote "legitimate" children against "illegitimate."

Son of the Father was begotten from his *ousia*, just as we have proven from the start of the discussions through so many written testimonies, or not?

The counterquestion of the philosopher:

How and in what way, pray tell?

19.12. *The holy bishops through the same Eusebius Pamphili said:*

Do not ask "how," philosopher. Otherwise, just as has already been told you through several methods and we bore witness to in the beginning of the debate, you are hastening to hurl yourself down by attempting to investigate unsearchable things. 13. For on the one hand if it is possible to inquire how he is unbegotten, it is also possible to inquire how he is begotten. On the other, if the unbegotten does not leave room for debate on how he is unbegotten, thus neither does the begotten leave room for debate on how he is begotten. Do not seek after the inscrutable, for you will not find it. Seek what is discoverable and you will discover.[217] 14. For if you seek [answers to these questions], from what are you able to learn? From the earth? It had not been established. From the sea? The water had not yet been created. From the heaven? It had not been made. From the sun and moon and stars? They had not yet been fashioned. From the angels and archangels? They did not yet exist, since the Son was maker even of them. What about from time? The only begotten is before time. 15. Do not pose questions to things that are not eternal about that which is eternal. Ineffable and unbegotten is the Father. Ineffable and ineffably begotten from the Father is the Son. 16. Be silent about the how and forgo this question in regard to the begetter and the begotten. For the Father alone knows the Son, who he is, and the Son "and he to whom the Son desires to reveal him"[218] knows the Father, just as his gospel says.

19.17. But if you do not want to stop asking after the how, but instead contentiously strive to investigate unsearchable things, we laugh at your audacity, but even more than that we grieve for you, that you do not want to understand by faith that God is always the Father of his Son and that his only begotten Son is always his Son, coexisting eternally with the Father

---

217. See Matt 7:7.
218. Matt 11:27, Luke 10:22.

and not later born, as you impiously say. 18. But understand by faith and profess that the Son is perfect from perfect, as you so often heard, unending light from unending light, veritable God from veritable God and Father, uncreated from uncreated, uncompounded from uncompounded, being always with the Father. For, "In the beginning was the Word," just as John the Evangelist says, "and the Word was with God and the Word was God."[219] 19. The Word *was*, philosopher, does not imply something preexisting; the Word *was*, philosopher, precludes a "there was not," just as we have previously proven; and the word *God* precludes a "not God." Believe what has been written; do not think about or seek into what has not been written. 20. Believe that the Son himself, by his Father's nod, fashioned all things that have come into being, not at a glance from his eyes (for God is uncompounded, just as we have previously said) but by his nod, as he himself alone knows.[220] And indeed, understanding this by faith, we profess according to the teaching of the Holy Scriptures that he fashioned by the Father's will and his own all creation both in heaven and on earth, both seen and intelligible, not by tools and machines or by the assistance of something else, but by the will of the Father, as we just said, who said to him and to the Holy Spirit, "Let us make humankind in our image, according to our likeness."[221] 21. He did not say, "you, make," or "you both, make," but "let us make," showing the equal *ousia* and equal honor of that blessed and inexpressible Trinity.[222]

19.22. Do not mutter and roll your eyes, philosopher, but see with the eye of the intellect the precision of the apostolic doctrines and accept them faithfully, being no more "an unbeliever, but a believer."[223] 23. Therefore, hear and understand; the Word of God, his Son before the ages, to whom he said, "Let us make humankind" and so on, he himself, once again, by the Father's will and his own, at the end of days became human, having been made flesh from a virgin, on account of the fallen man Adam, 24. the bodi-

---

219. John 1:1.

220. "Nod" translates νεῦμα ("nod of assent"). The emphasis in this passage is that the Son's activity in creation should not be imagined to imply otherness in God; that is, the Son does not look at the Father, as one being looking at another being, in the work of creation.

221. Gen 1:26.

222. τό ὁμοούσιον in the Greek, which we normally transliterate *homoousios*, we have rendered "the equal *ousia*" to show the parallel with the less theologically loaded term ὁμότιμον (*homotimon*), "equal honor."

223. See John 20:27.

less emptying himself into a body for the sake of the body, as the apostle Paul said.[224] God, the Word, took on a cloud, the body, in order that he might not set aflame the created natures in the world (for "nobody has ever looked upon God"[225]); 25. he was prevailed over by flesh, in order that flesh through its immutable union with him would be freed from death;[226] the invisible in the visible form in order that he might endure the visible as a human subject to time, but truly God and human in accordance with both, the same one human and God. For there is one Christ from both, the differentiation in *ousia* being both intelligible and known, both his Godhead and his flesh.[227] He was God and is; he became human through the divine economy. 26. On his account there were prophets; on his account there were apostles; on his account there were martyrs: prophets on account of the one who had been prophesied; apostles on account of the one who had been sent by divine plan; martyrs on account of the archetypal martyr. God the Son came to earth, having concealed in flesh the greatness of his Godhead, as he planned, though not leaving a void in the heavens; for the world was not devoid of him before his becoming flesh. 27. God was and is; he became human through the divine economy, having become flesh and born of a virgin on account of his own love for humankind. 28. The Father begat a Son worthy of him and equal, as the one who begot him, God the Father, knows, as does the one begotten of him, God the Son, philosopher.

20.1. *The rebuttal of the philosopher:*

Do not keep doing violence to the truth to such a degree, and do not try to overshadow like a cloud the clear light of the Scriptures with your skill at words, but come to the clarity of the Scripture that has been extended to you and do not flee from the phrase, "The Lord created me as the first of his ways for his works"[228] and the phrase, "The Lord made the habitable

---

224. See Phil 2:7.
225. John 1:18.
226. The phrase "immutable union" (ἄτρεπτος ἕνωσις), like the surrounding passage, is heavy with Chalcedonian Christology.
227. Compare the Chalcedonian Definition: "*homoousios* with the Father as respects divinity and likewise *homoousios* with us as respects humanity." According to the Acts of the Home Synod of 448, this was what Eutyches would not affirm; see C. Chalc. 1.511–527; Price and Gaddis 2007, 1:221–22.
228. Prov 8:22.

lands and those uninhabited, the outermost dwellings of the world below the heavens."[229] 2. These passages have one and the same idea about the one Lord. They are about the God who created even the proto-creation as "the first of his ways for his works,"[230] whom he also called his Son, and who created through him, as through a tool, "the habitable lands and those uninhabited." [231] 3. For even if the created wisdom of God, that is to say, the Son, engaged in work, nevertheless God was the one who created the things that did not exist through him as through a tool.

20.4. The response of the holy bishops through the same Eusebius Pamphili:

Though standing widely apart from the kingly highway, that is to say, apostolic faith, somehow you allow yourself to be carried beyond it, choosing once and for all to hurl yourself down headlong and barely keeping your head above the depths of the impiety surrounding you. And this when you have heard from this holy council the prophecy of the great Jeremiah, who points the way, as one might say, saying, "This is our God, no other can be compared to him" and so on,[232] 5. to which he adds "Afterward, he appeared on earth and associated with humankind."[233] And you knew when the bishops just asked you, "Who was the one 'seen upon the earth and who associated with humankind,' the Father or the Son," didn't you, philosopher? And you agreed that "It was the Son, just as the Holy Scriptures say."[234] 6. Have you not said these things? Furthermore, how is it that you are again throwing yourself into the depths of Arius's depravity, or rather plunging right in? For you have not broken away, although you have separated from

---

229. Prov 8:26.
230. Prov 8:22.
231. The term *proto-creation* (πρωτόκτιστον) refers to the Son as a secondary being to the Father created before all other created things. Key theologians on the Nicene side took issue with the term, as it implied that the Son had at some point not existed, e.g., Epiphanius (*Pan.* 3.58.17) and Basil (*Eunom.* 5).
232. This phrase seems to be a combination of two verses, both in Isaiah rather than Jeremiah: 25:9 ("This is our God") and 40:18 ("To whom will you liken God?"). Jeremiah is referenced specifically in regard to the verses about the hardness of the heart, but the way the syntax is construed seems to suggest that the quote should be attributed to him too. On Jeremiah and the hardness of the hearts of those to whom he preached, see, e.g., 16:12, 17:9, 30:12.
233. Bar 3:38.
234. See above, 2.16.14.

that man to whom you had yoked yourself. You prefer, wretched man, the blasphemous sayings of Arius to the apostolic doctrines, when you name the Son of God a creation and a tool. 7. Therefore, hear it from us, lover of wisdom, if indeed you do love wisdom,[235] and trust that the Son of God himself is not the created, rational wisdom granted to humankind by that same Son himself who created "the habitable lands and those uninhabited." 8. Take thought, looking not to hatred but to truth, and the truth itself will guide you, and you will know that the only begotten Son of God is not a creation but himself the creator and maker of all created natures, just as even you yourself, when you saw clearly for a moment, understood and will understand, as I myself believe, if indeed you long to be saved.

21.1. *The rebuttal of the philosopher against the Holy Spirit*:[236]

Let these things be believed about the son, *he said*, and let them be unambiguous, as you say, that he created or even co-created with God the Father, as the testimonies make clear, and that he is not a production, but a begetting of God, begotten of him by nature, and behold, we accept as much.[237] 2. But are you not also able to say something about the Spirit? For who would dare to call the Holy Spirit the creator of any natures that have come into existence? And where do testimonies also say about it that the Spirit itself was the maker of any of the creations visible and invisible? And who at all wrote about it as about the Son? Let one of you shout it out if he is able.

---

235. There is a pun here on the root meaning of the term *philosopher*, which means "lover of wisdom."

236. The divinity of the Holy Spirit was not debated at Nicaea. From this point on in the dialogue, the bishops are portrayed as articulating theological definitions that were actually formulated at subsequent councils. The doctrine of the full divinity of the Spirit, for example, was confirmed at Constantinople in 381. The fictional debate thus dramatizes the notion, key to the theological conflicts of Cyzicenus's day, that all of doctrine had been defined sufficiently in the Nicene Creed, with all other councils confirming or refining that doctrine.

237. The philosopher is portrayed as accepting that the Son is not a creature and that he is *homoousios*, though he uses the terms ποίημα ("made thing") and φύσει ἐξ αὐτοῦ ("in nature from him"), rather than the more contentious terms κτίσμα ("creation") and *homoousios*.

21.3. The rebuttal of the fathers through Protogenes, bishop of Serdica:

It is not difficult, philosopher, to show you the testimonies to the activities of the Holy Spirit that our fathers set forth concerning it, as to the fact that it did create. Let us once more mention the passage concerning the creation: "And God said, 'Let us make humankind in our image and according to our likeness.'" And it goes on to say, "So God created humankind in his image, in the image of God he created it; male and female he created them."[238] 4. Therefore as God is the Father who says to the Son "Let us make," and God the Son is the one who created humankind, if we then say that the one who spoke as well as the one who created Adam and Eve is God, then hear about the Holy Spirit. Was God the one who created Adam or not?

21.5. The philosopher:

Yes, it is God.

The bishop:

In the book of Job, Elihu the Buzite says to Job, "The Spirit of God is the one who made me."[239] If, then, God is the one who created Adam, how would you call the one who made Elihu? Or does Elihu seem to you to be different in *ousia* from Adam? For the identical accomplishment of the makers, who were equal in knowledge, came to be manifest in the form of humankind. 6. Therefore, how will you call, philosopher, the one who created Elihu? Is it not God, the creator of humankind? For as Scripture said concerning the one who created Adam, "and God made Adam,"[240] thus it is correct for us to say also about the one who created Elihu that the Holy Spirit is God. And their fashioning of the creation is equal, and equal is the appellation given the craftsmen,[241] if indeed the Godhead of the Holy Trinity is conceptualized to be one in three perfect and equal hypostases. 7. And in the book of the Assumption of Moses, Michael the archangel, when speaking to the devil, says, "For we all were created by his Holy Spirit." And furthermore it says, "The Spirit of God came forth from the face of God

---

238. Gen 1:27.
239. Job 33:4.
240. Gen 1:27.
241. I.e., both are properly called God, and as God they do the work of creating.

and the world came into existence."[242] This passage is the equivalent of "All things came into being through him."[243] 8. For the divine and inexpressible Trinity that fashioned all creation, intelligible and sensible, is ever inseparable, the Father, the Son, and the Holy Spirit. 9. For as it also says in the thirty-second Psalm, "The heavens were fashioned by the Word of the Lord and all their power by the Spirit from his mouth."[244] Indeed, listen to God saying in Isaiah, "I, your God, am Lord, I, the God of Israel, shall listen to you."[245] 10. But speaking about his benefactions toward his people, he goes on to say, "In order that they may at the same time see and consider and understand that the hand of the Lord made all these things, and the holy one of Israel made them known,"[246] meaning by "hand" the Holy Spirit of God, and by "the holy one of Israel" his Son. 11. And furthermore he said to Jacob, "My hand laid the foundations of the earth and my right hand made firm the heavens,"[247] just as Ezekiel also says, "The hand of the Lord came upon me."[248] 12. Scripture is accustomed, philosopher, to call the Holy Spirit of God either "hand" or "arm," but to call his Son "right hand."

21.13. *The holy fathers continue to speak through Leontius, bishop of Cappadocian Caesarea:*

Are these statements concerning the activities of the Holy Spirit sufficient to persuade you, philosopher, that [the Spirit] is a co-maker of all created natures together with the Father and the Son and is of the same Godhead and *ousia* as the Father and the Son?[249] 14. Then, having readied your mind with what has been said already, hear now even clearer proofs on this matter from the Holy Scriptures. The prophet David in the ninety-seventh Psalm says, "Sing to the Lord a new song." Why? "Because the Lord has

---

242. The passages from the Assumption of Moses that are used here do not survive in the extant manuscripts of that text. The Spirit is said to come from the "face" of God because the Greek word πνεῦμα means both "breath" and "spirit." A play on the double meaning continues throughout this and the next paragraph.
243. John 1:3.
244. Ps 32 (33):6.
245. Isa 41:17.
246. Isa 41:20.
247. Isa 48:13.
248. Ezek 3:22.
249. We take this sentence as a rhetorical question rather than a statement, punctuating it differently from Hansen.

done wondrous deeds; his right hand has saved him" (instead of saying "his Son") "and his holy arm,"[250] meaning the Holy Spirit. 15. And in the General Epistles, John the Evangelist proclaims concerning the Holy Spirit, describing it as God,[251] as do all the rest, "The Spirit is the one who testifies, because the Spirit is the truth," and after a few other comments he says, "The one who believes in the Son of God has the testimony of God in himself" (in place of "the Spirit of God"), "but the one who does not believe in God has made himself a liar."[252] 16. And the great vanguard of the apostles, the godly Peter, says to Ananias, "How far did Satan fill your heart that you have lied to the Holy Spirit?"[253] And after a little, "You did not lie to human beings but to God." And again, in the Old Testament it says, "'I shall fill the heaven and the earth,' says the Lord,"[254] and Solomon also shows who it is who does the filling when he says, "The Spirit of the Lord has filled the inhabited world."[255] 17. Therefore, believe in the dominion of the Holy Spirit and likewise accept the testimonies about it, having faith that the Holy Spirit is of the same Godhead, *ousia*, and selfsame property as the Father and the Son, ever coexisting with the Father and the Son. Are you listening, philosopher?

21.18. *The response of the philosopher to our holy fathers:*

Well then, just as you say and as the testimonies of the Scriptures that you bring forward make clear, it is also necessary to describe the Holy Spirit as God. And it seems to me that the idea would have been forced, if you had not adduced the passages from the Scriptures. 19. Except for the passage about Elihu the Buzite, the explanation is clear, but concerning the aforementioned Assumption of Moses about which you have just spoken, I have never heard of it until now. Therefore, I ask you to furnish me with a clearer proof concerning what has been said. 20. For your statements thus far do not seem to me to be enough for complete assurance about the Holy

---

250. Ps 98 (97):1.
251. "Describing as God" translates θεολογῶν, "theologizing" or "providing an account of as God."
252. 1 John 5:6, 10.
253. Acts 5:3.
254. Jer 23:24.
255. Wis 1:7.

Spirit. The topic at hand requires clearer and more elevated diction, for the subject of debate is not about trivial matters.

21.21. The response of our holy fathers through the same bishop Leontius to the philosopher:

Since the explanation of the question you have posed has been extensive and the clearest testimonies from the Holy Scriptures are able to persuade you about the present subject, philosopher, we are amazed at how you, who seem to be full of such intelligence, are still uncertain. 22. But since we want you to look to the truth and pray for this, we urge your intelligence to begin to understand by faith that uncreated and unchangeable nature, and not to presume to inquire into matters beyond the mind through human reasoning, as we have said so often. Do not continue to be mixed up in the erroneous and impious ideas of Arius any further, for you, philosopher, are as you say, a philosopher, but faithfully accept, as we have just said, both what we are now telling you and what we are about to say. 23. Accept the one Godhead of the Father who begot the Son inexpressibly and the Son begotten from him and the Holy Spirit that proceeds from the very Father and is the Son's own, just as the apostle Paul says, 24. "If anyone does not have the Spirit of Christ, they are not his."[256] And elsewhere the same writer says, "And the Lord is the Spirit," and again, "And there are varieties of gifts, but the same Spirit, and there are varieties of service, but the same Lord, and there are varieties of activities, but the same God acting on all things in all matters," and not far after this, "And one and the same Spirit effects all these things, distributing to each one individually as it wills."[257] 25. Behold, philosopher, this surest and clearest explanation that speaks of the Holy Spirit as God and that indicates that it has its own authority. Observe how he says thus, "And there are varieties of activities, but the same God acting on all things in all matters," and "And one and the same Spirit effects all these things, distributing suitably to each just as it wills."[258] 26. And what does the Lord likewise say in the gospels, as you know, discussing plainly with the Samaritan woman? "God is Spirit."[259] Therefore, if God is Spirit, the Spirit is also entirely God, but not one [God] and another [God], but a

---

256. Rom 8:9.
257. 2 Cor 3:17; 1 Cor 12:4–6, 11.
258. 1 Cor 12:6, 11.
259. John 4:24.

single Godhead of both persons, according to the concept [we have] of their hypostases.[260] 27. But when hearing "persons," let us not take it to mean the divine as having human shape. For it is unbounded and without form, just as also even you agreed, as did we as well, in the beginning of our discussions. 28. For in fact both the heaven and the earth are evidenced as having a "face,"[261] just as the Lord himself says in the gospels when discoursing to the scribes and Pharisees, "Hypocrites, you know how to examine the face of the heaven and the earth," and so on.[262] 29. For everything that subsists, insofar as it subsists, is said to have a "person" of its own nature, or rather a form.[263] But the heaven and the earth are created, just as is the nature of everything that has come into being, but the divine *ousia* is ineffable and uncreated, since indeed it is pure and unbounded and without form and eternal and undying.

21.30. But let us return to the present matter. We showed through many witnesses from the Holy Scriptures that the Holy Spirit is co-maker with the Father and the Son of all creation, both the visible and the intelligible, since it is also ever inseparable from the Father and the Son, just as the Son also is from the Father and the Father from the Son. 31. Here now, if it seems necessary, accept too the useful counsel of examples, even if they are examples of lesser things.[264] Your word, just as that of every human being, is on the one hand spoken out but is engendered indivisibly from your mind.[265] Similarly, your spirit also proceeds from you, and you

---

260. This difficult phrase is κατὰ τὴν τῶν ὑποστάσεων ἔννοιαν, literally "according to the concept of the hypostases." In other words, the Trinity is understood to consist of three distinct persons because the concepts of Father, Son, and Spirit intelligible to humans are concepts of really existing hypostases, not metaphors. The sentence that follows is aimed at another extreme—taking the concept of person in an overly literal, corporeal sense.

261. The Greek term employed here, πρόσωπον, can mean "face" (e.g., of a human being), "surface" (e.g., of the earth), or "person" (i.e., a particular individual). Leontius uses all three senses of the term in his response to the philosopher. On the theological use of the term πρόσωπον, see the note at 2.14.5.

262. Luke 12:56.

263. The sentence contains many technical terms: "subsistent" and "subsist" translate ὑφεστός and ὑφίσταται, which are etymologically related to hypostasis. "Person" (πρόσωπον) is here glossed by σχῆμα ("form").

264. I.e., an analogy from the sensible world may help the philosopher understand the point being made about the transcendent nature of God.

265. The uncommon phrase, "engendered indivisibly" (γεννᾶται ... ἀτμήτως), joins the mental process of conceiving a word to the physical act of speaking, arguing

would not call either your word or your spirit foreign to you. 32. And you would think it unworthy to think this about human beings, would you not? But in regard to that ineffable and incomprehensible and immeasurable *ousia* of God, would you consider his Word foreign, which is not spoken forth but is ever-living and active and sharper "than every double-edged sword,"[266] and which is also judge of all, since it is also indeed the maker of all, for whom "There is not a creation hidden from his sight, but all things are naked and laid bare to his eyes"?[267] 33. And who dares to say that his Holy Spirit, which examines "even the depths of God,"[268] is alien, or dares to accept those who say this of either the Word or Spirit? Do you agree, philosopher?

22.1. The response of the philosopher to the assembly of the holy bishops:

Since you led me to a loftier understanding by saying that it is necessary that there be conceptualized and believed to be one Godhead of the Father and the Son and the Holy Spirit, I recall the things that you said previously, that the Father is God and the Son is God and the Holy Spirit is God. 2. But now you say that there is one Godhead of the three perfect hypostases of the Father and the Son and the Holy Spirit. Clarify these statements more plainly for me, please.

22.3. The response of the holy fathers to the philosopher through the same bishop, Leontius:

It is inexpressible, since that divine and ineffable *ousia* is incomprehensible and immeasurable and utterly inscrutable, which surpasses all things and embraces all things. 4. However, listen to us: we have not told you that God is two different [beings], as the impious Arius blasphemed, when he said that one God is uncreated and another created and proclaimed that

---

that the physical act is ultimately inseparable from the motivating thought. This analogy was a subject of debate in the early fourth century, especially in the competing theologies of Marcellus of Ancyra and Eusebius of Caesarea (see, e.g., Eusebius, *Eccl. theol.* 2.13).

266. Heb 4:12.
267. Heb 4:13.
268. 1 Cor 2:10.

the Spirit of God was likewise created (may it not be so!),[269] but we have said that there must be conceptualized and believed to be one Godhead, one *ousia*, one dominion and will of the Father and the Son and the Holy Spirit, 5. and we have said that we know that the hypostases of the holy Trinity are not separated or localized, but the Godhead of the holy, *homoousios*, and venerable Trinity is to be conceptualized and believed to be one by faith alone, just as we have said many times. 6. Behold, the true faith demonstrates in every way that one must not understand there to be difference in the holy Trinity. So, be less eager to give us your opinion and you will be strengthened in your faith even more, when you accept the precepts of salvation from the Holy Spirit through us, in order that you may understand the Godhead of the holy Trinity to be always one and subsistent, a trinity truly triune, with nothing in it ever preexisting [anything else in it] but which is always and in exactly the same manner indivisible and *homoousios*.

22.7. *The response of the philosopher:*

Do not suppose that I shy away from the doctrines of the truth (else I would have rejected your arguments from the very beginning of our discussions). Rather, I am inquiring into the meanings of your ideas for this reason: so that the subject about which you speak may become more evident and clear to me.

22.8. *The response of the holy fathers to the philosopher on this subject, concerning fire, radiance, and light, through the same Leontius the bishop:*

Then listen indeed, now, philosopher, listen! We have already set down as a basis for your understanding through very many such passages from the Holy Scriptures that the Divine is something singular and uncompounded, as you yourself likewise agreed in the beginning of your questions,[270] 9. and that it is in nature fire undying, eternal, and uncreated as well as light infinite and incomprehensible and is not to be conceptualized in one single

---

269. See, e.g., Arius's *Thalia* as quoted by Athanasius, *Syn.* 15, "The unbegun made the Son a beginning of things originated, and advanced him as Son to himself by adoption; he has nothing proper to God in his own essence" (*NPNF* 2/4:457, slightly modified).

270. See above, 2.14.6–7, and the philosopher's consent at 2.15.1.

person, as is supposed by the Jews, but among all Christians the belief is in three, ever inseparable persons and the proclamation is of the inseparable Trinity of the Father and the Son and the Holy Spirit, just as has been shown. 10. But also learn now, philosopher (if we be even too daring, yet the divine majesty will be gracious to us, for our work on behalf of your salvation and the salvation of all others is nearing completion), learn about the intelligible therefore from what can be sensed, what is beyond understanding from what can be understood, and what is beyond expression from what [can be] said, 11. even though all things seen and intelligible and all creations "in heaven and on the earth and under the earth"[271] are incomparable to the uncreated and incomprehensible and immortal *ousia* of God. In addition to the example at hand being of no mean advantage for those who accept it faithfully, we may also say that it is an image sufficient for the piety of those who wish to understand things piously. 12. This perceptible fire, although it is of a single nature, nevertheless is a triune *ousia*, at once fire, radiance, and light, and none of these elements is found to preexist the others, but the three exist inseparably from one another: the fire, the radiance from it, and the light. 13. Now then, if you are able, philosopher, separate the three and show us which one preexists the others, whether the fire, on its own, precedes the radiance and the radiance is born at some period of time after the fire, or again whether the light is born later or comes later in time than the fire and radiance, or whether it comes beforehand. 14. Show us, if you are able, when you have divided the three from one another, that it is not the case that the fire is likewise radiance and light, since the nature of the fire is one.

22.15. Keeping in mind these perceptible and created things—even though, as we have just said, they are not comparable to the eternal and unendurable *ousia* of God,[272] nevertheless take them as salvific starting points[273]—and setting on the wing the eye of your understanding by faith, mount up to the lofty knowledge of God. 16. There will greet you, at least as we pray and believe, the grace of the Father and of the Son and of the Holy Spirit shining on you, showing you its Godhead as one, being undy-

---

271. Phil 2:10.
272. Some manuscripts (V, T, H) read "uncreated" (ἄκτιστον) rather than the "unendurable" (ἄστεκτον) preserved in other witnesses (a, B, W, p, C, M).
273. The Greek term ἀφορμαί signifies "launching points" or "points of departure" for contemplation in the sensible world, from which one can ascend to the contemplation of purely intellectual realities.

ing fire and radiance and light, singular and uncompounded, inseparable, indivisible, incomprehensible and ineffable, a Trinity truly *homoousios*, of the Father and of the Son and of the Holy Spirit.

22.17. *Wherein the philosopher puts faith in the Holy Trinity:*

> *Upon hearing these things, the philosopher, just as though falling into an ecstatic trance,[274] was struck dumb for an exceedingly long time and "his arguments confounded him,"[275] and much fear fell upon him.[276] 18. Then, coming to himself, he cried out loudly, saying*

Glory to you, God, who inspired in these holy men of yours the mystery beyond all understanding of the immaculate and inseparable and uncreated Godhead. But I beseech you, Christ, that you, the all-good Son of the all-good Father, disregard the ways in which I sinned against you, caught up as I was in these impious doctrines of Arius, and let me not, by your just decision, have the penalties exacted by you for those impious statements that I, wretch that I am, spoke out against you. 19. Woe to Arius and his impious company! They blaspheme against the Son of God. They say, "There was a time when he was not," and that the Son of God and the Holy Spirit are created and made and of different *ousia*, and they have said that the Son of God and the Holy Spirit are not of the same *ousia* as the Father. 20. I now and for all time anathematize Arius and his impious doctrines and all those who agree with him and those who blaspheme against the Father and against the Son and against the Holy Spirit. For the one who does not have the Son "neither has the Father,"[277] and the one who has blasphemed against the Son and the Holy Spirit has blasphemed against the Father. 21. I beseech your holy assembly of elders, assist me through your supplications on my behalf to Christ, the Son of God, since I am following above all the precepts set forth and defined by the Holy Spirit through you. And I confess that these things are true and certain. 22. For I believe this to be what Paul, the teacher of sacred truths, asserts: that "the mystery that

---

274. The ecstatic trance suggests the operation of the divine in the philosopher's conversion.

275. Dan 5:6.

276. The last phrase recalls Gen 15:12, where darkness falls on Abraham immediately before one of the covenantal conversations between him and God.

277. 1 John 2:23.

has been hidden from ages and generations,"[278] which "now was revealed," just as it has been said, "to his holy apostles and prophets" and to you "in spirit":[279] that his Son and his Holy Spirit exist always, co-rule, and are co-permanent with God the Father.

23.1. Continuing, the holy fathers spoke to the philosopher about spring and river and water, through the bishop Leontius:

One must take thought of this as well, O philosopher, henceforth a friend of truth. Let us consider a spring that produces a river of water. For the whole river, as you know, has a spring as its begetter. Now then, the river on the one hand proceeds from the spring of water, but no one calls the river a spring or the spring a river, but the spring is called a spring and the river a river, and both are one water. 2. When someone wants to draw water from the river or from the spring, they use the name "water" interchangeably. For one will not say "Go out; when you have made your way, draw and bring me 'the spring' or 'the river,' but 'water.'" For there is one nature, but there must be reckoned three "persons": spring, river, and water. 3. But the Holy Scripture is also shown to discuss these things—for we are not telling you things contrary to Scripture, you who are henceforth a genuine child of grace, if we also introduce the word of truth in symbols and types and images. 4. Now, the Holy Scripture says about the Son, "He will bend himself down unto them as a river of peace,"[280] that is to say, he clearly proceeds from the true spring of life, from the Godhead of the Father, just as the Lord himself says in the gospels, proclaiming, "I have come from the Father and I am here,"[281] and this is the very thing that he says most clearly, "I and the Father are one,"[282] and "I am in the Father and the Father is in me."[283] 5. And the Holy Spirit, which all of us who believe receive from him, which is of the same *ousia* as the Father and the Son, which proceeds from the Father and is the Son's own, just as we showed earlier, which has been poured on us by him, this the Lord himself indicates most clearly in saying, "If anyone thirsts, let him come to

---

278. Col 1:26.
279. Eph 3:5.
280. Isa 66:12.
281. John 8:42.
282. John 10:30.
283. John 14:11.

me and drink. He who believes in me, just as the Scripture said, rivers of living water will flow out from his core," to which the evangelist, inspired by God and explaining the statement, adds, "He said this concerning the Spirit which those who believe in him were going to receive."[284] 6. And the prophet David, seeing something of this truly living spring, the holy Trinity, proclaims that "beside you is the spring of life; in your light we shall see light,"[285] calling God the Father the spring of life. Speaking in regard to the Son, since the Father is in the Son and the Son in the Father, he designates the Son as "light," in which light he says we shall see light, that is, the Holy Spirit. For "in your light we shall see light." 7. For the Father is truly the spring of life and light, and the Son is the light from the light of the Father, and the Holy Spirit is light from his light, 8. since, as we have had to say so often, there is one Godhead of the Father and the Son and the Holy Spirit, just as God himself proclaims through the prophetic words, "I am God and there is no other,"[286] and "I God am first and I am after these things,"[287] and "I am for all ages,"[288] and again "I am and do not change,"[289] and so forth, in accordance with what was explained previously. 9. For it is necessary, I think, to reconsider the sayings, and if not all of them on account of their number, still those that most clarify the fact that what has been said has the most secure support. 10. Therefore, we will adduce what came from the mouth of the prophet Jeremiah. He says:

> The one that created the earth for all eternity, he filled it with four-footed animals. He sends out the light and it proceeds on its way. He called it and with trembling it obeyed him. The stars shone in their posts and rejoiced. He called them, and they said, "We are here." They shone with joy for the one who made them. This is our God. There is no other that can be compared to him,[290]

and so forth. 11. Now, it is necessary at this point, most God-beloved philosopher, to understand the notion and to unpack the meaning of the Scrip-

---

284. John 7:37–39.
285. Ps 36 (35):9.
286. Isa 45:21.
287. Isa 44:6.
288. Isa 48:12.
289. Mal 3:6.
290. Bar 3:32–36.

ture. For it showed, just as you yourself also agreed, that these matters have been foretold about the Son. For it says, "After these things he was seen upon the earth and associated with humankind."[291] 12. Therefore, if, as according to the impious depravity of Arius, the Son has a different, created *ousia* and is a god that came into being after the Father, but the Scripture says about him, "This is our God; no other can be compared to him,"[292] then the Father is not God, according to Arius's impiety, for Scripture says concerning the Son, "No other can be compared to him." And so the impious Ariomaniacs are refuted together with the author of their blasphemy even before denying the Godhead of the Son, since they cast aside the Father himself. And so the enemies of the truth are found to be completely godless. 13. For he who does not have "the Son," just as it says in the General Epistles, "neither has the Father."[293] But the universal faith knows and holds preeminent a single Godhead of the Father and the Son and the Holy Spirit, to which no other can be compared. This mystery of the holy, venerable, and *homousios* Trinity is unknowable, and inexpressible, and utterly incomprehensible, and can be conceptualized by faith alone.

24.1. *The philosopher:*

What truly divine and illuminating things have been spoken by the Holy Spirit through you all. But I beg of you; since the holy words of your instruction are pleasing to me, incline your hallowed attention to me and instruct me in the matters about which I ask, in order that you may get the fullest reward from God on behalf of my salvation.

24.2. *The response of the holy fathers through the same bishop, Leontius:*

Say what you wish. For it is our desire to satisfy you fully, since you are especially now in all ways readily able to receive the demonstration of our statements, as you have been enlightened by the Holy Spirit.

---

291. Bar 3:38.
292. Bar 3:36.
293. 1 John 2:23.

24.3. *The philosopher's thanksgiving and inquiry concerning the Lord's becoming human:*

Grace be on your sanctified heads. Tell me, holiest men, how one should conceptualize the fact that God the Word, the Son of God, was seen on the earth and "associated with humankind"[294] though being invisible to every created nature seen and intelligible, and teach me the cause of his doing this, please.

24.4. *The response of the holy fathers to the philosopher through the bishop Leontius:*

Indeed, the cause of his advent was part of his divine economy, on account of the fall of the first created human beings, Adam and Eve, which occurred in paradise and which spread among all of their lineage. 5. Since, therefore, they were exposed for having transgressed the command of divine grace, the maker wanted to give this as recompense to the human race.[295] And thence it must be understood that, just as "God said, 'Let us make humankind in our image, according to our likeness,'" "And God made humankind,"[296] as demonstrated earlier, the same God once more said, "Let us save lost humankind, which we made 'in our image, according to our likeness.'" 6. And just as God the Father said "Let us make" and the Son acted as maker, being God from God, the same Son once more, by his Father's will, wanted to rescue humankind in himself.[297]

24.7. *The inquiry of the philosopher concerning the same question:*

And how "was he seen on the earth" and how did he "associate with humankind"[298] as a human being, since God is unchangeable?

---

294. Bar 3:38.
295. "Exposed" (ἐγυμνώθησαν) both in the sense of being "discovered" and "naked."
296. Gen 1:26–27.
297. It is unclear whether the phrase "in himself" (ἐν ἑαυτῷ) refers to the Savior redeeming humanity by becoming human in his own person or to the Son's volition as God in his own right.
298. Bar 3:38.

24.8. *The response of the holy fathers through Macarius, bishop of Jerusalem:*

According to the prophetic statement of the divine Paul, "Great is the mystery of piety; for he was manifest in the flesh" (that is, the Son of God). Then he says "he was seen" also "by angels."[299] For the only begotten is not visible to angels or archangels or to any of the heavenly powers, since indeed "no one has ever seen God."[300] 9. And when hearing of his descent from the heavens, do not suppose that this was a spatial change of place for his unbounded Godhead, but understand that this truly "great mystery of godliness," in which we are renewed, is in accord with the divine economy. 10. For renewal is a restoration of newness. Indeed, on account of this, the same Word of God, who grants us likeness unto himself, came down into our likeness. 11. But it was impossible for God to become like unto us without being made flesh (for an incorporeal form was not added to the one who was of incorporeal *ousia*, which he himself was, but rather a corporeal form), but the *ousia* did not become corporeal without assuming something. For this reason, he truly assumed a body, in order that we, who had fallen from the brotherhood that existed in the beginning, might on account of the incorporeal form's change (that is to say, through the grace of the Spirit, which we lost through the first human beings, Adam and Eve) be led into fellowship through the assumption of a body and once more ourselves assume the divine, incorporeal form.[301] 12. And he takes flesh from a woman; for thus also he became of like kind to us, in order that he might also impart his own glory to us as beings like in kind and in order that he might save the woman through the birth. For it says that the woman "will be saved through the bearing of children."[302] 13. But flesh was assumed, which is by nature full of life. For there is no flesh without that which gives life, which Scripture calls, in its particular idiom, soul.

---

299. 1 Tim 3:16.
300. John 1:18.
301. In Cyzicenus's historical context, this emphasis on the reality of Christ's full humanity is anti-Eutychian.
302. 1 Tim 2:15.

24.14. *The philosopher:*

Who would not be astounded at these great things of God, and the way that you have said them? But how does he take flesh from a woman, as you have just said?

24.15. *The reply of the holy fathers through the same Macarius, bishop of Jerusalem:*

We have already told you, best of men, not at all to ask how concerning the mysteries of God, for they are ineffable and incalculable. And as we have been taught by the holy words, we will tell as much as speech will be able to express. 16. For no human or angel has an entirely full understanding of that mystery of the divine economy of the Lord made flesh, how it happened. Not even Gabriel himself, the one who was the minister of that mystery, knows, nor will the all-hallowed and pure and holy Virgin Mary be able to offer a full grasp of this very enfleshment of God the Word.[303] For the only begotten Son of God himself alone knows the exact account of his own becoming human for our sake. 17. For if, just as Luke says, "the eyewitnesses from the beginning and those who became helpers of the Word related to us"[304] concerning the divine economy of his being made flesh, that he was "from the seed of David" and Abraham "according to the flesh"[305] and "Jesus was born from her," that is, from the virgin, "he, the one called Christ,"[306] and that "these are his ancestors from whom Christ was, according to the flesh,"[307] and that he was concerned with "not angels, but the seed of Abraham,"[308] and he was made like unto us in all respects except sin—these things we have come to know. 18. But the manner in which these things happened exceeds the understanding of every rational nature. For the prophet Jeremiah says concerning this, "And he is human, and who shall know him?"[309]

---

303. See Luke 1:26–38.
304. Luke 1:2.
305. Rom 1:3.
306. Matt 1:16.
307. Rom 9:5.
308. Heb 2:16.
309. Jer 17:9, reflecting a peculiar translation in the LXX.

And while the philosopher and the whole assembled throng were marveling at what was heard, the holy fathers spoke further through Macarius bishop of Jerusalem:

24.19. We have already proven through as many proofs as possible that the only begotten Son of God, who is God, became human because of his love for humankind and took flesh and was born from the Virgin Mary by an ineffable birth. 20. For since he desired, as our discourse has already demonstrated,[310] to renew the things that were destroyed because of the fall of the first-formed human beings, he came to be in our condition in order that he might cause us to be in his condition, coming down to us as the best doctor for our sickness. 21. And again, we will say that the "coming down," the "descending," and the "being sent" must be understood according to the manner of his taking on human form, as we demonstrated before. For he always fills all things with his Godhead, together with the Father, as accords with our previously argued concepts.[311]

24.22. Now then, listen: we are born of woman; he came on account of his love of humanity into this state, but we are born from the pleasure of sleep and the seed of man,[312] while he alone was born from the Holy Spirit and the Virgin Mary. We are fed on milk; he came into this state in the flesh, having given nourishment to all flesh by his Godhead. We are born for growth and increase of stature; he did not judge it unworthy that he become such in body, just as it is written that Jesus grew in wisdom and in stature and in grace with God and humankind.[313] 23. And when he had completed thirty years' time, in order that he might give praise for his entire youth, then he came to the baptism of John son of Zachariah who was preaching to the people a "baptism of repentance,"[314] not giving a gift of pardon for sins, nor of adoption. For these things were not John's to give, nor even an angel's, but God the Word's himself, made flesh and having taken human form. 24. And he undergoes baptism on our behalf and God, though blameless, was baptized corporeally as a human being, not being in need of baptism himself, but in order that he might glorify our baptism, in order that we might believe, that, just as the Holy Spirit came upon him,

---

310. See 2.24.10–11.
311. I.e., the incarnation does not contradict the omnipresence of God.
312. A paraphrase of Wis 7:2 and a euphemism for sexual procreation.
313. See Luke 2:52.
314. Mark 1:4.

so it would come upon we who are baptized in him. 25. Then, after he had associated with humankind and expounded the meaning of his divine commands and worked the wonders of his miracles for three years' time and when the fourth had begun, thus he voluntarily came to bodily suffering on our behalf.

For the punishment of the cross was our debt, but had all of us been crucified, we would not have had the strength to snatch ourselves from death. 26. For "Death ruled from Adam to Moses even for those who had not sinned."[315] There were many holy men, many prophets, many just men, and yet not one of them was able to redeem himself from the power of death, but the Savior of all came himself and took from us onto his blameless flesh the punishments owed to us, in our stead, on our behalf. 27. We are borne down into Hades after death; he undertook even this and went down into it willingly. He was not borne down just as we are but went down; for he was not subject to death but has authority over death. And descending by himself, he rose up with a multitude.[316] 28. For he himself was the intellectual grain of wheat that fell on the ground on our behalf and died in the flesh,[317] who by the power of his Godhead caused his bodily temple to rise up, in accordance with the Scriptures,[318] bearing the fruit of the resurrection of the entire human race. And appearing to his disciples after his three-day burial and his return to life from the dead, he showed to them the sufferings of his body on the cross, saying, "Touch me and see that I am he, the wonderworker, who took upon my flesh sufferings on behalf of your kind."[319] 29. Then, gathering with them for forty days and giving them the precepts of his saving commandments, he went up into the heavens as they watched,[320] and the holy words provide proof that he has been seated at the right hand of the Father.[321] And we wait for him, who is

---

315. Rom 5:14.

316. A reference to the tradition that Christ descended into the realm of the dead between the time of his death and resurrection. Support for this tradition is found in 1 Pet 4:6, Eph 4:9. The earliest textual evidence for the tradition includes the apocryphal Gospel of Peter and the Acts of Nicodemus.

317. See John 12:24.

318. See John 2:19–22.

319. This is not a biblical quotation but a short example of speech in character (*prosopopoeia*), though some phrasing is taken from Luke 24:39. See Cyzicenus's own speech in character at *proem.* 16–17.

320. See Acts 1:3–11.

321. See Heb 10:12.

eternal and reigns together with the Father for the boundless ages, to come at the end of time to judge the living and the dead.[322] 30. This is the apostolic and unblemished faith of the church, which is the same belief handed down from the beginning by the Lord himself through the apostles from forebears to successors. The church proclaims this and holds it even up to now and forever, since the Lord said to his disciples, "Go forth and teach all the nations, baptizing them in the name of the Father and the Son and the Holy Spirit."[323]

Concerning the Harmony of All Regarding *Homoousios*

25.1. Thus when these things had been spoken by the Holy Spirit through our holy fathers who had gathered together in that holy council, that entire multitude that had come there to listen magnified God. 2. And the most God-beloved emperor himself, who was present with them for most of the council, listened and, since he was most greatly pleased, glorified God upon hearing such divine doctrines. Truly indeed delighting in the harmony of our bishops, he was overjoyed in spirit; for he was eager that no one, great or small, be out of harmony with this salvific confession.

25.3.[324] So, then, after this long and lengthy fulfillment of the worshipful inquiry, it seemed to all our people together that *homoousios* needed to be defined as it relates to the ecclesiastical faith, according to the way our holy fathers in succession to the apostles handed down this faith, that is, to confess that the Son and the Holy Spirit are of the same *ousia* as that of the Father. 4. And all the holy bishops who were gathered in Nicaea confirmed this very faith, and the multitude of the priestly men and holy confessors and the all-praiseworthy and God-loving emperor and the entire crowd

---

322. Acts 10:42, 2 Tim 4:1. See also Matt 25:31–46, Rev 20:11–15.

323. Matt 28:19.

324. By comparison with BHG 1279 and Rufinus, in 2.25.3–5 we can see that Cyzicenus returns to Gelasian source material (F12f). In the other accounts, however, the impetus to discuss *homoousia* comes from the first debate with an Arianizing philosopher that Cyzicenus narrated in 2.13. It is possible, as with Constantine's burning of the petitions (2.8.4, 2.8.6), that in comparing his sources Cyzicenus understood there to have been multiple recurrences of similar events based on the different versions of the same event in each of his sources. Compared to the parallel passages, Cyzicenus's version of the decision to define *homoousia* emphasizes more the tradition of the apostles, the equality of the Holy Spirit with the Son and Father, and the quantity of orthodox believers.

of the faithful that had come together there rejoiced 5. and welcomed the confession of faith—apart from the bishops, seventeen in number, about whom we have spoken earlier.[325] Arius seemed to delight in them but was convicted along with those very men who harmonized with him, for together with him they said that God fashioned the Son externally, of out some hypostases that did not exist,[326] and that he was not begotten of the same Godhead as the Father.

In Which Arius and Those with Him are Banished by Proclamation by the Entire Council

26.1.[327] For that reason, all our holy fathers determined by unanimous vote that they be banished yet again from the universal church together with Arius, and they anathematized them and their unholy doctrine and their blasphemies in speech and thought, which they employed against the Son of God when they were saying that he came from what does not exist, and that "there was a time when he was not," and that "the Son of God was capable of vice and virtue through his free will," and that "he is something created and made." 2. And the holy council anathematized them and all their doctrines, not enduring so much as to hear their impious opinion and madness and their blasphemous words.

26.3. And moreover they immediately tore up their tract, which, though full of their impiety, they had dared to submit.[328] Such was the end their doctrines received thanks to the holy council. 4. As regards the matters concerning the orthodox faith, all the bishops in harmony sum-

---

325. See 2.7.43.

326. Or, "for they, being outside [the community of the faithful], were saying together with him that..." For a possibly similar usage of "outside" meaning outside the orthodox faith, see 3.2.1 and note *ad loc.*

327. The summary of the events of the council in 2.26.1–4 is unique to Cyzicenus, though it loosely parallels the narrative of Theodoret (*Hist. eccl.* 1.7).

328. "Tract" translates πιττάκιον, a transliteration of the Latin *pittacium*, originally a small strip of leather, linen, or parchment used as a label or ticket. In Greek the term came to mean any small piece of writing, such as a promissory note or list, but also a writing tablet or short message. The use of πιττάκιον rather than λίβελλος adds a layer of scorn, emphasizing the minuteness of the tracts and their ideas by using the term that properly denotes a very small message or label rather than a pamphlet. Compare with the account of Constantine's destruction of petitions at the opening of the council (2.8.1–4) and our notes to 2.8.1.

marized all of it in a few statements, on account of the simpleness of the faithful multitude of the laity, and set out the creed of the universal faith in writing, just so.

A Decree on the Universal and Apostolic Faith Put Forth by the Council in Nicaea in the Reign of the Most God-Beloved Emperor Constantine, in the Consulship of Paulinus and Julianus, *viri clarissimi* 636 Years from the Death of Alexander, in the Month of Desius on the Nineteenth, Thirteen Days before the Kalends of July in the Thirteenth Indiction in Nicaea, the Metropolis of Bithynia

27.1.[329] We believe in one God, the Father Almighty, maker of all things visible and invisible, 2. and in one Lord, Jesus Christ, the Son of God, the only begotten, who was begotten of the Father, that is, of the *ousia* of the Father, God from God, light from light, true God from true God, begotten not made, *homoousios* with the Father, through whom all things came into being, those in heaven and those on earth, 3. who for the sake of us human beings and for the sake of our salvation descended and was made flesh and became human, 4. who suffered, was buried, and rose on the third day and ascended into the heavens and has his seat at the right hand of the Father and will come again to judge the living and the dead; 5. and in his Holy Spirit. 6. And as for those who say, "There was a time when he was not," and "He did not exist before he was begotten," and those who assert that the Son of God came into being out of what does not exist, or is of a different hypostasis or *ousia*, or that he is a creation or liable to turns and changes, these the universal and apostolic church anathematizes.

---

329. The dating formula in the heading combines three different systems for calculating dates: the standard Roman system by consular year; the Seleucid era, dated from the death of Alexander; and the indiction cycle. The indiction was a fifteen-year tax-collection cycle, which began in September. The date according to the indiction would be 19 June 325. This corresponds accurately to the year in which Paulinus and Julianus were consuls, but the date from the death of Alexander appears to be miscalculated by about twelve years. Cyzicenus and Socrates (*Hist. eccl.* 1.13.13) agree in this error. The Macedonian month of Desius/Daisius was used alongside the Seleucid era and in some other calendars inherited from the Hellenistic kingdoms of Alexander's successors. It overlaps with our May and June.

27.7. This is the creed that our holy fathers in Nicaea, the orthodox bishops, first set forth against Arius, who was blaspheming and calling the Son of God a creation, 8. and against Sabellius and Photinus and Paul of Samosata and Manichaeus and Valentinus and Marcion and against every heresy whatsoever that rose up against the universal and apostolic church. 9. Upon them the council of the holy and orthodox gathered in the city of Nicaea passed judgment, and the names of the council members have been appended below, as well as their provinces.

27.10.[330] Now then, the judgments passed by the council, the declaration against the God-battlers, and the decree of the orthodox faith were brought to the pious and all-praiseworthy emperor, and he received it gladly with utmost piety, as if it had come down from God. And he resolved that the enemies of this faith be exiled, inasmuch as they were opposing God. 11. Therefore, six of the bishops siding with Arius endured exile along with Arius himself and his partisans. 12. But eleven others who feared the presence of the God-beloved emperor and the multitude of the bishops at the council—fearing that they might be exiled—put on an act and signed the statement of *homoousios* with their hand but not their conviction.[331] 13. The leader of this deceit was Eusebius of Nicomedia, who is proven even to his end to have employed arguments on either side (just as Eustathius of the Antiochenes, Eusebius Pamphili, the great Athanasius, and all those who wrote about the proceedings of the council relate),[332] seeming both to be a man on our side, through his dissembling,

---

330. 2.27.10–13 returns to the Gelasian source (F13f) last identified at 2.25.3–5. BHG 1279 and Rufinus present the two passages sequentially, and Rufinus presents the creed after this passage instead of before. Cyzicenus may have rearranged the order to clarify what Constantine accepted from the council. At 2.27.10, the decision submitted for Constantine's approval is separated into three distinct pieces: the judgments, the declarations against the Arians, and the creed. This arrangement lends an air of extra authority to the decisions passed but also separates mention of the signatories (27.9) from the list of their signatures (28.1).

331. The motive of fear for this deception, while logical, does not appear in sources outside Cyzicenus.

332. Cyzicenus probably has in mind documents such as Athanasius's *On the Decisions of the Council of Nicaea* and *Discourses against the Arians*, anti-Arian works by Eustathius now lost but known to Jerome (*Vir. ill.* 85; *Ep.* 73.2), and Eusebius's *Against Marcellus*. The specific list of Eustathius, Athanasius, and Eusebius of Caesarea is in keeping with Cyzicenus's interest in habilitating Eusebius and distancing him from the party of Eusebius of Nicomedia. From Theodoret (*Hist. eccl.* 1.8.15), he had read

and seeming to be fighting on behalf of the faction of those in opposition, in a manner true to his nature.

The Signatures of the Bishops Concerning the Faith

28.1.[333] Hosius, bishop of the city of Cordoba, for the holy churches of God throughout Rome and Spain and all Italy and those among the other nations that are far beyond me who live as far as the ocean,[334] through the presbyters of Rome with him, Vito and Vicentius.
2. Alexander of Alexandria together with Athanasius, who was then archdeacon, for the churches throughout all Egypt and Libya and Pentapolis and the lands bordering these as far as the provinces of India.[335]

---

that Eusebius of Caesarea was accused of association with the faction of Eusebius of Nicomedia and that he was instrumental in securing the depositions of Eustathius and Athanasius in the years after Nicaea. See Eusebius, *Vit. Const.* 3.59–62; Sozomen, *Hist. eccl.* 2.18–19; Cyzicenus, *Hist. eccl.* 3.16.13 and notes *ad loc.*

333. The exact source of this list of signatories is uncertain. See Wallraff, Stutz, and Marinides 2018, 116–19. It appears to belong to a synodical letter sent out after the council, a context in which it will reappear at 2.38. BHG 1279 contains a brief passage (16.8–14) that mimics the beginning of the list, while Rufinus transitions directly from the creed to the canons of the council, with no mention of signatures. This condensed list and the list at 2.38 bear similarities in organization to a long list of signatories found in the early sixth-century history of Theodore Anagnostos, but Theodore does not name his source. Consequently, it is difficult to reconstruct where Cyzicenus found his information, but Wallraff, Stutz, and Marinides hesitantly postulate Gelasius (2018, F14), who could have been a source for Theodore Anagnostos. For Theodore's list see Hansen's (1995) edition of Socrates (*Hist. eccl.* 1.13.13). Graumann (2021, 287–88) notes that Cyzicenus's assumption that these thirteen bishops were tasked with universal dissemination of the decisions of the council reflects late fourth- or fifth-century expectations of the protocols of church councils, not those contemporary with Nicaea.

334. The "me" is Hosius, who presumably means Gaul and Britain by referencing lands "beyond him" even "as far as the ocean." The perspective is from Italy and suggests territory beyond the Alps, stretching to the North Sea. The "tribes beyond" could include Christian communities living outside Rome's political control, perhaps in Britain or Ireland.

335. By "regions" of India here, Cyzicenus means Ethiopia, which was often referred to as "India" in antiquity. Sometimes, as here, "greater India" is used for the subcontinent to differentiate it from lesser "India," i.e., Ethiopia.

3. Eustathius of the great Antioch, for those churches throughout Coele Syria and all Mesopotamia and both Cilicias.[336]
4. John the Persian,[337] for the churches in all Persia and in Greater India.[338]
5. Leontius of Cappadocian Caesarea, the pride of the church of the Lord,[339] for the churches throughout Cappadocia itself, Galatia, Pontus of Diospontus, Paphlagonia, Pontus Polemoniacus, and Lesser and Greater Armenia. [340]
6. Theonas of Cyzicus for the churches throughout Asia and Hellespontus, Lydia and Caria, through the bishops beneath him, Eutychius of Smyrna and Marinus of Troas.
7. Macarius of Jerusalem together with Eusebius Pamphili, bishop of Caesarea,[341] for the churches throughout Palestine and Arabia and Phoenicia.[342]

---

336. Coele Syria was a Roman province in the Levant stretching from the Lebanon mountains to Mesopotamia. Cilicia on the southern coast of Turkey was split into two provinces in late antiquity, Cilicia Prima and Cilicia Secunda.

337. Little is known about this mysterious John the Persian, but he is presumably the same as the Persian bishop Eusebius mentions at the council in a passage already quoted (*Hist. eccl.* 2.5.3).

338. The Indian subcontinent should be understood for "greater India."

339. Leontius was bishop of Caesarea in Cappadocia, said to have ordained his friend Gregory the Illuminator, a foundational figure in the Armenian church. In this text he is also one of the major disputants in the Dispute with Phaedo (2.16.5–23; 2.21.13–24.4). Why he alone is given the honorific "the pride of the church" is not clear.

340. Roman Armenia was also divided into two provinces, Armenia Prima and Armenia Secunda, together constituting "lesser Armenia," the Roman province. "Greater Armenia" was an independent kingdom caught in the wrangling for power between Rome and Persia. Mentioning both provinces demonstrates that the council had force outside Roman territory as well as within it. Galatia was located in central Anatolia and Paphlagonia in northern Anatolia on the Black Sea. Pontus, located between Paphlagonia and Armenia, was subdivided into several provinces, the two longest-lived mentioned here, though Diospontus was later renamed Helespontus by Constantine, in honor of his mother, Helena.

341. Macarius and Eusebius are both given the opportunity to communicate the decisions of Nicaea to avoid already fraught tensions between Jerusalem and Caesarea over which see had rightful control over the region's ecclesiastical affairs (see the canons from the council, 2.32.7 and associated footnote).

342. Phoenicia and Palestine were both coastal provinces in the Levant. The Roman province of Arabia was located to the south of these, taking up a small fraction of the Arabian Peninsula, most of which was controlled by various local powers.

8. Alexander of Thessaloniki, through those acting under him, for the churches throughout Macedonia Prima and Secunda, along with Hellas and all Europa, both Scythias, and for all the churches throughout Illyricum and Thessaly and Achaia.[343]

9. Nunechius of Laodicea, for the churches throughout Phrygia Prima and Secunda.[344]

10. Protogenes the admirable, of the city of Serdica,[345] for the churches in Dacia, Calabria, Dardania, and the churches bordering these.[346]

---

343. Alexander of Thessaloniki is little known figure, outside his role as the recipient of a letter from Alexander of Alexandria opposing Arius (*Urk.* 14), and here for signing for several provinces near modern-day Greece. *Hellas*, the archaic term for the Greek-speaking region, had mostly fallen out of usage by Constantine's day and does not appear in other, similar lists. It is possible that a gloss has slipped into the text. Europa was the portion of the continent closest to Anatolia in Asia (where Constantinople would later be located). The two Scythias greater and lesser were north of Europa, as Macedonia was north of the Greek provinces. Illyricum stretched from these lands toward northern Italy (where modern-day Albania and Croatia are located), whereas Thessaly would cover some of the territory of Macedonia, and Achaia would cover the Greek provinces. Theodore Lector's list has Alexander sign only for Macedonia. See Socrates Scholasticus 1995, 51.

344. Nunechius of Laodicea is another Nicene father about whom little is known. Phrygia Prima (or Salutaris) and Secunda were provinces in central Anatolia.

345. Protogenes of Serdica (modern Sofia in Bulgaria) was present years later with Hosius at the Council of Serdica (343) trying to win assent for the Nicaean formulation *homoousios* against the critiques of the partisans of Eusebius of Nicomedia (Socrates, *Hist. eccl.* 2.20; Sozomen, *Hist. eccl.* 3.11-13). With Hosius he received a letter from Pope Julius (who served from 337–352) concerning this struggle (*Ep.* 3.12).

346. *Dacia* seems used in a general sense here to designate a larger region of the central Balkans including formerly Roman lands conquered by Trajan (r. 98–117) but relinquished to Gothic tribes by Aurelian (r. 270–275) and a remaining Roman territory that was divided into two provinces in this period, Dacia Mediterranea (because it is in between other lands, not because it is near the Mediterranean Sea) and Dacia Ripensis ("Dacia on the river bank," i.e., the Danube). Dardania was a neighboring province in the same larger administrative district, the Diocese of Moesia. Presumably, by mentioning these three provinces in it, the entire diocese is implied. Calabria is the boot of Italy, apparently considered separate from the Italy to which Hosius wrote. Protogenes's territory also cuts across the Adriatic. Alexander of Thessaloniki's territory seems to jump over that assigned to Protogenes (see previous note).

11. Caecilian of Carthage,³⁴⁷ for the holy churches of God that are throughout all the provinces of Africa and Numidia and both Mauritanias.³⁴⁸

12. Pistus of Marcianopolis,³⁴⁹ for the churches throughout Moesia and the peoples of Athens and of the Gauls and for the cities bordering on them.³⁵⁰

13. Alexander of Constantinople,³⁵¹ who was then still a presbyter but who later was allotted the episcopal priesthood in the church

---

347. Caecilian of Carthage was a bishop whose election helped spark the first major internecine Christian conflict of Constantine's reign, the Donatist controversy. Caecilian was ordained by Felix, who was afterwards condemned as a *traditor* ("traitor"), that is, one who succumbed to pressure during the persecutions and either sacrificed or compromised their faith in some other way. Another bishop, Donatus, was appointed in Caecilian's stead by a rival faction. Conflict broke out, and the emperor had to intervene. Caecilian was declared the rightful bishop twice, at councils in Rome (313) and Arles (314), respectively. The followers of Donatus refused to be reconciled to him and continued as a rival Christian organization until the Arab conquests in the seventh century. The standard history of the schism is Frend 1985.

348. Africa here signifies one province rather than the continent, specifically Africa Proconsularis, with its capital at Carthage. Numidia was another province in Roman North Africa, to the south and west of Africa Proconsularis. The two Mauretanias (Mauretania Caesariensis and Mauretania Tingitania) were provinces west of Numidia. The names given here are all from the Severan-era provincial reforms and do not reflect the names employed in the Diocletianic reforms, which created a third Mauritania and split Africa Proconsularis into three provinces. The entire North African region of Tripolitania, which connected these former provinces with the Libyas, is left off the list. As a whole, the signatory list mixes provincial titles from different time periods and leaves some provinces out entirely.

349. Pistus was bishop of Marcianopolis, capital city of the province of Moesia inferior, and was the recipient of two now-lost letters from Constantine, which were originally included in the missing part of book 3 (see appendix 2, *Pinakes*). Little else is known about him.

350. These regions are the most perplexing of the entire document. Moesia presumably means the diocese, since this would have included Athens in the early fourth century. The mention of Gauls complicates matters. Either Gaul the Western Roman diocese is meant, or it is a reference to the closer province of Galatia. But Galatia has already been covered by Leontius and Gaul by Hosius, making unclear here to whom Pistus is to convey the council's decisions.

351. Alexander (d. ca. 340) was bishop of Byzantium and first bishop of Constantinople. As mentioned above (2.7.44), he was only a presbyter at the time of the council but was later appointed bishop. Why he is writing in the place of the actual bishop, Metrophanes, is not explained. That the list refers to a later appointment and to

there, together with Paul, who was still then his reader and notary, for the churches on all the Cyclades islands.[352]

14. All these holy and apostolic men, conveying the things that were decided in the holy, great, and ecumenical council in Nicaea, transmitted them everywhere on earth to all the holy churches of God under heaven.

In Which the Emperor Rises from His Throne and
Offers Words of Thanksgiving to God

29.1.[353] The emperor Constantine, taking joy in the exposition of the right and apostolic faith declared by the Holy Spirit through our three hundred holy fathers as if with one mouth and confirmed by all, rose from his throne in the presence of the entire multitude of the holy high priests and all who had assembled for that holy audience of the faith. 2. Spreading his hands and lifting his eyes to heaven toward God, he praised God, the Savior and benefactor of us all, with reverent words, because God had bestowed on him the unanimity of the bishops that he desired, as well as their harmony concerning the right and salvific faith. 3. Such a man

---

the name of Constantinople, a city that would not be formally dedicated for five years yet, suggests strongly that the list of signatories comes from a later historical tradition rather than any document emanating from the council. By the time of Cyzicenus's writing, the bishop of Constantinople had come to be seen as one of the patriarchs, bishops of influential sees with widely accepted authority, among whom were also the bishops of Rome, Alexandria, Antioch, and later Jerusalem. According to this list, then, the "patriarch" has still signed, even if he was at the time only a presbyter; Constantinople had yet to be founded; and a patriarchate was not yet established. See also the notes to Photius, *Bibl.* 88, in appendix 3.

352. The Cyclades are an archipelago between Greece and Asia Minor. Paul later became bishop of Constantinople (d. ca. 351), again suggesting his name is included because the document dates to a later period when the careers of these men were known and revered. As in the case of Alexander above, for an orthodox historian writing after the Council of Chalcedon, it probably seemed incumbent that the bishop of Constantinople be counted among the signatories at Nicaea.

353. The origin of the following passage is uncertain, but it must have been composed after the historical tradition had elevated the number of participants at the council from Eusebius's 250 to the over 300 handed down by Rufinus, Socrates, and Theodoret. Elements of the paragraph imitate the language of Cyzicenus's first prologue as well as the introduction to book 3, suggesting he may have composed this passage as well.

was that emperor, God-beloved and in all ways best, when it concerned the care of the churches of God and the most peaceful unanimity of their shepherds.

29.4. I do not think it out of place to insert into this text the account of Eusebius Pamphili, which he handled well in his third book on the life of Constantine, the God-beloved emperor, when he begins to give an account of these matters (I mean the goings on of the council). It is as follows:

> 29.5.[354] Indeed, when a great many complaints were being put forward on each front and a great quarrel was being raised by certain men at the outset, the all-praiseworthy emperor was listening to all and receiving the propositions of each faction with keenest attention. 6. He was attending in part to the things being said on both fronts, and he gently reconciled those who were resisting out of love for contention, and calmly held talks with each side. And speaking in good Greek, since he was not unlearned in this, he presented himself as being sweet and pleasant,[355] 7. persuading some and entreating others by his speech, and praising still others who were speaking well urging everyone toward unanimity, until such time as he had brought them all to the same understanding and the same opinion as him, in such a way that he harmoniously strengthened the pious doxology and affirmed the salvific faith pronounced truly by the Holy Spirit through all our aforementioned holy fathers. 8. And at the same time he ordained that one date be agreed on by all concerning the salvific feast of Easter.[356] 9.

---

354. This passage of Eusebius (*Vit. Const.* 3.13–14) appears with the same beginning and endpoints in both Socrates (*Hist. eccl.* 1.8.20–23) and Theodoret (*Hist. eccl.* 1.13.1–2). Unique to Cyzicenus are the details about the "pious doxology," that the statement of faith was "pronounced by the Holy Spirit through all the aforementioned fathers," the reference to Constantine's action concerning Easter, and the recommendation to record the "regulations and canons" in writing.

355. Constantine himself spoke primarily in Latin. Eusebius highlights his ability to speak Greek (literally "Hellenize his speech") as a sign of his consideration and concern for the inhabitants of the eastern part of the Roman empire.

356. For Cyzicenus (as for Socrates, Sozomen, and Theodoret), the ultimate source on debates over the observance of Easter at Nicaea is Eusebius, who references the topic in his list of events precipitating the Council (*Vit. Const.* 3.5.1–2) and includes a letter of Constantine on Easter, presumably sent after the council (3.17.1–20.2 = *Urk.* 26). This letter is reproduced by Cyzicenus below at 2.37.10–22 along with other letters

Indeed, he then determined that the things agreed on in common be ratified in writing through the signature of each man, and he recommended that the bishops set down in writing the regulations and canons of the church one by one.

Concerning Acesius the Bishop of the Novatianists and Those with Him

30.1.[357] But the faith of the emperor moves us to remember yet another deed; for he was the sort of man so moved by zeal and concern for the peace of the church that he did not disregard even the smallest matters. And he called Acesius, a bishop of the Novatianists' sect, and those with him into the council since they, too, believed in the *homoousios* and the Trinity. 2. Therefore, after the setting out and signing of the definition of the faith by both the council and the emperor, Constantine, the emperor, asked Acesius whether he, too, agreed with the creed and the determination of the festal day for Easter.[358] 3. And Acesius said to him, "Emperor, the council has determined nothing new. For so have we all before from apostolic times interpreted both the definition of the faith and the time for the festal day of Easter." 4. And the emperor said to him, "Then why do you separate yourself from our fellowship?" And Acesius described the things that had occurred in the time of Decius during the persecution concerning those who did not have the strength to contend in the contest for martyrdom but became deniers, and he cited the strictness of that

---

that Cyzicenus places in the immediate aftermath of the council. Athanasius (*Decr.* 36 = *Urk.* 23) preserves a synodical letter from Nicaea to the churches of Egypt that also references decisions on Easter; Cyzicenus reproduces this letter below at 2.34.2–13.

Although *Easter* is an anachronistic term, we have employed it to translate πάσχα for accessibility's sake, except when the history refers to the Jewish observation of the πάσχα, where we have used "Passover." Although the Greek term remained the same, part of Constantine's aim at the council was to create a distinction between the Christian calendar and observation and the Jewish (see 2.37.10–24).

357. 2.30.1–5 closely parallels Socrates, *Hist. eccl.* 1.10.1–4. Cyzicenus's text clarifies the speakers at several points, adds a brief contextualization for the Novatian controversy, and simplifies the theology presented by Acesius. Other variants highlight Constantine's piety and active role in the council: instead of Socrates's term, "zeal" (σπουδή), it attests "faith" (πίστις) and claims that Constantine also signed the definition of the faith. Also unique is that among the reasons for summoning Acesius appears the goal of glorifying *homoousia* and the Trinity.

358. See 2.29.8 above.

austere canon, saying that therefore one must not receive those who had sinned after their baptism even after they had repented, or to think them worthy of communion in the mysteries hereafter.[359] 5. After Acesius said these things, the emperor said to him, "Acesius, set up a ladder and climb to heaven all by yourself."

30.6. After these things, all the bishops set out various ecclesiastical regulations.

An Instructive Account Concerning the Regulations of the Church

31.1.[360] Let us keep company with the light, which is Christ, since we stand close to him; since we look upon him, let us thus live a life of hallowing prayers. For prayers make holy, if we petition the divine Word; for the divine Word is present where one's heart and way of life are kept pure with humility. Israel used to weary itself performing its sacrifices; the prophets used to clamor to God, "Send forth your light and your truth."[361] They were clamoring and we received it; just as the Lord said, "Others have labored, and we have entered into their labor."[362] For the Lord himself came to us saying, "I am the light,"[363] "I am the truth."[364] We have received grace without effort, but it is necessary for us to preserve our grace through effort.

---

359. The emperor Decius (r. 249–251) ordered all residents to sacrifice for the well-being of the emperor and empire, threatening death for any citizens who failed to comply. Christians in the empire thus had to choose to sacrifice against the precepts of their religion or to face torture and death. Many Christians who chose to sacrifice and save their lives were known as *lapsi* ("lapsed"). Novatian, a leading Christian theologian in the West, opposed the restitution of the *lapsi* and resisted the nomination of a more lenient bishop of Rome to replace Fabian, who had died in the persecution (d. 250). This resulted in a schism, with Novatian as a rival bishop of Rome, consecrating his own clergy and establishing a parallel church in many cities.

360. These διατυπώσεις, or "regulations" for the church, exist only in Cyzicenus, and he does not specify a source for them.

361. Ps 43 (42):3.

362. John 4:38.

363. John 8:12; see 14:6.

364. John 14:6.

31.2. Concerning those who say that is not necessary for Christians to work.

Since certain persons, who do not want to be busy but rather to be busybodies, have badly interpreted the holy words of the Lord when he said, "Have no worry in your soul as to what you shall eat,"[365] as if he were saying that it was not necessary for Christians who follow this precept to do work on the earth, we must demonstrate that the Lord has not spoken thus. For we can both be busy and have no worry, knowing and believing that the Lord himself grants the increase and fruits of our labors when he says, "The kingdom of God is like this, as when a human being should throw his seed on the earth and sleeps and wakes, night and day, the seed grows and increases, and he does not know how."[366]

31.3. Concerning those who are consecrated to the priesthood.

It is necessary that those who are consecrated to the priesthood be in the type and image of the heavenly beings and that the bishop occupy the <throne>[367] of the Lord himself, considering that he is, after the Lord, the head of the church he has received; and it is necessary for the presbyter to occupy the throne of the seraphim, and the deacon that of the cherubim. It is fitting for them to have an attendant in their service.[368]

---

365. Matt 6:25, Luke 12:22.
366. Mark 4:26–27.
367. Most manuscripts provide no noun as an object of the verb, though one, late manuscript (T) has τύπον ("type"). Lietzmann emends τύπον to θρόνον ("throne"), likely because the prefix "in" is included in the verb. See Hansen 2002, *ad loc*. Furthermore, this would be parallel with the "throne of the seraphim" and "throne of the cherubim" below.
368. This enigmatic passage compares the hierarchy of various positions among Christian clerics to the hierarchy of angels, inferred from passages such as Isa 6:1–6, in which heavenly beings called seraphim praise God on his throne (see Rev 4), and Ezek 1:5–14, 22–28, which depicts another angelic creature (specified as cherubim later in 10:1) also attending the throne of God. A hierarchy of angelic beings grew up in both Jewish and Christian traditions. Around the time Cyzicenus was writing, the pseudographer who named himself Dionysius after the convert of Paul at the Areopagus in Athens wrote a tract titled *Celestial Hierarchies* that played a large role canonizing the seraphim and cherubim as the highest grades of angels in the Christian tradition.

31.4. Concerning how the laity must not step up to the ambo.[369]

Concerning how the laity must not step up to the ambo, except for those who have been appointed to recite the readings or to sing the psalms in the parchment books.[370]

31.5. Concerning holy baptism.

Our baptism is to be perceived not with sensible eyes but those of the spirit. You see water; understand the power of God hidden in the waters. For the holy words teach that we are baptized "in the Holy Spirit and in fire."[371] For in the confession of faith of the one baptizing and the confession of faith of the one being baptized, as given in the holy [baptismal] formula, understand that the waters are filled with the holiness of the Spirit and divine Fire.[372] For it says, "He himself will baptize in the Holy Spirit and in fire." Therefore, the one being baptized goes down into the water at fault for sins and enters in "slavery to decay,"[373] but comes up freed from such slavery and sin, having become a son of God and heir to his grace, and a joint heir with Christ as one who has clothed himself with Christ, just as has been written, "As many as you as have been baptized into Christ, have been clothed in Christ."[374]

---

369. An ambo is a speaking platform approached by steps, from which the epistles and gospel are read during a church service. They are often colloquially called pulpits, which more properly refers to a different style of platform.

370. This regulation is intended to keep laity from offering prayer or orations of their own design, restricting laity to the role of lector or cantor. Parchment codices, although more expensive to produce than papyrus, were also easier to navigate for selected readings and could hold more text. Constantine himself recognized the value of codices to the function of reading and instruction in the church and ordered Eusebius to commission additional codices of Scripture (see below, 3.4.1–5).

371. Matt 3:11. A more complete quotation of the passage appears later in this paragraph.

372. The "holy invocation" refers to the words of consecration spoken by the officiant baptizing the new Christian.

373. Rom 8:21.

374. Gal 3:27.

31.6. Concerning the divine table and the mystery of the body and blood of Christ that takes place on it.

> At the divine table there again let us not attend in lowly manner to the bread and the cup set before us there, but let us elevate our intellect and let us understand by faith that there lies on that holy table the Lamb of God who takes away the sin of the world,[375] who has been sacrificed by the priests without any shedding of blood,[376] and that as we truly take his precious body and blood, we believe that these are truly the tokens of our own resurrection. For this reason, we do not take much but only a little, in order that we may understand that we do this not for satiety but for sanctification.

31.7. Concerning the resurrection from the dead.

> The Lord did not simply give his own flesh unto suffering and death on our behalf, but in order that he might bring about our salvation although being free from death, just as our discourse previously revealed.[377] And the prophet cries out as if in the person of the Lord announcing in advance the coming mystery of the divine economy for his flesh: "I was born," he says, "as a helpless human being among the dead, though free."[378] And who is free from death except God? But according to the proofs demonstrated beforehand,[379] having become flesh on account of his love for humankind he became "as a helpless human being," humbling his own flesh "unto death, even death on a cross."[380] And his flesh is proclaimed to have arisen in order that, having made us immortal, he might announce to us, who were in despair, the hope of our salvation, through our firstfruit offering, so that we

---

375. See John 1:29.
376. See Heb 10:1–18.
377. A reference to the Dispute with Phaedo at 2.24.27. Hansen (2002) argues that this reference backwards suggests the *Diatyposeis* were written by the same source as the dispute, but Anonymous Cyzicenus, if he did not write either piece himself, could easily have inserted the cross-reference.
378. Ps 88 (87):5.
379. Perhaps another reference back to the Dispute with Phaedo at 2.19.27, 2.24.19, 2.24.22.
380. Phil 2.8.

might no longer be slaves to eternal death, but free, just as our firstfruit offering, Christ, as the blessed apostle Paul says: "Christ is our firstfruit; next are the followers of Christ at his advent."[381] And he is also the Savior, he himself indeed, this our Lord, Jesus Christ, the only begotten Son of the Father. And that we await him coming from the heavens, who will resurrect our bodies from the tombs, Paul bears witness to this, saying, "Our citizenship is in heaven, whence we eagerly await the Savior and Lord Jesus Christ, who will change the body of our humility into something conforming to the body of his glory."[382] For thus it is necessary for our body to be made glorious, like that of our master, one that admits no evil nor all our present sufferings, one free from death and sin, holy, in order that we might be able to walk in newness of life with him in heavenly light, reigning together with Christ himself. For in this hope we have accepted also holy baptism and receive the salvific participation in his holy members. These are the doctrines of the universal church.

31.8. That the church of God is one.

The church in heaven is one and the same church also on earth. On it the Holy Spirit descends. Heresies that exist outside this, which human beings hold, are not teachings of our Savior or the apostles but of Satan and of "their father, the devil."[383] For they teach the principles of the Jews and of the Greeks in another form, in order that they might take away from human beings "what is truly life."[384]

---

381. 1 Cor 15:23.
382. Phil 3:20–21.
383. See John 8:44.
384. See 1 Tim 6:19. A commonplace in early Christian heresiology: the distinction between "Jewish" and "Greek" notions was shorthand for heresies that the orthodox considered, respectively, radically materialist or bodily (e.g., Christologies that did not sufficiently acknowledge or denied Christ's divinity; Jewish-Christian heresies that were not sufficiently supersessionist) or radically transcendent or spiritual (e.g., gnostic traditions; Christologies that did not sufficiently acknowledge or denied Christ's humanity).

31.9. Concerning the foreknowledge of God and concerning the world.

The world became shorter on account of foreknowledge.³⁸⁵ For God foreknew that human beings would sin. On account of this, we expect a new heaven and a new earth in accordance with the holy writings,³⁸⁶ when the manifestation even of the kingdom "of the great God and our Savior Jesus Christ"³⁸⁷ is revealed to us. "And then," just as Daniel says, "the holy will receive the kingdom of the Most High,"³⁸⁸ and the earth will be pure, holy, an earth of the living and not of the dead, which David foresaw with the eye of faith and proclaimed, "I believe that I will see the good things of the Lord in the earth of the living,"³⁸⁹ the earth of the meek and humble. For it says, "Blessed are the meek, because they will inherit the earth."³⁹⁰ And the prophet says, "And the feet of the meek and the humble will walk on it."³⁹¹

31.10. We have included in this text these small selections from the many ecclesiastical ordinances with which our holy fathers concerned themselves.

And they also set forth twenty ecclesiastical canons in the same council in Nicaea, which very canons I thought necessary to include in my writing.

Ecclesiastical Definitions: The Definitions Subjoined When the Holy and Great Council Had Been Assembled in Nicaea

32.1.³⁹² Concerning eunuchs who have dismembered themselves.

If someone has been operated on by a doctor due to illness or been castrated by barbarians, let this man remain in the clergy. But if

---

385. I.e., "shorter"; that is, that there will be an end (ἔσχατον) that fulfills God's plan for history.
386. See Isa 65:17, 2 Pet 3:13, Rev 21:1.
387. Titus 2:13.
388. Dan 7:18.
389. Ps 27 (26):13.
390. Matt 5:5.
391. Isa 26:6.
392. In Rufinus, the canons immediately follow the profession of the creed, which Cyzicenus included at 2.27.1–6. In general, Cyzicenus's version of the canons adheres closely to other surviving collections. Differences will be noted in specific footnotes.

someone in good health has castrated himself, it is both right for him to stop being considered part of the clergy and right that, from this point forward, no one of this sort ought to be appointed. And as this is clear, that this is said about those who maintain this practice and dare to castrate themselves, thus if any persons have been made a eunuch by barbarians or by their masters but are otherwise found worthy, the canon admits these persons to the clergy.

32.2. Concerning those from the gentiles who have been presented for ordination.

Since many events occur contrary to ecclesiastical canon either by necessity or because people are pressured in some other way, to the point that that men who have only recently come to the faith from a gentile mode of life and have only been catechumens for a brief period go directly to the spiritual washing and proceed at the same time that they are baptized into being a bishop or a presbyter, it seemed to be appropriate that hereafter nothing of this sort happen. For indeed, there needs to be time as a catechumen and after baptism there is need for more testing. For the apostolic writing is quite clear that says, "not a neophyte, in order that he might not become conceited and fall into condemnation and the snare of the devil."[393] But if, as time goes forward, any spiritual transgression should be discovered about his person and if it should be proven by two or three witnesses, such a man shall cease from his office. And anyone who acts against these orders will risk losing the office himself for daring to act in opposition to the great council.

32.3. Concerning those who have cohabiters.

Concerning cohabiting women, the great council as a general rule forbids that a bishop or a presbyter or a deacon or on the whole anyone in the clergy be allowed to have for himself a cohabitor, unless perhaps she be his mother or sister or aunt or only such types as have avoided any suspicion. And anyone who acts against these orders will risk losing his own standing.[394]

---

393. 1 Tim 3:6–7.
394. In the second century, a practice had developed of Christian men and women

32.4. Concerning the appointment of bishops.

It is particularly fitting for a bishop to be appointed by all the bishops in the province. But if such a process would be difficult either on account of pressing need or the distance of the journey, when at least three have gathered at the same place and when those who are absent are also of the same opinion and express their agreement in writing, then let those three carry out the ordination, and let the right to authorize what has occurred be granted the metropolitan bishop in each province.[395]

32.5. Concerning those who are excommunicated.

Concerning those who are excommunicated by the bishops in each province, whether those from among the clergy or the ranks of the laity, let the judgment that accords with the canon hold sway, that those who have been cast out by some not be accepted by others. But let there be an examination into whether they were expelled out of pettiness or quarrelsomeness or some other such unpleasantness on the part of the bishop. Therefore, in order that this matter may receive a suitable investigation, it seems fitting that in each year there be synods twice each year in every province. Do this in order that any such inquiries may be investigated in common by all the bishops of the province gathered in the same location and those who are generally agreed to have offended the bishop may be recognized by all as being excommunicated for good reason, unless it should seem to the group or to their bishop

---

living together in chaste, spiritual unions outside traditional marriage (*syneisaktism*, from the Greek συνείσακτος, "bring in together"). Several church leaders were suspicious of these unions and spoke out in strong opposition, but the practice continued despite their admonitions and this canon. See Miller 2005, 117–49. Cyzicenus is the only source to include a punishment for disobeying the third canon.

395. In the early church, the metropolitan bishop was the bishop in charge of the church in the capital of a Roman province, who oversaw the other bishops, presbyters, and deacons of that province. As the church expanded, political boundaries shifted, and schisms occurred, the terminology and location for the leading bishop of a given geographical region changed. Different Christian traditions today use the term *metropolitan* for different roles within the church hierarchy, but most metropolitans are still the leading church figures of distinct, geographical regions.

that a more clement sentence should be passed for those persons.[396] As for the synods, let one take place before Lent, in order that a pure offering may be given to God once all pettiness has been put aside, and the second around the time of late autumn.

32.6. Concerning the special honors that have been awarded according to ecclesiastical canon by the church for those managing the greater bishoprics.

Let the traditional customs in Egypt and Libya and Pentapolis hold sway, that the bishop in Alexandria has authority over all, since this is also customary for the bishop in Rome, and likewise that these dignities are maintained for the churches in the region of Antioch and in the other provinces.[397] And it is universally clear that if someone should become a bishop without the assent of the metropolitan, the great council has determined that such a man should not become a bishop. Nevertheless, if two or three persons should oppose an election on account of their own quarrelsomeness, despite the common vote of all being reasonable and in accordance with ecclesiastical canon, let the vote of the majority hold sway.

32.7. Concerning the bishop in Aelia.[398]

Since custom and ancient tradition have held that the bishop in Aelia is honored, let him maintain the continuation of that honor, preserving due dignity for the metropolitan.[399]

---

396. The standard text for the canons says that the punishment can only be mitigated by the group of bishops, whereas Cyzicenus's text gives the individual aggrieved bishop the right to pass a lighter punishment than excommunication.

397. Supplementing the fourth canon, the Council of Nicaea determined that the bishop of Alexandria should have a rank that superseded the metropolitans of nearby provincial capitals, such as Ptolemais in the Thebaid (southern Egypt) and Cyrene in the Pentapolis (modern Libya).

398. The Roman name for Jerusalem was Aelia Capitolina, following the rebuilding and renaming of the city under the emperor Aelius Hadrianus (i.e., Hadrian, r. 117–138). Hadrian had destroyed the city during the Bar Kokhba revolt and instituted measures preventing Jews from resettling the Romanized town. See Mor 2016.

399. Aelia (Jerusalem) technically lay in the province of Syria Palaestina, the capital city for which was Caesarea where Eusebius was the bishop. This canon created a

32.8. Concerning those called "the Pure."[400]

Concerning those who once called themselves "the Pure" but who are coming over to the most holy, universal, and apostolic church, it seemed right to the holy and great council that those who have been ordained remain as they are in the clergy. But before any of this, it is fitting that they confess in writing that they will affirm and follow the teachings of the universal and apostolic church, that is, that they will keep communion with the twice-married and those who lapsed in the persecution, for whom also a time has been arranged and an opportunity granted [for penance], so that they will follow all the teachings of the universal church. Thereupon, therefore, when every such individual who has been ordained is found, whether in the villages or cities, if they are found among the clergy, they will remain in the same position. But whoever comes forward who is a bishop or presbyter of the universal church, it is quite clear that a bishop of the church will have the dignity of the bishop, but one who is called a bishop among "the Pure" will have the honor of the presbyter, unless it seems right to the bishop that he share in the honor of his name.[401] If this is not pleasing to him, he will consider a position either as a suffragan bishop or as a presbyter so that he be seen as wholly in the clergy, in order that there not be two bishops in the city.

---

vaguely defined separation of powers and dignity for Eusebius and his counterpart in Aelia, Macarius. Both figures feature prominently among the orthodox fathers in the Dispute with Phaedo (2.14–24), although Arius's own letters pit Eusebius and Macarius on opposite sides of the debate. See *Urk.* 1; Epiphanius, *Pan.* 69.6; Theodoret, *Hist. eccl.* 1.5.

400. "The Pure" were followers of Novatian. In addition to their strong opinions about Christians who had lapsed under persecution, they opposed admitting Christians who had divorced and remarried, arguing from biblical passages such as Mark 10:1–9, Matt 19:3–9, Luke 16:18.

401. Many early church controversies centered on multiple claimants to the rights, privileges, and financial control of a particular ecclesiastical office (e.g., the Donatist controversy). This canon aims to settle such disputes ahead of time as well as bring the Novatianists into full communion with the larger church. Although the canon allows Novatianist bishops to retain the title itself, as long as the orthodox bishop presiding allows it, the title would not come with the associated privileges.

32.9. Concerning the ordination of presbyters.

If any be promoted as presbyters without examination or, while being examined, admit to their failings, and men acting contrary to canon have ordained them despite their admission, the canon does not admit such men. For the universal church will defend its irreproachability.

32.10. Concerning the lapsed who yet were appointed due to ignorance.

Any of the lapsed who have been appointed, whether due to ignorance or even with the foreknowledge of those who appointed them—this does not supersede the ecclesiastical canon. Those who are discovered shall be removed.

32.11. Concerning those who transgressed without compulsion.

Concerning those who transgress and do not do so under compulsion or threat of confiscation or without any threat or any such compulsion that occurred in the time of the tyrant Licinius, it seemed right to the council, even if they were not worthy of clemency, nevertheless to be merciful to them. Therefore, whoever genuinely repents shall spend three years among the hearers, for seven years shall do penance, and for two years shall associate with the laity in prayers but separated from the offering.[402]

32.12. Concerning those who have broken ranks and gone running back to the world.

Those who have been called by grace and have demonstrated an initial desire and set aside their belts[403] but afterwards went

---

402. A layperson who was "separated from the offering" (χωρὶς προσφορᾶς) did not have the right to make an offering during the service, which likewise precluded them from participating in the rites of Communion. The matter had been discussed in detail at the Council of Ancyra (314), which prescribed different treatment for different degrees of lapsing from the church. See canons 4–9 of the Council of Ancyra in NPNF 2/14. The hearers were those laypersons still receiving the most basic instruction and not yet qualified to present themselves for baptism or to participate in the service.

403. The setting aside of belts is a symbol for surrendering military rank and sta-

running back to their own vomit,[404] to the point that some have spent their silver lavishly and recovered their military standing through bribes,[405] let these men be prostrators for ten years after a three-year period as hearers.[406] But it is fitting in all these cases to examine their commitment and the form of their repentance. For however many demonstrate their rehabilitation with fear and tears and persistence and good works—deeds, not outward show—when these have fulfilled the determined length of time as hearers, they will join in communal prayers, with the possibility that the bishop will decide something more clement on their behalf. But however many bear themselves with no change in manner and think that the outward show of entering the church is enough for their rehabilitation, let them fulfill their time in its entirety.

32.13. Concerning those who seek communion as they are dying.

Concerning those who are departing life, the ancient and canonical rule shall be preserved even now, namely that if someone should be departing, let him not be deprived of the master's traveling provisions.[407] But if someone should despair, receive communion, and then, after sharing in the offering, once more be numbered among the living, let him be among those sharing in the fellowship of prayer only. And in general, concerning any person whatsoever, therefore, who asks to take part in the Eucharist when departing life, after examinations let the bishop give him a share of the offering.

---

tion. The soldiers in Licinius's army had been required to sacrifice on Licinius's behalf, driving certain Christian members away from the army's ranks. Those who returned for the sake of money became their own category of lapsed Christians in the eyes of the council. Military service itself was not the issue—as Constantine maintained an army in the name of Christ—but rather service to an emperor who had demanded non-Christian sacrifices, Licinius.

404. See Prov 26:11, 2 Pet 2:22.

405. I.e., those who have used their previously renounced wealth and position to garner promotions and benefits by purchasing their commissions.

406. As with the term *hearers* in the previous canon, *prostrators* signifies a penitential status separating offenders from full participation in prayer.

407. "The master's traveling provisions" refers to Communion, described here as provision provided by a master to a slave sent on a journey by the master.

32.14. Concerning those who are catechumens but fall away.

> Concerning those who undergo catechism and who fall away during catechesis, it seemed right to the holy and great council that they be hearers for a period of three years alone, and after that pray with the catechumens.[408]

32.15. Concerning how persons must not be transferred from one city to another.

> In light of the great civic disturbance and upheavals that arise, it seemed good to absolutely everyone to do away with the countercanonical custom found in some regions, so that neither a bishop nor a presbyter nor a deacon be transferred from one city into another. And if anyone after the decision of the holy council should endeavor to do such a thing or lend himself to this practice, the arrangement will entirely be made void and he shall be restored to the church over which he was ordained bishop or presbyter or deacon.[409]

32.16. Concerning those who do not remain in the churches in which they were appointed.

> Whosoever, having not the fear of God before their eyes and not knowing the church's canons, recklessly withdraws from the church, be they presbyters or deacons or those in any way ranked among the clergy, these people in no way ought to be found acceptable in another church; rather, every compulsion must be brought to bear against them that they return to their own communities. But if they remain, it is right for them to be excommunicated. And if anyone should dare to poach someone who is distinguished in another city and ordain him in their own church, without the assent

---

408. Only Cyzicenus specifies that the time of lapsing had to be during catechesis for this canon to apply.

409. Cyzicenus's text is consistent with his list of offices affected by the rule against transferring clergy at both places in this canon, where other versions of the text leave the office of deacon out of the second list.

of the bishop of the place from which the one being appointed to the office has departed, let the ordination be void.

32.17. Concerning clergy who lend on interest.

Since many who are numbered in the office have pursued covetousness and shameful gain and have forgotten the divine Scripture that says, "He has not given his money at interest,"[410] and since many lending money have demanded back an extra percentage, the holy and great council has deemed it correct that if anyone should be found after this decision to receive interest as a handling fee or to undertake this business some other way, or demand back a share and a half, or have any other plot in mind for the sake of shameful gain, he will be removed from the clergy and be estranged from the office.

32.18. Concerning presbyters who receive the Eucharist from deacons.

It has come to the attention of the holy and great council that in some places and cities, the deacons give the Eucharist to presbyters, which very thing neither canon nor custom has handed down, namely that those who do not have the authority to give an offering give the body of Christ to those who do give the offering. And even this act has become known, that already certain deacons even touch the Eucharist before the bishops. Therefore, let all these things cease and let the deacons remain in their own stations, knowing that they are the servants of the bishop and that they are lesser than the presbyters. And let them take the Eucharist according to their rank after the presbyters and with either the bishop or the presbyter giving it to them. But neither shall it be allowed for deacons to sit in the midst of presbyters. For what is happening goes against the canon and the order of ranks. But if someone should not wish to obey even after these decisions, let him cease being a deacon.

---

410. Ps 15 (14):5.

32.19. Concerning those from the party of Paul of Samosata who have come over or are coming over to the universal church.[411]

> Concerning those who Paulianized and then sought refuge with the universal church, the decision has been established to rebaptize them without exception. But if some men at a previous time were numbered among the clergy and if they should appear blameless and irreproachable, after their rebaptism let them be ordained by the bishop of the church. But if, after being scrutinized, they are found not fit for service, it is right that they should be removed. And likewise concerning deaconesses and more generally those appointed in the same office, the same plan will be observed. And we make particular mention of the deaconesses who were counted at that rank among them, since they do not have an ordination, such that they are numbered without exception among the laity.

32.20. Concerning those who bend the knee on the Lord's day.

> Since there are certain persons who bend the knee on the Lord's day and also on the days of Pentecost, for the sake of keeping everything uniform in the same way in every community, it seemed right to the holy council that people give their prayers to the Lord while standing.[412]

32.21. The said holy council wrote these twenty rules in the presence of the most God-beloved and all-praiseworthy emperor Constantine concerning ecclesiastical governance.

---

411. Paul of Samosata was bishop of Antioch from 260 CE until he was deposed and anathematized in 268 CE on the charge of Sabellanism. His followers continued to appoint their own priests and other clergy at the time of the Council of Nicaea. On Paul and his deposition, see Eusebius, *Hist. eccl.* 7.27–30.

412. Augustine (*Ep.* 55.28, 32) claims that the standing posture for prayers on the Lord's day and, particularly, Easter and Pentecost calls to mind the resurrection of Christ and is therefore more fitting than kneeling. Tertullian (*Cor.* 3.4) more forcefully claims that kneeling on these days is unlawful.

32.22. And certain bishops planned to set out even another rule, which the divine Paphnutius prevented, about which I think it necessary to narrate an account that does justice to this greatest marvel.

It seemed right to certain of the bishops to introduce a new rule to the church during the council and to decide this as they had concerning the other matters of the church.[413]

Concerning How It Is Not Necessary for Each of Those Who Have Been Consecrated to Cast Aside Their Wives

33.1.[414] Therefore they were beginning to record that those consecrated—whether bishops or presbyters or deacons or subdeacons or anyone in the priestly register—ought not sleep with the wives that they had taken when still laypersons. 2. But when these regulations were thus being prescribed, the divine Paphnutius rose up in the middle of the crowd of bishops and cried out with a loud voice, saying, "Do not burden the yoke of the consecrated, for it is said that 'honorable is marriage in all ways and the marriage bed undefiled.'[415] Do not further harm the church by the excess of your punctiliousness. For it is not said that everyone is able to bear the discipline that requires mastery of the passions.[416] 3. And no one, as I suppose, will keep himself under self-control when each man is deprived of his own

---

413. The story of Paphnutius opposing a newly proposed regulation is paralleled in Socrates (*Hist. eccl.* 1.11.3–7) and appears in the general discussion of Paphnutius and Spyridon's characters (see above, 2.9–11). Cyzicenus's narrative makes this drama a part of the discussions on the regulations and canons of the church, limiting the number of bishops supporting this noncanonical regulation by saying only "some" (τισι) of the bishops move to introduce it, as opposed to Socrates's claim that the rule seemed right "to the bishops" (τοῖς ἐπισκόποις). Cyzicenus's text also dramatically casts parts of Paphnutius's speech into direct discourse—at times awkwardly for the grammar.

414. The title suggests a stricter prescription than actually appears in the text of the canon. As it is uncertain whether the titles were original to the text or added later, no conclusions can be drawn about the discrepancy (see introduction, section 7).

415. Heb 13:4. The grammar is ambiguous as to whether the verb φησι ("it/he says") is a parenthetical, reminding the reader that Paphnutius is speaking ("for," he says, "honorable…"), or spoken by Paphnutius, introducing his quotation of Scripture ("for it is said that 'honorable'…").

416. More literally, "the discipline of not being affected." Both words are difficult to render in English. Ἄσκησις ("exercise; practice") signifies a training in virtue that is both physical and mental. Ἀπάθεια ("freedom from emotion/the passions") is an ideal

wife.⁴¹⁷ But I call good self-control also the intercourse of each man with his lawfully married wife. Do not therefore unyoke the wife whom 'God has yoked'⁴¹⁸ and whom a man who was once a reader or cantor or layperson led in marriage."⁴¹⁹ 4. And this is what Paphnutius said, although he himself was inexperienced in marriage on account of his living in monasteries from infancy. Therefore, the entire assembly of bishops, persuaded by this man's council, fell silent on this question, leaving it to the judgment of those who so wished to abstain from their own wives, with their consent.⁴²⁰

33.5.⁴²¹ These were the proceedings at the holy, great, and ecumenical council assembled in Nicaea of Bithynia.

But since Eusebius and Theognius and the Arians with them still could not endure the strengthened affirmation of the true faith and could not bear to anathematize Arius, they were found out and on that account were subject to exile in turn, by the vote of the most God-beloved emperor and the judgment of the holy council of bishops, and as a result other men were appointed in their stead in their communities by the vote of the same council and by the vote of the clergy and laity of each of their communities. 6. And Amphion took up leadership over

---

state in Stoic philosophy in which the mind or spirit is not unduly affected by outside stimuli.

417. Following Socrates's οὐδὲ ἴσως (*Hist. eccl.* 1.11.4) over Hansen's οὐδείς ὡς in order to avoid a disagreement in gender between the masculine pronoun οὐδείς ("not one") and the word "wife," on which it must depend to construe this sentence logically.

418. See Matt 19:6, Mark 10:9.

419. Cyzicenus omits part of this sentence where Paphnutius specifies that those already in the clergy should not then get married. The affirmation that God himself joins a layman and his wife is unique to Cyzicenus.

420. I.e., the wives' consent.

421. The story of Eusebius of Nicomedia and Theognius being ejected from their churches appears in various levels of detail in the other church histories. Socrates (*Hist. eccl.* 1.8.33) mentions their exile but not their replacements. Theodoret (*Hist. eccl.* 1.20.11) mentions the elevation of Amphion and Chrestus as a coda to the lengthy letter against Eusebius that Cyzicenus quotes in book 1 (1.11.22–31). Sozomen (*Hist. eccl.* 1.21) transitions from a list of Arian theological arguments very similar to those spoken by the first philosopher in Cyzicenus (2.13) directly to an account of Eusebius and Theognius's exile and replacement. A nearly identical verbal parallel between Theodoret (*Hist. eccl.* 1.20.11) and the final sentence of Cyzicenus (2.33.6) may, with the similarities of detail, suggest the Gelasian history as a common source to all four authors. Cyzicenus's only major difference from the three previous historians is the claim that Constantine joined the Nicene bishops in voting for the exiles.

the church of the Nicomedians, Chrestus that of Nicaea itself, and other men the churches of people likeminded to those men. But employing their customary machinations yet again and discovering that even the emperor's clemency was fodder for their treachery, Eusebius and Theognius were attempting to again renew and snatch back their former influence.

33.7. And I would refer those desirous to learn about their most wicked machinations, which were very numerous and were full of every impiety, to the *Ecclesiastical History* of Theodoret and the others who have written about it.[422] But I myself will go on from here to give an account concerning the following: what commands the council of bishops sent by letter to the bishops who were absent and to their communities, and indeed furthermore also what the victorious and most faithful emperor commanded in regard to the establishment of the most holy faith as it had been set out, as well as the establishment of the holy feast of Easter, and in regard to the refutation of the leaders of the impiety.[423] 8. For in addition to all these things, after the council had been nobly assembled, and after the faith had been proclaimed in a way worthy of God, and after the holy fathers had stipulated all matters relevant to the good governance of the church, they were eager to clarify all the definitions in writing to all the holy churches of God under heaven, touching also on matters related to Meletius.[424]

---

422. This is Cyzicenus's first direct mention of Theodoret as a source, although he was likely the source of the Constantinian letter quoted in 1.11.22–31. Theodoret's narrative appears to provide the structural outline for much of the Cyzicenus's narrative from here to the end of book 3.

423. Cyzicenus's plans for the work evidently changed, as he went on to write a third book about the very events for which he here refers the reader to Theodoret and other authors. See also the discussion of Cyzicenus's sources in the introduction, section 6.

424. Meletius was a bishop in Lycopolis, Egypt, who for uncertain reasons caused a schism from the metropolitans in Alexandria. According to Socrates (*Hist. eccl.* 1.7), Meletius had been among the lapsed and been deposed as a bishop for improper elevation (see above, 32.10). Other sources say that Meletius was himself advocating the strict treatment of the lapsed. Whatever the origin of the schism, Meletius eventually began ordaining his own clergy in opposition to the other metropolitans and bishops. He made common cause with Arius against Alexander, metropolitan of Alexandria. On the Meletian schism, see Barnard 1973.

Concerning the Unholy Meletius

34.1.[425] And since a certain Meletius had been thought worthy of ordination as a bishop not long before the madness of Arius, he was interrogated by the most divine Peter, bishop of the church of the Alexandrians, who also was wreathed with the crown of martyrdom. Although he was condemned, Meletius himself did not accept the vote of condemnation but filled the Thebaid and the surrounding parts of Egypt with turmoil and distress, assailing the primacy of Alexander the bishop with intent to usurp. But the governing body of the council wrote to the church of the Alexandrians the decrees it had established concerning this man's revolutionary behavior.

34.2.[426] The Letter of the Council, Written to Those throughout Alexandria and Egypt and Pentapolis and Libya and to the Holy Churches of God throughout the Whole Land under Heaven and the Clergy and Laypersons of the Orthodox Faith from the Holy Council in Nicaea.

> To the church of the Alexandrians, holy and great by the grace of God, and to our beloved brothers, throughout Egypt and Pentapolis and Libya and to all the churches under heaven, to the orthodox clergy and laypersons, the bishops gathered in Nicaea and assembled in the holy and great council send greetings in the Lord.

---

425. Cyzicenus continues his story about the aftermath of Nicaea with information found in Theodoret (*Hist. eccl.* 1.9.1), clarifying points in the introduction where there might have been grammatical ambiguity about the actors.

426. Beginning with this synodical letter (*Urk.* 23), Cyzicenus introduces a series of five letters with minimal contextualizing or transitional material. Three of the letters appear in the works of Theodoret, while all five appear in Athanasius and Socrates. None of these sources, however, presents the letters in the order preserved by Cyzicenus, and his versions do not exactly parallel any the versions presented in Athanasius, Theodoret, or Socrates. This particular letter appears in the works of Athanasius (*Decr.* 36), Socrates (*Hist. eccl.* 1.9.1–14), and Theodoret (*Hist. eccl.* 1.9.2–13), a passage from whom introduces the letter. Nevertheless, certain variants from the text in Theodoret that agree with Socrates and Athanasius may suggest that Cyzicenus was cross-referencing between copies, such as for the phrase "naming him 'created' and 'made'" (2.34.4), which does not appear in Theodoret but does in the other two authors. It is certainly possible, however, that later scribes have emended the text to match the more standard versions or that both Cyzicenus and Theodoret shared another source. In Cyzicenus, the audience of the letter is expanded from just Egypt, Pentapolis, and Libya to the entire known world, increasing the letter's relevance to his text.

34.3. Since, having been gathered from our various provinces and cities by the grace of God and the God-beloved emperor Constantine, the great and holy council assembled in Nicaea has discussed matters of concern to the ecclesiastical faith, it appeared necessary for us to send these decisions from us to you in writing, in order that you might be able to know what motions were brought forward and what was examined, what seemed best and what was confirmed. Accordingly, therefore, first of all to be examined in the presence of our most God-beloved emperor Constantine were matters related to the impiety and lawlessness of Arius and those with him. 4. By unanimous vote it was deemed right that the man himself and his impious opinion be anathematized as well as his blasphemies, both his sayings and ideas that he employed to blaspheme the Son of God, saying that he came from nonbeing and that before he was begotten, he did not exist, and that "There was a time when he was not," while also saying that the Son of God became capable of vice and virtue through the exercise of free will and naming him "created" and "made." 5. The holy council anathematized all these things, not even suffering so much as to listen to his impious opinion and insanity and blasphemous words. And as to that man, what sort of conclusion he met with you doubtless have either heard or will hear, lest we appear to trample on a man already receiving just rewards for his own failure. 6. But his impiety was of such strength that it even ruined Theonas from Marmarica and Secundus from Ptolemais. For they also met with these rewards, together with the others.[427]

But since the grace of God has freed Egypt from that wicked opinion and blasphemy and from persons who dared to cause a division and factionalism in a people previously at peace, there remained the matter of the rashness of Meletius and those ordained by him, and we are making clear to you, beloved brothers, what seemed good to the council concerning this part of the issue. 7. Therefore, since the council was moved to act with greater clemency (for by strict definition he deserved no leniency), it seems good for Meletius to remain in his city but to have no authority to

---

427. The "others" mentioned here are, presumably, Arius, Eusebius of Nicomedia, Theognius of Nicaea, and the others who refused to sign the decrees of the council (see 2.27.10–13).

raise his hand to vote, nor handle any official business, nor lay his hands to ordain anyone or make an appearance in the countryside or in another city for the purpose of doing so, but he is allowed the mere title of the office.[428] 8. And it seems good that those who were installed by him, because they were confirmed by a more mystical ordination, participate in communion on these conditions: on the condition that they retain their honor and continue to serve, but also that they are to be second in every way to all those numbered among each community and church who were selected under our most honored fellow minister Alexander.[429] And in this way they should have no authority to appoint those who please them or to put forward any name or in sum to do anything without the assent of a bishop of the catholic and apostolic church who is of those serving under Alexander, our most holy fellow minister. 9. But it seems good for those who—by the grace of God and your prayers—are found not to be in any schism but are in the universal and apostolic church spotless to have authority and make appointments and select for themselves the names of those worthy of the clergy, and in sum to do all things following ecclesiastical rule and rite.[430] 10. But if it should happen that anyone of those in the church should take their final rest, it seems good that those who have just been admitted should then advance to the honor of the one who has met their end, but only if they seem worthy and the people choose them, and the bishop of Alexandria ratifies him and seals it. 11. And this was granted to all the others, but with regard to the person of Meletius, these allowances did not yet seem right, on account of his earlier lack

---

428. Three Greek infinitive verbs used in this sentence all have the word "hand" (χείρ) as part of their root: χειροτονεῖν ("stretch out the hand"; i.e., "vote"), χειρίζειν ("handle"; i.e., "administer"), and χειροθετεῖν ("lay on the hands"; i.e., "ordain"). Our translation tries to get this wordplay across. The repetition of the word emphasizes that Meletius is to have no part in managing the affairs in the Alexandrine church.

429. The determination made by the council concerning Meletius's followers was justified by the combination of the will of the one ordaining and the grace of God in ordaining ministers. This allowed the Meletian bishops to transition seamlessly back into the larger church without having to go through all the normal processes of initiation. A similar tactic was used for the Novatian bishops, for which see 2.32.8.

430. This exception applies to clergy consecrated by Meletians but found not to be in schism.

of discipline and the hastiness and rashness of his judgment, such that no authority or command should be given to him, as a man capable of producing the same disorderly state of affairs again. 12. These are the decisions particular and specific to Egypt and to the most holy church of the Alexandrians. But whatever else was established as a standard or stated as doctrine, since our master, most honored fellow minister, and brother Alexander was present, he himself will present these things to you more accurately when he is present, seeing as he was both leader and participant in the things that happened.[431]

34.13. We bring you good news also about the agreement over the most holy feast of Easter, since this issue, too, was set aright by your prayers, such that all those brethren in the East who formerly practiced at the same time as the Jews from this point forward will celebrate the most holy feast of Easter in harmony with the Romans and with you and with all of us who keep the feast with you from the beginning.[432] 14. Rejoice, then, in these achievements and in the common peace and unanimity and in the fact that every heresy has been extirpated, and receive with greater honor and more love our fellow minister, your bishop, Alexander, who cheered us with his presence and who even at his age persists in such great exertion on behalf of peace among you and among all.[433] And pray also for all of us, that what we think has been done properly remains steadfast, as it has come about as desired—as we believe—through the almighty God and his only begotten Son, our Lord Jesus Christ, and the Holy Spirit, to whom be glory for all ages. Amen.[434]

---

431. The closing suggests that this letter was one originally sent by the Egyptian clergy to Alexandria and Egypt upon the conclusion of the council but before they had returned home. In this respect, it is similar to Eusebius of Caesarea's letter to his church, quoted next by Cyzicenus (2.35).

432. See 2.29.8 and note *ad loc.*

433. The phrase "and among all" again expands the audience of the letter in comparison to other versions.

434. The closing of this letter is uniquely phrased in Cyzicenus, bearing at some times similarities to Theodoret, at others similarities to Socrates and Athanasius. Unlike any of those sources, Cyzicenus's text presents all three members of the Trinity in the same grammatical cases. Whereas in the standard text, the desired outcomes happened "through" (διά) God and Jesus Christ "in" (ἐν) the Holy Spirit, this version emphasizes the equality of the Trinity by making the Holy Spirit part of the same prepositional

A Letter Written and Circulated by Eusebius Bishop of Palestinian Caesarea

35.1.[435] It is likely, beloved, that you have heard from another source what business was undertaken concerning the ecclesiastical faith during the great council gathered in Nicaea, since rumor has the tendency to outpace the true account of the events.[436] But in order that you might not have anything contrary to the truth reported to you by such hearsay, by necessity we circulated among you first the document set out by us concerning the faith, and then second that which they have put out, after making additions to our wording. 2. Therefore, our text, which was read out in the presence of our God-beloved emperor and declared to be good and acceptable, goes as follows

35.3. The creed as set out by us.[437] Just as we received our faith from the bishops before us and in our first catechesis and when we

---

phrase as the other two members. The phrase "his only-begotten Son" appears only in Cyzicenus's version.

435. The letter from Eusebius to his community (*Urk.* 22) appears in Athanasius (*Decr.* 33), Socrates (*Hist. eccl.* 1.8.35–54), and Theodoret (*Hist. eccl.* 1.12). It was originally sent by Eusebius to Caesarea in anticipation of his return from Nicaea. Eusebius had been placed under a kind of provisional excommunication at a council in Antioch in early 325, where he was accused of being in communion with Arius and rejecting the creedal formulation proposed there. He was granted the opportunity for rehabilitation at Nicaea. In its original context, then, Eusebius's letter explained to his church why he had acceded to the theological language of the council's creed when he had already objected to similar language at Antioch. Athanasius introduces the letter saying that Eusebius wrote the letter affirming the creed "even though he had denied it one day before" (*Decr.* 3.3). Socrates is probably drawing on Athanasius when he introduces the letter as written to allay potential censure for "pausing a little and investigating whether he should accept the definition of faith" (*Hist. eccl.* 1.8.34). Theodoret claims that Eusebius held Arian views but uses the letter as proof that he tried to reconcile Arians with the creed from Nicaea. For Cyzicenus, however, such a context would have contradicted his own claims that Eusebius never considered Arianism (below, 3.16.13) but was one of the most vocal orthodox fathers at the council (above, 2.17.2). Unusually, Cyzicenus transitions directly between letters without any intervening commentary.

436. In Cyzicenus's version, the word "accurate" (ἀκριβῆ), present in all other versions of the letter, has been replaced with a term that recurs throughout the history as a marker of orthodoxy, "true" (ἀληθῆ).

437. The word for "creed" in Greek is the same as that for "faith": πίστις. When, as here, the word refers to a specific textualization of the tenets of faith, we have translated it "creed," as mentioned in the translators' note.

received baptism, and just as we have learned it from the divine Scriptures, and just as we believed and taught it in our role as presbyter and do now in the office of bishop itself, and as we even now believe, we present our faith to you. And it is this:

> 35.4. We believe in one God, Father Almighty, the maker of everything visible and invisible, and in one Lord, Jesus Christ, the Word of God, God from God, light from light, life from life, the only begotten Son, the firstborn of all creation, begotten of the Father before all ages, through whom all things came into being, who for the sake of our salvation was made flesh and lived among humankind, who suffered and rose on the third day and ascended to the Father and who will come again in glory to judge the living and the dead. 5. And we believe also in one Holy Spirit,[438] being truly the Holy Spirit, just as our Lord also said, when sending his disciples out to preach, "Go forth and teach all the nations, baptizing them in the name of the Father and the Son and the Holy Spirit."[439]

And concerning these matters, we affirm also that we hold these things to be so and that we think thus, and again that we have held them so and that we are set in this faith to the point of death, anathematizing every godless heresy. 6. That we have always thought these things from the heart and soul since we have known ourselves, and that we think them and speak them now owing to the truth, we testify before the almighty God and our Lord, Jesus Christ, and are able to show you and through our evidence persuade you that we so believed and preached in times past.

35.7. There was no room for anyone to dispute this creed as set out by us, but our most God-beloved emperor himself was the first

---

438. Cyzicenus's text leaves out part of this creedal statement contained in Athanasius, Socrates, and Theodoret, which says, "believing that each of these exists and subsists, Father as truly Father, Son as truly Son, and Holy Spirit." Because of the repetition of the words "Holy Spirit," it is probable that a scribe has committed haplography—skipping ahead to an identical word while copying—rather than this being an intentional deletion. One manuscript (T) preserves this statement but also has other signs of being corrected against a copy of Theodoret.

439. Matt 28:19.

to testify that it was completely correct, and he professed that he himself thought thus and agreed with it in all ways, and he kept exhorting them all to agree to that creed, to subscribe to its doctrines, and to agree with those very things, adding only the one word, *homoousios*, which very word he elaborated on, saying that it is not in respect to a change in the bodily sense that one would say "*homoousios* with the Father," and that there existed neither a division nor any sort of severing from the Father. For, he said, it is not possible for an immaterial, spiritual, and incorporeal nature to undergo any bodily change, but it is appropriate to understand such matters through divine and ineffable reasoning. And our wisest and most pious emperor philosophized in this manner, and at the impetus of the addition of *homoousios*, they created this transcription

35.8. The creed as promulgated during the council.

> We believe in one God, Father Almighty, maker of all things visible and invisible, and in one Lord, Jesus Christ, the Son of God, the only begotten, who was begotten of the Father, that is, of the *ousia* of the Father, God from God, light from light, true God from true God, begotten not made, *homoousios* with the Father, through whom all things came into being, those in heaven and those on earth, who for the sake of us human beings and for the sake of our salvation descended and was made flesh and became human, who suffered, was buried, and rose on the third day and ascended into the heavens and is coming to judge the living and the dead; and we believe in the Holy Spirit. And as for those who say, "There was a time when he was not" and "He did not exist until he was begotten" and that "he came into being out of nonbeing," or that the Son of God is of a different hypostasis or *ousia* or that he is a creation or liable to turns and changes, the apostolic and universal church anathematizes them.

35.9. And after they had promulgated this text, we did not let them go unquestioned as to how they meant the phrase "of the *ousia* of the Father" and the phrase "*homoousios* with the Father." Therefore, motion was made for interrogations and responses on that point, and the discussion examined closely the intended meaning of the statements. And indeed, they agreed that the phrase "of the *ousia* of the Father" meant being from the Father but not being some fraction of the Father. 10. And it seemed that it was good for us also to agree with this interpretation, inasmuch as the pious teaching dictates that the Son is of the Father, not that he is a portion of his *ousia*. For that reason, we ourselves granted that interpretation and did not reject the expression, since the goal of peace lay before our eyes, as well as that of not falling away from proper interpretation. 11. For the same reasons, we admitted also the phrase "begotten, not made," since they were asserting that *made* was the common designation for the other creations that came to be through the Son, with which the Son has nothing in common. For that reason indeed they were asserting that he is not a created thing like what came into being through him, and he is of a mightier *ousia* than any made thing, an *ousia* that the divine oracles teach was begotten of the Father, although the manner of his begetting is inexpressible and incomprehensible for any nature that has come into being. 12. And so, when scrutinized, the statement of the Son's being *homoousios* with the Father is not meant in the manner of bodies, nor in any way relatable to mortal animals (for it is not through division of *ousia* or through severing, but also not through any passibility, mutability, or alteration of the power of the Father. For the unbegotten nature of the Father is a stranger to all these occurrences). 13. But his being *homoousios* with the Father is indicative of the Son of God bearing no resemblance to born creatures but being comparable in every way only to the Father who begot him. And he is not of some other hypostasis and *ousia* but from that of the Father. And it seemed good to agree to the idea as defined in this manner, since we knew that certain eloquent and distinguished bishops and writers from among the ancients employed the term *homoousios* in their theological discourse about the Father and the Son. 14. Let this be our report concerning the creed as it has been put forward, to which we all agreed, not without investigation but according to the meaning that has just been elaborated and which was investigated in the presence of the most God-beloved emperor himself and was agreed on with the aforesaid senses.

35.15. And we considered the anathematization set out by them after the creed to be unobjectionable, since it forbids using nonscriptural phrases, which have been the cause of nearly all the confusion and instability in the church. Therefore since there is no divinely inspired Scripture for "out of nonbeing" or "There was a time when he was not" or which uses the rest of these statements, it did not appear reasonable to say and teach these phrases. 16. We likewise assented that this seemed good, since at no time before this were we accustomed to using these words. Furthermore, the anathematization of the phrase "He did not exist before he was begotten" was deemed not to be out of place, with the agreement by all that the Son of God existed himself before his begetting in the flesh. 17. And in fact, our most God-beloved emperor even himself made the case in a speech that he existed according to his divine begetting, which was before all ages, since before the Son was begotten in actuality, he existed in potentiality, unbegotten in the Father; for the Father is always the Father as he is also always the King and Savior and is capable of all things, since he always exists in these capacities, ever the same. 18. We have sent these things to you as a matter of necessity, beloved brethren, making plain to you the judgment reached by our inquiry and our assent and how reasonably we resisted nearly even to the last possible hour as long as we were offended at differences of phrasing. But we, taking no pleasure in strife, then accepted those phrases that did not seem harmful, when it was clear to us upon prudently investigating the words that their meaning ran the same as those that we ourselves confessed in the creed we previously presented. We greet you together with the brethren with you. We pray that you be strengthened in the Lord, most honored brethren.[440]

36.1.[441] The Victor, Constantine Maximus, Augustus to the Bishops and Laity

Because Arius has imitated wicked and impious men, it is just that he be subject to the same disgrace as them. Accordingly, just as Porphyry, the enemy of reverence for God, who was composing

---

440. The formulaic closing of the letter does not appear in other surviving versions of the letter.
441. This letter (*Urk.* 33) is not found in the text of Theodoret, demonstrating that Cyzicenus did not solely rely on this sequence of correspondence concerning Nicaea.

certain illicit treatises against the worship, has found the reward owed him, and that reward—so that he might become a thing of reproach in times to come and reach the fulfillment of his most false opinion—is for his impious texts to vanish, so also it now seems right for Arius and those of the same thinking as him to be called Porphyrians, so that they have the same appellation as those whose ways they have imitated.[442] And add to this also that if any text compiled by Arius should be found, it should be consigned to fire, in order not only that the ills of his teachings vanish but that even memory of him may be entirely lost. 2. Indeed, I declare this: that if anyone should be caught hiding a text compiled by Arius and does not immediately consign it to fire and destroy it, the penalty for him will be death. For as soon as he is caught in this act, he will incur capital punishment. God will protect you, beloved brethren.

36.3. And the emperor wrote other more triumphally wrought letters against Arius and those of the same opinion as him, and he sent them throughout the cities everywhere.

A Letter from the Emperor Constantine to the Alexandrians against Arius and to All the Orthodox

37.1.[443] Constantine Augustus to the universal church of the Alexandrians and to the universal church of all the orthodox

Greetings, beloved brethren. We have received perfect grace by divine providence, in order that we who have been delivered from every error may come to know one and the same faith. Henceforth,

---

The letter appears in Athanasius (*Decr.* 39) and Socrates (*Hist. eccl.* 1.9.30–31). The text does not differ significantly in Cyzicenus and Socrates.

442. Porphyry (233–ca. 302) was an influential Neoplatonic philosopher who wrote a now-lost treatise, *Against the Christians* (*Contra Christianos*), portions of which survive as quotations in refutations by later Christian authors, such as Eusebius or Jerome. The date of the tract as well as its scope have been the topics of much scholarly debate. Porphyry's tract continued to occupy a prominent place in the imagination of later Christians.

443. This letter (*Urk.* 25) survives in Athanasius (*Decr.* 38) and Socrates (*Hist. eccl.* 1.9.17–25). In Cyzicenus's version, the address is broadened to suggest that this is a general letter to all churches. Otherwise, there are few textual variations between Cyzicenus and the other copies of the letter.

the devil will have no power against us. 2. Anything that he might attempt while working his evils has been destroyed from its very foundations. The brilliance of truth has conquered the disagreements, schisms, confusions and, if I may call them thus, deadly drugs of disharmony, according to God's command. Therefore, we all now venerate one in name and have come to believe that he is one. 3. That this be so, by the will of God I summoned to the city of the Nicaeans most of the bishops, with whom I also myself rejoiced to exceeding degree to be as one of you, your fellow servant, and I myself undertook an examination of the truth. 4. And thus, however many matters seemed to be engendering pretexts for dispute and difference of opinion, these all were investigated and closely scrutinized. And may the divine Majesty have mercy on how much and how terribly certain persons indecently blasphemed about our Savior, about our hope and life, declaring and confessing that they believe things contradictory to the divinely inspired Scriptures and the holy faith. 5. And thus, although three hundred bishops and more, admired for their sobriety and sagacity, affirmed one and the same faith, which faith had come to represent accurately the truths of divine law,[444] Arius alone was found to be succumbing to the workings of the devil and sowing this evil through his impious opinion, at first just among you all but then among others as well. 6. Therefore, then, let us receive the faith that the almighty God has presented; let us come back to our beloved brethren, from whom some shameless lackey of the devil has separated us; let us return to our shared body and our own, proper limbs thereof;[445] and let us go with all haste. 7. For it befits your sagacity, faith, and sanctity that, now that the error

---

444. The phrase "divine law," used here and in other imperial letters from this period, is ambiguous in its original context. Some readers would likely have taken this as a reference to the Scriptures, though it is also possible to read the phrase as referring to something like "natural law." The ambiguity may be deliberate, especially in texts such as the Letter to the Eastern Provincials, written in late 324 or early 325, and addressed to Christians and non-Christians; on this and related phases as part of a Constantinian effort at fostering a "consensus politics" around a common-cultural monotheism, see Drake 2000; Digeser 2000. In Cyzicenus, however, the inclusion of the Dispute with Phaedo (2.14–24) would naturally lead the reader to assume that Constantine meant Scripture specifically.

445. The shared body refers to the entirety of the church, the limbs to the indi-

of that man—who has been established to be an enemy even of the truth—has been refuted, you may return to God's grace. 8. For what won favor among the three hundred holy bishops is nothing other than the judgment of the only Son of God, particularly since the Holy Spirit also resided in the intellects of such great men as these and imparted the divine purpose.[446] 9. For that reason, let no one hesitate, let no one delay, but let all eagerly return to the truest road, in order that when I arrive among you, at some imminent time, I may profess the thanks due to the all-seeing God together with you, because indeed he has revealed the unalloyed faith and restored to us the love for which we prayed. God will preserve you, beloved brethren.

A Letter from the Emperor Constantine, Which He Sent from the City of the Nicaeans to the Bishops Absent from the Council

37.10.[447] Constantine Augustus to the churches and bishops absent from the holy and great council in Nicaea, greetings.

Having experienced from the success of state matters how great the grace of divine power has been, this above all have I judged to be a fitting purpose for me: that a single faith and unalloyed love and piety of the likeminded with respect to the almighty God be preserved among the most blessed multitudes of the universal church. 11. But since it was not possible for this to reach an unwavering and steadfast state otherwise unless all the bishops, or rather most, were gathered together to the same place, and a decision reached on each matter befitting most holy worship, when

---

vidual communities from which each member of the council had come and the roles each member plays. See 1 Cor 12:12–13.

446. The earlier manuscripts of Anonymous Cyzicenus (Hansen's A, T, H) simply have "holy bishops," while Socrates and Athanasius record "three hundred bishops." A tradition of manuscripts first attested in the fifteenth and sixteenth centuries (Hansen's b tradition) combines these to read "three hundred holy bishops."

447. The final letter in the sequence (*Urk.* 26) survives also in Eusebius (*Vit. Const.* 3.17–20), Socrates (*Hist. eccl.* 1.9.32–46), and Theodoret (*Hist. eccl.* 1.10). Hansen (2002, 106–7) notes that the introductory material in Theodoret states that the letter was for absent churches and bishops, while Cyzicenus has yet another expanded salutation. Much of Cyzicenus's text follows the other three authors, with some small explanatory insertions and a few variations noted below.

as many of the most God-beloved bishops as possible had been gathered in that city of the Nicaeans (and I myself was present, just as one of you; for I would not deny that in which I most delight: to have been your fellow servant), there occurred a suitable inquiry into every matter until such a time as the understanding pleasing to the all-seeing God in regard to harmonious unity was brought to light, in order that nothing would remain still a matter of difference in opinion or controversy over faith.

37.12. Then, after an inquiry concerning the most holy day of Easter had been conducted, it seemed by general opinion that it was good for all Christians everywhere to observe the Savior's feast of most holy Easter on one day. For what is better for us, what indeed can be more respectful, than unerringly to observe that feast, from which we have derived our expectation of the truth, following one arrangement and with a clear principle among all. And first of all, it did not seem worthy to fulfill that most holy feast following the practice of the Jews, who stain their hands with their unrighteous offense and, being polluted, blind their souls, as is only natural.[448] For now that their custom has been displaced by a truer arrangement, which we have preserved from the first day of his passion to the present, it is possible for the proper completion of this observance to take place for the ages to come. 13. Therefore, now let us have nothing shared with the most hateful mob of the Jews. We have received a different path from the Savior. A course lies open to our most holy worship, and a suitable law. Setting ourselves on this course with one voice, let us tear ourselves away from that shameful complicity, most honored brethren. 14. For it is truly outrageous for them to boast over us that we are not competent to preserve these matters without their instruction. And on what matter could they have right opinion, those who after that Lord-slaying were driven out of their minds and are led not by any reasoning but by unchecked impulse, wherever their innate madness might carry them? For that reason, therefore, they do not see the truth even in this matter, to the point that

---

448. The strongly anti-Jewish sentiment here is undeniable. For examples of Constantinian legislation prejudicial to Jews, see Cod. theod. 16.8.1, 16.8.2, 16.9.1. The degree to which Constantine can be described as enacting systematic anti-Jewish policies is debated. See, e.g., Edwards 2015, 160–61, 166–69.

they are almost always in error and, in place of proper calculation, in the same year they celebrate Passover twice. 15. Therefore, for what reason do we follow those who admittedly maintain a dreadful error? For we would never endure establishing a second Easter in one and the same year.[449] But even if these matters were not so, it was befitting of your sagacity <...> that the purity of our soul at all times be seen to share nothing at all in common with the perception of any of those utterly depraved people.[450] 16. For one can easily see in addition to this that it is unlawful for there to be disharmony on so important a matter and a feast of such great ritual significance. 17. For our Savior has handed down to us one day for our freedom—that is, that of his most holy passion; he has intended that his universal church be one. Even if the limbs are utterly scattered to many, varying places, nevertheless they are invigorated by one Spirit, that is, by the divine will. 18. Indeed, let the sagacity of your sanctity reckon how terrible and unbecoming it is that on the same days some devote themselves to the fast, others celebrate symposia; that after the days of Easter some be found in feasts and relaxation, others devote themselves to the appointed fasts. On this account, therefore, divine Providence

---

449. On the preceding sentences about the Jewish calendar and the problem of celebrating Easter "twice," see Eusebius 1999, 259–61, 269–70. For a detailed discussion of the complexities of establishing the proper date for the observance of Easter, see Mosshammer 2008. There were two factors that contributed to divergent celebrations of Easter. Christians inferred from the gospels that Jesus had died on either the first day of Passover (15 Nisan in the Jewish calendar) or the day before (14 Nisan). 14 Nisan fell on the first full moon after the spring equinox. By the early fourth century, it had become standard periodically to intercalate another lunar month before Nisan in order to keep Passover aligned with the spring equinox. Many Jewish communities in this period determined the need or not for an intercalated month (and thus 14 Nisan) based on meteorological observation (i.e., was there evidence that spring had come). Many Christians celebrated Easter on the Sunday following 14 Nisan, as determined by astronomical tables, whether or not this coincided with the start of Passover as determined by local Jewish communities. Others celebrated Easter based on when the local Jewish community determined the beginning of Passover.

450. Other authors' copies of this letter contain the phrase "both through zeal and through prayer" (διὰ σπουδῆς καὶ δι'εὐχῆς) at the lacuna. The reason for its absence in Cyzicenus is uncertain. Cyzicenus's text attests the word "customs" (ἔθεσι) instead of "senses" (αἰσθήσει). One fourteenth-century manuscript (T) seems to correct certain passages against Theodoret, adding to the confusion.

wishes that there be a suitable correction of practice and that this be guided following a single regulation, as I think you all see. 19. Consequently, because it is fitting for this to be set aright thus, namely that we have nothing in common with the Father-slayers and Lord-slayers, there is yet a fitting arrangement, which all the churches of the western, southern, and northern portions of the inhabited world observe, which certain locations across the East do not accept. On account of this, at the present time everyone has thought that it is good—and I myself promise to accommodate Your Sagacity—that Your Intelligence would accept gladly what is observed by one and the same, harmonious opinion throughout the city of the Romans and Italy and all of Africa; Spain, Gaul, and the British provinces; Egypt and the Libyan provinces; the whole of Greece and the Asian and Pontic diocese, as well as Cilicia, considering that not only is the number of churches throughout the aforementioned places greater, but also what in particular is most holy for all to desire in common is that which the keenest reasoning finds appropriate to demand, namely, to have no commonality with the perjury of the Jews. 20. And so that I may speak of the most essential point in a summary manner, it pleased the common judgment of all that the most holy feast of Easter be observed on one and the same day. For it was not fitting that there be any variance in so great a matter of holiness, but it was fitting to follow more nobly that opinion in which there is no admixture of any outsider's transgression and error. 21. Thus, since these regulations have been carried out by divine judgment through those holy bishops so numerous and great, receive gladly the heavenly grace and truly divine commandment.[451] For everything that was accomplished in the holy meetings of the bishops bears its reference back to the divine will. For that reason, make plain to all our beloved brethren the messages written above, as well as the aforementioned wording of the universal creed,[452] and help them welcome and make arrangements for the proper observance of

---

451. No other copy of the letter mentions the bishops in this sentence.
452. In Cyzicenus, Constantine's exhortation to publicize documents refers specifically to the creed, whereas other texts do not specify which documents to publicize. It is more likely, given contemporary habits of publicizing imperial letters, that the original command was to transmit the letters sent to the various churches after the council of Nicaea, such as those included immediately before this one.

the most holy day of Easter, in order that, whenever I come before the sight of your affection, which I have long desired, 22. I may be able to observe the holy feast with you on one and the same day and may take pleasure with you for all these things, seeing the savagery of the devil destroyed by divine power through our deeds. And since our faith, peace and unanimity are blossoming everywhere, I will send up songs offering thanks to the all-beneficent and saving God. God will preserve you, beloved brethren.

37.23.[453] And so he sent these letters to those who had been absent from the council. And he honored those who had come with words of praise and gifts and, ordering several couches to be prepared, he had them feast in the same place, taking some of the more notable members as diners at his own table and allotting others to other tables. 24. But when he saw that some did not have their right eyes but that they had been gouged out, after learning that their steadfastness in their piety toward Christ had become the cause of their suffering, pressing his lips to the wounds, he believed that he would thereby draw blessing with his kiss. And when the symposium reached its end, he gave them yet more gifts. 25. Most notably, he also gave letters to those serving as leaders over the peoples,[454] commanding throughout every city that annual donatives be furnished to perpetual virgins, to widows, and to those dedicated to divine service, providing these amounts more from his munificence than because of their need.

37.26. And Eusebius Pamphili, when treating these matters, says thus:[455]

> Indeed, in this way the all-praiseworthy and most faithful emperor Constantine, when he had refreshed the holy bishops with so much

---

453. Cyzicenus borrows transitional material that immediately follows the copy of the previous letter in the text of Theodoret (*Hist. eccl.* 1.11.1–2), whose words had introduced the sequence of letters (see 2.34.1). As only three of the five letters in Cyzicenus's sequence appear in Theodoret, however, it is clear that Cyzicenus was not solely dependent on Theodoret and may have been comparing multiple sources at this point.

454. I.e., provincial governors.

455. Although Cyzicenus cites Eusebius here (see *Vit. Const.* 3.21.4–3.22), the exact excerpt that he quotes appears in Theodoret as well (*Hist. eccl.* 1.13.3–4), which suggests that Cyzicenus is simply following his text of Theodoret. The setting for the passage is unique here in mentioning Constantine's feasts with the bishops, which makes it fit better within Cyzicenus's chronology. In Theodoret, the episode of the petition burning (see 2.8.1–7) and Eusebius's letter to his own congregation (see 2.35) appear between the feast and the dismissal.

of the greatest reverence, enjoined them to return homeward and dismissed them all. And they went forth with great merriment, and from that point on a single opinion prevailed among all of them, agreed on by the emperor himself, since those who had been widely separated were joined together like a single body. 27. Thence the emperor, rejoicing in his success, gave abundant profit to those bishops who had not been present at the council through his letters, and he ordered that a lavish distribution of money be made to all the peoples living both throughout the countryside and on the outskirts of the cities, in this way after a fashion honoring the celebratory occasion of the *vicennalia* of his rule,[456]

37.28. having gathered the holy council of bishops in the sixteenth year and sixth month of his rule, as the above account has demonstrated in accordance with the ancient accounts.[457] But in the twentieth year, after they had adjourned the meetings of the council, each went back to their own communities, just as was laid out before.[458]

37.29. But I who, to the best of my ability and in the interest of fullest confidence for anyone who may read this text, have arranged in this ecclesiastical history the judgments and definitions made in that holy council concerning the universal and orthodox faith and the august feast of holy Easter, as well as the regulations of the ecclesiastical divine service and the canons providing good order within it, shall cease my account here.[459] 30. I am intending to arrange the remaining zealous acts of piety of the all-

---

456. The *vicennalia* was a celebration of the twentieth anniversary of an emperor's elevation to power. Constantine celebrated the start of his twentieth year in the east in 325 CE, then the end of the anniversary year at Rome in 326.

457. See the note to 2.5.1 on the issues with Cyzicenus's chronology.

458. This attempt to reconcile the dates of the council does not appear in Theodoret or Eusebius.

459. This passage indicates that Cyzicenus may have concluded an early version of the *Ecclesiastical History* with the close of book 2. Though Cyzicenus indicates his intention to complete a third book, there was no guarantee he would have fulfilled it at this point (see the apparently unfulfilled promise for a work on Constantius and the early life of Constantine at *proem.* 26). Furthermore, Cyzicenus has referred the reader to Theodoret's *Ecclesiastical History* for the machinations of Eusebius and Theognius (3.37), though he does in fact tell that story in book 3, suggesting he may not have originally planned on including this material in book 3. Book 3 also begins with its own (second) *proemium* and a summary of the first two books. This evidence for a

praiseworthy and most faithful emperor on behalf of the faith in a third collection, for the glory of Christ the Savior of us all, and for the sake of offering a most straightforward demonstration of the piety of the most faithful emperor.

37.31. This one point alone I thought necessary to add here, since I did not consider it merely incidental but rather entirely fitting: the names of the bishops who were sent out by the assembly of all the bishops to the provinces everywhere on earth, through whom he sent the decisions made by the council out through the conciliar letters and through the writings of the all-praiseworthy emperor to all the holy churches of God under heaven for the glory of God, the Father and his Son, Jesus Christ our Lord, and the Holy Spirit. Amen.

A List of the Holy Bishops through Whom the Holy, Great, and Ecumenical Council, Together with Them in Nicaea, Sent Forth to the Churches of God throughout the Inhabited World the Decisions Reached in the Council through Them by the Holy Spirit

38.1.[460] Hosius, bishop of the city of Cordoba, for the holy churches of God throughout Rome and Spain and all Italy and those among the other nations that are far beyond me who live as far as the ocean, through the presbyters of Rome with him, Vito and Vicentius.

2. Alexander of Alexandria together with Athanasius, who was then archdeacon, for the churches throughout all Egypt and Libya and Pentapolis and the lands bordering these as far as the provinces of India.

3. Macarius of Jerusalem together with Eusebius Pamphili, bishop of Caesarea, for the churches throughout Palestine and Arabia and Phoenicia.

---

change in plan may mean that at least some time had elapsed between the composition of books 1–2 and book 3. See further discussion in the introduction, section 3.

460. The arrangement of this list adheres more closely to the order of key figures in Theodore Anagnostes's list of signatories, on which see the notes to sections 2.28.1–14 above. The main difference is that Macarius of Jerusalem and Eusebius of Caesarea have moved from the seventh place to the third, on which see Wallraff, Stutz, and Marinides 2018, 117 n. 1. Compare, too, the list at 2.28 above.

4. Eustathius of the great Antioch, for those churches throughout Coele Syria and all Mesopotamia and both Cilicias.
5. John the Persian, for the churches in all Persia and in Greater India.
6. Leontius of Cappadocian Caesarea, the pride of the church of the Lord, for the churches throughout Cappadocia itself, Galatia, Pontus of Diospontus, Paphlagonia, Pontus Polemoniacus, and Lesser and Greater Armenia.
7. Theonas of Cyzicus for the churches throughout Asia and Hellespontus, Lydia and Caria, through the bishops beneath him, Eutychius of Smyrna and Marinus of Troas.
8. Alexander of Thessaloniki, through those acting under him, for the churches throughout Macedonia Prima and Secunda, along with the whole of Hellas and all of Europa, both Scythias, and for all the churches throughout Illyricum and Thessaly and Achaia.
9. Nunechius of Laodicea, for the churches throughout Phrygia Prima and Secunda.
10. Protogenes the admirable, of the city of Serdica, for the churches in Dacia, Calabria, Dardania, and the churches bordering these.
11. Caecilian of the city Carthage, for the holy churches of God that are throughout all the provinces of Africa and Numidia and both Mauritanias.
12. Pistus of Marcianopolis, for the churches throughout Moesia and the peoples of Athens and of the Gauls and for the cities bordering on them.
13. Alexander of Constantinople, who was then still a presbyter but who later was allotted the episcopal priesthood in the church there, together with Paul, who was still then his reader and notary, for the churches on all the Cyclades islands.

38.14. All these holy and apostolic men, conveying the things that were decided in the holy, great, and ecumenical council in Nicaea, transmitted them everywhere on earth to all the holy churches of God under heaven, just as this account has demonstrated just above.

The Third Treatise of the *Ecclesiastical History*: The Efforts Taken by the Pious Emperor Constantine after the Great Council in Nicaea

1.1. We have made an account sequentially in the first and second book of the *Ecclesiastical History*. It began from the first years of the reign of the bearer of Christ and of victory, the emperor Constantine, and went over all the events during and up to the full accomplishment of the business undertaken at the holy council in the city of the Nicaeans, and presented a sort of image of what occurred,[1] as well as the siege on the very churches of God set in motion by the God-hating usurpers against them, and the most humiliating destruction of those same impious usurpers. 2. And it presented how Christ, the bridegroom of the church, most nobly fortified the servant worthy of him, Constantine, with the armaments of his honored cross and uplifted his servant against those same impious men, 3. and how he granted him the trophies of his victory against those very usurpers, killing every one of them with their entire kind, strewing them at the feet of Constantine the most God-beloved, bestowing through him a deep peace from above on his churches throughout the entire inhabited world. 4. And it presented the scheme set in motion once again after these events against the church by that good-despising, hostile demon through the utterly abominable Arius, 5. and how, on account of him and his impious blasphemies with which he blasphemed against the son of God, the holy, great, and ecumenical council occurred in Nicaea on God's command through his servant, the most God-beloved emperor Constantine. 6. And the actions taken during it by the Holy Spirit through the holy, orthodox chief priests there—three hundred in number—on behalf of the apostolic and orthodox faith our account has presented as plainly as I am able by the grace of our God, Christ. 7. Now, I will proceed onward from there to a

---

1. The word used here is εἰκών, "image" or "icon." Although this text predates fully developed icon theologies, the phrasing may suggest that Cyzicenus wishes his readers to view the narrative devotionally. See Tandy 2023, 114–15.

narrative on the emperor's piety and how he maintained his assiduous care for the churches of God.

> Concerning the Unceasing Zeal of the
> Emperor concerning Divine Matters

2.1.[2] The fire of Christianity within him was so indescribably great as to lead even all those outside[3] to the true recognition of the living God.[4] For he sent instruction to all the peoples living under the dominion of the Romans, exhorting them to reform from their prior deception and urging them to convert themselves to the teaching of God our Savior. And he exhorted them all to come to this truth, adopting an apostolic goal, rather than an imperial one.[5] 2. And he roused the bishops throughout the city to the construction of churches, urging them to this, and not by words alone but even making liberal grants of money and providing all the expenses for the construction. And indeed, the things written by him make this clear, and those writings run as follows.[6]

---

2. As in the later parts of book 2, in the third book Cyzicenus infrequently cites his sources, to which he makes increasingly numerous alterations in tone and content. Cyzicenus follows the general sequence of events found in Theodoret, interspersing his narrative with passages from other sources. As Cyzicenus does not often mark his transitions or make explicit citations, we have left most material between cited documents unmarked by breaks or indentation. Where possible, we have identified the source materials in the footnotes, noting major differences.

3. "Those outside" translates οἱ ἔξω and refers to those "outside" the Christian polity. Eusebius states in *Vit. Const.* 4.24.1 that Constantine described himself as "bishop over those outside."

4. An unmarked transition here begins a lengthy passage through 3.7.13 seemingly borrowed from Theodoret, *Hist. eccl.* 1.14.12–1.18.9, with one identifiable excerpt from the Gelasian history (see below notes 26, 28, 29).

5. The differentiation between apostolic and imperial goals does not appear in Theodoret.

6. The following sequence of three letters is preserved at various places in Eusebius's *Life of Constantine*: Cyzicenus, *Hist. eccl.* 3.3.1–4 = *Vit. Const.* 2.46; Cyzicenus, *Hist. eccl.* 3.4.1–5 = *Vit. Const.* 4.36; Cyzicenus, *Hist. eccl.* 3.5.1–8 = *Vit. Const.* 3.30–32. Socrates (*Hist. eccl.* 1.9.46–63) is the earliest surviving source to juxtapose all three letters in the same sequence that Cyzicenus follows, positioning them chronologically near the Council of Nicaea. Theodoret (*Hist. eccl.* 1.15–17) reproduces the same series of letters but inserts them after the death of Arius. Cyzicenus uses Socrates's chronology, but Theodoret's transitional material suggests either that Cyzicenus was compar-

A Letter of the Emperor Constantine to Eusebius Pamphili concerning the Building of Churches

3.1.[7] The victor, Constantine Maximus Augustus, to Eusebius,

Since an unholy design and tyranny were persecuting the ministers of God and our savior up until the present time, I have come to believe and through careful consideration convinced myself that the edifices of all the houses of God either have been destroyed by neglect or have fallen short of the honor they deserve out of fear of threatened injustice, most beloved brother. 2. But now that freedom has been restored and that serpent has been driven off from the administration of government by the providence of God, who accomplishes all things, and by our service, I deem that the divine power has become manifest to all and that those who fell away due to fear, faithlessness, or any errors but who recognize God as he truly is will come to the true and correct faith and direction for their life.[8] 3. Now then, however many of these churches either you yourself direct or for which you know the other bishops and presbyters or deacons who direct them in each locale, put it in their minds to be eager about the work of building the churches,

---

ing the two sources, taking his surrounding narrative from Theodoret and electing to use Socrates's chronology, or that Theodoret's contextual material itself derives from the Gelasian history.

7. In Eusebius's *Life of Constantine*, this letter forms part of the depiction of Constantine's restoration of Christianity in the Eastern Roman Empire after his battle with Licinius, and is placed contemporaneously (probably correctly) with two other imperial letters to the provinces of the East that date to late 324 or early 325 (*Vit. Const.* 2.24–42, 2.48–60). Socrates includes this letter without comment in a series of documents issued immediately after the Council of Nicaea and before the death of Arius (*Hist. eccl.* 1.9.46–50). Theodoret places this letter immediately after his narration of the death of Arius (*Hist. eccl.* 1.15.1–2). Altering the timing of the letter shifts the calamity described by the emperor from one of political upheaval, where Licinius plays the role of the serpent and the errors of the faithful are due to military force, to a narrative about theological upheaval, in which Arius as serpent drags Christians away from true faith through fear and deception. That Socrates, Theodoret, and Cyzicenus all displace this document to after the Council of Nicaea may indicate that the Gelasian history did as well.

8. In the context of Cyzicenus's narration, the serpent refers simultaneously to Arius and to the devil, a conflation that Cyzicenus had made in the *proemium* as well (*proem.* 19).

either to repair those that exist or to make them even larger, or else, where need should demand it, to build new ones. 4. And you yourself and the rest of them through you shall request the necessary materials from the provincial governors and the office of the prefect.[9] For they have been instructed by letter to obey with all zeal the words spoken by your holiness. God will preserve you, beloved brother.

3.5. These instructions, then, did he send concerning the construction of the churches both to Eusebius Pamphili himself and to the bishops who held authority throughout each province. 6. And the sorts of things he also wrote to Eusebius of Palestine himself concerning the production of holy books are easily learned from the missive itself.

A Letter of the Emperor Constantine concerning the Production of Holy Books

4.1.[10] The victor, Constantine Maximus Augustus to Eusebius, the bishop,

Throughout the city named after us, by the aid of God's providence, a great multitude of people has devoted itself to the most holy church, such that everything there is experiencing great growth. It has become clear to us that it is especially worthy for more churches within the city to be properly outfitted. 2. For that reason, receive most eagerly what our deliberation considers appropriate.

---

9. I.e., the Praetorian prefect of the East.

10. From nearby chronological evidence in Eusebius's *Life of Constantine* (*Vit. Const.* 4.36.1–4), it would appear that this letter was sent in the mid-330s, near the celebration of Constantine's thirtieth year of rule. Cyzicenus's chronology, like that of Socrates (*Hist. eccl.* 1.9.50–55), instead places the letter in the immediate wake of the Council of Nicaea. Theodoret (*Hist. eccl.* 1.16.1–4), by contrast, places this letter later, after the death of Arius, and thus in the mid-330s. Cyzicenus, Socrates, and Theodoret all place this letter between the letter on the construction of churches just quoted above (3.3.1–4) and the letter to Macarius of Jerusalem on the Holy Sepulcher (3.5.1–8). In Eusebius's *Life of Constantine*, the source of these documents, the letters on the building of churches and the Holy Sepulcher, appear in book 3, while the letter on the production of Scriptures appears much later, in book 4. If Cyzicenus, Socrates, and Theodoret are all dependent on the Gelasian history, then this arrangement of the documents may derive from it.

It seemed fitting to us to clarify this for your understanding, that you should command that fifty codices on well-crafted parchment, easy to read aloud and easy to use,[11] be written by skilled calligraphers with precise understanding of their craft, particularly for the divine writings,[12] the provision and use of which you know are necessary for the teaching of the church.[13] 3. And letters have been sent out by our clemency to the manager of our finances so that he can see to supplying all the necessities for their provision.[14] 4. For it will be your responsibility that the written codices might be prepared as quickly as possible. And it is likewise suitable for you to receive on the authority of our missive the right to use two state carriages for their transportation. 5. For thus most easily would what has been written most beautifully be conveyed before our eyes—of course one of the deacons of your church will accomplish this. And when he arrives in our presence, he will come to know our benevolence. God will preserve you, beloved brother.

4.6. Now, even just these points provide sufficient evidence, or rather teach clearly, how the all-praiseworthy emperor, as we also have said above, turned all his efforts toward the business of the divine.[15] 7. Nevertheless, I will add to what has been said an account of his achievements concerning the salvific tomb. For when he learned that persons possessed with Corybantic and Bacchic frenzy in service to idols had buried the tomb of our master, our Lord, and were zealously striving to consign the memory of the Savior of humankind to oblivion, and on the spot built a house for the licentious demon Aphrodite, the most faithful emperor ordered for that abominable edifice to be destroyed as quickly as possible. And he commanded that the land

---

11. The term translated "easy to use" (εὐπαρακόμιστα) could also mean "portable" or "easy to carry."

12. In the other versions of this text, it is clear that Constantine is only discussing texts of religious significance, specified with the phrase "that is, of the divine writings" (τῶν θείων δηλαδὴ γραφῶν). In Cyzicenus, the specifying word δηλαδὴ, "that is," has vanished, and the word μάλιστα ("particularly") has moved from its position in the following clause, where the other witnesses have it. This creates some ambiguity as to what Cyzicenus is envisioning for the scope of Constantine's project.

13. The Greek phrase τῆς ἐκκλησίας λόγος could mean "teaching of the church," "preaching of the church," or perhaps "reading of the church."

14. Probably the *comes rerum privatarum*, the minister of imperial finances.

15. This sentence is added by Cyzicenus as a cross-reference to 3.1.7.

that had been contaminated by polluted sacrifices be dug out and thrown far away from the city.[16] And then he ordered the largest and most beautiful temple to be constructed for God our Savior. 8. These matters are explained more clearly by the letter of our most God-beloved emperor, which he sent to the leader of that church, I mean of the church in Jerusalem. And at that time, it was Macarius, of whom I also made mention previously, who had participated in the great council in Nicaea and quenched the flame of the blasphemy of Arius together with the others.[17]

A Letter from Constantine the Pious Emperor to the Bishop of Jerusalem concerning the Salvific Tomb

5.1.[18] The victor, Constantine Maximus Augustus, to Macarius, bishop of Jerusalem.

So great is the grace of our Savior that I believe no abundance of words seems worthy of the present wonder. For the mark of that most holy tomb, although long ago hidden under ground through so many cycles of the years, was not able to be forgotten, until such a time as, through the grace of God our Savior, the usurpation of the common enemy of us all was undone. And the emperor of all, Christ, granting his own servants freedom from all tyranny whatsoever, has illuminated the knowledge of the most holy tomb, so

---

16. Cyzicenus's narrative (= Theodoret, *Hist. eccl.* 1.16.5–6; see also Eusebius, *Vit. Const.* 3.25–29) gives a more vibrant depiction of the rites practiced at the temple of Aphrodite. The Corybants were notoriously rambunctious worshipers of Cybele, a goddess with Phrygian origins, and were often depicted as consisting solely of eunuchs. Bacchus was the ancient Greek god of wine and ecstasy. By associating these two divinities with Aphrodite, goddess of sexual attraction and love, the text evokes the image of a wild, drunken orgy occurring over the tomb of Christ.

17. With the term κατέλυσε ("quenched" or "utterly destroyed"), Cyzicenus's text implies a more definitive end to Arianism than Theodoret, who says simply that Macarius "contended against" (κατηγωνίσατο) the blasphemy of Arius. Macarius was bishop of Jerusalem from 312 to 335 CE and was one of the signatories to the decisions of Nicaea (see 2.28.7, 2.38.3). Theodoret had previously named Macarius as one of the principal enemies of Arius (*Hist. eccl.* 1.5.6; see also 1.14.3–8). It is uncertain whether Cyzicenus has directly borrowed Theodoret's citation, which points to prior discussion of Macarius, or whether they both have borrowed it from a shared source.

18. In the *Life of Constantine* (3.30–32), this letter (the last of those to appear in this text from that source) is originally positioned immediately after the events of the Council of Nicaea, much as it remains in Cyzicenus.

that it truly surpasses all admiration.[19] 2. For if all those throughout the entire inhabited world who are reputed to be wise were to come to one and the same place and wished to say anything worthy of this occurrence, they would not be able to win even the smallest success, since indeed faith in this wonder is beyond every nature characteristic of human reasoning by the extent to which heavenly powers are known to be mightier than human powers. 3. For that reason, then, this is always my first and only goal: that just as faith in the truth proves itself daily by newer wonders, so also may all of our souls become more zealous toward the holy law, through prudence and likeminded enthusiasm.[20] 4. And since I think that this very fact is clear to all, it is my will that you most of all be persuaded of this: that of greater concern to me than all else is that holy place, which by the ordinance of God I have commanded to be relieved of the most shameful error of the false idol, as from an oppressive burden.[21] And though it has been holy in the judgment of God from the beginning and has been shown to be holier still from the time it brought to light belief in the suffering of our Savior, I have commanded you to adorn it with the beauty of buildings. 5. Now then, it is fitting for your sagacity thus to arrange and take forethought for each of the necessary items, so that not only may that basilica on that most holy site be more beautiful than those anywhere else, but also all other such structures there may be presented in such a way that all those buildings that beautify every other city are conquered by the splendor of this creation. 6. With regard to the raising of the walls and their beautification, know that our intention has been entrusted by us to our friend Dracilianus, who administers portions of the most

---

19. Cyzicenus's version of the letter changes the focus of the wonder Constantine describes. In Theodoret (*Hist. eccl.* 1.17), who follows Eusebius (*Vit. Const.* 3.30–32), the wonder is that the tomb has safely escaped notice under the assaults of the other emperors. Cyzicenus's version emphasizes that the tomb was *not* forgotten.

20. "Holy law" is a characteristically Constantinian phrase, found in many of his imperial letters, and refers, as here, to the doctrine, tradition, and practice of the church as a polity, and, on some occasions, to Scripture as the embodiment of and legislation of that doctrine, tradition, and practice.

21. Cyzicenus transmits the word "error" (πλάνης) where Eusebius and Theodoret have "addition" (προσθήκης).

illustrious provinces, and to the governor of the province.²² For it has been ordered by my piety that by their own provision they immediately send craftspeople and workers and whatever else that they may learn from your sagacity happens to be necessary for the construction. 7. And as for the pillars or the marbles that you might consider especially fitting or especially precious, hasten to write us when you have an estimate, in order that, however many and whatever kind we may learn from your missive are needed, all these can be transported from anywhere whatsoever, for the splendor of that dwelling. For it is right that this site so wondrous of the world should be made resplendent according to its worth. 8. And whether it seems right for the vaulting of the basilica of that same dwelling to have a coffered ceiling or be decorated through some other most splendid workmanship I wish to learn from you. For if it is to be coffered, it can be beautified by gilding as well. As for what remains, concerning these matters also your holiness shall make haste to inform the aforementioned magistrates how many workers, craftspeople, and expenditures you need. And hasten to deliver to me right away all matters pertaining not only to marbles and pillars but also to the coffering, if indeed you should judge this is the more beautiful. God will preserve you, beloved brother.

Concerning the Journey to Jerusalem of the Blessed Helena

6.1. No less than the mother of the emperor himself conveyed these letters,²³ she who was blessed with a beautiful child and is praised in song by all the pious, she who bore so great a luminary to the inhabited world and brought him up from childhood on the nourishment of piety.²⁴ For

---

22. Dracilian was vice Praetorian prefect in the diocese of the Orient in 326 CE. The lone manuscript of Cyzicenus's third book attests "most illustrious provinces" (ἐπαρχίων) rather than "most illustrious governors" (ἐπαρχιῶν), a translation of the Latin term for the office, *praefecti illustrissimi*. We have elected to preserve this discrepancy rather than correct the Cyzicenus manuscript to the majority reading, as Hansen (2002) does.

23. Theodoret's text emphasizes Helena as the agent ("the mother *herself*"), whereas Cyzicenus's text emphasizes her relationship to Constantine ("the mother of the emperor *himself*"). Cyzicenus frequently emphasizes Constantine's role in Helena's exploits (see, e.g., 3.7.5, 3.7.7, 3.7.10, et al.).

24. Relatively little is known about Helena outside the imperial tour of Palestine and Syria she took late in life, which Eusebius describes as a pilgrimage (*Vit. Const.*

she herself, no less than the father of her son, that is, her own husband, Constantius, raised him by the divine laws of piety toward Christ.²⁵ 2. And she bore the toils of the journey and took no consideration for the travails of old age. Indeed, she set off on that journey a little before her own end. For she reached the terminus of this life when she was eighty years old.

Concerning the Discovery of the Holy Cross of Christ

7.1. At any event, since she conceived a yearning and since a fiery spark kindled in her heart to see the holy places for herself and to seek out both the tomb of our Savior and the precious wood of the cross of Christ, she came to Jerusalem.²⁶ 2. And when she saw that land, the land that took on itself his sufferings for our shared salvation, straightaway she ordered that abominable temple to be razed to its foundations and for that polluted earth to be tossed somewhere far away. And when the formerly hidden site became visible, three crosses were seen to have been buried near the Master's grave. 3. And everyone believed without a doubt that one of them was in fact that of our Master and Savior, and the others were for the robbers who had been nailed up along with him.²⁷ But all the same they did not know which cross had drawn near to that holy body of the Lord and had taken on itself the drops of his precious blood. 4. But that wisest and truly godly Macarius, who was the leader of that church, resolved their

---

3.42.1–43.5). Most sources locate her birthplace in Drepanum, not far from Nicomedia and Nicaea, and imply she was of low birth. She was the first partner to Constantius, and Constantine was her only known child. In 289 CE, Constantius separated from Helena to marry Theodora, the daughter of the Western Augustus, Maximian. See Drijvers 1992.

25. This sentence appears only in Cyzicenus's text. Helena's low status and reputed early life as an inn worker led to some disparagement and implied uncertainty about Constantine's lineage. See Drijvers 1992, 15–18.

26. The origin of this story about Helena is difficult to determine. Although much of the text parallels that of Theodoret, substantial parallels with Rufinus's more concise version suggest that Cyzicenus consulted the Gelasian history. How much of the expansion found in Cyzicenus's text can be traced to that work cannot be determined with any precision. For the reconstruction of the Gelasian narrative, see Wallraff, Stutz, and Marinides 2018, 120–29. Theodoret's narrative progresses directly from what Cyzicenus says in 3.6.2–3.7.2; the intervening material in Cyzicenus (3.7.1) is of indeterminate origin.

27. Mark 15:27; Matt 27:38; Luke 23:32–33, 39–43; John 19:18.

perplexity in the following way.²⁸ He planned for the wood to be brought to a most eminent woman of that city who was gripped by a long illness and who had death in sight, and he discerned the power of the Savior's cross, employing a prayer to God such as follows: 5. bending his knees to the frail woman's pallet, he cried out with a great voice, while the most God-beloved Helena and a crowd of many people were with him. "You, Master, God the Almighty, who through your Only-begotten Son, Jesus Christ, obtained salvation for the race of humankind on the wood of the cross and who now has inspired your handmaid in these last days together with her son, your servant, to seek for the blessed cross on which Christ, the Savior of all humankind—most of all, the faithful—was nailed in the flesh, show to us, Lord, which of these three pieces of wood is the cross of Christ, who through the contact he has through us with this woman, weak and near death, may come to lead her by the hand to health and to rising once more."²⁹ 6. And once he ceased his praying, he brought forward the first piece of wood and touched it to the weakened woman, but it benefited her not. Then he proffered the second, but that one also proved itself useless. But when he extended his hand to the third, as soon as the shadow of the wood approached the weakened woman, an exceedingly great wonder also occurred. For suddenly the half-dead woman opened her eyes. Then, once the precious cross of the Lord was laid on her, she immediately leapt up and, rising to her feet, offered up glory to God. And when she became much stronger than she had been, going about the whole house and rejoicing with her whole household, she proclaimed with a great voice

---

28. The narrative's aggrandizement of Jerusalem and its bishop suggests that it derives from Gelasius, who, as nephew of Cyril of Jerusalem, benefited from legends about Jerusalem that increased the reputation of the see.

29. This dramatic narrative appears to derive from the Gelasian history (F15), since Theodoret passes over Macarius's prayer and the surrounding action, skipping directly to the successful conclusion of the test and the next part of the Helena narrative, while Rufinus preserves a nearly identical prayer. Cyzicenus presents three major details differently from Rufinus: the cooperation of Constantine in the search for the cross, the special emphasis on the salvation of the faithful over the general populace, and the presence of Christ "in the flesh" on the cross. Debates persist about the possibility of Gelasian origin of these three points. See Wallraff, Stutz, and Marinides 2018, 123 nn. 6–7. These themes, however, fit with the agenda of Cyzicenus, whose narrative focuses on the role of Constantine as the champion of Nicene orthodoxy, the necessity of proper faith, and the debates over the proper way to conceptualize the reality of Christ's humanity stemming from the Council of Chalcedon.

the power of the divine cross. 7. Thus the most pious empress, mother of the all-praiseworthy and most God-beloved emperor Constantine, having a pure understanding in her mind and showing her faith concerning the salvific tomb and the precious cross of Christ, immediately erected a house of prayer on the very spot in accordance with the orders of her most pious son, Constantine, and designating it as a "place of testimony," she progressed further and further still in her faith.[30]

7.8. Therefore, once she found what she was desiring, from then on she also dedicated herself ceaselessly to the search for the nails by which the Lord's body was nailed to the wood of the cross.[31] And when she found them, she inserted some of them into the imperial helmet, out of concern for her son's head, in order that the helmet might repel the arrows of his enemies. And she had this helmet transported to her son as a divine gift. The rest of the nails she had forged and incorporated into the bridle for the imperial horse, devising protection for the emperor and fulfilling an ancient prophecy. For the prophet Zacharias has proclaimed long before, "That which is on the bridle shall be holy to the Lord Almighty."[32] 9. She apportioned a certain part of the salvific cross for the palace. She had a case made for the remainder out of silver material and gave it to the bishop of that city, to that godly Macarius, of whom we made mention above as well, ordering him to preserve these reminders of salvation for the generations thereafter. 10. Then, together with Macarius, who was the leader of the church there, in accordance with the orders given by the emperor, her son Constantine, she gathered craftspeople skilled in working every kind of material from everywhere. And she built wondrously those greatest and most resplendent temples, the beauty and the greatness of which I have considered utterly superfluous to include in this account, since, in a word, all those who love Christ from the entire land under heaven stream in together there and gaze on the sumptuousness of those works.[33]

---

30. A "place of testimony" (μαρτύριον) was a site commemorating testimony to Christ. Generally this meant a memorial either to one who had borne such testimony (i.e., a martyr) or, as here, to the site where such testimony was manifested by, for example, a miracle.

31. The section that follows agrees in large part with the text of Theodoret, *Hist. eccl.* 1.18.5–9, with additional statements deriving from either Gelasius or Cyzicenus himself.

32. Zech 14:20. In the original Hebrew context, "holy to the Lord Almighty" is an inscription written on the bells of the horses, but the LXX translation leaves the grammar ambiguous, allowing for the interpretation here in Cyzicenus that the nails themselves are holy objects and thereby fulfill the prophetic text.

33. In particular, the Church of the Holy Sepulcher; see above, 3.4.7–3.5.8.

7.11. And that all-praiseworthy and admirable empress, the mother of the most faithful emperor, did another act worthy of remembrance. For when she had gathered all those who were practicing virginity throughout their life and had them recline on several couches, she fulfilled the role of a handmaid herself, serving them, providing food, taking their goblets and pouring the wine, carrying a pitcher on a basin and pouring water over their hands. 12. And when she had accomplished these things and others like them, she returned to her son, rejoicing; but not much later, in all cheerfulness, she crossed over to the life imperishable, after enjoining her son at great length to a pious mode of life and wreathing him with her farewell blessings. Therefore, she met with honor after her death, which was of the sort that was fitting for one who served the God of the universe so diligently and fervently to meet. 13. And she left behind a daughter, Constantia by name, who had been the wife of the impious Licinius.[34]

7.14. Of her many and great virtues in regard to God our Savior, just these few details have I set down in this historical account concerning the most blessed, most pious, and most God-beloved Helena.

Concerning the Forum of Emperor Constantine

8.1.[35] But I shall turn my account once more to the godly zeal of the Christ-bearing emperor Constantine, the son of this woman, who so surpassed the zeal of his father and mother for the salvation of Christ that he—trusting in the symbol of the saving cross of our master Christ's suffering according to the flesh, which his mother had brought to him,[36] and trusting that the

---

34. In a curious departure from historical reality, Cyzicenus's account combines the various Christian relatives of Constantine into one cohesive family unit, a maneuver not found in the other closely associated sources. Constantia was in fact the daughter of Constantius and Theodora, whom Constantius married in 289 CE to cement his political alliance with her father, Maximian, who was at that time Augustus. In 3.12, Cyzicenus again emphasizes a close familial connection between Constantia and Helena, although there acknowledging the former as Constantine's half-sister.

35. 3.7.14–8.1 presents a jumbled transition from material derived from either Theodoret or the Gelasian history to material derived from either Socrates or the Gelasian history. Whichever the case, Cyzicenus's text confuses the grammar and results in a complex prolepsis, which we have tried to resolve by including the participle *trusting* (πιστεύσας) twice, to cover both of its grammatical functions in the sentence that follows.

36. Cyzicenus's authorial aside transitions without notice into a passage that echoes the language of Socrates (*Hist. eccl.* 1.17.8), who may have used the Gelasian history.

city, the one named after him, would always be preserved if that symbol was protected in the city—hid it, placing it within a statue of himself that was in the so-called agora (or rather, forum) "of Constantine" and which he set atop a great porphyry pillar.[37]

Concerning Frumentius and Edesius and Those in Inner India

9.1.[38] Thus the most God-beloved emperor, fortified by such piety and faith toward God, made preparations for a great many other barbarian peoples to come to peace with him, since God placed in subjection to him those who had often been at variance with the Romans in the past.[39] For the more he humbled himself in reverence for God, by that degree and indeed even more so by far did God make all things prosper for him. 2. And throughout that time, several advances were made for apostolic preaching. For although Matthias preached to the Parthians, Bartholomew to the Ethiopians, and Thomas to the Indians of Greater India, still word about Christ was not yet known to the Indians farther from the Parthians or to some peoples who bordered them.[40] 3. It happened then that, in imitation of a

---

Cyzicenus, in turn, may have referred to Socrates for the information, or directly to the Gelasian history, from which much of the material to follow appears to derive as well. The repetition of Christ's suffering in the flesh does not parallel Socrates's version or other accounts derived from the Gelasian history and thus suggests that the insistence on the corporeality of Christ belongs to Cyzicenus (see also Macarius's prayer above at 3.7.5).

37. The column still stands in Istanbul. According to Eusebius, *Vit. Const.* 3.48.2, Constantinople was devoid of idols. The Chronicon Paschale 528–529, however, makes it clear that Constantine adorned the city with statuary and other art brought from other locales to the new capital. See further Bassett 2004.

38. Comparisons with Rufinus, Socrates, Sozomen, and Theodoret show that 3.9.1–3.10.27 derives from Gelasius. Cyzicenus often offers more detail than the other four, and it is uncertain what parts derive from the Gelasian original and what is original to Cyzicenus. Inner India refers to the ancient kingdom of Aksum, located in the region of modern Ethiopia and Eritrea.

39. Both Rufinus (*Hist. eccl.* 10.8) and Socrates (*Hist. eccl.* 1.18.4) specifically mention Sarmatians and Goths, in addition to the catchall category of "barbarians."

40. For Romans, "Ethiopia" could refer to either the horn of Africa, territory south of the Nile (including, for example, Aksum and also the ancient kingdom of Kush), or generally all of sub-Saharan East Africa. The use of *Ethiopia* here implies one of the later meanings since Aksum is later specified as the place of missionary activity and referred to as (Inner) India. *Parthians* here means "Persians," using an old Roman

certain philosopher, Metrodorus, who had journeyed around to nearly all peoples for the sake of personal inquiry, a certain Tyrian man by the name of Meropius, notable among philosophers, embarked on the same task that Metrodorus had, for the sake of personal inquiry.[41] And he brought with him two boys who grew up together, who, after they had been exceedingly well-enculturated in all forms of literary education, were eagerly curious to make all sorts of inquiry and who themselves had requested of the philosopher Meropius that he bring them with him. Of these, one was named Frumentius, the other Edesius. 4. And since it was custom and law for the barbarians there, if the Romans were not adhering to the treaties of peace with them, to kill those of us who were found among them, it so happened then also that the treaties dissolved on both sides for a short time at the time that Meropius was investigating Inner India together with Frumentius and Edesius. 5. Therefore, in desperate straits due to a lack of necessities, particularly water, they departed from the countryside and took to the sea. And they came to anchor in various places throughout those of Inner India, since they were not able to sail onward, prevented by the contrariness of the winds. And indeed, for a number of days they stayed there unnoticed, procuring from the land there their bodily needs. 6. But on one of the days, when the children were taking time out for their readings underneath a tree, barbarians appeared and slaughtered all of them along with Meropius except for the aforementioned boys, Frumentius and Edesius, since when they saw them, they took pity on them on the grounds that they spared children, and they brought them as a gift for their own king. Of the two of them, since the king immediately noticed Frumentius's noble bearing, he made him the manager of the expenses accrued at his palace, and he appointed Edesius to pour his wine.[42]

---

name for the people. The territory of the Parthians means the Sasanian, Persian Empire neighboring Rome.

41. The character of Metrodorus appears as an instigator of the Persian wars in Ammianus Marcellinus (*Res gest.* 25.4.23–24) and as a philosopher in Jerome's *Chronicle*. On his travels and relationship with the wars, see Warmington 1981. Meropius is known only from this story.

42. Theodoret (*Hist. eccl.* 1.23) refers to several biblical tales of God's faithful becoming trusted advisers in hostile territory, including Joseph in Egypt and Daniel, Shadrach, Meschach, and Abednego in Babylon. The king who accepted Christianity through Frumentius's intervention is widely held to be Ezana of Aksum (r. ca. 320–360).

9.7. And while the boys were among them and were making advancements day by day, it so happened that the king quietly departed this mortal life, leaving behind a son who was in all ways [still] a child as a successor to his own kingdom, with the approval of the high king of the Indians. 8. Now then, those around Frumentius became successive stewards of the entire kingdom for the boy, since his mother gave those two above all the power to have and exercise authority on account of their nobility of character and experience of human affairs. For they were possessed of both good nature and knowledge, previously polished particularly by their education and travels abroad, throughout which in particular they had the bearing of older men even as youths. 9. Now then, since they were also pious and both were preeminent in their faith toward God and excelled most people in all manner of affection toward humankind, they traveled land and sea, directing the affairs of the boy's kingdom, and they gave instructions to the bordering lands that they bring to them those of the Romans living abroad, taking care to sow knowledge of God among the Indians through these persons.[43] 10. For they found the times responsive. Indeed, at that time they found certain persons and convinced them to build places of prayer, using the customs of the Romans, and to construct houses for the church assemblies in order to gather those who were receiving the knowledge of God, even if they were not able also to erect altars on account of their not having priestly authority.[44] 11. Thus, from this act, there was occasion for those in farther India to come to knowledge of God, mostly through the benefaction, coaxing, and exhortations of Frumentius, who traveled to them out of noble ambition.

9.12. And when the royal child for whom they were exercising regency of the kingdom had grown up and had reached full maturity, they for their part requested the favor that he grant them their return to their own homes. But since the king, together with his mother, kept beseeching them with many entreaties and was restraining them and not letting them go, Frumentius said that they were extremely upset over this situation. Thereby they compelled the king and his mother to grant them release. And they assented, though with a great degree of distress; for they were unwilling to rebuff Frumentius, as their master. 13. And they both handed all the business of the kingdom that had been entrusted to them back to the boy and his mother,

---

43. Again, the text implies an ethnic or national link between Christianity and being Roman; see note to 2.7.19.
44. I.e., they had not been consecrated by a bishop, since there was as yet no clergy in this region.

and they departed from India with great honor, making a journey to their native lands. 14. Then finally Edesius came to Tyre, and Frumentius arrived at Alexandria, reckoning that it would not be fitting to leave unnoticed the divine deed accomplished among the barbarians. And when he had come to the bishop of the church of the Alexandrians, Athanasius (for at that time he himself held fast the helm of the high priesthood there), Frumentius informed him of each of the events that had occurred and suggested that he dispatch bishops to those people.[45] 15. Thereupon, the great Athanasius, heeding what was said with exceeding wisdom and intelligence, then said to Frumentius, "And what other man like this shall we find in whom is the Spirit of God within him as it is for you, brother, such that he is capable of directing these matters correctly and can guide the churches there as well as possible?" And after ordaining him as a bishop, he ordered him to leave home once more for the Indians and to consecrate the churches there and take care of the people therein. 16. And the greatest grace of God was laid on this man after the ordination, such that he was emanating rays of apostolic light. For after he arrived at the aforementioned Inner India, he confirmed the gospel of Christ through signs and wonders and drew many multitudes of the Indians to the true faith of Christ, since they received in full legitimacy the divine word through him. For that reason, both the churches and the ordinations increased to a great number among those peoples. 17. Edesius, who remained in Tyre, related these matters to us.[46] For he became a presbyter of the church there and remained in it until the end of his life.[47]

Concerning the Iberians and Lazi and the
Holy Woman Captive among Them

10.1. Around the same time, both the Iberians and the Lazi near the land along the Pontus received the word of God, although they had not believed

---

45. Athanasius became bishop of Alexandria in 328.

46. Cyzicenus has copied his source's own citation. He could not have gotten this information from Edesius, whose mission occurred at least 140 years before Cyzicenus composed his text. Rufinus attests the same citation formula (*Hist. eccl.* 10.11), which Socrates (*Hist. eccl.* 1.19.14) attributes to Rufinus himself. Wallraff, Stutz, and Marinides (see Wallraff, Stutz, and Marinides 2018, 141) suggest that the story originated with Gelasius (F16), but Rufinus confirmed it personally.

47. Frumentius was eventually recalled to Rome by Constantius II to sit for a theological inquisition (Athanasius, *Apol. Const.* 29, 31). There is no evidence that King Ezana or Frumentius complied with the request.

it before this point.[48] And the reason for this greatest boon turned out to be a certain woman who was a captive among them, who by maintaining a practice of the highest of lifestyles through temperance and other virtuous works brought them all to a state of amazement.[49] 2. And when they inquired as to the reason for such great discipline, that holy woman said simply, "due to Christ, the Son of God." Now still, she did not bring anyone to pious belief just by that statement, but they were just amazed at the woman and they mulled over many things while observing her unusual lifestyle. 3. But since it was their custom, if they should have a child who fell ill, that they would go around to all the locals and procure a remedy from each of them, it so happened for this reason that a certain woman who had gone around to everyone came also to the captive woman.[50] 4. And the captive woman said to the woman who was standing by the door with her little child, "I will not be able to give any assistance to your little child, but I know that Christ, whom I have often spoken of to you, is able even to raise the dead and grant healing to those who are without hope."[51] And the child's mother beseeched the captive woman. Then, moved to pity for the woman who was begging, the captive swaddled the child in her own sackcloth and, after praying to God, gave the child back to the mother in good health.

10.5. Report of the event circulated to many people and even reached as far as the queen, who herself lay beset by a most grievous illness. And indeed, because she had been ill for such a long time, the effects of the most distressing illness that had befallen her were now incurable. Therefore, she thought it worthwhile to send for the captive through her servants and have her come into her presence. But the captive, out of reverential fear, refused to go to the queen, since she recognized the danger that steals in through the glorification of humans. 6. Indeed, when the queen learned

---

48. The Romans knew the region of modern Kartli, Georgia, as Iberia, and it is to the people living there, not on the Iberian Peninsula, that this passage refers. The Lazi (or Laz) inhabited the southeastern coast of the Black Sea, where there is still a significant Laz population to this day.

49. In other words, the native population was edified by contemplation of the woman's virtue, as manifested in ascetic practices. Asceticism is here positioned as a sign of Roman-Christian civilization in contrast to pagan barbarism.

50. According to Socrates (*Hist. eccl.* 1.20.3), this woman was the nurse to the prince, whose parents summoned the Christian captive shortly after she healed their son.

51. Only Cyzicenus has the captive woman refer to the story of Christ raising Lazarus from the dead (John 11).

that she was steadfast in her choice not to come for this reason, she ordered that she herself be brought on her stretcher to the captive woman. Won over by that woman's humility, the blessed captive in the same way swaddled the queen in the sackcloth on which she knelt to offer prayers to God by her customary prayer to Christ. And she sent the queen homeward in good health, rejoicing and walking on her own two feet, displaying a new and extraordinary wonder to the local population, confessing the grace of Christ, just as she had been taught by the captive woman. And as she was on her way, she exclaimed clearly: "Glory to you, Christ," she said, "master of the captive woman. Grace to you and all honor to you, Savior of those of us who have thought it fit to believe in you."[52]

10.7. And furthermore, the queen recounted each and every detail to her spouse and urged him to consider repaying the captive woman with what was necessary for repayment in good faith, on account of the benefaction she had made to his spouse. 8. And the queen said to him, "That captive woman, O king, does not desire silver, and she is not trying to acquire gold. But she is asking a considerable gift from us, namely that we believe this only: that Christ is the Son of God the Most High.[53] For her, all of life is fasting and temperance; superfluous are treasures in gold and silver. For I have in fact put the pious woman to the test. I am telling you the truth, O king. But if you take any consideration for my deliverance, let us repay this woman in a more uncustomary way: accepting her Christ for veneration." 9. But for a while he was disposed to be more reluctant, and indeed although he was reminded several times by his wife, he put off making good on her request with promises and he said that he was hoping for a suitable opportunity that would be advantageous to him for this. And such time came about in accordance with the providence of God, who wills that "all humankind be saved and come to knowledge of the truth."[54] 10. For it so happened that, while he was distracted on a hunt in an extremely deep and forested wood, night fell unexpected at midday. For suddenly at noon,

---

52. Or, if the verb is taken as passive, "we who are deemed worthy to believe in you." This prayer is unique to Cyzicenus.

53. According to Rufinus, the woman's request is that "we worship Christ, the God who healed me when she prayed" (*si eum, qui me illa invocante sanavit, Christum deum colamus*). The woman's specific insistence that the queen believe a basic tenet of Nicene orthodoxy in this version may stem from Cyzicenus's desire to emphasize the normativity of the Nicene faith across time and space.

54. 1 Tim 2:4. This biblical citation appears only in Cyzicenus's version.

throughout the entire wood a darkness spread, most deeply where the king was. And when those who were with him for the hunt found themselves separated higher and thither, a very great fear gripped the king, who could scarcely figure out how he might escape the incursion.[55] 11. And since all those with him were enduring the same distress (for the darkness held fast each of those who were trying to come to him in the place where it seized them, preventing them from going to assist one another), the king then recalled his wife and the captive woman who had healed her when she was incurable. And he cried out, saying, "Christ, the Lord of the captive woman, be near me now, so that I may flee the distress that lies on me. For I have my spouse as the clearest proof of your divine power."[56] And just as he ended his prayer, straightaway the shadow was lifted away and the light of day spread about even more than before throughout the entire wood where they had been held fast. 12. And when they arrived home, immediately they found the king safe and ordering for the captive to come before him straightaway, proclaiming that he was no longer venerating any god other than Jesus Christ, whom his wife revered.

10.13. Therefore, the captive woman came and became the king's teacher, after presenting to him every formulation from the creed.[57] And he rejoiced and was not ashamed that he was learning piety toward God from a lowly woman.[58] But, on the contrary, taking pride in her, he ordered that she be led into the middle of the crowd and spoke boldly, saying of her, "My wife escaped death through the prayer of this woman by

---

55. I.e., the "incursion" (ἔφοδον) of the sudden darkness.

56. Rufinus (*Hist. eccl.* 10.11) directly contradicts Cyzicenus here, saying that the king prayed "not with words, but in his mind alone." Socrates, Sozomen, and Theodoret do not shed any light on the text of the Gelasian history or whether Cyzicenus has deliberately altered this passage.

57. The expression used here, πάντα τὸν τύπον τῆς πίστεως, could be translated as "the entire form of the faith" and may have had that connotation in Cyzicenus's source. Cyzicenus's implicit connection of all these deeds after the Council of Nicaea to the council itself suggests, however, that Cyzicenus would have read it as a reference to the Creed of Nicaea. Contemporary theological debates also suggest this reading, as many parties emphasized the sufficiency of the Creed of Nicaea and the unsuitability of devising a new creed.

58. Again, Rufinus and Cyzicenus are at odds here, as Rufinus (*Hist. eccl.* 10.11) says that she only taught him "as far as it was right for a woman to explain these matters." The point of contention likely stems from 1 Tim 2:11–12, which forbids a woman to have authority over a man.

the grace of Christ, the King of all." And he convinced his subjects that, if they wanted to be saved, they should believe the same and take up veneration of Christ, disregarding their idols. 14. And when he learned from the holy woman that it was necessary to establish churches for the veneration of Christ, he immediately set about that task zealously. And once builders raised the outer wall of the dwelling, and once it was necessary thereafter to set up columns in the middle of the dwelling to divide the men and women who would gather there, God—in his desire to implant a firm conviction in the king and all those subject to him concerning the gospel of Jesus Christ, his Son, proclaimed through the captive woman—caused the third column, erected in the middle and still at a slant, not to be righted completely as the other two were.[59] And the craftspeople, while they were making great exertion, ripped and broke the netting along with their equipment, and they backed away, fleeing because they feared that those left on site would be killed by the column. For the column hung slanted in the air, since no such assistance as was customary practice for craftspeople was being taken into consideration by them. 15. The captive woman heard these things and, beset by great fear that the multitude might once again dedicate itself to idols,[60] came to that place as the sun was setting and, kneeling to God until morning, raised the column through her prayer, not yet set on the base but suspended upright above the base at the space of one cubit;[61] for God did not have it in his divine plan for the captive woman to leave the dwelling until the arrival of the crowd, in order that they might come to know her faith in the veritable God proclaimed by her. 16. Thus they came early, along with the king, and when they saw so great a column suspended upright, they were beside themselves. Then, when the captive woman came to the notice of them all on account of the course of events, and she had risen from her prayer, straightaway the column

---

59. Only Cyzicenus relates the detail that the row of columns was intended to divide the men from the women, but the strict division by sex is paralleled where Rufinus claims that the king proselytized the men, the queen the women (*Hist. eccl.* 10.11). Rufinus does not include a divine motivation for the trouble with the column, but Socrates (*Hist. eccl.* 1.20.15) states that the situation arose to prove the power of faith. Cyzicenus alone specifies that this faith concerns the gospel of Jesus Christ, the Son, rather than a general faith in God.

60. No other version of this story suggests that the populace was in danger of reverting to worshiping idols.

61. The cubit was a standard unit of measurement that varied by region. It was roughly the length of a human forearm.

was set in place perfectly, just as if some craftspeople were fitting it onto its proper base, and it had a stability fair to look on, just as great as the columns before and behind it. 17. After this, it so happened that the rest of the crowd also assembled and confessed the faith of their king, marveling at Christ. For that captive, holy woman bore full witness of this to them. For she had been anxious for the simplicity of the crowd that, goaded by their ancestral superstition, they might at some time transfer to her the devotion owed to Christ, that is to say, that they might hold an opinion about her that would not urge them on to piety. 18. On that account, she invited them to join in her prayer as well when she made the suspended column fit into its proper place, overshadowing their ingrained preconception through this act and saying that the active power of the Savior, Christ, is transferred to all people who are pious toward him in his deeds on behalf of humankind.

10.19. And after the church was completed, the captive woman advised the king and queen to send to their foster-brother in piety, the most God-beloved emperor Constantine, asking on their behalf that he send to them someone to consecrate that church. And then the ambassadors sent by the king and the citizenry of the Iberians reached Constantinople, announcing to the emperor Constantine that the faith of Christ had grown strong there and requesting that he send them a bishop for the consecration together with the regulation of the churches in their land. 20. And the pious and Christ-loving emperor Constantine received them kindly and, rejoicing in the Lord, granted their request, urging Alexander, the bishop of Constantinople, to ordain a bishop for the Iberians, seeing likewise that this was the will of God, who was subjecting foreign nations to him.[62] 21. The most faithful Bacurius was our teacher on these subjects, a man most devout and notable from the royal lineage among the Iberians, who was appointed satrap for the Romans. And after waging war in the mountains of Palestine against the Saracen barbarians, he completely and utterly achieved victory over them.[63]

---

62. Only Cyzicenus mentions Alexander, bishop of Constantinople, as the consecrating bishop. For Alexander, see 2.28.13 and note *ad loc*.

63. In the Roman period, the term *satrap* was reserved for foreign, allied commanders active along the Persian border. The technical title for Bacurius's position mentioned here is the *dux limitis Palaestinae*, commander of the Palestinian border, as reported by Rufinus (*Hist. eccl.* 10.11). As at 3.9.17, Cyzicenus reproduces a citation formula that cannot be his own, as Bacurius was long dead by the late fifth century.

10.22.[64] But we must return to that part of the history of the empire entrusted to us.[65] Accordingly, Emperor Constantine, since he was especially attentive to the Christian way of life and was fired up with the ardor of an apostle for Christ, began to build yet again other churches throughout various cities and provided for one at the so-called Oak of Mamre, beneath which the sacred writings recall that the angels were entertained as guests by Abraham.[66] 23. For the most excellent in every respect and most God-beloved emperor Constantine, upon learning that an altar was set up beneath that oak and that hellenizing sacrifices were performed on that altar, made his grievance known by letter to Eusebius, the bishop of Palestinian Caesarea, who had overlooked such a loathsome act of impudence.[67] And he ordered that the altar be demolished and for a church of the living God to be provided for near the oak. 24. And when he further learned that those in Heliopolis of Phoenicia were still living impiously and engaging in a disgraceful practice, he did away with their shameful lifestyle through a solemn law and, after creating a church in that city, making preparations for a bishop to be ordained, and ordering that a holy clergy be

---

Rufinus preserves more information about Bacurius and likely had the opportunity to converse with him, since Bacurius is known to have been to Rome during the Battle of the Frigidus in 394 CE. On the confusing relationship between Cyzicenus and Rufinus here, see Wallraff, Stutz, and Marinides 2018, 157 n. 7.

64. The passage from 10.22–25 on Constantine's opposition to non-Christian traditions is probably derived from the Gelasian history (F16c). Eusebius and Socrates both describe construction of the church at Mamre immediately following the construction of the basilica in Jerusalem and the death of Helena (Eusebius, *Vit. Const.* 3.51–53; Socrates, *Hist. eccl.* 1.18.5–11). Cyzicenus and Socrates do not agree on all points, for which see Wallraff, Stutz, and Marinides 2018, 157–59.

65. Following the manuscripts against Hansen's suggested deletion of the phrase "of the empire" (τῆς βασιλείας).

66. Gen 18:1–15; whereas Eusebius follows more closely the narrative of Genesis, in which the visitors to Abraham are God, Socrates and Cyzicenus interpret the three as angels.

67. According to Eusebius, this letter was addressed not only to him but to Macarius and the other bishops of Palestine; the letter itself is quoted in full at *Vit. Const.* 3.52.1–3.53.4. Given that Socrates likewise names Eusebius as the recipient (*Hist. eccl.* 1.18.6), it is possible that the Gelasian history omitted reference to the other recipients, possibly by misconstruing Eusebius's introduction of it in the *Life of Constantine*. The address to Eusebius of Caesarea fits within a larger pattern in Cyzicenus's history of praising the historian and exonerating him of theologically questionable positions (see 2.1.8–11, 2.17–20, 2.35, 3.16.13–14).

consecrated with him in that church itself, in this way he turned the evils of the Heliopolitans rather toward temperance.[68] And not only that, but he also selected those who were Christians and attested for their honorable lifestyle and appointed them as political leaders for the city and the entire surrounding countryside. And he threatened the people there with death if they did not change as quickly as possible from the shameful conduct to which they were previously accustomed and from their superstition surrounding their loathsome idols.[69] 25. And furthermore, he uprooted the [temple] of Aphrodite in Aphacus <...> for its unmentionable vice and drove out the Pythonic demon in Cilicia, ordering that the temple in which he lurked be torn up from its foundations.[70]

10.26. Such worthy deeds did the most faithful emperor Constantine perform throughout the whole earth. And I shall set forth in this ecclesiastical history yet another piece of evidence for the faith of this same, most God-beloved emperor Constantine toward the God of the universe. For his longing and zeal for Christ was so great that he planned to go forth even to Persians on behalf of the Christians there, and to order that a tent of finely woven linens be erected in the form of a church and—as Moses had done in the desert—that this tent be carried along the road, so that he might have a suitable place of prayer throughout the desert places, in which he was to send up his prayers to God.[71] 27. But it did not come to pass that

---

68. Socrates (*Hist. eccl.* 1.18.7–11) gives further detail on the alleged sexual practices of the Heliopolitans, some of which derives from Eusebius's account (*Vit. Const.* 3.58.1–3). Eusebius also focuses on a statue constructed to replace the idol of Aphrodite and Constantine's communications with the Heliopolitans, neither of which appears in Cyzicenus.

69. Only Cyzicenus claims that Constantine reorganized the local politics by appointing Christians and threatened the death penalty for violating the new principles.

70. The manuscripts for this passage include a lacuna, and we have supplied the noun "temple" for the clause concerning Aphaca, following the text of Socrates (*Hist. eccl.* 1.18.10). Eusebius gives more detail about the destruction of both temples (*Vit. Const.* 3.55–56), but Socrates is similarly brief. Aphaca, or Afqa today, is situated near Heliopolis (Baalbek) and was the legendary site of the death of Aphrodite's lover Adonis (see Lucian, *Syr. d.* 6; Zosimus, *Hist. nov.* 1.58.1). According to Sozomen (*Hist. eccl.* 2.5.5), the temple of Asclepius was located in the city of Aigai, near modern Yumurtalik, Turkey. The "Pythonic demon" is Asclepius, a healing god associated with both snakes and prophecy, much like his father, the god Apollo, whose oracle was situated where he slew the snake, Python.

71. Cyzicenus presents a very different motive for the intended journey to Persia from Socrates. Socrates openly states that war with Persia was imminent (*Hist. eccl.* 1.18.12), while Cyzicenus makes his intention one of apostolic mission.

he would complete the journey to Persia then as was his intention, taking care as he was for the peace of God's churches. And the emperor,[72] taking forethought for those nourished on piety under his care there—I mean the Persians—because he understood that they were being persecuted by the impious there and that that emperor there himself, since he was enslaved to error, was devising schemes of all sorts against them (and this was Shapur), wrote to him, advising him to be pious and requesting that the pious and Christian enjoy respect.[73] And his very writings will show clearly the zeal of the Christ-loving emperor.

A Letter from Emperor Constantine to Shapur, King of the Persians, concerning the Care of the People of God

11.1.[74] Preserving the divine faith, I take part in the light of the truth; led by the light of the truth, I recognize the divine faith. Therefore, as the facts confirm, I recognize that most holy worship is our teacher in the knowledge of the most holy God. I profess that I maintain this form of worship. Since I possess the power of this my God as an ally, beginning from the ends of the ocean, I have raised the entire inhabited world part by part with the surest hopes in salvation. And

---

72. The following two sentences appear to depend on the text of Theodoret (*Hist. eccl.* 1.24.12–13), introducing Constantine's letter to Shapur, though Cyzicenus's text has several confusing additions. Theodoret does not imply that Constantine's Christian duties extend beyond his political realm the way that Cyzicenus does by claiming the Persian Christians were "under his care." Cyzicenus also specifies that it is not only the pious who deserve honor but the pious "and Christian," which Theodoret does not. The phrase "I mean of Persians" is necessitated by the awkward transition between material paralleled in Socrates, and probably deriving from the Gelasian history, and material from Theodoret. The subject of Persia links the narratives, but Socrates concludes his discussion of Constantine's church-building activities with an authorial aside about the goals of his history. By preserving the concluding statement that Constantine never reached Persia, Cyzicenus's narrative has to pivot back and reconnect the ideas. Theodoret's own narrative is much clearer.

73. Shapur II (309–379 CE) was the Sasanian emperor during the reign of Constantine and his sons. On Christians and Roman relations with the Sasanians, including this letter, see Smith 2016.

74. Constantine's letter to Shapur appears in Eusebius (*Vit. Const.* 4.9–13) and Theodoret (*Hist. eccl.* 1.25). Cyzicenus appears to have consulted the latter, as he copies Theodoret's transitional material surrounding the letter. On the question of the letter's true authorship and motivations, see Frendo 2001; see also Smith 2016.

thus all nations however many, enslaved by just as many tyrants, which had become next to nothing, beleaguered by daily misfortunes, these nations, now that they are taking advantage of the state's legal protections, as if revived by some great cure, they speak with confidence, rejoice and celebrate festivals in praise to God.[75] 2. I myself am an ambassador for this God, and my army, dedicated to him, bears his standard on their shoulders and is directed to whatever tasks the word of justice may summon it. From these very men forthwith I receive favor through brilliant victory trophies. I have been fully enlightened with unsullied and pure understanding that this God is in the highest regions. 3. And this God I call on with knees bent, avoiding all abhorrent blood and odious, ill-omened scents, shunning all the luster whereby the utterly abominable and unlawful error delights many of the nations and stains all peoples, casting them down and handing them over to the nethermost regions.[76] 4. For the things that God has brought to light for our benefit, while taking forethought for humankind by his own love of humanity, these things revert evilly to the lust of every individual.[77] He requires from humankind only a pure mind and undefiled soul, weighing the deeds of virtue and piety performed among them. 5. For he takes pleasure in deeds of gentleness and kindness, having affection for the meek and hating the troublemakers; loving faith, punishing faithlessness; condemning all authority held arrogantly, he casts it down; he punishes the hubris of the haughty; those puffed up with vanity he uproots from their foundations.[78] 6. Because he values a just sovereignty highly, he strengthens it with his aid, and he protects a sovereign's wisdom with the tranquility of peace. There-

---

75. In the text of the letter preserved by Eusebius and Theodoret, the revival of the nations is the end result of Constantine's efforts, to which Cyzicenus's text adds the speaking, rejoicing, and celebrations.

76. Where Cyzicenus says that error "delights" (χαίρουσα) many of the nations, Eusebius and Theodoret say that it "stains" (χραινομένη) them. Cyzicenus repurposes the verb for staining (χράνασα) immediately thereafter.

77. This sentence is extremely difficult to make sense of as preserved in Cyzicenus. In Eusebius (*Vit. Const.* 3.10) and Theodoret (*Hist. eccl.* 1.24), the idea is rather that God "does not allow these [benefits] to be diverted at each person's desire." A variety of alterations and absences make this interpretation impossible for the text as preserved for Cyzicenus.

78. Isa 13:11. Eusebius and Theodoret both contain the additional statement "granting just rewards to the humble and those who endure ills."

fore rejoicing, I am overjoyed, brother.[79] I confess that this God is the Ruler and Savior of all,[80] whom many of those who have been emperors here have tried to deny, compelled by maddening errors. But an avenging end of such kind has consumed all of them that the entire race of humankind that has come after them sets the misfortunes of those men as no different an example from the misfortunes among others eager to do likewise.[81] 7. Of these, I believe that one man has existed whom divine justice, like some thunderbolt, has driven away from those living here and sent over into your regions, where he has made the victory on your side very famous because of the shame brought on him.[82] But surely it seems to have turned out for the best that retribution against such persons has become widely recognized in the age in which we live. 8. For I myself beheld the ends of these people, who just recently were bringing the people devoted to God into disarray through their unlawful ordinances.[83] For that reason let there also be great thanks to God, since the entire human race that preserves his divine law is rejoicing and exulting in his perfect providence because peace has been granted to them.[84] 9. Thus, we ourselves also have been persuaded that he has arranged for us to keep everything as well and securely as possible, since he deems it worthy to gather every person to himself through the pure and proven worship of these people—I mean the peoples of God— by harmony about the divinity.[85] 10. How happy do you think it

---

79. Cyzicenus's text replaces the phrase "I do not think that I err" (οὔ μοι δοκῶ πλανᾶσθαι), attested in Eusebius and Theodoret, with the phrase "Rejoicing, I am exceeding glad" (διὸ χαίρων ἄγαν ὑπεραγάλλομαι).

80. The other witnesses attest "Ruler and Father of all" here.

81. Eusebius's and Theodoret's texts say instead that humankind "sets their misfortunes above all other examples for those among them eager to do likewise."

82. The subject of Constantine's criticism here is the former Roman emperor Valerian, whose attempts at a war with Persia famously resulted in his capture by Shapur I, great-grandfather to Shapur II. The "trophy" may refer to accounts that Valerian was made to serve as the Sasanian emperor's footstool and, upon death, was skinned and his hide displayed in a Persian temple (Lactantius, *Mort.* 5).

83. Constantine refers here to the deaths of the tetrarchs.

84. Cyzicenus attests "preserves" (φυλάττον) where other sources have "serves" or "restores" (θεραπεῦον).

85. In this sentence we read "every person" (πάντας), as in Eusebius, rather than Hansen's "everything" (πάντα). Within Cyzicenus's narrative, "harmony about the Divinity" may be read as a reference to the Council of Nicaea.

makes me to hear this catalog of people who are my fellow servants, I mean, of course, the Christians (for my entire message has been on their behalf), since the mightiest regions of Persia, for the most part, are adorned as I would wish them to be.[86] And therefore, in as much as it is fitting if you should consent to distribute the best favors to them, may the best favors likewise be yours, since those people are also yours. 11. For thus you will keep the Master of the universe and God mildly, kindly, and favorably disposed. For that reason therefore, since you are such a great man, I commend these people to you, and because you are renowned also for your own piety, entrusting the governance of these people—I mean the Christians—to those among them who take leadership in pious worship toward God.[87] Love them as is in harmony with your benevolence. For you will do yourself (and also us) an indescribable favor through your good faith.

11.12.[88] The emperor Constantine, best in all ways, showed this much concern for those adorned with piety toward Christ, taking care not only for his own subjects but even, as much as it was possible, showing regard for those subject to other scepters. On account of this, he for his part had the favor of divine guidance from above; and taking the reins of all those not only in the world of the Romans but even of the barbarians as well, he kept rulers and ruled loyal to him, and they obeyed the guiding bridle of his will with pleasure.[89] 13. For even the barbarians thereafter served him willingly,

---

86. Constantine's claim to be a fellow servant to the Christians in Persia, though not out of character for Constantine's self-characterization (see 3.18.9–10), appears only in Cyzicenus.

87. A segment that appears only in Cyzicenus creates a grammatical ambiguity as to who is entrusting the Christians to the church leaders. The nominative case of the participle "entrusting" could refer either to Constantine himself, the overall subject of the sentence, or to Shapur, the subject of the most recent subordinate clause. In the second instance, this becomes a further command on what Shapur should do. Both Eusebius and Theodoret end the sentence with the participle for "entrusting," which would logically be referring to Constantine entrusting the Christians to Shapur.

88. This closing paragraph largely reproduces material Theodoret (*Hist. eccl.* 1.25.12–13) includes after the letter.

89. Cyzicenus's text attributes more total power to Constantine than Theodoret, the source for this passage, who says only that "all of Europe and Libya, and the greater part of Asia" were under Constantine's sway. Cyzicenus also adds that Constantine held both rulers and ruled in check.

overpowered by fear of war, since they feared the God who stood by Constantine. For trophies were set up everywhere, and the emperor proved victorious over everyone. But these affairs a great many others have recorded more accurately, giving praises to the glory of the God of the universe.[90] Let us direct the narrative once again to the sequence of the present history.

Concerning Constantia, the Sister of the All-Praiseworthy Emperor Constantine and the Arian Presbyter Whom She Introduced to Him

12.1.[91] Therefore, the most faithful emperor Constantine, taking forethought for the peace of the churches, carried his cares for them in his soul, in the manner of an apostle, just as we have said many times. But those who were called priests on their appearance, inasmuch as they had welcomed Arius's outrage, could not tolerate keeping quiet and undertook an implacable war against the truth, hatching intricate plots against right faith.[92] 2. For Constantia, the sister of the God-beloved emperor Constantine, who had become the wife of the impious Licinius and of

---

90. Both mentions of God in 3.11.13 are unique to Cyzicenus. The statement that "many others" have discussed this history is not original to Cyzicenus here but also found in Theodoret.

91. The story of the Arian presbyter gaining the trust of Constantia and Constantine (3.12.1–10) appears with varying detail in BHG 1279 (21.16–22.8), Rufinus (*Hist. eccl.* 10.12), Socrates (*Hist. eccl.* 1.25.1–4), and Theodoret (*Hist. eccl.* 2.3). From the similarities in the texts across sources, it is probable that the Gelasian history narrated the events (F17), although none of the later sources entirely agree on the timing of this episode. Rufinus and Theodoret place it shortly before the death of Constantine and carry over the remaining drama over the presbyter to the reign of Constantius II. Socrates and Rufinus agree that the episode occurred shortly after the conversion of the Iberians (see 3.10.1–22). Cyzicenus and Socrates agree on a long sequence of councils and trials that occurred because of the presbyter's success restoring Arius to the church and Arius's partisans to positions of influence. Cyzicenus includes most of the details found in BHG 1279, which Wallraff, Stutz, and Marinides (2018, 160–63) consider to be the most reliable source for the Gelasian text. However, at several places Cyzicenus reproduces information or phrases found in Theodoret. This may be evidence that Cyzicenus cross-referenced several histories or that BHG 1279 and Theodoret each selected different materials from their source. Hansen (2002) posits Philip of Side as a synthetic source that did the work of combining accounts for Cyzicenus. Cyzicenus's own authorial capacities, however, should not be underestimated.

92. 3.12.1 mostly parallels the content of Theodoret (*Hist. eccl.* 1.25.13), with different phrasing and vocabulary.

whom we made mention previously,[93] happened to make the acquaintance of a certain presbyter, of like mind with those in league with the blasphemy of Arius, a flatterer of the first order by the name of Eutocius.[94] 3. And at first he corrupted certain of Constantia's attendants,[95] but quite soon came face to face with Constantia herself as well. And since from her he was enjoying boundless freedom to speak openly as well as her protection because of their quite frequent meetings, his conversation with her concerning Arius began to make progress. 4. And so emboldened, thereafter he started to beguile her through his deceptive words: that malice, as he said, alone brought about opposition to Arius. And he persuaded her through these and similar deceptive words of his that Arius, as he said, was thinking and teaching the same things as Alexander and the bishops throughout the inhabited world.[96] 5. And Constantia believed what he was saying to her, especially when she heard from him that Arius was of like mind with Alexander, bishop of Alexandria, and that Pope Alexander had opposed him for no good reason, out of jealousy of his popularity among the masses.[97] And so it happened that Constantia, after accepting the words of the presbyter's deception regarding Arius, was herself pleased with what had been said and deemed that presbyter worthy of greater honor and kept him among her closest associates.[98] 6. But not long thereafter, she fell into a most grievous illness, in the course

---

93. See 1.8.1.

94. Cyzicenus is our only source for the name of this presbyter, Eutocius. This name is suspiciously similar to the leader of the group that Cyzicenus himself is writing against, Eutyches. Cyzicenus's text is also more condemning of Arius's supporters, saying they "shared in the blasphemy" (βλασφημίας κοινωνῶν) of Arius. Both BHG 1279 and Rufinus simply call them Arius's partisans (σπουδαστῶν/partibus Arrii faventem). Photius reproduces the name Eutocius in a sermon on the Arian heresy, deriving the name from this passage (*Hom.* 16). See Photius 1958, 261–62.

95. BHG 1279 tells that the presbyter made his first approach to the servants of Licinius's friends, suggesting that the issue began long before the point where Cyzicenus places it.

96. BHG 1279 says simply "as the bishops at Nicaea had expounded" (ὡς οἱ ἐν Νικαίᾳ ἐπίσκοποι ἐξέθεντο).

97. The comment about Alexander of Alexandria's jealousy does not appear in BHG 1279 but finds a parallel in Socrates (*Hist. eccl.* 10.11). "Pope" (πάπα) is first attested as a title for the bishop of Alexandria in a letter of Dionysius of Alexandria (r. 248–264), who applies it to his predecessor, Heraclas (Eusebius, *Hist. eccl.* 7.7.4).

98. Only Cyzicenus attests that the presbyter became a particularly close associate to Constantia.

of which she would also die. Now then, when the most pious emperor Constantine came to know of this, he came swiftly to her in order to look after her. For indeed after the death of her impious husband and the departure of the most God-beloved and all-praiseworthy Helena, their mother, for the life without pain, that all-praiseworthy and most God-beloved emperor considered Constantia worthy of all his concern, and he did not allow her to experience the distresses of widowhood and the loss of her parents.[99] And for this reason even up until her death itself he provided the care suitable for her both while he was away and when he was present. 7. And so, after much conversation between the emperor and Constantia, she said to him, as if she were confiding in her full brother, "Grant me one favor, O all-praiseworthy emperor, as I depart to God."[100] And the emperor said to her, "Whatever may that be?" And Constantia spoke to him: "I beseech you, emperor," she said, "that you order Arius to be released from his exile and that you mitigate the misfortune besetting him due to intrigue, and in a word that you not bring a stain on your pious reign with innocent blood."[101] 8. And so the emperor Constantine yielded to his sister, because he believed that she was saying these things to him out of sisterly affection and not that she had been beguiled by the presbyter of Arian persuasion, and because he believed that his sister was a steadfast adviser for him. 9. Up to this point he had prohibited Arius from approaching Alexandria and Egypt, but now he ordered that Arius straightaway be released from exile, due to the entreaty of Constantia, his

---

99. This sentence and the following mimic many of the phrases found in Theodoret's version of the story at *Hist. eccl.* 2.3.2. Theodoret, however, makes no mention of Helena or Constantia's status as an orphan. As at 3.7.13, Cyzicenus combines the two halves of Constantine's family into one Christian whole. It is not inconceivable that Constantia and Helena had a close relationship, as part of a blended family centered on the emperor himself. The date of death for Constantia's biological mother, Theodora, is a historical uncertainty. Coins issued in her name appeared only after the massacre of her surviving male children in 337. The reminder of Helena's devout belief serves to help characterize Constantia as likewise a pious Christian, despite her role in introducing Arian ideology into the emperor's palace.

100. The phrase "to God'" is unique to Cyzicenus, in similar fashion to how Helena's death is uniquely contextualized as a Christian death (3.7.11–13).

101. Cyzicenus has the most dramatic version of this conversation. BHG 1279 gives only a single statement to Constantia and none to her brother, while the remaining sources merely summarize the conversation.

sister.¹⁰² And Constantia commended to him even that presbyter of Arian persuasion,¹⁰³ enjoining the emperor to trust him and take pleasure in what he was saying, "Since I have experience of his righteousness, I present this man to you, most pious emperor." 10. And so Constantia slipped away from her mortal life. That presbyter, for his part, gained entry to the palace (for, of course, the most mild and God-beloved emperor, because he made a promise to Constantia who had requested that he do this, subsequently fulfilled his promise) and often was bidden to travel alongside the emperor. The emperor extended to him the greatest freedom to speak, and he became in every sense a member of the innermost circle of the Christ-bearing emperor Constantine.¹⁰⁴

12.11.¹⁰⁵ Upon hearing of these events, Eusebius of Nicomedia and Theognius of Nicaea, who were still living in exile, were emboldened to write a document on their supposed conversion and send it to the highest ranks of the bishops, begging that they be recalled from exile, maintaining in word, not in conduct, that even at an earlier time they received and supported the creed from Nicaea. 12. Moreover, since the bishops were merciful to them and accepted the document of their feigned repentance, they too, in accordance with their entreaty, were recalled from their exile by an imperial ordinance. And they recovered the churches from which they had been expelled, forcing out the bishops who had been ordained in their stead, Eusebius displacing Amphion, and Theognius displacing Chrestus. 13. And it would be fair to insert in this text a copy also of the document of their illegitimate repentance itself.¹⁰⁶ And it is as follows.

---

102. In BHG 1279, Constantine folds to the dual influence of Constantia and the presbyter. In Cyzicenus, the presbyter's influence is subordinate to Constantine's fraternal piety.

103. Only Cyzicenus's text reminds the reader that the presbyter is an Arian.

104. 3.12.10 loosely follows Theodoret, *Hist. eccl.* 2.3.5–6, with wording different enough to preclude direct reliance.

105. 3.12.11–3.13.6 narrates the Arian ringleaders Eusebius and Theognius's feigned conversion to Nicene theology. This same episode appears in Socrates (*Hist. eccl.* 1.14) immediately after the close of the Council of Nicaea. Cyzicenus's introduction to the letter is substantially longer than Socrates's, due to both additional contextual information and assertions as to the falsity of their conversion. In Cyzicenus's narrative, the world experiences a time of unanimity and conversion to true faith before Arius's partisans once again disrupt the peace.

106. Socrates calls their writing simply a "book" (βίβλιον), without casting aspersions on its legitimacy.

The Document of the Feigned Repentance of
Eusebius of Nicomedia and Theognius of Nicaea

13.1.[107] Now that we have been convicted by your holiness, we ought to bear in silence the verdicts of your sacred judgment. But since through our silence we are giving room to criticize us, for this reason we are reporting to your holiness both that we too have agreed with your holy council and that, upon close consideration of the idea, we have entirely come to peace with the idea of *homoousia*, in no way following the heresy. 2. And after we had made mention of whatever thoughts were occurring to us regarding the security of the churches and having reassured (and having been reassured by) those whom we needed to convince, we subscribed to the creed. But we did not sign on to the anathematization, not on the grounds of taking issue with the creed—far from it! Rather, it was because we do not believe that the accused was such a person, since we have been assured by those who had already come to us from him both through his letters and through our conversations face to face that he was not such a person. 3. But if your holy council was convinced, we do not resist, but we will consent to what has been decided by you and confirm this judgment, giving our assent in writing this, not because we find our exile burdensome but because we are aggrieved over the suspicion of heresy.[108] 4. For if you should now perchance think it worthwhile to receive us back into your own presence, you will have in us all confederates who follow what you have decided. For if it seemed right to your holiness that the very man who was accused in those matters of heresy[109] has received mercy from our most pious emperor and

---

107. The following letter appears both in Socrates (*Hist. eccl.* 1.14.2–6) and Sozomen (*Hist. eccl.* 2.16.3–7), but their source for the document is uncertain. Rufinus contains neither the letter nor reference to it, and Theodoret only mentions in passing the return of Eusebius and Theognius after their exile (*Hist. eccl.* 1.20.11). Neither Socrates nor Sozomen contains the direct reference to the Council of Nicaea at 3.13.1, and the section presenting Eusebius's and Theognius's self-justification for restoration is substantially more developed in Cyzicenus.

108. The manuscript for book 3 gives ἀποδυρόμενοι ("to be aggrieved"), where Socrates attests ἀποδυόμενοι ("to remove").

109. Neither Socrates nor Sozomen has the authors of the letter refer to Arius as a heretic, as Cyzicenus does here. Instead they merely call Arius "the man who was

has been judged worthy of clemency, and you accepted the plea for him to be freed from exile, how much more righteous it is that we who are guiltless also be deemed worthy of freedom from exile and of returning home to your holiness? 5. For it would be out of place for us to keep silent when the one deemed responsible has been let go, since we would give clear reasons for accusation against ourselves through our silence, as we have said before. Therefore, may you see fit, we beseech you, as is in harmony with your Christ-loving holiness, to remind our most God-beloved emperor about this matter and to place our requests in his hands and to make a decision as quickly as possible concerning us as to what suits you regarding us, most holy ones.

13.6. This is the document of recantation of the aforementioned Eusebius and Theognius. From their words it is clear that they signed the creed promulgated in the city of the Nicaeans by the holy council there by hand alone, not in intention, just as was also previously shown above.[110] But in the condemnation against Arius and in the anathematization against him, they did not wish to cast their vote along with the holy council. 7.[111] They were in fact released from their exile by the zeal of those bishops who had received their entreaties, and when they had regained their former communities, just as I had also said above,[112] and had barely glanced at them, so to speak, they rushed to the imperial court, employ-

---

accused in these matters" (τὸν ἐπὶ τούτοις ἐναγόμενον). The remainder of this sentence is unique to Cyzicenus. Socrates's version says simply that it seemed right to Constantine "to show kindness to and recall" Arius (φιλανθρωπεύσασθαι καὶ ἀνακαλέσασθαι) and proceeds directly to what appears in section 5 in Cyzicenus.

110. See 2.27.12. Socrates says only that they subscribed to the creed, without discussing their true beliefs.

111. The source of Cyzicenus's information is unknown for 3.13.7–3.13.15. Cyzicenus's description of the Arian presbyter's hesitation to reveal his allegiances before Constantine briefly parallels the wording of Theodoret (*Hist. eccl.* 2.3.4). However, Cyzicenus preserves an internal citation formula at 3.13.8 that does not appear in Theodoret and does not actually repeat previously presented information as it promises. This formula almost certainly betrays a common source behind both Cyzicenus and Theodoret. Hansen (2002, 134) suggests Philip of Side, but it is possible both preserve elements of the Gelasian history that BHG 1279, Socrates, and Rufinus do not. At times, Cyzicenus aligns with BHG 1279 (22.9–23.21) and Socrates (*Hist. eccl.* 1.25.5–1.26.7). Wallraff, Stutz, and Marinides see here a fragment of Gelasius (2018, F17b).

112. See 3.12.12.

ing the utmost haste. And upon arriving at Constantinople, they boldly broke in on the palace, trusting in the support of that presbyter whom Constantia had entrusted to the God-beloved Constantine, as if she were his full sister, since the presbyter was held worthy of the greatest care and honor by the emperor. 8. And nevertheless even he did not have the confidence, as I already said, to disclose the Arian heresy embedded within him, since he perceived that the soul of the emperor was as ardent as could be concerning divine matters and strict adherence to the true faith.[113] 9. In fact, he led Eusebius along with Theognius to the emperor, exhorting them that for the time being they should hide the disease of the impious heresy of Arius; and he prevailed heavily on the emperor on their behalf that they be permitted to speak freely, particularly Eusebius, testifying that they concurred with what had been said in the council. And what is more, he who was truly the enemy of the truth was speaking the truth. 10. For the flatterer was saying that they concurred with the things they had muttered there in disparagement. But since the emperor had nobility of character that was innate and great reverence for those who were priests and possessed the forgiving heart of a great emperor, just like the prophet David, he did not harbor the memory of the plots dared against him by Eusebius in the time of the impious Licinius.[114] He received them graciously and reverently as priests of God and esteemed them worthy of as much honor and welcome as possible, and bade them to come to him more often.

13.11. And as they were making progress day by day toward being able to speak freely to the emperor Constantine, best in all ways, they began importuning that presbyter of Arian persuasion to take the lead on making entreaties on Arius's behalf before the emperor, for him to consider Arius worthy of being in his sight, since he could be his ally and could show that he concurred with the ideas of the holy fathers in Nicaea. 12. And the presbyter, yielding to the exhortations of Eusebius and Theognius, began conversation on behalf of Arius with the emperor, very often as the spokesperson for the aforementioned men, saying that Arius agreed with all the assertions made in the council and that he was satisfied with the creed proclaimed there. But what was said by the presbyter concerning Arius

---

113. The manuscript tradition has οὗτος where Hansen conjectures οὕτως. Hansen's conjecture creates a parallel with the adverbs but leaves the new subject of the sentence less clear. We have chosen to read with the manuscripts.

114. See 1.11.19–32 and appendix 1.

appeared outlandish to the emperor.[115] 13. But the presbyter kept doing this for a great many days and did this at times privately but for the most part when Eusebius of Nicomedia was there. For the emperor sent for him quite often. For the most faithful emperor did not ruminate over the dramatic intrigues staged against him long before by this impious Eusebius.[116] 14. Now then, by his great skill in deceptive words, Eusebius, through the presbyter and through his own efforts, persuaded the most beneficent and most kindly emperor to order that Arius be summoned before him, since Eusebius was insisting that he meet face to face with the pious emperor Constantine and agree to all those propositions to which both the council and "we ourselves"—as he said—agreed. 15.[117] These statements clearly seemed faithless to the emperor,[118] but succumbing to the God-loving mercy present within him and to his zeal concerning the unanimity of the churches, trusting them since they were priests, he said the following to them, "If Arius agrees with the council and should choose truly to concur with its decisions, I will both receive him into my presence and send him forth to Alexandria with honor." He said these things and ordered him to come to his *comitatus*, sending for him in writing.[119]

---

115. Constantine's incredulity toward the presbyter is also recounted in BHG 1279 (22.13–14).

116. Cyzicenus's text frames several of the Arian faction's efforts as parts of a staged drama, beginning here with the term δραματουργηθέντων ("staged as a drama"). Theatrical terminology becomes more prevalent in the trials of Eustathius and Athanasius (3.16–17). While some of this terminology is reflected through inexact parallels in Theodoret (e.g., Cyzicenus, *Hist. eccl.* 3.16.6, δράμασιν, Theodoret, *Hist. eccl.* 1.25.15, δρᾶμα; Cyzicenus, *Hist. eccl.* 3.16.10, πρόσωπον, Theodoret, *Hist. eccl.* 1.21.3 προσωπεῖον), some, as here and at 3.16.16, is unique to Cyzicenus. This strongly suggests that both drew on a common source that had implemented this characterization, whether the Gelasian history or Philip of Side, as Hansen (1998, 196–197; 2002, *ad loc*) suggests.

117. 3.13.15–17 agrees closely in narrative and occasional phrases with Socrates (*Hist. eccl.* 1.25.6–11) and BHG 1279 (22.13–23.4), all likely stemming from Gelasius (F17). Cyzicenus's narrative makes Eusebius the agent for Arius's summoning, where Socrates and BHG 1279 make the presbyter the sole actor. Cyzicenus's version also focuses on the unanimity of the Council of Nicaea, adding mentions of the council itself in 3.13.17 and another in 3.17.21.

118. The other two authors describe Eusebius's statement as "foreign" or "outlandish" (ξένα), but Cyzicenus has "faithless" (ἄπιστα).

119. The *comitatus*, a Latin term borrowed directly into Greek here and elsewhere as κομιτάτον, was the collection of ministers, armed guards, and other personnel that

13.16. And Arius, since he had been deemed worthy of the emperor's missives, hastened to come to Constantinople straightaway. And Euzoeus was there with him as well, whom the godly Alexander, the bishop of the church throughout Alexandria, had deposed along with Arius. Indeed, through the zeal of the partisans of Eusebius the Nicomedian it was related to the pious emperor by the presbyter that Arius was present. 17. Therefore, the emperor received him into his presence along with Euzoeus, and he sought to find out from them whether they agreed to the creed set forth in the city of the Nicaeans by the three hundred holy fathers. And Arius said under oath that he did and had always believed so, "just as also our holy fathers in Nicaea and all those together with us so believe" (for he was speaking of the partisans of Eusebius the Nicomedian and Theognius, from Nicaea itself), swearing an oath, as it were, for the deception and persuasion of the Christ-loving emperor's guilelessness.[120] 18.[121] Since Arius said these things under oath, he put the most God-beloved and tolerant emperor beside himself with joy, to the point that straightaway on the spot he sent Arius to Alexandria with honor. 19. Then, when Arius reached Alexandria, the bishop did not receive him, since Athanasius was urging the bishop that he should instead avoid him as a defilement. 20. At that point the partisans of Eusebius wrote on Arius's behalf and prompted the emperor to write in strong rebuke to Alexander and Athanasius.[122] 21. So

---

accompanied the emperor, whether he was at one of the imperial capitals, as he is at this moment, or on the road, as at 3.17.39.

120. Both Socrates (*Hist. eccl.* 1.26) and BHG 1279 (23.5–21) present far more substantial statements of faith that use Nicene-approved language. Socrates's version does not specifically mention the fathers at Nicaea, nor does Sozomen's (*Hist. eccl.* 2.27.6–10), but the copy in BHG 1279 does.

121. 3.13.18–3.15.6 parallels parts of Socrates (*Hist. eccl.* 1.27.1–5) and BHG 1279 (23.22–28). Wallraff, Stutz, and Marinides (2018, 170–75) accept this passage as Gelasian (F18a) on the strength of these parallels as well as similarities to a *Life of Athanasius* (BHG 185). The letter at 3.15.1–5 is unique to Cyzicenus, however.

122. 3.13.20–3.18.13 includes several episodes that derive from Athanasius's biographical *Apology against the Arians* (*Apol. sec.* 59–89). From Cyzicenus's self-admitted inability to find complete copies of the documents he quotes (see 3.15.23–24), he evidently did not have access to Athanasius's own text. Athanasius himself depicts his struggles against a myriad of opponents, whom Cyzicenus's text condenses to Arians and a few hired Meletians. The general sequence of events in Cyzicenus also appears in Socrates, Sozomen, and Theodoret. It is improbable that all four made nearly identical selections of documents from Athanasius's original. Moreover, as Sozomen and Theodoret at times include more information than Socrates, they cannot have relied solely

then Athanasius refused to accept Arius and those with him under any condition and together with the bishop, he explained in writing to the emperor, saying that it was "impossible for those who once had rejected the faith and had been anathematized and sentenced by so great a holy council and by your God-loving piety to be received back immediately after their retraction."[123] 22. Thereupon the emperor, taking exception at this, was roused to anger by the partisans of Eusebius the Nicomedian and threatened Athanasius, writing the following words:

Part of the Letter of the Emperor to Athanasius

14.1. Now then, since you have a clear indication of my will, make the road unhindered for all those who desire to come into the church. For if I find out that you have kept away anyone laying claim to the ecclesiastical faith or prevented any such person from entering, I will immediately send someone to depose you at my command and to remove you from those positions.[124]

And likewise, he wrote equally strong threats also to the bishop Alexander on behalf of Arius.

A Letter of the Most God-Beloved Emperor Constantine to Alexander, Bishop of Alexandria

15.1.[125] The victor, Constantine Maximus Augustus, to father Alexander, the bishop.

Even now shall utterly abominable jealousy bray with its unholy sophistry at delaying? What then is the matter at the moment? Do we take for doctrine anything other than what was

---

on their best-known predecessor. This evidence points to a probable origin with the Gelasian source for many of the following passages.

123. Four of the canons from the Council of Nicaea concern the length of time necessary for repentance and reinstruction of Christians who lapse in various ways (see 2.32.11–14).

124. Cyzicenus's version makes Constantine's primary concern access to the faith of the church rather than access to the church itself, as in the other versions of this letter.

125. Constantine's letter to Alexander exists only in Cyzicenus but appears to have been known by both Socrates and the author of BHG 185, based on their shared concluding remarks. See Wallraff, Stutz, and Marinides 2018, 173 n. 5.

decreed by the Holy Spirit through you, most honorable brother? 2. Arius; Arius is the one I say has come before me, the Augustus, at the entreaty of very many persons, professing that he concurs with those things concerning our universal faith that were defined and confirmed through you in the council in Nicaea, at which I myself, your fellow servant, was present and was taking part in the definition. 3. This man, together with Euzoeus—once they clearly recognized the will of the imperial ordinance—came directly to us. Therefore, I have conversed with them concerning the word of life while several other persons were present. I myself am that man who has dedicated my mind to God with unalloyed faith. I myself am your fellow servant, who has turned my full attention to our peace and unanimity....

15.4. And after other statements:

...For that reason I have sent this message not only as a reminder but also because I deem it worthy to welcome the men who come to us as suppliants. Therefore, if indeed you should find them laying claim to the right and ever-living, apostolic faith set forth in Nicaea—for in our presence also they affirmed that this is the opinion they hold—provide for them all, I entreat you. For if you should take forethought for them, you would conquer hatreds with unanimity. 5. Therefore, I entreat you, provide for unanimity; share bounties of friendship with those who do not hesitate on matters of faith; make it so I hear the things I want and desire: peace and unanimity for you all. God will preserve you, most honorable father.

15.6. The emperor wrote these things out of practical concern and not wanting the church to be torn asunder; for he was hastening to lead them all to unanimity.

15.7.[126] After the godly Alexander received the emperor's letters and had lived on a little longer, he left his life with a blessed end, having held

---

126. 3.15.7–20 tells the story of Athanasius's childhood, elevation to being bishop of Alexandria, and why the Arians plotted against him. The story appears in similar narrative sequence in Rufinus (*Hist. eccl.* 10.15) and rearranged into a direct chronology in the later BHG 185. On the basis of broad parallels and close but inexact phrasing

The Third Treatise of the *Ecclesiastical History*   249

the bishopric over the church of God in Alexandria for sixteen whole years: nine years and one month before the council in Nicaea, three years and six months during the council, and three years and five months after the council, which altogether are sixteen years.[127] 8. And Athanasius succeeded him in the service of the priesthood. And what sort of man he was in regard to discretion, piety, and regulation of the church what follows will show us. 9. Now then, when the heretics realized that the godly Athanasius was overseeing the church, they at first were crestfallen but quickly assaulted him with singular focus, in order to erase—if it should even be said—all memory of him from the world, just as the Jews had schemed against Christ. For straightaway they made efforts to persuade the most God-beloved emperor to employ imperial constitutions against him.[128]

15.10. But it is necessary for us first to narrate a little bit about the man's way of life from his childhood. To that end, the blessed Alexander had been entrusted with leadership of the priesthood after the blessed Achillas and had invited the clergy to dinner after the feast day of the contest of the holy Peter, bishop and martyr. While waiting until they were all gathered, when he was standing at a distance he saw some children starting up a game that followed the ecclesiastical rule. 11. Now, the house was oriented toward the sea, along the banks of which the consecrated children were playing. Among them Athanasius was the bishop, and the others of the same age gathered there were presbyters and deacons, who were also leading children to him as catechumens for them to be baptized by him. And when he had baptized them all following ecclesiastical formula, as if he were a bishop, Athanasius was about to offer them a word of instruction. 12. Therefore, amazed at what was happening, the godly Alexander ordered the children to be brought to him. And when he had learned everything that had happened, with the approval of the clergy with him, he completed the rite, sealing the baptized children with the seal of Christ and anointing them with the marks of the holy baptism of salvation. And after summoning them, he commended Athanasius to his parents, exhorting them

---

found when comparing BHG 185 to Cyzicenus, Wallraff, Stutz, and Marinides identify this passage as a fragment of the Gelasian history (2018, F18b).

   127. As in the second book (2.37.28), Cyzicenus attempts to synchronize the chronologies of his various sources with limited success at making a coherent one.

   128. The term διάταξις is the Greek equivalent of *constitutio*, a proclamation made by an emperor with legally binding force. Athanasius's opponents were attempting to use secular as well as ecclesiastical procedures against him.

to have the boy undergo a literary education and to have him progress as far as possible in the Lord; and he urged that they return Athanasius to him once he had made progress, or rather to return him to the church, as Hannah—so he said—presented Samuel.[129] 13. Therefore, when the time had arrived the parents brought Athanasius before the bishop Alexander, whereupon the bishop straightaway bestowed on him the priestly ephod, putting him forward in the church as a new Samuel, as a bulwark against those truly foreign to it.[130] For he endured many contests at the hands of all the heretics who made a confederacy, not only forty men, as in the case of the hallowed apostle Paul,[131] but the entire mob of heretics throughout the entire inhabited world made a confederacy, particularly the Ariomaniacs.[132] Meanwhile Athanasius, along with David, was singing psalms and saying, 14. "Should an army be arrayed against me, my heart shall not fear. Should war rise against me, I have hope even in this,"[133] clearly meaning the hope to have the crown of victory placed on him, desiring to receive it from the Lord, who also said to him, "Take courage,"[134] and, "Do not fear, since I am with you, and no one will harm you from now on."[135]

15.15. Now then, since we want to avoid describing most of the things that befell him, lest we fatigue future readers of this account by prolonging the story (for the trials he endured are endless, persecuted by the most impious heretics), we shall satisfy ourselves with his more notable deeds, for which all this man's acquaintances sing his praises. 16.[136] For as soon

---

129. 1 Sam 1:25.

130. 1 Sam 2:18. The phrase τῶν ἀλλοφύλων ("those foreign") is used frequently in the LXX translation of Judges to identify the Philistines.

131. Acts 23:12–35, where "more than forty" Jews in Jerusalem plot to kill Paul. Both Rufinus and BHG 185 include a verse from Acts (9:16) in which the Lord describes the suffering that Paul must endure on God's behalf, translating the subject from Paul to Athanasius.

132. Neither Rufinus nor BHG 185 emphasizes the Ariomaniacs as a group of particular note.

133. Ps 27 (26):3.

134. Acts 23:11.

135. Acts 18:9–10. Neither of the other sources for this passage includes this verse of comfort to Athanasius.

136. From 3.15.16–20, Cyzicenus and BHG 185 diverge from the narrative of Rufinus, according to whom it was not Constantine but his son Constantius II (r. 337–361) who so distrusted Athanasius. Socrates (*Hist. eccl.* 1.27.6–9, 14–15), however, has a similar narrative, although Cyzicenus clarifies certain actors more directly and

as he had been put in charge of the church, just as we said,[137] the partisans of Eusebius of Nicomedia, since they were exceedingly hostile to Athanasius himself, taking the emperor's grievance with the great Athanasius at that time as a suitable opportunity for their plan—or so they imagined—brazenly set everything in motion against him, in their effort to remove him from the episcopacy, condemning the man on the grounds that he had succeeded to the priesthood in unworthy fashion. For only in this way did they have hope that the Arian doctrine would conquer, if they could get Athanasius out of the way. 17. Therefore, those mentioned previously of the impious Arianist heresy conspired against him <...> Hosion, Eudaimon, Callinicus, and set in motion various accusations against the godly Athanasius through them.[138] First was that Athanasius, so it went, upon assuming the role of bishop, imposed a tax of a linen garment on the Egyptians on behalf of the church of the Alexandrians.[139] They pieced together a second bit of slander more wicked than the first, namely that Athanasius, plotting against the emperor's directives, sent a casket to one Philomenus, so it went, full of gold intended for an insurrection against the emperor Constantine.[140] 18. Third, a certain man called Ischyras undertook a deed for which he deserved many deaths. For taking on himself the name of presbyter although he had not yet ever been in the priesthood, he dared to do the duties of the priests in the villages of the region called Mareotis. At this time then the holy bishop Athanasius, when he arrived at Mareotis, began reviewing the churches there, and when he learned of the details about Ischyras, he sent Macarius the presbyter to look into whether what was being said was true. Thereupon, since he was detected, Ischyras, when he had made his escape from there and beat a hasty retreat, arrived at Nicomedia and took refuge with the partisans of Eusebius. 19. And they, out of hatred toward Athanasius,

---

explains certain actions differently (e.g., why Athanasius sending gold to Philomenus was a worrisome accusation, 3.15.17).

137. See 3.15.9.

138. The text here is corrupt and must be reconstructed from Athanasius (*Apologia secunda*), Socrates, and BHG 185. These sources tell that the Arians hired Meletian heretics named Ision, Eudaimon, and Callinicus. Cyzicenus's heretics instead help to emphasize Athanasius's anti-Arian stance, as at 3.15.13.

139. As Athanasius's original text clarifies (*Apol. sec.* 60), the implication behind this accusation is that Athanasius was acting in the usurped role of a government official by levying a tax.

140. Philomenus is known only from this passage and its parallel versions.

welcomed Ischyras as a presbyter and furthermore promised that they would award him the title of bishop, on the condition that he would take it on himself to initiate an accusation against Athanasius. And he cobbled together these accusations: "Macarius, who had been sent by Athanasius as a presbyter of Athanasius," he said, "made an attack on our church in Mareotis and burst into the sanctuary, overturned the holy table, shattered a cup of the eucharistic mystery, and burned the holy books." 20. And the aforementioned accusers told the emperor this and similar things through the partisans of Eusebius of Nicomedia, rousing him to anger against Athanasius by also charging that "although he received the divine missive, he did not accept it and did not welcome Arius even though he had confessed to the creed in the presence of your piety."[141] Upon hearing what was said against Athanasius, the emperor was so thunderstruck that straightaway he sent orders to the bishop Athanasius himself to come to Constantinople as quickly as possible.[142] 21.[143] And when he arrived and saw the emperor, he refuted the falsity of the lying informants and reassured the emperor. 22. And with the support of imperial missives, he was sent by the most faithful emperor with the highest possible honor to Alexandria and took over the church that had been entrusted to him by God. These matters does the writing of the pious emperor make clear, which he sent to the church of the Alexandrians, the last portions of which I will include in this text.

15.23.[144] But let none of the readers of this text blame me for not adjoining the entire letter to the narrative of this ecclesiastical history. For

---

141. The "divine missive" refers to the letter from Constantine to Athanasius at 3.14.1. The word we have translated as "divine," θεῖον, was frequently associated with imperial communications by this period, reinforcing associations with the emperors and the divine realm. Although it could have less marked meanings, its deployment within this text would have by default called to mind its religious connotations.

142. Cyzicenus and BHG 185 differ as to the end result of the machination. Cyzicenus has the emperor summon Athanasius to a private council, whereas BHG 185 has him convene a new council. See Wallraff, Stutz, and Marinides 2018, 185.

143. The end of the story about the accusers (3.15.21–22) finds its closest verbal parallels in Theodoret (*Hist. eccl.* 1.26.5).

144. Cyzicenus's authorial comment at 3.15.23 about searching for the letter to Athanasius may give us further insight into his composition methods, as he does proceed from Gelasian material to sentences that parallel Theodoret's language (*Hist. eccl.* 3.15.21–22), incorporating a portion of a letter otherwise only found in Theodoret (*Hist. eccl.* 3.16.1–3), from whom he could not have learned the full story of the plots

although I carefully investigated everyone who wrote about these matters, I was not able to find the entire letter recorded by them, and not only this, but for a great many other such letters they included just some select portion of them, as in an abridgment, in the histories to which they devoted themselves. Wherefore I grieve even more than all of you about this. 24. But let me return to the matter at hand: affixing the end of the aforementioned letter to this history, as the statement above promised. And it was written as follows:

The End of a Letter of the Emperor Constantine Written on Behalf of Athanasius to the Church of the Alexandrians

16.1.[145] The wicked did not at all prevail against your bishop, believe me, brethren. They have been striving for nothing other than that they, who have wasted our time, might be unable to have any opportunity whatsoever for repentance in this life. Now then, I beseech you, provide for your own selves your holy affection, love one another with all strength,[146] and welcome your bishop Athanasius with boundless joy, beloved ones, 2. although I know full well that his separation has not given you so much grief as you have exceeding joy in his return to you. 3. Drive away those who are striving to eradicate the grace of your unanimity, and love one another, setting your eyes on God, I beseech you. For I for my part have received your bishop Athanasius gladly and I have so

---

against Athanasius. The comment may thereby be evidence for Cyzicenus collating multiple accounts at this moment. It is possible, however, that he is simply inserting a comment into material that was continuous in the Gelasian history. Both Socrates (*Hist. eccl.* 1.27.10) and Sozomen (*Hist. eccl.* 2.22.8–9) mention the letter reproduced by Theodoret but include no indication that they knew the full letter from Athanasius directly. It seems probable that all four authors gathered their information from the same abridgment of Athanasius's *Defense against the Arians*, probably found in the Gelasian history.

145. The following excerpt of the letter shows no knowledge of the content outside the excerpt presented by Theodoret (*Hist. eccl.* 1.27.1). Theodoret's excerpt comes from the end of a letter to the Alexandrians, found in complete form in Athanasius's *Defense against the Arians* (*Apol. sec.* 62). Cyzicenus alone attests the statement concerning Athanasius's welcome and separation (3.16.2), which makes the document relevant to the argument of his own history.

146. In Theodoret and Athanasius, the phrase "with all strength" (παντὶ σθένει) modifies the verb "drive away" (διώξατε) ahead (3.16.3).

addressed him as I have been persuaded he is: a man of God. God will preserve you, beloved brethren.

16.4.[147] After receiving these missives from the emperor, the great Athanasius arrived at Alexandria. And the entire clergy and people rejoiced gladly to welcome him, seeing that their shepherd had returned to his flock with the greatest possible honor. And they all glorified God and honored the emperor Constantine, best in all ways, with words of praise. 5. While these circumstances brought inexpressible joy to our fellows, on the other hand they brought endless pain and shame to those who were hostile and primed to fight against the Son of God. 6. Despite this, though they had thus stripped all sense of shame from their persons, they made a pretense "of piety, but repudiated the power thereof,"[148] especially the partisans of Eusebius of Nicomedia, and, though they should have slunk to the ground in shame, they cloaked their excessively great shamelessness, and they turned themselves to their most grievous and evil skill at wicked dramatics against another tower of piety. 7. And the parent and most prominent leader of all these wicked plans was Eusebius of Nicomedia, since he was extremely shrewd at evildoing, just like his father, the devil.[149] For he himself controlled the reins not of the church of God but of the impious worship of the Arians. And while lingering in Constantinople, he saw the emperor quite often through the presbyter of Arian persuasion and became increasingly bold in speaking to him, finding the emperor's basic

---

147. From 3.16.4 to 3.16.25, Cyzicenus tells the story of a plot against Eustathius, bishop of Antioch. After Eustathius's appearance, the text roughly follows Theodoret (*Hist. eccl.* 1.20.11–1.22.3), albeit with a different chronology. In Theodoret, the plot against Eustathius precedes not only the first plot against Athanasius (*Hist. eccl.* 1.27–18) but also the Christianizing missions outside the empire and Constantine's letter to the Shapur (see above, 3.9–11). Socrates, whose tale of Eustathius's deposition is quite different, likewise places it before all the plots against Athanasius, though after the Christianizing missions (*Hist. eccl.* 1.23–24). Inexact echoes of Theodoret in 3.16.7 point to a mutually shared source that could at least have provided the materials from 3.16.4–8 that are fully independent of Theodoret. Cyzicenus does, however, directly and accurately cite Theodoret in 3.16.10 and 3.16.13, where he takes issue with Theodoret's characterization of Eusebius of Caesarea. It appears he did have multiple sources before him while writing this account, and the evident mixture of sources in this passage makes ascertaining the author responsible for particular phrases or details difficult to discern.

148. 2 Tim 3:5.

149. See John 8:44.

integrity to be an avenue for his own evil scheming, and he easily prepared plots against the champions of the truth. 8. Since the hope of his most evil zeal against the great Athanasius had been frustrated, he cleverly devised a seemingly innocent path for an assault against the godly Eustathius, who presided over the church of the Antiochenes. He approached the good-loving emperor Constantine, ostensibly out of loyalty and, rejoicing in the acts performed by the emperor, in order to request permission to journey to Jerusalem, since he longed for the sight of the holy houses of God built there by the emperor. And by beguiling the Davidic soul of the emperor with these deceptive words, he departed from Constantinople with as much honor as possible, since the emperor made available to him imperial transport and every other service.[150] 9. And Theognius of Nicaea also set out along with him, since he was an accomplice, as we have also said before, in his wicked and impious councils. 10. Upon their arrival, they reached Antioch, adopting a façade of amity, just as Theodoret says—although Theodoret left out the vast majority of the events that occurred, because he had planned to write his history using as few as possible. But since we have read writers who preceded him, who depict everything accurately, in order, and sequentially, let me incorporate that sequence. For excerpting from others, as I have said before, we are incorporating their works here. 11. But let us return to the matter at hand.[151]

Now then, when those sinful men arrived at the city of Antioch, they were welcomed in the spirit with surpassing joy by the great Eustathius who presided there. For he had heard about their fabricated repentance as if it were true, he said, and he rejoiced over them. And welcoming them with loving heart on account of his piety toward Christ, the great Eustathius deemed them worthy of utmost consideration. 12. And after these events, when they had left from Antioch, they reached the holy sites of Jerusalem and found there certain likeminded men who agreed with them, who

---

150. The comparison of Constantine to David does not appear in the similar statement in Theodoret (*Hist. eccl.* 1.21.2).

151. Cyzicenus critiques Theodoret's chronology, and his criticism is largely supported by other extant sources. Rufinus and Socrates agree against Theodoret on the timing of the Christianizing missions outside the empire, and both likewise place the introduction of the anonymous Arian presbyter before the plots against Athanasius, which Theodoret reverses. Socrates hints that his source may have included the first plot against Athanasius prior to the account of Eustathius by beginning the account of Eusebius of Nicomedia and Athanasius's opposition but signaling a delay to the completion of the story (*Hist. eccl.* 1.23.4).

encouraged them without restraint to the drama they had plotted against the champion of the truth 13.—but not Eusebius of Palestinian Caesarea, the way Theodoret seemingly slanders the man, writing falsely about him. All our holy fathers recall that he was eminent in the orthodox faith, and they all sing of his successes in labors and contests in the council in Nicaea on behalf of the holy and *homoousios* Trinity. 14. Just as they remember also the godly Macarius, bishop in Jerusalem, the great Eustathius, Alexander of Alexandria, Leontius of Cappadocian Caesarea, Eupsychius of Tyana, Protogenes of Sardica, and above all Hosius of Cordoba,[152] as well as Athanasius of Alexandria and Alexander of Constantinople and all the others who contested in that hallowed and holy council on behalf of the apostolic doctrines, in this way they also memorialize the admirable Eusebius Pamphili, bishop of Palestinian Caesarea.[153] 15. But the partisans of Eusebius of Nicomedia did not find him of like mind, but finding in agreement Patrophilus of Scythopolis, the Lydian Aetius, and the Laodicean Theodotus, they also found many other comrades in the impiety of Arius, with whom they held liaisons, making clear to them the plot they cooked up against the holy Eustathius, then departed and reached Antioch together with them.[154]

16.16.[155] But while the pretext for the journey of the others was allegedly to have an honorable escort, the real desire among them was a war

---

152. This list of the bishops matches the major speakers in the Dispute with Phaedo in book 2.

153. Theodoret indeed named Eusebius of Caesarea as one of the primary conspirators against Eustathius (*Hist. eccl.* 1.22.4), and other authors corroborate this. Sozomen (*Hist. eccl.* 1.23.8) describes Eusebius of Caesarea and Eustathius producing written polemics against one another (one of Eustathius's own references to Eusebius of Caesarea survives in Theodoret [*Hist. eccl.* 1.8.1–5]). Socrates (1.23–24) confirms that it was an argument between Eustathius and Eusebius of Caesarea that led to the council in the first place; and Eusebius himself (*Vit. Const.* 3.59–62) publicized his role in the council that deposed Eustathius in 328 CE. Cyzicenus names no source for these corrections, which may well be his own attempts to clear Eusebius's name of charges of Arianism.

154. "Cooked up" translates τυρευθέν, which comes from the verb τυρεύω, which literally means "to make cheese" or "to curdle." By extension, the word comes to mean "make a mess" and "concoct," often being used for illegitimate, roughish plots. We have translated it as "cooked up" in an attempt to preserve the flavor of the Greek term.

155. When compared to Theodoret's version (*Hist. eccl.* 1.21.5–1.22.1), the tale of the woman who accused Eustathius of adultery is more dramatic in Cyzicenus's telling. Unique portions to the text continually praise Eustathius, denigrate his accuser,

against piety toward Christ. For after they had purchased a little courtesan woman with gold and persuaded her to lend them her tongue for one hour, they convoked a council with the great Eustathius together with the holy bishops with him and then, commanding that all the others go outside, those who had produced the drama against the high priest enjoined that thrice-wretched woman to come with all speed into the council.[156] 17. Those who were assisting their wrongdoing brought the little woman forward. And she stood there showing off a child at her breast and saying that it had been conceived and begotten from a union with Eustathius, and she kept shouting these things, lacking all restraint. The great Eustathius, recognizing the transparency of the false accusation, ordered that if she had anyone to corroborate this story, she should bring them forward. 18. And when she said that she had no one, those who had contrived the false accusation had that hussy take an oath, although the apostolic, divine canon explicitly prohibits an accusation being received against a presbyter unless brought forward by two or three witnesses.[157] 19. But because they were contemptuous of the divine laws in this way and flouted the judgment of God pronounced against slanderers, they contrived an unsupported charge against so great a man given by the sordid little woman, and, acting as condemned judges, accepted it.[158] And since the thrice-wretched little woman added an oath that they themselves had proffered to her, crying out that the infant was Eustathius's, these men filled with all manner of disgrace then

---

and remind the reader that the conspirators are faithless, lawless liars. The scene is also lengthened by additional, evocative subsidiary actions for each character that do not change the core details of the story (e.g., the conspirators *contrived and* accepted the charge). The increased theatricality extends to describing the conspirators as "those who have produced the drama" (δρᾶμα συντεθεικότες).

156. Cyzicenus's narrative shows discomfort with the proceedings at the council in Antioch. It acknowledges that there was a larger assembly there by mentioning Eustathius and other holy bishops, using *holy* as a marker for "pro-Nicene." However, it sidesteps the issues of how a pro-Nicene assembly could eject Eustathius and the actual charge against him of Sabellian theology (see Socrates, *Hist. eccl.* 1.24). Instead, the Nicene fathers are summoned and then removed from the proceedings, leaving only the few partisans of Eusebius of Nicomedia on the metaphorical stage with Eustathius.

157. 1 Tim 5:19. The need for two or three witnesses to accuse a bishop of unbecoming conduct had been affirmed by the second canon of the Council of Nicaea (see 2.32.2).

158. Theodoret attests οὗτοι ("these men") where the manuscript for book 3 has οὕτως ("in this way"). We have translated following the manuscript over Hansen's proposed correction.

passed a vote against him on the grounds that he was an adulterer. 20. But some of the other high priests (for there were many who fought on behalf of the apostolic doctrines with the great Eustathius, although unaware of all the plots that were cooked up) spoke out clearly against the lawless ones and prevented the bishop Eustathius from accepting that unjust vote. But those who had contrived the drama ran with all haste to the emperor and persuaded him that what was being said had been examined and was found to be true and that the verdict of condemnation was just. For on the grounds that he was at once an adulterer and a tyrant, they were arranging that the champion of piety and temperance would be driven out of the holy precincts and be driven far off into exile to an Illyrian city beyond Thrace.

16.21. But the enemy of the apostolic doctrines, Eusebius of Nicomedea, knew how to enact his slanders against the heralds of the true faith, and kept visiting Constantinople together with Theognius, and those whom they left behind in Antioch they had as accomplices to their own reprobacy, who ordained Eulalius to take the place of the godly Eustathius. 22. And because he survived for a very short while, they ordained a certain Euphronius.[159] But because he also died very soon thereafter (for he lived for a single year and a few months after his ordination), they arranged for the presidency over that church to be granted to Flacitus.[160] 23. And all these men similarly maintained in secret the impiety of Arius, for which reason all those who upheld the right and pious faith, both priests and laity, abandoned the ecclesiastical assemblies and gathered on their own. And everyone was calling them Eustathians since they banded together after his exile. 24. But that thrice-wretched little woman, succumbing to a most grievous and lengthy illness not long thereafter, revealed the plot and laid bare the false accusation, summoning not two or three but many of the priests and explaining what had been cooked up by that astonishing faction of the impious. For she asserted that she had been emboldened to that false accusation for money, but she said that the oath was not entirely false. For she exclaimed that the infant belonged to a certain metalworker

---

159. Theodoret (*Hist. eccl.* 1.22.1) adds that Eusebius of Caesarea was a candidate to replace Eulalius, but this was prevented by Eusebius's refusal and the emperor's prohibition. Eusebius (*Vit. Const.* 3.59–62) confirms Theodoret's information. Its omission from Cyzicenus's text fits a pattern of removing Eusebius from among the pro-Arian actors.

160. Athanasius (*Apol. sec.* 79) gives this bishop's name as Flacillus, but Cyzicenus and Theodoret call him Flacitus.

named Eustathius. 25. This, then, was what the impious Eusebius and his partisans dared at that time in Antioch.

But even so,[161] the impious ones did not feel ashamed then, nor did they get their fill from their false accusations against the champions of the truth, but since they saw that their plots against the great Eustathius had turned out according to plan for them, once again they patched together another drama against the godly Athanasius, the likes of which none of the most wicked of men ever before had dared. 26. For once again paying off some accusers from the same faction of Meletius, they led them to the emperor crying out against Athanasius that this athlete of virtue had dared many shameful, unholy acts. And the leaders of these men were Eusebius and Theognius and Theodorus of Heracleia in Thrace, and they said that these matters could not be tolerated or even listened to. 27. Indeed, they thus persuaded the emperor to order that a council be gathered in Antioch of Syria, where the enemies were the majority, and order that Athanasius be put on trial there.[162] And the emperor, persuaded since they were priests (for he was entirely unaware of the plots cooked up by them), commanded that this take place. 28. But the defender of truth, the great Athanasius, because he recognized the ill-will of the aforementioned impious men, did not come to the council. Now thereupon, taking this as stronger pretext for their false accusation, they took up the fight against the truth once and for all and condemned him to the emperor in writing for usurpation and for brazenness. 29. And the emperor, while highly forbearing, sparked to anger against Athanasius by this, sent a letter to him, revealing his anger and recommending strongly that he come to Tyre. For he ordered that the council be transferred and assembled there, since he suspected that Athanasius would be suspicious of the city of the Antiochenes, because there were many throughout the East who welcomed Arius's outrage.[163] And he

---

161. From the start of this paragraph through 3.16.29, Cyzicenus roughly follows the text of Theodoret, *Hist. eccl.* 1.28, with the main difference being an emendation that removes Eusebius of Caesarea from the list of Athanasius's opponents, as at the Eustathius episode (see 3.16.12–22 with notes).

162. According to Sozomen (*Hist. eccl.* 2.25.1) and Theodoret (*Hist. eccl.* 1.28.2), the initial meeting place of the council was Caesarea, where Eusebius of Caesarea would have presided.

163. Sozomen (*Hist. eccl.* 2.25.1) and Theodoret (*Hist. eccl.* 1.28.2) both allege that Athanasius's true reason for not attending the council was that he distrusted the motives of Eusebius of Caesarea, who was to be the presiding bishop. Eusebius briefly mentions the council, alluding to Athanasius without naming him by locating the

also wrote to the council what one adorned with piety ought to write. These are the following things:

A Letter of the Emperor Constantine to the Council Assembled in Tyre

17.1.[164] The Victor Constantine Maximus Augustus to the holy council assembled in Tyre.

It would perhaps be appropriate and particularly fitting for the well-being of these times that the universal church be guarded against partisanship and that all the servants of Christ now be free from all reproach. 2. But certain persons are driven unsoundly by an impulse toward quarrelsomeness (not to say anything else: leading a life unworthy of themselves[165]), and are making attempts to cause all manner of confusion, a fact that seems to me to have transcended beyond all calamity. For this reason I urge you to take off running, so to speak, without any delay in order to assemble at the same place and fill the council with spiritual celebration and to come to the aid of those who need help, and heal your imperiled brethren, to return those of your limbs that have been scattered to wholeness and correct the offenses, as the present age demands. In this way you might bestow fitting harmony on these provinces so great, a harmony that—alas for the absurdity of it—the disdain of lesser men has destroyed. 3. But this is also something pleasing to our master, God, and beyond the prayers of us and you yourselves as well, if somehow you should restore the peace: this, I think, all men would confess as worthy of uncommon glory. 4. Now then,

---

source of the church's disturbance in Egypt (*Vit. Const.* 4.41). Socrates instead ascribes his reticence to concern about new theological definitions disrupting Nicene theology (*Hist. eccl.* 1.28.4). Cyzicenus omits any suggestion that Eusebius of Caesarea was not on the Nicene side of the debate, identifying unnamed Christians in the East as the cause of Athanasius's suspicion.

164. Copies of this letter exist in Theodoret (*Hist. eccl.* 1.29) and Eusebius (*Vit. Const.* 4.42). Cyzicenus reproduces several of the synonym substitutions from Theodoret (such as ἰατρεῦσαι for ἰάσασθαι in 3.17.2, both verbs of healing), suggesting Theodoret was his source. Cyzicenus has some grammatical variation, of which two are highlighted below.

165. In Theodoret, Constantine says, "For I could not call it living in a manner unworthy of themselves," implying that those members of the church were predisposed toward such action. In Cyzicenus, the impulse comes from without.

do not delay any longer, but from now on, increasing your willingness, hasten to set a limit appropriate to the tasks before you, coming together with all sincerity, of course, and faith. See to it that in all points peace might be bestowed on you and on all.[166] 5. I have sent a request to those of the bishops whom you desired, so that they might be present and share in these deliberations with you. I have sent out Dionysius, a man of consular rank, who also will notify those who ought to attend the council with you and will be present as an observer of the proceedings, with particular attention for keeping good order.[167] 6. For if anyone—as I do not think will happen—should attempt even now to thwart our command and refuse to attend the council, thereupon we will dispatch someone who will cast him out by imperial decree and teach him that it is not ever right to oppose decisions put forth by an *imperator* on behalf of the truth.[168] 7. Finally, your holiness's duty shall be, with unanimous judgment, neither with a view toward hatred nor toward favoritism but rather in line with the ecclesiastical and apostolic canon, to formulate a remedy appropriate for these offenses, that is to say, for these that happen by mistake. In this way you might also free the church from every blasphemy, relieve my concerns, and, by granting the grace of peace to those who now stand in rebellion, effect the greatest prosperity for yourselves. May God preserve you, beloved brethren.

17.8.[169] So then he had written these things after commanding that the council convene in Tyre. For he trusted the false accusers since they were

---

166. This sentence does not appear in Theodoret or Eusebius. It stands in the place of a statement about the Savior demanding faith from the church, an assertion of Constantine's own piety, and a mention of letters previously sent by the church at Tyre to Constantine, to which the emperor is responding.

167. Perhaps the Dionysius described as *vice praefectorum agentem* in a law of 314 CE (Cod. justin. 7.22) or the Dionysius addressed by Libanius in 355 CE (*Ep.* 433), possibly acting as governor of Syria at that time.

168. A clear threat directed at Athanasius for refusing to come to the council initially (see 3.16.27–29 with notes). As at 1.1, the Greek term αὐτοκράτορος translates the Latin *imperator*, a direct reminder of the emperor's core function as a military commander with power over the life and death of his subordinates.

169. Similarities to BHG 185 and Socrates (*Hist. eccl.* 1.28) suggest that 3.17.8–11 derives from the Gelasian history (F19). Although BHG 185 and Socrates both make the Council of Tyre secondary to the plan to assemble at Jerusalem, Cyzicenus follows

priests. Even though he had an unwavering intense piety, yet because he thought that those on the opposing side had been wronged, as a just judge, he put up with even this annoyance. He also gave the order that, after the council had finished making decisions on the particulars, the entire council go to Jerusalem for the sake of consecration rites for the church he had built there. 9. And he wrote another letter to the council, ordering that not only Athanasius should present himself before the council but even Arius as well, and that what had been done by each should be investigated in good faith. To that end if, just as Arius said, he had suffered isolation due to jealousy although he was within the bounds of the right faith, he should first indict himself for his affronts against the truth and then he should keep silent. 10. This was only on condition that his acceptance of correction was not a cunning stratagem of revenge against his own bishop, Athanasius, weaving into it hints of suspicion against him. And he ordered that if jealousy were found to be responsible, the bishops in the council should make every effort to bring both to peace, but if Arius employed any fabricated sort of repentance, he should once more go to Alexandria and he should be judged on this matter there.

17.11. The all-praiseworthy emperor wrote these things, out of his concern for the unanimity of all, in order that, when all useless bickering had been gotten out from underfoot there, they might complete more peaceably the rites of consecration for the church in Jerusalem, which they were dedicating to God. 12.[170] But while the unholy Arius would

---

Theodoret in placing the summons to Tyre first. See Wallraff, Stutz, and Marinides 2018, 187. Cyzicenus also introduces a long conditional statement that simultaneously reaffirms Arius's heretical status while nevertheless providing a reason to continue investigating his claims. Neither BHG 185 nor Socrates states that Constantine ordered Arius to keep silent if jealousy were found to be the motive or suggests here that his repentance might have been a trap for Athanasius. Rufinus (*Hist. eccl.* 10.12) omits the charges against Athanasius from his account of the council, using similar phrasing to the Greek sources but making the entire episode about Arius.

170. Cyzicenus's account of the events of the Council of Tyre (3.17.12–38) largely corresponds to that found in Theodoret (*Hist. eccl.* 1.29.7–1.31.3), enlarged by material that at times parallels BHG 185, Rufinus (10.18), or Socrates (1.29), and at times has no known predecessor. Hansen (2002, 146–50) identifies Gelasius as the source of the expanded material, but Wallraff, Stutz, and Marinides (2018, 189 n. 5) do not include it in their edition due to a lack of clear corroboration for the wording. It is clear, however, that a dramatic account of Athanasius's trial must have been available, as none of the surviving authors show signs of independently consulting the docu-

not tolerate presenting himself in the council in Tyre, the great Athanasius, along with Timotheus and Macarius, his presbyters, and a great many other clerics and venerable men associated with him, reached the city of the Tyrians with great alacrity. 13. Thus indeed, when the bishops had come into Tyre and all had come to the same place, together with the consular Dionysus and the most prominent men honored with the highest ranks along with him and the governor of the province, the emperor's missive was given by the consular Dionysius to the council of the bishops. 14. And certain other bishops arrived, accused of doctrinal corruption, one of whom was Asclepas of Gaza.[171] But I would first like to insert into this text the tragic plot of the charge against the holy Athanasius, and thereupon to narrate the events that took place in that infamous court of law.

17.15. When a certain Arsenius, who had previously held the post of reader under Athanasius, was being prosecuted on certain charges and was about to be destroyed by the mob, he was saved in the following way once the great Athanasius learned of this (for he had closely examined the case). For once Athanasius learned that Arsenius was falsely accused, he arrived by night and saved the man, urging him to escape his murder by flight. 16. And after these events, the associates of Meletius found that man in Egypt and prepared for the title of bishop to be bestowed on him. And after some time, at the suggestion of Eusebius of Nicomedia (for he himself was the one everywhere contriving intricately woven false accusations against the pious), those of Meletius's faction concealed that very Arsenius and required him to lie low for a while longer. 17. Then, cutting the right hand off of some corpse and laying it embalmed in a wooden chest, they carried it around everywhere, saying that Arsenius had been slaughtered and

---

ment-rich testimony of Athanasius himself, nor does Athanasius share the story of dramatically revealing Arsenius to the council (3.17.24–30) found in Cyzicenus, Rufinus, Socrates, Sozomen, and Theodoret. As these authors differ from one another on matters of sequence and entire episodes from the council, the later accounts appear to have a source separate even the earliest surviving in Rufinus and Socrates, leaving the Gelasian history as a likely source behind many similarities. Whether Cyzicenus was comparing multiple sources as he himself describes (3.16.10), following the Gelasian history directly, or embellishing independently cannot be ascertained.

171. Asclepas was bishop of Gaza during Nicaea and was deposed for heterodox teaching and having overturned an altar. He seems to have sided with Athanasius at Tyre and opposed the Arians on numerous occasions. See Sozomen, *Hist. eccl.* 3.8, 11–12, 24; Mark the Deacon, *Vit. Porph.* 20.

dismembered by Athanasius, and they named Athanasius as the murderer.[172] 18. But the eye of God that sees all did now allow Arsenius to lie low for a long time, but first in Egypt and the Thebaid he made it clear that he was alive; then God propelled him—as he himself would narrate later—to contemplate the safety afforded him beyond all expectation by Athanasius, and that still he himself was doing wrong and committing a great injustice if he should overlook that his benefactor was being put to death on his account instead of him dying on his behalf. Therefore, the one who governs the universe led him to Tyre, wherein the hand was being presented to the judges by the false accusers, like in a scene from a tragedy. 19. The companions of Athanasius, upon seeing this man, brought him to their quarters, and when they had learned from him the details of God's dispensation and of his own intention, they urged him to lie low for the time being.

17.20. The great Athanasius reached the council chamber just before dawn together with Timotheus and Macarius, his presbyters, and those who had come there with him from Alexandria. 21. And first they led in a little woman who had lived in licentiousness. And she cried out unceasingly, saying that she had pledged herself to virginity but that Athanasius had been receiving hospitality at her quarters and had overpowered her and defiled her against her will. While she was saying these things, the accused came in and with him together with the others was the presbyter Timotheus, a most admirable man. 22. And when the judges commanded Athanasius to defend himself against the charge, Athanasius kept silent, as if he were not the one accused, but Timotheus spoke to the woman: "Have I, woman, ever met you? Have I ever come to your house?" And she cried out ever more shamelessly, fighting with Timotheus and holding her hand out against him and warding him off and saying to Timotheus himself, "You took my virginity. You stripped me of my chastity. You have corrupted the noble part of my soul," and many other things such as those women who have no shame due to the excess of their licentiousness are accustomed to say. 23. And there really was amazement at what was happening, and most astonishing of all was that although Athanasius was being charged with the crime, Timotheus was the one being accused. And so, because those who had devised the drama were disgraced and all the judges who were in on the plan turned red with embarrassment, they ordered that the little

---

172. That the hand is embalmed may be a detail intended to suggest that this is a deliberately faked relic, since a genuine relic was often held to have been miraculously preserved.

woman be thrown out. 24. At that point, the godly Athanasius said that it was not necessary to dismiss the little woman but rather to question her and learn.[173]

But the false accusers kept crying out that the other charges were more serious and could under no circumstances be dispelled by some craft or cleverness, "for seeing and not hearing shall be the judge of the evidence." When they had said these things, they produced that much-vaunted chest and laid bare the embalmed hand. 25. And after witnessing this, each of those in the council yelled out. Some of them (the false accusers who were in on the plot) were saying that the defilement was true, while others who knew it was false started laughing, saying that Arsenius had been hidden away and was still alive. 26. And when the council was filled with massive confusion and a brief peace was barely restored, the accused, Athanasius, asked the judges whether anyone among them had known Arsenius. Once many of them had said that they knew the man well, Athanasius commanded that he be led in. 27. And after he arrived and stood in the middle of the council, Athanasius once more asked whether, "This is Arsenius whom I did away with, who was mistreated by these men after his slaughter and was deprived of his right hand?" When the vast majority of those who were in the council agreed that this was Arsenius, the godly Athanasius stripped him of his cloak and pointed to Arsenius's hands, both right and left. "And let no one," he said, "seek another hand! 28. For each of us humans received two hands from the maker of the universe." But even when this evidence had been displayed in this way by the judgment of God, who watches over all things, in spite of the fact that the accusers and those of the judges in on the plot should have fallen down and prayed for the very earth to yawn open for them and to swallow them utterly, they did the opposite. For they filled the council chamber with confusion and discord, naming Athanasius a sorcerer and saying that he beguiled the sight of human beings with some sort of trickery. 29. And they made an attack against him and tried to rend and slaughter the champion of piety, disturbing, so to speak, the very earth and throwing up a cloud of dust into the air, like those men who were squawking out against the godly apostle Paul and saying, "Away with him at once! He is not fit to live."[174] 30. But those there from the emperor, entrusted with maintaining order, prevented

---

173. The text of Theodoret supplies, as an object to the verb "learn" (μαθεῖν), "who had contrived these plans" (τὸν ταῦτα συντεθεικότα).

174. Acts 22:22.

the murder. For snatching the victor away and making it possible for him to board a skiff, they procured his deliverance. And the godly Athanasius boarded the skiff and rushed to the imperial court, fleeing the hands of those seeking his blood.

17.31. But they, once they were able, sent some of the bishops who sympathized with them to Mareotis—Theognius of Nicaea, Maris of Chalcedon, Theodorus of Heracleia in Thrace, Narcissus the Cilician, Ursacius, and certain others who agreed with them[175]—in order that they might compile a one-sided record of the proceedings against Athanasius (and this Mareotis is in Alexandria, named for Lake Mariout, since it is near to the lake).[176] 32. And they instructed them as they were setting out from Tyre to Aelia—that is, to Jerusalem—together with the bishops in the council to send Arius, the master of the evils, there to them as quickly as possible. For the emperor also straightaway suggested that the entire council come from Tyre to Jerusalem along with all the bishops from everywhere, as I said earlier as well, in order to consecrate the temples built there by him.[177] 33. And he also sent with them certain of the more loyal governors, distinguished by their piety and faith, with the order that all expenses generously be defrayed for all on their authority, not only for the high priests and priests and those in their entourage but also for all those in need assembled from everywhere. For a crowd beyond description was flowing together practically from the entire land throughout the East there to the consecration of the new Jerusalem.[178] And he had the divine altar adorned with imperial drapery and with jewel-encrusted golden treasures.

17.34. And when the impious Arius had just arrived in Aelia on the day of the consecration with great eagerness—especially because he had

---

175. Theodoret here lists Theognius of Nicaea, Theodorus the Perinthian, Maris the Chalcedonian, and the Cilician Narcissus. By including Ursacius, one of the foes mentioned in Athanasius's *Apology against the Arians*, Cyzicenus shows that he cannot simply be relying on Theodoret as his source and elaborating the rest of the unique material solely from his own invention, as Theodoret does not mention Ursacius at any point in the material within the scope of events included in Cyzicenus's history.

176. On the production of meeting notes, and their sometimes contentious and partisan nature, see Graumann 2021.

177. See 3.17.8.

178. That Constantine ordered the expenses defrayed means that he authorized the use of imperial conveyance, as he had for attendees of the Council of Nicaea. Cyzicenus's text presents a larger assembly than Theodoret and mimics phrasing found in the *proemium* (*proem*. 1) to express the universal appeal of Constantine's summons.

heard that Athanasius was keeping his distance from that festival—he was welcomed gladly by his sympathizers, by whom I mean by the partisans of Eusebius of Nicomedia and Patrophilus of Scythopolis. 35. But when those who fought on the side of the right faith saw Arius, they turned their backs on him as if he were a defilement and drove him out of the church. They also commanded that he be expelled from the council and decreed that they would listen to him in the council in Alexandria, in which he was also found guilty, just as, they said, our Christ-loving emperor Constantine also ordered. 36. In this way when the destroyer had been gotten out from underfoot and that most peaceable and resplendent festival had begun, the all-praiseworthy and beyond all most faithful emperor, upon beholding the resplendence and sumptuousness of the festal assembly, became filled with immense joy and extolled to the heights he who governs all good things, because he had granted him this request also. 37. Then, when this festival for the consecration had thus reached its magnificent conclusion, most of the bishops returned to their own countries, especially all those who had not assembled for the council that had taken place in Tyre. 38. But those from Eusebius of Nicomedia's faction, as many as had accepted Arius's outrage with him, repaired to Tyre with Eusebius himself and the other bishops, awaiting there their sympathizers from Mareotis.[179]

17.39. And in the meantime, the great Athanasius arrived at the imperial *comitatus*,[180] approached the most pious, most God-beloved emperor Constantine, and explained the entire tragedy boldly enacted against him. And the most compassionate and virtuous emperor Constantine was deeply wounded in his spirit by the deeds dared against Athanasius and shaken by the unjust judgment that had been passed against him. 40. Especially because Athanasius had begged mightily with tears that his accusers and the

---

179. The slightly jumbled chronology here helps to explain why the letter to the Arians was sent to Tyre despite the proceedings in Jerusalem. Socrates (*Hist. eccl.* 1.33) solves this dilemma by claiming that the emperor and the council sent letters to each other at the same time, unaware what had been accomplished by each, so that the emperor's decisions reached the council after they had already gone to Jerusalem. Theodoret's account (*Hist. eccl.* 1.31) omits the letter from the emperor entirely, allowing him to simply say that Constantine summoned bishops to his court in Constantinople without specifying where the bishops had been. Constantine's letter, which follows, shows that he himself had not yet heard final decisions from the Council at Tyre, making Socrates's solution plausible. Athanasius (*Apol. sec.* 84–85) does not provide sufficient information to answer the question about the sequence of events.

180. See note to 3.13.15.

judges be summoned and that the trial be renewed before the pious emperor himself, he sent missives to those who had moved quarters to Tyre from Aelia indicating that Athanasius was with him and that they should come as quickly as possible to Constantinople. And this is what was written: [181]

A Letter from the God-Beloved Emperor Constantine to the Bishops Who Had Moved Quarters to Tyre from Aelia

18.1. The victor, Constantine Maximus Augustus, to the bishops gathered again in Tyre.[182]

I am unaware of what has been decided by your council with so much clamor and turmoil, but it seems that the truth has somehow been twisted by some manner of troublesome disorder, evidently on account of some bickering with your neighbors, which you never want to let abate, not looking to what is pleasing to God. 2. But let it be the work of divine providence to scatter off the dangers of your quarrel-loving nature—or rather wicked strife—which have been caught out in the open, and for you to prove explicitly to us whether upon assembling there you have taken any consideration for the truth and whether you made your decisions without any favoritism or hatred. 3. Therefore, I desire that you all speedily come to my reverence, in order that you may furnish in person in my presence an accurate account of the proceedings. Now, the reason why I saw fit to write these things to you and to summon you before me in writing you shall learn from what follows.

18.4. Athanasius, the bishop of the church throughout Alexandria, the disciple of divine law, is with me, since he approached me in the middle of the highway with certain other persons he had with him as I was entering into my eponymous and all-fortunate Constantinople after a public appearance.[183] And as he

---

181. Athanasius (*Apol. sec.* 86) preserves the earliest copy of this letter, which appears also in Socrates (*Hist. eccl.* 1.34) and BHG 185 (227C–228A). Similar phrasing between the later sources before and after the letters suggests a Gelasian origin to the copies that survive outside Athanasius (F21).

182. The additional word "again" (πάλιν) in Cyzicenus helps to fix the confused chronology (see note to 3.17.38).

183. Cyzicenus's text has Constantine confirm Athanasius's position and orthodoxy more strongly than other versions.

was mourning and lamenting, he approached us so suddenly in this way that it gave us cause for consternation. 5. For God who watches over all is my witness that I would not have been able to recognize him, who he was, at first glance, had not certain of our attendants explained upon our inquiring after who he was and the injustice that he had suffered at your hands.[184]

The man that we saw was so dejected and sorrowful that we fell to inexpressible pity on his behalf when we realized that that man was Athanasius, whose holy countenance was enough to draw even the gentiles to piety toward the God of the universe. This was the man whom certain wicked men, strangers to peace and unanimity, long ago encumbered with far-fetched, false accusations, 6. to the point that even I myself, caught up by their various, crafty deceptions, was about to commit an error against that man, had I not been moved by divine judgment to order that he then proceed in haste from Alexandria to the imperial court of our clemency. 7. And thus, when an examination had been made at the behest of my reverence concerning the theatrics deceitfully staged against him, the man stood up for himself in our presence and proved the falsity of the charges. And when he had been pronounced innocent of all those charges, I sent him with the greatest honor from us to his own country, returned in peace to the orthodox people guided by him. But now he cries out that a second set of actions has been dared against him, worse than the first, requesting of us with even greater frankness nothing other than that you come to us, which it seemed right to grant to him, in order that he might be able to express his grief over what he suffered while you are present, as is necessary.

18.9. And since it was plain to us that this was reasonable and befitting the present times, I ordered that these messages be written to you, in order that as many of you as constituted the council that occurred in Tyre might make haste to arrive immediately at our court, proving by your actions the pure and undistorted nature of your judgment, accounting for <...> the

---

184. The paragraph that follows (3.18.5–8) is unique to Cyzicenus and supports the overarching portrayal of Athanasius's orthodoxy and Constantine's piety. In the letters preserved elsewhere, Constantine himself claims not to have spoken with Athanasius when he first appeared, necessitating further petitions before the audience occurred.

decisions passed by you in my presence, of course, since you would not deny that I myself truly am a genuine servant of God.[185] 10. Therefore, through my service toward God, there is universal peace, including in the majority of the barbarian nations who genuinely revere the name of God and who up until now were ignorant of the truth.[186] And it is clear that someone who does not know the truth also does not recognize God. Nonetheless, just as has been said, even those very barbarians now have recognized God and learned how to show reverence on account of me, the genuine servant of God, since they perceive that God has protected me with his shield and provided for me everywhere with those very deeds. For this reason especially they know God, whom they revere on account of their fear of us. 11. But although we all seem to profess the holy mysteries of his favor, for I could not say we observe them, we are accomplishing nothing other than that which tends toward discord and hatred and, to say it plainly, that which leads to the destruction of the human race. 12. But hasten swiftly to us, just as has been said, assured that I will try with all my might to set things right so that these mysteries, to which no blame or false opinion can be connected, are observed in the law of God. And this will happen once the enemies of the law of God have been manifestly scattered, utterly crushed, and completely eliminated, 13. whosoever under the pretense of a holy title produces crafty and divisive blasphemies for the deception of the simple-minded, as if they desired some sort of cleansing of the universal church, which very church our savior keeps undefiled, holy, and blameless, since he redeemed it by his salvific and honorable blood, just as his divine and unbreakable laws declare.[187]

---

185. A lacuna has left this sentence impossible to reconstruct with certainty. We have elected to fill it with the neutral expression "accounting for," which makes the remaining grammar sensible without overinterpreting. Lietzmann offers the conjecture "defending" (ἀπολογούμενοι). See Loeschcke and Heinemann 1918.

186. Only Cyzicenus has Constantine refer to the nations outside of Rome in the letter.

187. In Athanasius (*Apol. sec.* 86.12) and other sources, the letter ends with the phrase "produces crafty and divisive blasphemies." The concluding phrases, unique to Cyzicenus, are modeled on Eph 5:25–27.

18.14.[188] This missive brought those in the council to grief, particularly the partisans of Eusebius of Nicomedia. Indeed, those who had been gotten ready by them in Mareotis and had written falsities as if they were true and who had compiled a one-sided record of the proceedings against the great Athanasius prior to this imperial missive arrived in Tyre at the council of those stupendous bishops. 15. But not everyone accepted that action fabricated against Athanasius full of the pollutions of those false accusers. For this reason, most of them, upon learning the contents of the imperial missive from its reading, departed fearfully for their own lands. 16. But the partisans of Eusebius of Nicomedia and Theognius and those with them lingered in Tyre for a while, extending their time of their own volition. And they kept writing to the pious emperor that they were held there against their own volition, although they were eager to send to him also the record of the fabricated proceedings as well, which the most faithful emperor avoided as something polluted; and he did not tolerate them to be accepted whatsoever, ordering that those who committed the offense come to him once and for all. 17. Meanwhile, while they were delaying, I mean the partisans of Eusebius, he sent Athanasius once more to Alexandria with the highest honors, also writing yet again to the church of the Alexandrians that their bishop Athanasius had been slandered falsely and that his purity shone plainly in all ways. 18. And once Athanasius was on site in Alexandria and receiving support in accordance with the imperial commands and the ordinances of the orthodox bishops who had come together for the consecrations in Jerusalem, there occurred some events related to Arius, and there was a large gathering of a crowd and expectations wavered over the outcome hanging in the balance, particularly for those who saw that the harmonious opinions and decisions of so many and such great bishops were again being distorted.[189] 19. Now then, the godly Athanasius, seeing that Alexandria and all of Egypt was in a commotion, did not keep silent but made this apparent through missives to the pious ears of the best in all ways and God-beloved emperor.

18.20. And when the emperor realized that Arius had turned back again, he ordered that he be sent for and led to Constantinople to render an account of the things he had dared to bring up again, writing to him and

---

188. From 3.18.14 to the end of what survives in the third book of the *Ecclesiastical History*, Cyzicenus borrows from the Gelasian history (F21a and b), as shown by close parallels to Socrates (*Hist. eccl.* 1.34) and BHG 185 (227C–228B).

189. The opinions and decisions referred to are those of the Council of Nicaea.

to those with him a letter full of indignation at them. And the text read as follows:[190]

---

190. The surviving manuscripts of Cyzicenus end here. According to the *pinakes* (see appendix 2), the text originally contained four further letters: one to Arius and the Arians, one about the death of Arius, and two to Pistus of Marcianopolis. The letter to Arius and the Arians is *Urk.* 34, a copy of which came to be appended to book 2 in the manuscripts of Anonymous Cyzicenus's *Ecclesiastical History*. This letter and two others that survived alongside the *Ecclesiastical History* have been included in appendix 1.

Appendix 1: The Byzantine Epistolary Supplement

In every manuscript of the *Ecclesiastical History*, the end of the second book is followed by three letters from the Emperor Constantine related to the Arian controversy. All three letters seem to stem from Athanasius's collection of documents, *On the Decisions of the Council of Nicaea* (*De decretis Nicaeanae synodi*). In fact, the three letters follow the same sequence as in *On the Decisions*, where they are documents 40–42. The first of the three letters is known to have originally been part of the lost portions of book 3 of the *Ecclesiastical History*, based on the evidence of the *pinakes* (see appendix 2), which show that it appeared immediately where the manuscript breaks off. Anonymous Cyzicenus would have no doubt manipulated the text of this letter as he had the text of other documents in his history, but we can only speculate the ways in which he would have. Portions of the second letter appear in 1.11.22–31, and comparison with the unaltered letter, presented here, provides a good demonstration of Anonymous Cyzicenus's methods of selection and alteration.

It is not certain how these three letters came to be added to the manuscript tradition of the *Ecclesiastical History*. Each letter relates directly to the Arian controversy and all are penned by Constantine, so perhaps they were simply regarded as a nice complement to the *Ecclesiastical History* and worth having in the same manuscript. Whatever the means by which these letters were added to the text, they soon became part of the textual tradition and were continually recopied with the text in Byzantium and after, as well as translated into Latin during the Renaissance and Counter-Reformation. All three were therefore an important component of how the text was read and understood by Byzantine and early modern readers.

For easy reference, each letter is given its title as used in the manuscripts as well as a reference to the numbering in the standard collection of documents relating to the Arian controversy, Hans-Georg Opitz's *Urkunden zur Geschichte des Arianischen Streites*, as well as the compiler's source text, Athanasius's *De decretis*, and the *Ecclesiastical History*.

A Letter of the Most God-Beloved Emperor Constantine to
Arius and the Arians (*Urk.* 34; Athanaius, *Decr.* 40;
Anonymous Cyzicenus, *Hist. eccl.* 3.19)

19.1.[1] Constantine Augustus to Arius and the Arians.

A wicked expositor is truly an image and human likeness of the devil. For they are just like clever artisans sculpting the form of that one [the devil] to serve as deceptive bait, as if they are contriving a fair form of beauty for him although he is absolutely disgraceful in his nature, in order that he might destroy the wretched by presenting a delusion to them.[2] This expositor, I think, would act in the same way; for him, this alone appears to be worthy of his effort, namely, to spew forth copiously the poisons of his own impertinence. 2. Accordingly, he also introduces a faith of faithlessness, a faith that has never at any time come to light, now or from the very time that human beings came into existence. For this reason that which was articulated long ago in a divine saying does not at all seem to be discordant from the truth, that they are faithful to evil.[3] 3. But how could anyone say that he who has lost the favor of giving counsel no longer desires to find for himself some means of relief? Why then do I say, "Christ, Christ, Lord, Lord? Why in the world does a den of robbers wound us daily? Some fearsome sort of violent audacity has taken a stand against us, bellowing and grinding its teeth, misshapen by dishonor and wounded by every manner of accusation. 4. This audacity indeed, spread abroad in the law and preaching about you as if by some storm and sea swell of evil,

---

1. The original date of this letter was set by Opitz at 333 CE, but a more recent assessment suggests that the letter actually dates from just after the Council of Nicaea in 325 or thereabouts. See *Urk.* 34 and Brennecke et al. 2007, document 27. If the earlier date is correct, then this document, like the two others in this appendix, comes from a period before Constantine was reconciled to Arius, Eusebius, and Theognius. By placing it near the end of the third book, Anonymous Cyzicenus would have presented it as part of the later events of the Arian controversy, implying instead that Constantine had a later falling out with these men. The letter is given the numbering "3.19," following the Loeschke-Heinemann edition, since some form of this letter is known to have followed 3.18 in the completed text (see *pinakes* below).

2. Constantine here is speaking about makers of idols.

3. This statement paraphrases Jer 4:22. A more literal version of the verse following the LXX would say, "They are wise at evildoing." Throughout this passage, Constantine plays with forms of the Greek word πίστις, "faith," "creed," or "trust."

vomits forth ruinous words.[4] And by writing it reveals these words, words that you, who have coexisted with the eternal Father of your own source, have never at any time given in definition to understandings about yourself. Speaking generally, it gathers and collects certain fearsome and lawless impieties, now making tongues wag, now once more elevated again by the zealotry of wretched people, whom, although they expect amnesty, it seduces and corrupts."

19.5. But now I desire to examine the nature of the chief actor in this audacity. For what indeed does he say? "Either let us hold fast," he asserts, "to that of which we have already become possessors, or let it happen just as we ourselves desire." He has fallen, and he has fallen being destroyed in these ways, so he claims, "by treachery or by some villainous cunning." It makes no difference. He considers sacred only that which crept into him through a wicked understanding. "We have the crowds," he asserts.[5] 6. I myself, of course, shall advance a little bit forward, in order that I might come as an observer to the wars of madness. I even myself, I say, shall advance, I who am accustomed to halting the wars of the foolish. Come then, you Ares, Arius, there is need of shields.[6] We beseech you, at least, not to do this. Let Aphrodite's companionship detain you, in any event.[7] Yet indeed, would that, to the extent that you believe it right to fashion yourself as best you can for the masses, it would be your custom to flourish in piety toward Christ to the same extent. 7. See, I come again once more as a suppliant, and though I am capable of battling your entire crowd with weaponry, I do not want to. But, armored with the faith of Christ, I desire that you be cured and heal others. 8. Why then do you assert that you are doing these things, things that are unbefitting of your character? Or with what sort of peace, tell me, or with what authority have you girded yourself,

---

4. Here, as in other Constantinian letters, "the law" is Scripture. "Preaching" refers to homilies and other exegeses on Scripture.

5. A probable allusion to the threat of civil unrest or even mob violence. On the role of popular opinion and public violence in religious controversies, see Gregory 1979.

6. Here Constantine adopts a mock-epic tone, with a possible allusion to Homer's *Il.* 5.31 with the "Ares, Ares" tag. Constantine mocks Arius by alluding to the latter's name, meaning literally "of Ares," the Greco-Roman god of war. Constantine also implies he is waging intellectual warfare against Arius, a motif that continues throughout the letter.

7. Aphrodite and Ares (or Venus and Mars) were often depicted as adulterous lovers in the ancient world (e.g., Homer, *Od.* 8.266–366). Constantine implies that Arius, like Ares, is sexually degenerate.

or rather to what point of heedlessness have you advanced? What audacity that deserves to be destroyed by thunderbolts! For hear what he has recently disclosed to me, writing with a pen dripping poison. "Thus," he asserts, "we believe." Then, I suppose, adding on some things or other I do not know, elaborated somewhat haughtily and in rather scrupulous detail, he kept silent about not one of those horrors as he proceeded onward. But he opened up, as one might say, the entire storehouse of his insanity. 9. "We are driven off," he asserts, "and they are depriving us of the freedom to be granted admittance." But these matters are not at all related to the matter at hand. But pay attention to what follows, for I will employ his own words. "If the bishop of Alexandria," he says, "should persist in the same opinion, we want to be given license hereafter to carry out our lawful and undeniable service toward God in accordance with the regulation of the law."[8] 10. O fearsome shamelessness, which it is fitting to expose out of zeal for the truth. For what has happened to him was as he pleased: this has been marked by the brevity of his expression. What are you asserting, outrageous man? Are you building up your separation to seem innocent to us, as a defense for the unsoundness of your mind that rages against us? And are you eager to destroy those who have been implicated in your evil? 11. "What then," you say, "shall I do, if no one thinks me worthy of welcome?" You have cried this out many times from your unholy throat. But I ask you in return: Where have you shown secure proof and testimony of your meaning? For it was necessary for you to take a clear stance, disclosing your meaning to things divine and human, and particularly because venomous reptiles are by nature even more wild at the time that they perceive that they have reached maturity in the recesses of their dens.

19.12. But that is at least most urbane of him: that quite eagerly he manufactures silence as if under some sort of mask of modesty. You at least present yourself as tame and manageable through the artifice of this façade, and you have deflected most people from noticing that you are inwardly full of countless evils and plots. Yet, oh the wretchedness! As the evil one has planned, thus he has established Arius as a foundry of lawlessness among us. 13. Come here and give me a statement as proof of your faith, and at least do not in any way keep silent, you who possess a perverted mouth and a nature prone to wickedness. You say, "There is one God"? You

---

8. This passage references Athanasius's refusal to admit Arius to the Alexandrine church after Constantine recalled Arius from exile and accepted Arius's nominal agreement with the decisions of Nicaea. See above, 3.13.11–3.15.6.

have my vote on this; consider it so. Do you assert that "the Word is the Word of his *ousia*, without beginning and without end"?[9] I gladly assent to this; believe it so. 14. If you attach a further stipulation, I reject it. If you cobble together something that inclines toward an impious separation, I profess that I neither see nor think this. If you acknowledge "a lodging within the body according to the economy of the divine activities," I do not reject this.[10] If you say that "the spirit of eternity was born in the transcendent Word," I accept this. Who knew the Father, except the one who comes from the Father?[11] Whom did the Father know, except the one whom he has begotten from himself eternally and without beginning? But while you with your obviously poor notion of the faith think that it is necessary to subordinate a "foreign hypostasis," I know that the plentitude of the superior and all-pervasive power of the Father and the Son is a single *ousia*. 15. Now then, if you are detracting from the one from whom nothing has at any time been able to be taken away, not even by the interpretation of quibblers, you are forming the notion of an addition, and in sum you are setting limits to the characteristic methods of inquiry over the one to whom he has granted, from himself a perfect eternity and a thought incorruptible, and distributed the faith in immortality through himself and through the church. Therefore, surely cast it aside. Cast aside that foolish iniquity, you sweet-tongued cosmopolitan who keeps singing out your evils to make the foolish faithless.[12] 16. Fittingly indeed has the wicked one overthrown you with his evil. And perhaps such an evil seems sweet to some (for you have persuaded yourself thus), but that evil is entirely destructive. 17. Come now, free yourself from wasting time among these absurdities and listen, demon-driven Arius, for I am trying to reason with you. Do you not actu-

---

9. The passages represented in quotation marks appear to be Arius's own words that Constantine is parroting back at him, possibly drawn from the letter Constantine alludes to at 3.19.8 in which Arius explained his position. Whether these are verbatim quotations from such a document or are Constantine's loose paraphrase is unknown. Similarly, the lines in sections 29–30 of this letter may be quotations from a work by Arius or Constantine's own paraphrase (or parody) of Arius's words.

10. "A lodging within the body" translates τὴν τοῦ σώματος ξενίαν: the metaphor is that of a stranger offered hospitality by a host.

11. See Matt 11:27, Luke 10:22.

12. An allusion to Arius's well-known theological songs employing popular meters to spread his message to as wide a segment of the Alexandrian public as possible. These songs are exemplified by the surviving, though fragmentary, *Thalia*. See Athanasius, *C. Ar.* 1.2; *Decr.* 16.3; Socrates, *Hist. eccl.* 1.9; Philostorgius, *Hist. eccl.* 2.2.

ally perceive that you have been expelled from the church of God? You are ruined—know this well—if you do not take a look at yourself and condemn your present folly. But you will say that crowds are helping you and are relieving your cares.

19.18. Listen then for just a little while and lend your ears, unholy Arius, and perceive your own folly. And you, God, protector of all, may you be kindly to what is being said, as long as it adheres to faith. For I, your human representative, who graciously has consideration from you, shall plainly show from the oldest of the Greek and Latin writings that the madness of Arius was foretold and spread abroad some three thousand years ago by the Erythrean sibyl.[13] 19. For she herself said, "Woe to you, Libya, lying in coastal lands. For a time will come for you in which you along with your citizens and your daughters will be compelled to undergo a fearsome, savage, and utterly grievous struggle, when judgment will be passed on all those of faith and piety, but you shall tumble to the extremes of ruin. For you have dared to upend the vessel of heavenly flowers and rend it asunder with biting and certainly have defiled it with teeth of iron."[14] 20. What then, you villain? Where on earth do you admit you are now? Clearly you are there, for I am holding your missives, which you have scribbled to me with the reed pen of madness, in which you assert that all the Libyan people are of the same opinion, as a safeguard for yourself, of course. But if you deny that this is so, I now testify by God that I am actually sending the oldest documentation of the Erythean sibyl, compiled in the Greek tongue, to Alexandria, in order that you might perish more swiftly. 21. Are you then blameless, two-faced scoundrel? Are you not then plainly ruined, wretched man, you who have surrounded yourself with such fearsomeness? We know. We know your ventures. The sort of thinking, the sort of fear that disturbs you, has not eluded us, unfortunate and miserable man. Oh, the obtuseness of your mind! You who do not remove the sickness and perplexity from your own soul. Unholy man! You who undermine the truth with artful words and are the sort not to feel shame at censuring us and even now are trying to disprove us, as you think anyhow, and now

---

13. The Erythrean sibyl was one of ten canonical sibyls, a special class of ancient prophetess who offered enigmatic prophecies. The Erythrean sibyl hailed from Erythrae, an ancient Greek city in Asia Minor. In the fourth century, quoting sibyls as proof of the divine origins of Christianity was in fashion. For example, on the Erythrean sibyl and Christianity, see Constantine, *Orat. sanct.* 18–19; Lactantius, *Inst.* 1.6.10.

14. Sib. Or. 3.332–338.

again once more are admonishing us as if you were the sort of person who excelled in faith and words, from whom the wretched of course desire to procure assistance for themselves. 22. And yet one ought not to associate with such a person, nor address him whatsoever, unless someone should think that for the average person the hope of living rightly lies in these treacherous words of his. 23. But this is not so, and indeed far from it. But truly—oh for your foolishness, however many of you are mixed up with this man—what madness has compelled you to endure this man's grievous tongue and countenance?

19.24. Very well. But now I shall advance on you yourself in my argument, you—a fool in spirit, yet glib of tongue, and faithless of mind! Give me here a level field for discourse, not enormous, I say, and suited to horsemanship, but rather an easily demarcated circuit, only not decaying but vibrant and firm by nature, you who are plainly unholy and most wicked of dissemblers. For I am being impelled to say these things. And furthermore, I shall fasten a noose about you now, tie your feet together with my argument, and stand you right in the middle, so that the entire populace may fully comprehend your deficiency.[15] 25. And I shall now proceed to the issue itself. My hands, you see now, are washed. Let us approach with prayers. Call on God indeed. Or rather, refrain for a little while and tell me, you greatest of firebrands, what god will you call on for aid? For certainly I cannot keep my peace. 26. Master who has lordship over all things, Father of singular power, on account of this unholy man here your church bears both reproaches and griefs and indeed even wounds and pains. Arius is already affixing a space for you, and quite cleverly, at which he is setting up a council for himself, I suppose, or rather taking hold of and restraining your Son who comes from you and is the author of our aid, by the law of adoption.[16] 27. Listen, I entreat you, to this astonishing creed. He thinks,

---

15. In this oblique passage, Constantine alludes to bringing Arius as a condemned man before a large crowd in a Roman circus (or hippodrome). The metaphor of a demarcated circuit metaphorically calls to mind such venues for horse racing. The circus, like the arena, was a venue for the emperor to interact with the people, and therefore defeated enemies of state were paraded in front of the people to demonstrate the ruling emperor's might. See McCormick 1986, 59–60, for the later but illustrative example of the defeated pretender John being paraded in the circus of Aquileia by Valentinian III and Galla Placidia in 425 CE. Constantine metaphorically threatens Arius with similar treatment.

16. Arius was subject to accusations of adoptionism—the notion that the sonship of the Son is an accident of God's adoption of him, rather than essential to him—due to his emphasis on ontological distinction between Father and Son. See, for example,

Master, that you, the source of motion, are moved throughout space. He dares to circumscribe you within a circuit of a confined station. But is there anywhere your presence is not? Or anywhere that all do not perceive your activity from your laws, which pervade all things? For you yourself envelop all things, and outside you it is not at all appropriate to conceive that there is either space or anything else. And so your power is boundless with activity. May you, God, indeed listen, and you, all you people, pay attention. 28. For this shameless and useless man, who has pushed on to the peak of reprobacy and lawlessness alike, dissembles piety. "Far be it," he says, "I do not want for God to seem to be subject to the suffering of outrages. 29. And for this reason, I for my part am suggesting and devising astonishing things, at least as far as faith is concerned, that God, when he had made the newly begotten and newly created *ousia* of Christ, prepared an aid for himself, as it appears to me, at least. For whatever you should detach from him," he says, "this you have made lesser."[17] 30. Then, corrupter and destroyer, is this your belief? Do you, according to this proposition, also accept as a fabrication the one who condemned the fabrications of the gentiles? Are you calling him extrinsic and some sort of servant of duties, and one who, without thought or reason, perfected all things just by coexisting with the Father's eternity? Ascribe now, if indeed you dare, ascribe to God, I say, both precaution and expectation for what shall come to pass, as well as reflection, reasoning, declaration and articulation of considered judgment, and, in short, delight, laughter, grief. 31. What then are you asserting, man more wretched than the wretched, veritable counselor of evil? Understand now, if you are able, that, being reprobate, you are destroyed by your very act of villainy itself. 32. "Christ," he asserts, "experienced sufferings for our sake." But I myself have already said previously that he was sent in the form of a body. "Yes," he says, "but there is concern lest we seem to diminish him in some respect." Then, agent of the beasts, when you say these things, are you not mad and clearly raving? For indeed, behold, the very world is a form or at least a configuration, and the stars have produced at least images, and in

---

the *Thalia*, where Arius emphasizes that the Son is a result of an act of the Father's will ("The one who is greater is able to beget one equal to the Son, but one more distinguished, greater, or grander he is not. The Son is as great as he is and what he is by God's will").

17. In other words, Arius is emphasizing that his astonishing theological articulations are intended to emphasize the mediating activity of the Son in creation and the Father's absolute impassibility and ontological distance from created things.

short the spirit of this spherical globe is an image of what exists, a sort of form. And nevertheless, God is present everywhere. Where then are there any outrages in God? Or in what way is God lessened? 33. You parricide of clemency! Consider then indeed, making your judgment for yourself, and ponder whether God's presence in Christ seems to be an error. So then, he recognized the denigration of his Word and did not send retribution slowly. Moreover, without a doubt, sins occur in the world daily. And nevertheless, God is present, and the instruments of justice do not follow long after. How then does any lessening occur from this in regard to the greatness of his power, if the instruments of justice are perceived everywhere? Not at all, I reckon. 34. For the mind of the world comes through God. Through him comes all permanence, through him all justice. The faith of Christ exists eternally from him. And in short, the law of God is Christ, who possesses at the same time what is infinite and unending through him.[18]

19.35. Nonetheless, you appear to make up your own notions. Oh, the excessive madness! Turn now the devil's sword to your own destruction. And see indeed, all of you see that he already produces mournful cries, held fast by the bite of a viper, as his veins and his flesh are gripped in turn by poison and provoke terrible pains, as his entire, wasted body slips away—he is full of thirst and squalor, lamentation and pallor and countless evils, and he is terribly withered—that the tangle of his beard is repulsive and defiled, that he is fully half dead and already weakening in the eyes, that his face is drained of blood and melts away beneath his fear, that all these things converge on him together—frenzy, madness, and folly—and have made him wild and bestial by the long duration of his suffering. 36. For example, not perceiving what evil he has indeed met with, he says, "I am exalted by pleasure and I leap, bounding with joy, and take wing." And then on the other hand, with all the excessive impetuousness of youth, "Well then," he says, "we have been undone." 37. This at least is true. For on you alone has the evil bestowed the zeal that comes from it in abundance, and what was bought at a great cost, this has most easily been granted to you. Indeed, come now and say, where are your holy precepts? Wash yourself, then, in the Nile, if you can, man full of outrageous insensibility. And indeed, you at least have endeavored to confound the entire inhabited world with your impieties. 38. Do you at least understand that I, the human

---

18. The preceding sentences equates the Son/Logos with the Stoic concept of the divine rationality ("mind") that structures the world.

agent of God, already know all these things? But yet I am at a loss as to whether I ought to stay or to leave. For I am not able to look upon this any longer, and I am ashamed at this sin, Arius, oh Arius! You have led us into the light but have cast yourself down into shadow, miserable man. The end of your labors has revealed this to you.

19.39. But I return to this point once again. You say that there is a crowd of people to be found on your side. That is likely, I think, and certainly receive them. Receive them, I say. For they have devoted themselves to be food for wolves and lions. Except, however, that even each of these, when encumbered by an increase of ten tax-shares and the duty to repay these, will certainly begin to sweat straightaway, unless they run as swiftly as they can to the saving church and enter into the peace of love through affection for harmony.[19] 40. For they will not indeed be deceived hereafter by you when you have been convicted for your wicked conscience, nor will they endure being completely destroyed for being entangled in your polluted inquiries. Your sophistry is clear and easily known to all, for the times to follow, anyhow. And you yourself will not be able to accomplish anything but will plot in vain, feigning clemency and mildness of words and putting on an outward show of simplicity, so to speak. All your handiwork shall be in vain. For straightaway shall the truth encircle you; straightaway shall the downpour of divine power, so to speak, extinguish your flames. 41. And assuredly, charge over the functions of public services will occupy your comrades and associates who have already become liable to the senate, if they do not flee as swiftly as possible and exchange their intercourse with you for the uncorrupted faith. 42. But you, iron-minded man, give me proof of your intention, if you have faith in yourself, and be firm in the steadfastness of faith and have an entirely clean conscience. Come to me. Come, I say, to the human representative of God. Trust that I shall delve deeply into the secrets of your heart by my questions. But if it should seem that anything mad remains, calling on divine grace, I shall make you better than the paradigm of health. But if you should appear healthy in matters of the soul, upon recognizing the light of truth in you, I shall direct thanks to God, and I will rejoice in myself for your piety.

19.43. *And in another hand*,[20]

---

19. Constantine threatens to overtax Arius's supporters until they abandon him.

20. Letters were often dictated by their authors to an amanuensis, who wrote down the letter. The sender would then sign with his own name, as a sign of authenticity and familiarity. Attention was often drawn to portions of text written in one's own

Appendix 1: The Byzantine Epistolary Supplement 283

God will protect you, beloved ones.
This was conveyed by Synkletius and Gaudentius, agents of the magister officiorum, *and these things were read in the palace when Paterius was governor of Egypt.*

Against Eusebius and Theognius (*Urk.* 27; Athanasius, *Decr.* 41; Anonymous Cyzicenus, appendix 1)

This letter provides the opportunity for a useful case study on the variances between surviving versions of Cyzicenus's source texts and the versions presented in his *Ecclesiastical History*.[21] Preserved in its complete form in Athanasius's documentary appendix to *De decretis*, the letter appears in truncated form in Theodoret (*Hist. eccl.* 1.20.1–10), beginning from the middle of section 9. Cyzicenus's version of the letter (1.11.22–31) begins at the exact same point as Theodoret's. However, it is uncertain whether Cyzicenus drew his text directly from Theodoret or whether both relied on the same intermediary text, possibly the history ascribed to Gelasius of Caesarea (see the introduction to this volume) or, if Hansen is correct about the material that immediately precedes the letter in Cyzicenus's narrative, Philip of Side's ecclesiastical history. No other material near the excerpt appears to be drawn directly from Theodoret.

The following translation adheres to the version of the letter preserved in the epistolary appendix to Cyzicenus, which can be found at the end of the 1918 edition by Loeschcke and Heinemann and largely agrees with the independent Athanasian tradition. We have used typeface to indicate where the two versions vary from each other. The footnotes clarify where these variants are unique to Cyzicenus and where they are shared by other versions of the letter. **Boldface** indicates words that are absent from Cyzicenus, *Hist. eccl.* 1.11. <u>Underlining</u> indicates where Cyzicenus, *Hist. eccl.* 1.11, has an alternative term. [Square brackets] indicate where Cyzicenus,

---

hand versus that of a scribe, including in the New Testament (e.g., Rom 16:22, 1 Cor 16:21, Gal 6:11).

21. Opitz dated this letter to 325, while the new edition of the *Urkunden* dates it slightly later, to 326–327. A Latin version of this letter also survives in Paris Lat. 1682 and was edited by Schwartz in *ACO* 4.2, p. 102, included in the Loeschcke and Heinemann (2018) edition as a supplementary apparatus. With this letter, Constantine directs the Nicomedians to accept a new bishop in place of Eusebius, who had just been deposed at Nicaea.

Hist. eccl. 1.11, presents text absent from the appendix. The last category demonstrates some of the characteristic variants found throughout Cyzicenus's history.[22] In addition to the usual minor discrepancies often found across different branches of a textual tradition, the unique text in Cyzicenus (1) offers additional guidance to the reader, in the form of prepositional phrases that identify the actor or object of an action left unspecified in other versions; (2) characterizes the figures in the narrative, often with judgments on their morals or doctrinal beliefs; and (3) reinforces the piety and sincerity of the champions of Nicene orthodoxy, particularly Constantine, but also Eusebius of Caesarea.

■ ■ ■ ■ ■ ■ ■ ■ ■ ■ ■

1. Constantine Augustus to the universal church of the Nicomedians

Of course, you all clearly know that our master, God, and Savior, Christ, are Father and Son, beloved brethren. I assert that the Father, without beginning and without end, is the parent of eternity itself and that the Son is this: the will of the Father, which he did not take on himself through any sort of contemplation, nor was he compelled to accomplish his works by means of some externally sought *ousia*.[23] For the man who does think or will think this, this man will have an unceasing expectation of every kind of punishment. 2. But yet the Son of God, Christ, the crafter of all things and provider of immortality itself, was begotten as far as pertains to the faith in which we have put our trust. He was begotten, or rather he himself proceeded, since even at all times he is in the Father, for the regulation of the things that came into being through him. He was begotten, now, by proceeding without causing separation. For at the same time the divine will fixed itself in its dwelling place, and it accomplished and governed those matters that necessitated differing degrees of care according to the qualities of each. 3. What then? Is there anything between God the Father and God the Son? Nothing at all, clearly. For the fulfillment of these acts itself undertook the command of the divine will by knowledge and did

---

22. See introduction, §6.1.

23. The preceding clauses are directed against two notions associated with Arius: first, that the Son's existing at the Father's will implies a distinction in their essence, and second, that the Father chose or adopted an essence other than himself as a tool for creation.

not separate its will to be divided from the _ousia_ of the Father.[24] And the following is consequent on those points: who is there who, as an attendant of my master, Christ, has more to fear for showing reverence than if they should appear foolish? 4. Does the Divine then suffer, when the inhabitation of the sacred body has the impulse to come to know its own holiness, or is that which is separate from the body subject to physical sensation? Does not that which is separated from the lowest humility of the body stand apart? And do we not live, even if the glory of our soul should call our body to death?

5. Now then, what has the inviolate and unmixed faith accepted that is worthy of hesitation? Or do you not see that God selected a most holy body, through which he intended to manifest proofs of faith and illustrations of his own virtue, and to repel the destruction of the human race that had been stirred up already by deadly error; to provide a new teaching on worship and to cleanse the unworthy undertakings of the mind through his example of purity; and then to put an end to the torment of death and to proclaim the rewards of immortality? 6. But you all, whom fellowship of love fittingly causes me hereafter to address as brethren, are not ignorant that I am your fellow servant; you are not ignorant of the fortress of your salvation, care for which I have legitimately taken on myself, and through which we not only battled against the armaments of our enemies but also bound them in spirit, still living, for the sake of exhibiting the true faith of benevolence. 7. But I took joy in these good things particularly on account of the renewal of the inhabited world. For it was worthy of wonderment truly to win so many nations over to agreement when just a little before they were said to be ignorant of God. Only, what were these nations, which used to pay no heed to contentiousness, bound to learn? Why then do you think, beloved brethren, that I am blaming you yourselves? We are Christians and are in a pitiable state at variance. 8. Is this our faith? Is this the teaching of our most holy law? Yet what is the reason for which the ruin of this present evil has awakened? Oh, the absurdity! Oh, the excess of hatred that exceeds the magnitude of any censure! What fearsomeness of this band of robbers has come to light, which denies that the Son of God proceeds from the undivided _ousia_ of the Father? Is not

---

24. "The fulfillment of these acts" (αὕτη ... ἡ τῶν πραγμάτων συμπλήρωσις) here refers to Christ as the embodiment of the divine plan for the world fulfilled through incarnation.

God everywhere, and furthermore do we not perceive that he is present with us at all times? Or did the orderly arrangement of the universe not come together through his power? And was it not spared the divisiveness of separation?

9. Then what have you done? O beloved brethren, understand now, I pray, the torments of the grievance at hand. You used to profess that you were confessors of the one whom you deny exists, since that all-destructive teacher has convinced you of this. I ask you,[25] who is it who thus has taught the innocent crowd these things? Eusebius, obviously, the fellow initiate in this tyrannical savagery. For since he has become the usurper's protector[26] on all sides, it is possible to see him from every quarter. **For**[27] the murders of the bishops testify to this—of those truly bishops, at any rate—and the harshest persecution of Christians expressly cries out to this fact. 10. For I will at present say nothing of the **injuries** done to me [...[28]], through which, when the onslaughts of the opposing factions were most strongly engaged [...[29]], he used to send spying eyes against me **secretly**[30] and did all but contribute armed assistance to the usurper [...[31]]. 11. And let no one think that I am unprepared to prove these claims. For there is definitive proof, namely that it is publicly known that I have caught the presbyters and deacons who <u>followed along with</u>[32] Eusebius. But **I am passing over**[33] these matters, which I bring up now not out of wrath but in

---

25. Everything after this sentence appears at 1.11.22–31. Differences between the texts in Cyzicenus and the text of the Byzantine epistolary supplement are reflected in the translations.

26. Both versions of the letter found in Cyzcienus's manuscripts give προσφύλαξ ("guardian"). Theodoret and Athanasius give instead πρόσφυξ ("client"), which Hansen (2002) prints at 1.11.22.

27. 1.11.22 omits the particle γάρ ("for") found in the other three versions.

28. 1.11.23 supplies παρ' αὐτοῦ ("on his account"). Theodoret is the only source to give the preposition περί in the phrase "nothing of/about [περί] the injuries," while Theodoret, the appendix, and Athanasius have a definitive noun ὕβρεων ("injuries") absent at 1.11.23.

29. 1.11.23 supplies καθ' ἡμῶν ("against us"). Whether this is intended as the royal "us," meaning Constantine, or the collective of the orthodox is unclear.

30. The appendix is the only version of the letter to give ὑπέπεμπε ("to send secretly") instead of the neutral ἔπεμπε ("to send").

31. 1.11.23 supplies αὐτῷ χάριν ("out of gratitude to him").

32. 1.11.24 has παραπεμπομένους ("who were sent by"); all other versions have παρεπομένους ("who followed along with").

33. The verb παρίημι ("I pass over") in the other three versions has become πὰρ'

order to shame them. This alone have I feared; this alone do I ponder: that I see you have been called into association with this charge. For through the conduct[34] and perversion of Eusebius, you have taken on[35] a conscience devoid of truth. 12. But the treatment is not too late, at least if you now receive a faithful and inviolate bishop and look to God. And indeed, this is in your hands at present and [...[36]] would necessarily have depended on your judgment even long before, had not the aforementioned Eusebius come here by the cunning [...[37]] of those who then[38] supported him and shamelessly disturbed the uprightness of your situation.

13. But since occasion has come to say a few things to your affection concerning this same Eusebius [...[39]], your forbearance will recall that a council [...[40]] took place at the city of the Nicaeans, where I myself was also fittingly present in service to my own conscience, since I desired nothing other than to bring about a general concord and to reprove and shake off in the presence of all that affair that had its beginning through the frenzy of Arius of Alexandria, and then immediately became entrenched through the absurd and deadly zeal of Eusebius. 14. But this very Eusebius, most dear and honored ones, supported [...[41]] false doctrine that has been

---

ἡμῶν ("by us") at 1.11.24.

34. 1.11.24 supplies διαγωγῆς ("lifestyle"), where the other three have ἀγωγῆς ("conduct").

35. 1.11.24 agrees with Theodoret, presenting εἰλήφατε where the appendix and Athanasius have ἀνειλήφατε, both variants of verbs of taking or receiving.

36. 1.11.25 repeats the connective relative article here (i.e., "and this would necessarily").

37. This passage is vexed in the manuscript traditions. The appendix and Athanasius present the dangling adjective δεινῇ ("cunning") with no noun, although marginalia in the Athanasius manuscript offers the alternative ἢ δεῖνα (i.e., "Eusebius or his clever tricks"). Theodoret's text has instead δίνῃ (i.e., "by a whirlpool" of his compatriots), a reading taken up into the later Latin translation of the letter (cod. Paris Latin 1682, ACO 4.2, p. 102, also printed alongside the appendix in Loeschcke and Heinemann 1918). 1.11.25 supplies the noun προαιρέσει ("plot"), which not only resolves the dangling adjective and confusing genitive case of συλλαβομένων ("supporters") in the appendix and Athanasius but fits the context well enough to suggest Cyzicenus's source text had a high-quality copy of the letter and was independent of Theodoret.

38. Both the appendix and 1.11.25 supply a τότε ("then") absent in Theodoret and Athanasius.

39. 1.11.26 supplies μακροθύμως ἀκούσατε ("listen patiently").

40. 1.11.26 supplies ἐπισκόπων ("of bishops").

41. 1.11.27 supplies αὐτοῦ ("his").

refuted on every front—you know well with what a crowd, since he succumbed to his very own conscience, and with how great dishonor—sending various men secretly to me who made a case on his behalf and requesting some manner of alliance from me, in order that he might not, once proven guilty in so great an offense, be cast out[42] of the office belonging to him. My witness to this is God himself, and may he remain beneficent to me and you, since that man [...[43]] turned even me around and unfittingly misled me, [...[44]] which you all also [...[45]] will come to understand. For at that time all things were accomplished [...[46]] just as he himself desired, since he was then concealing all such evil in his own[47] mind.

15. But first, in order that I might leave unmentioned the rest of this man's perversity, hear, I beseech you, in particular what he has plotted with Theognius, whom he holds as an associate in [...] folly.[48] He had commanded that certain Alexandrians who had withdrawn from our faith be sent here, since the fire of the discord was being stoked through their min-

---

42. 1.11.27 gives ἐκπέσοι ("fall from") where the other three versions have ἐκβάλλοιτο ("be cast out of").

43. Where the other versions have simply ἐκεῖνος ("that man"), 1.11.28 has instead αὐτὸς ἐκεῖνος Εὐσέβιος ("that Eusebius himself").

44. 1.11.28 provides a lengthy clause here: ἀλλ' ἡ θεία με πρόνοια ἐπὶ τὴν ἀληθεστάτην αὐτῆς ὁδὸν ἐπαωνήγαγεν ("but divine providence led me down its truest path"). The position of this clause changes the focus of the audience's recognition; rather than their recognizing how Eusebius misled the emperor, they instead recognize the working of divine providence. Similar textual variants that diminish Constantine's culpability and reinforce his sincerity, orthodoxy, deference to bishops, and good standing with God appear frequently in Cyzicenus's history.

45. 1.11.28 supplies ἐπέγνωτε καῖ ("recognized and"), uniquely implying that the audience is already in agreement with Constantine about the causes and effects of his interactions with Eusebius.

46. 1.11.28 gives several additional specifications here compared to the other versions: παρ' αὐτοῦ ... Εὐσεβίου τοῦ ἀνοσίου λέγω ("by him ... I mean by the unholy Eusebius"). These additions present two frequent patterns in Cyzicenus's textual variants: first, additional guiding pronouns, often in places where the context is clear enough that they are not necessary to understanding the passage; second, characterizing adjectives for the protagonists and antagonists of the narrative.

47. In a minor difference, 1.11.28 has αὐτοῦ ("his") where other versions have ἑαυτοῦ ("his own").

48. In the place of ἀνοίας ("folly") presented by the other witnesses, 1.11.29 has ἀνοσίας αὐτοῦ προαιρέσεως ("his unholy intent"), repeating the adjective for Eusebius uniquely attested in 1.11.28 (see note above).

istry. 16. But these noble and good bishops,[49] whom the truth of the council had once kept penitent, not only welcomed[50] those men and ensured their safety at their own residences but even shared with them in the malice of their ways. On account of this, I have decided to do the following concerning those ingrates: I have ordered that those who have been caught be banished as far away as possible. 17. Now it is up to you to look to God with that faith, which[51] has in certainty always come to be and which is established always to exist, and act in such a way[52] that we may rejoice that we have holy, orthodox, and beneficent bishops. But if anyone should dare without due consideration to be all on fire either[53] for remembering or praising those destroyers, he shall immediately be repressed from his own daring through the action of the servant of God, that is, me. God will preserve you, beloved brethren.

(Untitled) (*Urk.* 28; Athanasius, *Decr.* 42;
Anonymous Cyzicenus, appendix 2)

1.[54] The Victor, Constantine Augustus to Theodotus,

How great the strength of divine wrath has grown is easy for even you to learn from what Eusbius and Theognius have suffered who, drunkenly abusing the most holy worship rite, defiled the name of the savior God by the company of their den of thieves even after meeting with clemency. For when, especially following the like-minded concord of the council, it was most necessary for them to set aright their previous error, at that time

---

49. Constantine here co-opts the language of nobility in referencing these bishops, referring to them as "noble and good" (κάλος κἀγαθός) or *boni* ("good men") in the Latin. An approximation of the sarcasm might be "these gentlemen-bishops."

50. Where the appendix and Athanasius have ὑπεδέξαντο, 1.11.30 and Theodoret have ἐδέξαντο, variants on verbs of welcoming and receiving.

51. 1.11.31 supplies the pronoun ὑμᾶς ("you"), making the addressees the subject of the following verbs, and faith the means by which the addressees have their being.

52. Neither Athanasius nor Theodoret includes the conjunction ἵνα ("that") found in both versions in Cyzicenus.

53. Neither Theodoret nor 1.11.31 has the extra conjunction ἤ attested by Athanasius and the appendix.

54. Opitz dates this letter to 325, while the new edition of the *Urkunden* dates it slightly later to 326–327. Theodotus was bishop of Laodicea and aligned theologically with Eusebius of Caesarea, Paulinus of Tyre, and others aligned to varying degrees with Eusebius of Nicomedia. On Theodotus see DelCogliano 2008.

they were caught clinging to the same absurdities. 2. On account of this, then, divine providence drove them away from its own people. And since it could not bear to see guiltless souls be corrupted by the frenzy of a few, even now it has demanded a worthy punishment of them, and it will exact an even greater punishment still in the time to come throughout every age.

3. We thought that this ought to be made clear to Your Sagacity in order that if any wicked advice of such people should settle on your character, as I do not think will happen, by removing this from your soul as befits your pure mind, you may be eager to present your sincere fidelity and undefiled faith to the Savior, God. For it is fitting for this to be done by the one who wishes to be deemed worthy of the unalloyed prizes of the life eternal.

And in another hand,
God will preserve you, beloved brother.

Appendix 2: The *Pinakes* for Book 3

Pinakes, the ancient equivalent of tables of contents, listed the chapter headings (*kephalaia*) of a book. In the case of the Ecclesiastical History, the chapter headings in the manuscript are directly related to the contents listed in the pinakes. The chapter headings for books 1–2 were written sequentially without regard for the book break (chapter 13 [ιγ'] = 2.1), since these two books were taken as a unit.[1] If these chapter headings were copied into a set of *pinakes* for books 1–2, this set of *pinakes* does not survive, likely due to the acephalous nature of the manuscript transmission. On the other hand, one set of *pinakes*, those for book 3, are partially preserved in manuscript A, the only manuscript to contain book 3. These *pinakes* are clearly based on the chapter headings of the book, with minor variations.[2] The preserved *pinakes*, however, continue past the point at which the text of book 3 breaks off and are therefore indispensable for reconstructing the ending of Anonymous Cyzicenus's history. Unfortunately, these *pinakes* are also incomplete. The evidence of Photius (see appendix 3) indicates that the history ended with the death and baptism of Constantine, which the surviving *pinakes* do not mention. How much of the story is left out between Constantine's rejoicing over Arius's death and his own baptism and passing is difficult to tell, but perhaps not very much, since Constantine and Arius were believed to have died in close temporal proximity to one another.

---

1. For the chapter headings and the *pinakes*, see Loeschke and Heinemann 1918, xxv, 26, 138–39, with Hansen 2002, xvii. Books 1–2 were described as "the proceedings in the holy council of Nicaea," while book 3 was described as "after the great council" in the headings found in manuscript A. Though the first set of *pinakes* is lost, the surviving chapter headings reflect this numbering scheme.

2. Major deviations from the surviving chapter headings in the main text of the *Ecclesiastical History* are noted in the footnotes, though minor variations (e.g., differences in word order, lack or presence of an article) are passed over.

The Contents of the Third Book of the *Ecclesiastical History*

1. Concerning the proceedings after the great synod.[3]
2. Concerning the unceasing zeal of the most God-beloved emperor Constantine concerning divine matters.[4]
3. A letter of the emperor to Eusebius Pamphilius concerning the building of churches.[5]
4. A letter of the same man concerning the production of the holy books.[6]
5. A letter of the same man to Macarius, bishop of Jerusalem, concerning the salvific tomb.[7]
6. Concerning the journey of the blessed Helena to Jerusalem.[8]
7. Concerning the discovery of the holy cross of Christ.
8. Concerning the forum of pious Constantine.[9]
9. Concerning Frumentius and Edesius and those in innermost India.
10. Concerning the Iberians and the people of Laz and of the holy captive woman among them.
11. A letter of the emperor Constantine to Shapur the king of the Persians concerning the care of the people of God.[10]
12. Concerning Constantia the sister of the all-praiseworthy emperor Constantine and the Arian presbyter whom she introduced to him.
13. The document of the feigned repentance of Eusebius of Nicodemia and Theognius of Nicaea.
14. Part of the letter of the emperor Constantine to Athanasius.[11]
15. A letter of the most God-beloved emperor Constantine to Alexander, bishop of Alexandria.
16. The end of a letter of the emperor Constantine written on behalf of Athanasius to the church of the Alexandrians.

---

3. This heading does not correspond to the heading in the text, which reads, "The Efforts Taken by the Pious Emperor Constantine after the Great Council in Nicaea."

4. The chapter heading omits "most God-beloved" (θεοφιλεστάτου) and the name Constantine.

5. The chapter heading includes the name Constantine.

6. This letter is also addressed to Eusebius of Caesarea. The chapter heading, which varies slightly in wording, also does not make this clear.

7. The chapter heading has "from Constantine the pious emperor" rather than "of the same man," and omits Macarius's name.

8. The chapter heading has εἰς for ἐπὶ, although both roughly mean "to" in context.

9. The chapter heading has "Emperor Constantine" for "pious Constantine."

10. The word for "emperor" and "king" is the same in Greek, βασιλεύς. The terms carried slightly different valences when used to describe Roman and non-Roman rulers.

11. The chapter heading omits Constantine's name.

Appendix 2: The *Pinakes* for Book 3

17. A letter of the emperor Constantine to the council assembled in Tyre.
18. A letter from the most God-beloved emperor Constantine to the bishops in Tyre who had moved quarters from Aelia.[12]
19. A letter of the most God-beloved emperor Constantine to Arius and to the Arians.[13]
20. A prayer of the victory-bringing and God-beloved emperor Constantine concerning the most shameful death of Arius.
21. A letter of emperor Constantine to Pistus, bishop of Marcianopolis.[14]
22. Another letter of the emperor Constantine to the same bishop.

---

12. The manuscript has ἰταλίας ("Italy") for αἰλίας ("Aelia," i.e., Jerusalem), an obvious mistake that was corrected by Ceriani (1861) in his *editio princeps*. It also gives only "God-beloved" instead of the superlative form.

13. The evidence of the *pinakes* allows us to know that this letter, which survives in other sources and is included in appendix 1, was originally included in the *Ecclesiastical History*.

14. Pistus of Marcianopolis is essentially unknown (see note to 2.28.12). If these two letters had survived in Cyzicenus, we would know a great deal more about the man.

Appendix 3: The Testimony of Photius

Photius (ca. 810–after 893) was twice patriarch of Constantinople (858–867 and again from 877–886) as well as one of the preeminent scholars of the ninth-century resurgence of classical knowledge, sometimes called the Macedonian Renaissance.[1] One example of Photius's extensive classical knowledge is his *List of and Description of Books We Have Read*, more commonly known as the *Myriobiblion* or *Bibliotheca*.[2] The *Bibliotheca* contains descriptions of some 386 different books, arranged under headings commonly referred to as codices (singular codex).[3] Photius twice remarks that he is avoiding books widely known, such as school authors (*Bibl.* preface 1; postface 545). We can infer from these comments that Photius was interested in reading uncommon and even rare authors, suggesting that Anonymous Cyzicenus's *Ecclesiastical History* was not a particularly well-known book. Photius commented on the text on two occasions, once while describing the proceedings, or *acta*, of several ecumenical church councils (cod. 15–20) and later in a tangled set of descriptions that demonstrate the patriarch's confusion about the authorship of Anonymous Cyzicenus's *Ecclesiastical History* and that of Gelasius of Caesarea (cod. 88–89). Photius's description of Cyzicenus's work also provides key details about the missing portions of the work, most significantly that the work ended with the death and baptism of the emperor Constantine.

Photius, *Bibliotheca*, Codex 15, 4b

The *acta* of the first council were read in three parts. The book bore the inscription of Gelasius though it was less of an *acta* than a history. It

---

1. For Photius generally, see Wilson 1996, 89–119; White 1981.
2. On the *Bibliotheca*, see Treadgold 1980 along with Wilson 1996, 93–111.
3. The number of books is more than the number of codices the text is divided into (280). This figure comes from Treadgold 1980, 5.

was lowly and humble in style, but nevertheless it details carefully what occurred in the council.[4]

Photius, *Bibliotheca*, Codex 88–89, 66a–67b

A book was read along the lines of a history[5] concerning what happened at the council in Nicaea. And the book is in three parts.

And it says that Hosius of Cordoba, and Vito and Vicentius, priests from Rome, were present representing Sylvester of Rome; and that the famous Eustathius of Antioch was there himself, and Alexander, who at that time had the rank of presbyter, was present in the stead of Metrophanes of Constantinople. For Metrophanes himself was prevented by his very advanced age, since his lifespan had extended over one hundred years.[6] And it says that Alexander of Alexandria was present as well, along with Athanasius, who later stood as the successor to his seat.[7] And furthermore, Macarius of Jerusalem and an additional number of high priests and priests were there.[8]

And it asserts that the council was assembled in the sixteenth year of Constantine's rule and that the proceedings of this council extended to halfway through the twenty-second year, that is, when this council was in

---

4. The testimony of cod. 15 shows that already in the ninth century the *Ecclesiastical History* was taken by some readers to be the *acta* of Nicaea, an assumption that persisted through the Byzantine period and into the Renaissance.

5. Photius reasserts the generic intermediacy of this text, on which he already commented in cod. 15.

6. See above, 2.5.3–4. Photius adds the detail that Metrophanes lived past the age of one hundred, probably relying on another source for the information (see BHG 1279 12.4–7, 21.7–8).

7. See above, 2.7.44.

8. Macarius is introduced in the Dispute with Phaedo (2.24.8) before being formally introduced as a participant of the proceedings. Photius's list of the major participants is therefore not derived from the order presented in the text but seems based on a desire to go through the bishoprics of the so-called pentarchy, the five most authoritative bishoprics ("patriarchies") who had special privileges and responsibilities: Rome, Constantinople, Alexandria, Antioch, and Jerusalem. This system developed gradually over a century or more, beginning with the *Novellae* 131 of the emperor Justinian (after 534 CE), which formalized the patriarchal status of these five sees. They do not therefore reflect any hierarchy of bishoprics that existed when Cyzicenus wrote, let alone one that existed during the Council of Nicaea, though the Nicene canons did grant special authority to the bishoprics of Alexandria, Rome, and Antioch (see 2.32.6).

session for six and a half years.⁹ And it asserts that Arius was condemned and subject to an anathema, and that he then tried once more to be readmitted.¹⁰ And it asserts that in pursuit of this he was often supported by Eusebius, who had control of Nicomedia, and by Eutocius, the Arian who had been ordained presbyter, whom the sister of the emperor, Constantia, introduced to her brother as she reached the final day of her life.¹¹

Although these men were eager to reintroduce Arius to the church, divine justice did not allow the enemy to dance in triumph through its temple and along its portico but adjudicated that he end his life among the latrines, on the very day he and his partisans appointed to profane the church of God and its holy rites through his entry. And his destruction took place in public. For the latrines happened to be located near to the forum.¹² And it records that the great Constantine rejoiced over this, since the incorruptible judge resolved the whole controversy by the sentences he pronounced, and that he himself wrote letters to many people, in which he makes an official record of Arius's justified destruction.¹³

And this is what he says, agreeing in this matter with the great Athanasius, Theodoret, and many others.¹⁴ To some others it seemed right to record that Arius thus shamefully disappeared from humanity not in the time of the great Constantine but when his son Constantius was emperor.¹⁵

---

9. See 2.37.27–28. In that passage, Anonymous Cyzicenus actually states that the synod lasted until the twentieth, rather than the twenty-second, year. Photius is either misremembering what he read or intentionally interpolating the date from another source ("correcting" Cyzicenus), or else his manuscript copy had a textual variant or corruption.

10. See 2.26. The attempt to have Arius readmitted to the church is a prominent theme throughout book 3.

11. See 3.12.

12. Photius is our chief testimony that the *Ecclesiastical History* included the well-known scene of the death of Arius, found in other ecclesiastical historians (Gelasius, F22; Rufinus, *Hist. eccl.* 10.14; Socrates, *Hist. eccl.* 1.38.6–9; Sozomen, *Hist. eccl.* 2.29.5, 2.30.2–4; Theodoret, *Hist. eccl.* 1.14.8). The *pinakes* merely state that the history included a document recounting Constantine's joy over Arius's death.

13. This detail about the lost portions of book 3 accords with the evidence of the *pinakes*. See appendix 2, 20–22 with notes *ad loc.*

14. Athanasius was the ultimate source of the account of the death of Arius (*Ep. mort. Ar.* 2–4; *Ep. Aeg. Lib.* 19), and Theodoret included a citation of Athanasius's account in his version (*Hist. eccl.* 1.14).

15. See, e.g., Rufinus, *Hist. eccl.* 10.14–15; Gelasius, F22.

And these things constitute this book. But the name of the person who wrote it has not been inscribed on it.[16] However, in another book that contained the same events, I found inscribed on the book "Gelasius, bishop of Palestinian Caesarea."

The manner of expression tends excessively toward the lowly and ordinary style of speaking. Whoever this Gelasius is, I have not been able to learn with certitude. For up to now, it can be surmised, we have come across the books of three bishops of Caesarea named Gelasius, or at the very least two. And as to the books in which we came across them, one was composed *Against the Anomoeans*, but the other two, one of which we have just referred to in summary form, deal with ecclesiastical matters.[17]

In the place where we have found its title, this book has the following title: "Three Treatises on Ecclesiastical History by Gelasius, bishop of Palestinian Caesarea." And it begins thus: "An account of the holy, great, and ecumenical council of bishops gathered in the city of the Nicaeans from practically all the provinces of the Roman world and from Persia," and so forth.[18] And it ends at the death of the great Constantine, at which time he received remission of sins by divine baptism, washing away the stains in his life, of the sort which one who is human is apt to incur.[19]

And it asserts he received baptism from an orthodox priest who initiated and completed the rite, and not, as some supposed, by the hands of one of the heretics. But some delay put off his baptism because he had most earnestly desired to be baptized in the waters of the Jordan.[20]

---

16. Photius's comment suggests that either the start of the work had fallen out in manuscript tradition ("acephalous") or else that the name of the author was not included with the text.

17. Gelasius of Caesarea did indeed compose a treatise titled *Against the Anomoeans* that Photius later commented on in the *Bibliotheca* (cod. 102, 86a). The theological fragments are collected, discussed, and translated by Wallraff, Stutz, and Marinides (2018, 256–69).

18. See *proem.* 1.

19. Photius is our only testimony that the *Ecclesiastical History* ended with the baptism and death of Constantine.

20. Socrates (*Hist. eccl.* 1.39–40) and Sozomen (*Hist. eccl.* 1.34) also record that Constantine was baptized at the end of his life, as does Eusebius in an independent tradition (*Vit. Const.* 4.61), while Theodoret adds the detail that he only delayed baptism because he wished to be baptized in the Jordan (*Hist. eccl.* 1.32.1). Jerome (*Chron.* 337) records that Eusebius of Nicomedia baptized Constantine. The assertion that Constantine was baptized on his deathbed by an anonymous "orthodox" priest is unique

This writer asserts that he flourished in the time of Basiliscus, who overthrew Zeno and ruled as a usurper, and that he read the proceedings of the council on old pages while he was still living in his father's house. And he asserts that he composed this history while he still retained memory of them and was collecting as much as was useful from other writings. And he recalls also certain passages from a certain Gelasius, naming him Gelasius and Rufinus at the same time. And he says that his fatherland was Cyzicus and that his father was a certain one of the presbyters there.[21] And this person is the father of that book, and these things constitute the book.

89. The remaining book contains the following title: "*Proemium* of the bishop of Palestinian Caesarea to the events after the *Ecclesiastical History* of Eusebius Pamphili," and it begins thus: "Others who have set out to write a history and have determined to recall to memory the histories of events" and so forth.

And he says that he himself was a nephew on his mother's side to Cyril of Jerusalem and was urged by him to compose this account. And we have discovered when reading elsewhere that Cyril himself and this Gelasius translated the history of Rufinus of Rome into the Greek tongue and did not in fact compose their own history.[22] And it is clear that this Gelasius, if indeed he flourished during the time of Cyril of Jerusalem, is older than the one mentioned previously. This Gelasius, moreover, differs from him by his greater eloquence in speaking. However, each of them is inferior by far to the one who has written *Against the Anomoeans*.[23] But he, too, is described as bishop of the same Palestine. But that Gelasius, at least, in his manner of speaking, broad knowledge, and his approaches to discursive methods, which—I do not know how—he even managed to use tastelessly, leaves the other two far behind, who in their writing style occupy a lower rank. But whether one of them is himself the writer who both collected

---

to Anonymous Cyzicenus. Photius repeated this information in one of his sermons on Arianism (*Hom*. 15). See Photius 1958, 255.

21. Photius has created this biography from the information in *proem*. 2–14, 20–24.

22. For the common confusion of Gelasius and Rufinus, see the introduction, section 6.2.3, with Wallraff, Stutz, and Marinides 2018, xxx–xxxvii.

23. Photius's attempt to assign authorship based on style is erroneous insofar as ancient writers wrote in different stylistic registers for different genres of writing. Gelasius of Caesarea may have written both texts.

these accounts over time and added on what was missing, I have not yet been able to discover.[24]

---

24. Photius seems to mean Anonymous Cyzicenus here, since this description matches Cyzicenus's own description of his project, especially in regard to collecting accounts and adding them together. See *Hist. eccl. proem.* 20–24, 1.5.3, 2.31.10, 2.37.29–30, 3.16.10–11.

Appendix 4: The 1599 *Editio Princeps* and the Attribution to "Gelasius of Cyzicus"

One year before the publication of their *editio princeps* of Anonymous Cyzicenus's *Ecclesiastical History*, publisher Fédéric Morel wrote to translator Robert Balfour the letter included below, which was later printed in the editio princeps. In flowery language full of legal puns, Morel explains how celebrated French jurist François Pithou found reference to the text that Balfour was translating and Morel was making preparations to publish in the writings of Photius (see appendix 3). The passages of the *Bibliotheca* that are appended as "proof" of the author's name being "Gelasius" are heavily edited and gloss over Photius's own confusion and uncertainty. It is unclear whether Morel or Pithou is responsible for the selective editing seen here, but Morel used this testimony to justify printing the work under the name Gelasius (changing the toponym to "of Cyzicus"). On the authority of Morel and Balfour's edition, the *Ecclesiastical History* was attributed to Gelasius of Cyzicus until Gunther Christian Hansen challenged the attribution in 2002 (see the introduction, §1).[1]

Fédéric Morel,[2] *clarissimus vir*,[3] sends greetings to Robert Balfour.[4]
I will tell you, my dear Balfour, that books without an author are pitiable; like children with no sure father, they are liable to dubious legal claims.

---

1. The Latin text used in this translation comes from Kecskeméti 2014, 128. Unfortunately, Kecskeméti (16, 128) reproduces the false attribution to "Gelasius" in this work.

2. Fédéric Morel II (1552–1630) was the son of the *impremeur de roi* Fédéric Morel I (1523–1583) and later took over that position himself (from 1571 to 1603). Though he was appointed to the chair of Latin eloquence at the royal college in 1586, Morel was primarily a Hellenist who published and edited numerous late antique Greek authors in his career. For Morel's life and works, see Kecskeméti 2014, 15–23.

3. This is one of several antiquarian Roman-styled titles used throughout the letter, a common affect of much early modern European literature.

4. Robert Balfour (ca. 1553–ca. 1621) was a Scottish Catholic, humanist, and

It gratified the jurisconsult François Pithou to summon a father from the camps of Photius (whose testimony I will presently append below) so that anyone at all could plead its case.[5]

In addition, I have summoned another advocate to defend the text from the injury that the "winged ministers of words" (as Ausonius calls *tachygraphs*[6]) have introduced.[7] I refer to a codex jotted down by a learned and industrious hand, a codex that the most decorated and most learned senator, Pierre de l'Estoile,[8] has fetched for us from his own well-stocked library, has liberally shared, and—according to that humanity that is characteristic of the man—has often with me compared it to your example and our drafts. For I suppose there will be no lover of virtue and literature who should not recognize, hold to, and, if possible, return this favor. But if these things have not yet been emended by the judgment of the mind, what is just and good ought to be well considered and nothing dared *para dunamin*.[9] Farewell and love me as you do. Paris. 9 days before the kalends of January 1598.[10]

From the *Summary of Books He Has Read* by Photius, patriarch of Constantinople:

A book of the *acta* of Nicaea was read, exhibiting itself as a history. It was also divided into three parts.

A little later. In another codex containing these same things I found inscribed the name of Gelasius bishop of Palestinian Caesarea. Indeed, the beginning of the book was of this sort, "what in the holy, great, and universal," etc., and it ended with the death of the great Constantine.

Aristotle scholar who sought refuge in France during the religious tumult of the sixteenth century.

5. François Pithou (1543–1621) was a parliamentary lawyer in Paris and brother to Pierre, a classical scholar and jurist. This entire section is full of legal metaphors, probably in part because the testimony from Photius was provided by this eminent legal expert.

6. Morel includes the Greek term ταχυγράφους ("shorthand writer"). The words in quotation marks are a near quotation of Ausonius, *Ephemeris* 2.7.1–2.

7. Elsewhere in the edition Balfour complains about the poor quality of the manuscript he has been working with. Morel suggests the new exemplar will help correct this additional "injury" to the book.

8. Pierre de l'Estoile (1546–1611) was a high-ranking French bureaucrat.

9. "Beyond one's ability." This final expression is also written in Greek in Morel's text.

10. I.e., 24 December 1598.

Then he appends.[11] The same one recalls certain words of Gelasius,[12] whose fatherland, he asserts, was Cyzicus. And this one is certainly the parent of this book.

---

11. The "he" here presumably refers to Photius. The corresponding Greek text simply reads "and a little bit later" (καὶ μετ'ὀλίγα).
12. Pithou is already calling the anonymous author "Gelasius" by this point.

Works Cited

Works on *The Ecclesiastical History*

Editions and Translations of the *Ecclesiastical History*

Balfour, Robert, ed. and trans. 1599. *Gelasii Cyziceni Commentarius actorum Nicaeni concilii*. Paris: Apud Federicum Morellum.

Ceriani, Antonio. 1861. "ΓΕΛΑΣΙΟΥ ΤΟΥ ΚΥΖΙΚΗΝΟΥ ΛΟΓΟΣ ΤΗΣ ΕΚΚΛΗΣΙΑΣΤΙΚΗΣ ΙΣΤΟΡΙΑΣ ΤΡΙΤΟΣ." Pages 129–76 in *Monumenta sacra et profana*. Vol. 1.2. Milan: Typis et impensis Bibliothecae ambrosianae.

Hansen, Günther Christian, ed. 2002. *Anonyme Kirchengeschichte (Gelasius Cyzicenus, CPG 6034)*. GCS NS 9. Berlin: de Gruyter.

———, ed. and trans. 2008. *Anonymus von Cyzicus, Historia Ecclesiastica Kirchensgeschichte*. FontChr 49. Turnhout: Brepols.

Loeschke, Gerhard, and Margret Heinemann, eds. 1918. *Gelasius Kirchengeschichte*. GCS 28. Leipzig: Hinrichs.

Studies on Anonymous Cyzicenus and the *Ecclesiastical History*

Croke, Brian. 2018. "Gelasius of Cyzicus." In *The Oxford Dictionary of Late Antiquity*. Edited by Oliver Nicholson. Oxford: Oxford University Press.

Ehrhardt, Christopher T. H. R. 1980. "Constantinian Documents in Gelasius of Cyzicus, Ecclesiastical History." *JAC* 23:48–57.

Hansen, Günther C. 1998. "Eine fingierte Ansprache Konstantins auf dem Konzil von Nikaia." *ZAC* 2:173–98.

Heyden, Katharina. 2006. "Die Christliche Geschichte des Philippos von Side mit einem kommierten Katalog der Fragmente." In *Julius Africanus und die christliche Weltchronik*, 209–43. Edited by Martin Wallraff. Berlin: de Gruyter.

Louth, Andrew, ed. 2022. "Gelasius of Cyzicus." *ODCC*.

Mai, Angelo. 1841. "Historiae Ecclesiasticae Fragmentum: Ex Codice Mediolanensi Bibliothecae Ambrosianae." *SRom* 6:603–10.
Nautin, Pierre. 1983. "Gélase de Cyzique." Pages 301–3 in *Dictionnaire d'histoire et de géographie ecclésiastiques*. Vol. 20. Paris: Letouzey et Ané.
———. 1992. "La continuation de l'*Histoire ecclésiastique*' d'Eusèbe par Gélase de Césarée." *REByz* 50:163–83.
Shedd, Martin. 2022. "The Mask of Compilation: Authorial Interventions in Anonymous Cyzicenus." *GRBS* 62:494–525.
Tandy, Sean. 2023. "Hagiographic History: Reading and Writing Holiness in the *Ecclesiastical History* of Anonymous Cyzicenus." *JLAnt* 16:106–29.
Treadgold, Warren. 2007. *The Early Byzantine Historians*. Basingstoke, UK: Palgrave Macmillan.

General Bibliography

Late Antique and Byzantine Texts

The Acts of the Council of Constantinople 553. 2009. Translated by Richard Price. TTH 51. Liverpool: Liverpool University Press.
Brennecke, Hans Christof, Uta Heil, Annette von Stockhausen, and Angelika Wintjes, eds. 2007. *Bis zur Ekthesis Makrostichos*. Fascicle 3 of *Dokumente zur Geschichte des Arianischen Streites 318–430*. Part 1 of vol. 3 of *Athanasius Werke*. Berlin: de Gruyter.
Cyril of Alexandria. 1987. *Letters 1–50*. Translated by John I. McEnerney. Washington, DC: Catholic University of America Press.
Epiphanius of Salamis. 2013. *The Panarion of Epiphanius of Salamis, Books II and III: De Fide*. Translated by Frank Williams. Leiden: Brill.
Eusebius. 1903. *Eusebius Werke*. Edited by Eduard Schwartz. Vol. 2. Leipzig: Hinrichs.
———. 1952–1958. *Ecclesiastical History*. Edited and translated by Gustave Bardy and Pierre Périchon. SC 31, 41, 55, 73. Paris: Cerf.
———. 1975. *Life of Constantine*. Vol. 1.1 of *Eusebius Caesariensis Werke*. Edited by Friedhelm Winkelmann. Berlin: de Gruyter.
———. 1999. *Life of Constantine*. Translated by Averil Cameron and Stuart G. Hall. Oxford: Oxford University Press.
———. 2019. *Ecclesiastical History*. Translated by Jeremy Schott. Oakland: University of California Press.

Wallraff, Martin, Jonathan Stutz, and Nicholas Marinides, eds. 2018. *Ecclesiastical History: The Extant Fragments, with an Appendix Containing the Fragments from Dogmatic Writings*. Translated by Nicholas Marinides. GCS NS 25. Berlin: de Gruyter.
George the Monk. 1904. *Chronicle*. Edited by Charles de Boor. Leipzig: Teubner.
Photius. 1958. *The Homilies of Photius, Patriarch of Constantinople: English Translation, Introduction, and Commentary*. Translated by Cyril Mango. Cambridge: Cambridge University Press.
Price, Richard, and Michael Gaddis, trans. 2007. *The Acts of the Council of Chalcedon*. 3 vols. TTH 45. Liverpool: Liverpool University Press.
Socrates Scholasticus. 1995. *Kirchengeschichte*. Edited by Günther Christian Hansen. GCS NS 1. Berlin: de Gruyter.
Theodoret of Cyrrhus. 1998. *Kirchengeschichte*. Edited by Léon Parmentier and Günther Christian Hansen. GCS NS 5. Berlin: de Gruyter.
Tromp, Johannes. 1993. *The Assumption of Moses: A Critical Edition with Commentary*. Leiden: Brill.
Wickham, Lionel. 1983. *Cyril of Alexandria: Select Letters*. Oxford: Clarendon.
Winkelmann, Friedhelm, ed. 1982. "Vita Metrophanis et Alexandri: BHG 1279." *AnBoll* 100:147–83.

Secondary Sources

Arnold, Gottfried. 1729. *Unpartheyische Kirchen- und Ketzer-Historie: vom Anfang des Neuen Testaments biss auf das Jahr Christi 1688*. Frankfurt: Bey Thomas Fritschens.
Aubineau, Michael. 1966. "Les 318 serviteurs d'Abraham (Gen., XIV, 14) et le nombre des pères au concile de Nicée (325)." *RHE* 61:5–43.
Ayres, Lewis. 2004. *Nicaea and Its Legacy: An Approach to Fourth-Century Trinitarian Theology*. Oxford: Oxford University Press.
Backus, Irene, ed. 1997. *The Reception of the Church Fathers in the West: From the Carolingians to the Maurists*. Leiden: Brill.
Barnard, Leslie W. 1973. "Athanasius and the Meletian Schism in Egypt." *JEA* 59:181–89.
Bassett, Sarah. 2004. *The Urban Image of Late Antique Constantinople*. Cambridge: Cambridge University Press.
Bjornlie, Shane. 2017. *The Life and Legacy of Constantine: Traditions through the Ages*. London: Routledge.

Brock, Sebastian. 2016. "Miaphysite, Not Monophysite!" *CNS* 37:45–54.
Brown, Peter. 1992. *Power and Persuasion in Late Antiquity: Towards a Christian Empire*. Madison: University of Wisconsin Press.
Constas, Nicholas. 2003. *Proclus of Constantinople and the Cult of the Virgin in Late Antiquity: Homilies 1–5, Texts and Translation*. Leiden: Brill.
DelCogliano, Mark. 2008. "The Eusebian Alliance: The Case of Theodotus of Laodicea." *ZAC* 12:250–56.
Digeser, Elizabeth DePalma. 2000. *The Making of the Christian Empire: Lactantius and Rome*. Ithaca, NY: Cornell University Press.
Drake, Harold A. 2000. *Constantine and the Bishops: The Politics of Intolerance*. Baltimore: Johns Hopkins University Press.
Drijvers, Jan Willem. 1992. *Helena Augusta: The Mother of Constantine the Great and the Legend of Her Finding of the True Cross*. Leiden: Brill.
Edwards, Mark. 2015. *Religions of the Constantinian Empire*. Oxford: Oxford University Press.
Frend, William H. C. 1972. *The Rise of the Monophysite Movement: Chapters in the History of the Church in the Fifth and Sixth Centuries*. Cambridge: Cambridge University Press.
———. 1985. *The Donatist Church: A Movement of Protest in Roman North Africa*. Oxford: Oxford University Press.
Frendo, David. 2001. "Constantine's Letter to Shapur II, Its Authenticity, Occasion, and Attendant Circumstances." *BAI* 15:57–69.
Fruchtman, Diane Shane. 2018. "Early Modern Receptions of Late Antique Literatures." Pages 597–610 in *A Companion to Late Antique Literature*. Edited by Scott McGill and Edward J. Watts. Hoboken, NJ: Wiley & Sons.
Gaddis, Michael 2009. "The Political Church: Religion and State." Pages 512–24 in *A Companion to Late Antiquity*. Edited by Philip Rousseau. Chichester: Wiley-Blackwell.
Gavrilyuk, Paul L. 2021. "The Legacy of the Council of Nicaea in the Orthodox Tradition: The Principle of Unchangeability and the Hermeneutic of Continuity." Pages 327–46 in *The Cambridge Companion to the Council of Nicaea*. Edited by Young Richard Kim. Cambridge: Cambridge University Press.
Gentz, Günter, and Friedhelm Winkelmann. 1966. *Die Kirchengeschichte des Nicephorus Callistus Xanthopulus und ihre Quellen*. Berlin: Akademie.
Graumann, Thomas. 2021. *The Acts of the Early Church Councils: Production and Character*. Oxford: Oxford University Press.

Gregory, Tim. 1979. *Vox Populi: Popular Opinion and Violence in the Religious Controversies of the Fifth Century A.D.* Columbus: Ohio State University Press.

Gwynn, David M. 2009. "The Council of Chalcedon and the Definition of Christian Tradition." Pages 7–26 in *Chalcedon in Context: Church Councils 400–700*. Edited by Richard Price and Mary Whitby. Liverpool: Liverpool University Press.

Hall, Stuart. 1998. "Some Constantinian Documents in the *Vita Constantini*." Pages 86–104 in *Constantine: History and Historiography*. Edited by Samuel N. C. Lieu and Dominic Monserrat. New York: Routledge.

Hanson, R. P. C. 1988. *The Search for the Christian Doctrine of God: The Arian Controversy, 318–381*. London: T&T Clark.

Hauschild, W. D. 1970. "Die antinizänische Synodalsammlung des Sabinus von Heraklea." *VC* 24:105–26.

Humphries, Mark. 2008. "Rufinus's Eusebius: Translation, Continuation, and Edition in the Latin *Ecclesiastical History*." *JECS* 16:143–64.

Jefferson, Lee M. 2010. "The Staff of Jesus in Early Christian Art." *RelArts* 14:221–51.

Kaster, Robert A. 1988. *Guardians of Language: The Grammarian and Society in Late Antiquity*. Berkley: University of California Press.

Kazhdan, Alexander P. 1987. "'Constantin Imaginaire': Byzantine Legends of the Ninth Century about Constantine the Great." *Byzantion* 57:196–250.

Kecskeméti, Judit. 2014. *Frédéric Morel II: Éditeur, traducteur et imprimeur*. Turnhout: Brepols.

Lieu, Samuel N. C. 1996. "Introduction: Pagan and Byzantine Historical Writing on the Reign of Constantine." Pages 1–38 in *From Constantine to Julian: Pagan and Byzantine Views, a Source History*. Edited by Samuel N. C. Lieu and Dominic Monserrat. London: Routledge.

———. 2012. "Constantine and Legendary Literature." Pages 298–322 in *The Cambridge Companion to the Age of Constantine*. Edited by Noel Lenski. Cambridge: Cambridge University Press.

Löhr, Winrich Alfried. 1987. "Beobachtungen zu Sabinos von Herakleia." *ZKG* 98:386–91.

MacMullen, Ramsay. 2006. *Voting about God in Early Church Councils*. New Haven: Yale University Press.

McCormick, Michael. 1986. *Eternal Victory: Triumphal Rulership in Late Antiquity, Byzantium, and the Early Medieval West*. Cambridge: Cambridge University Press.

Meyendorff, John. 1989. *Imperial Unity and Christian Divisions: The Church, 450–680 AD*. Crestwood, NY: St. Vladimir's Seminary Press.

Miller, Patricia Cox. 2005. "The Subintroductae." Pages 117–49 in *Women in Early Christianity: Translations from Greek Texts*. Washington, DC: Catholic University of America Press.

Mor, Menahem. 2016. *The Second Jewish Revolt: The Bar Kokhba War, 132–136 CE*. Leiden: Brill.

Mosshammer, Alden. 2008. *The Easter Computus and the Origins of the Christian Era*. Oxford: Oxford University Press.

Oakley, Francis. 2003. *The Conciliarist Tradition: Constitutionalism in the Catholic Church, 1300–1870*. Oxford: Oxford University Press.

Parvis, Sara. 2006. *Marcellus of Ancyra and the Lost Years of the Arian Controversy, 325–345*. Oxford: Oxford University Press.

Schott, Jeremy. 2008. *Christianity, Empire, and the Making of Religion in Late Antiquity*. Philadelphia: University of Pennsylvania Press.

Scott, Roger. 2010. "Text and Context in Byzantine Historiography." Pages 251–62 in *A Companion to Byzantium*. Edited by Liz James. Chichester: Wiley-Blackwell.

———. 2015. "The Treatment of Ecumenical Councils in Byzantine Chronicles." In *Christians Shaping Identity from the Roman Empire to Byzantium: Studies Inspired by Pauline Allen*, 376–77. Edited by Geoffrey D. Dunn and Wendy Mayer. Leiden: Brill.

Smith, Kyle. 2016. *Constantine and the Captive Christians of Persia*. Berkeley: University of California Press.

Smith, Mark. 2018. *The Idea of Nicaea in the Early Church Councils, AD 431–451*. Oxford: Oxford University Press.

Stinger, Charles. 1985. *The Renaissance in Rome*. Bloomington: Indiana University Press.

Treadgold, Warren. 1980. *The Nature of the Bibliotheca of Photius*. Washington, DC: Dumbarton Oaks.

Van Dam, Raymond. 2014. *Remembering Constantine at the Milvian Bridge*. Cambridge: Cambridge University Press.

Van Liere, Katherine, Simon Ditchfield, and Howard Louthan, eds. 2012. *Sacred History: Uses of the Christian Past in the Renaissance World*. Oxford: Oxford University Press.

Van Nuffelen, Peter. 2002. "Gélase de Césarée: un compilateur du cinquième siècle." *ByzZ* 95:621–40.

Vessey, Mark. 2009. "Cities of the Mind: Renaissance Views of Early Christian Culture and the End of Antiquity." Pages 43–58 in *A Companion to Late Antiquity*. Edited by Phillip Rouseau and Jutta Raithel. Chichester: Wiley-Blackwell.

Wallraff, Martin. 2015. "Tod und Bestattung Konstantins bis Nikephoros Kallistou Xanthopoulos." Pages 101–8 in *Ecclesiastical History and Nikephoros Kallistou Xanthopoulos*. Edited by Christian Gastgeber and Sebastiano Panteghini. Vienna: Verlag der Österreichischen Akademie der Wissenschaften.

Warmington, Brian H. 1981. "Ammianus Marcellinus and the Lies of Metrodorus." *ClQ* 31:464–68.

Watts, Edward. 2013. "Theodosius II and His Legacy in Anti-Chalcedonian Communal Memory." Pages 269–84 in *Theodosius II: Rethinking the Roman Empire in Late Antiquity*. Edited by Christopher Kelly. Cambridge: Cambridge University Press.

White, Despina Stratoudaki. 1981. *Patriarch Photius of Constantinople: His Life, Scholarly Contributions, and Correspondence Together with a Translation of Fifty-Two of His Letters*. Brookline, MA: Holy Cross Orthodox Press.

Wiles, Maurice. 2001. *Archetypal Heresy: Arianism through the Centuries*. Oxford: Oxford University Press.

Wilson, Nigel G. 1996. *Scholars of Byzantium*. Rev. ed. London: Duckworth.

Winkelmann, Friedhelm. 1964. *Das Problem der Rekonstruktion der Historia Ecclesiastica des Gelasius Von Caesarea*. Berlin: VDI-Verlag.

———. 1966a. *Untersuchungen zur Kirchengeschichte des Gelasios von Kaisareia*. SDAWB 3. Berlin: Akademie, 1966.

———. 1966b. "Charakter und Bedeutung der Kirchengeschichte des Gelasios Von Kaisareia." *ByzF* 1:346–85.

Young, Frances M., and Andrew Teal. 2010. *From Nicaea to Chalcedon: A Guide to the Literature and Its Background*. 2nd ed. London: SCM.

Scriptural Passages Index

Old Testament

Genesis
- 1:3 — 132
- 1:16 — 132
- 1:26 — 121–27, 138, 142, 146
- 1:27 — 122, 127–28, 132, 133, 146
- 1:26–27 — 137, 158
- 1:31 — 128
- 3:23–24 — 108
- 18:1–15 — 232

Exodus
- 3:4 — 64
- 14:29 — 64
- 15:1–2 — 67
- 15:11 — 67
- 19:16 — 65
- 19:18 — 64
- 20:11 — 120

Joshua
- 5:14 — 65
- 10:11 — 65

1 Samuel (1 Kingdoms)
- 1:25 — 250
- 2:10 — 56
- 2:18 — 250

2 Samuel (2 Kingdoms)
- 22:14 — 56
- 22:15 — 65

2 Kings (4 Kingdoms)
- 19:8–37 — 105

2 Chronicles
- 32:1–23 — 105

Job
- 5:13 — 119
- 9:10 — 73
- 33:4 — 146
- 38:15 — 73

Psalms (LXX)
- 7:9 — 138
- 15 (14):5 — 187
- 19:4 (18:5) — 57
- 27 (26):3 — 250
- 33 (32):6 — 140, 147
- 33 (32):15–19 — 70–71
- 36 (35):9 — 156
- 43 (42):3 — 174
- 45 (44):2 — 90
- 48 (47):1 — 73
- 72 (71):18 — 73
- 82 (81):1 — 111
- 82 (81):6 — 111
- 88 (87):5 — 177
- 94 (93):10–11 — 138
- 98 (97):1 — 73, 147–48
- 110 (109):3 — 90
- 113 (112):7 — 73
- 119 (118):60 — 119
- 136 (135):4 — 73
- 136 (135):17–8 — 73

Psalms (cont.)
- 136 (135):23 — 73
- 139 (138):2–3 — 138
- 146 (145):6 — 120

Proverbs
- 8:22 — 129–34, 136, 140, 143–44
- 8:22–23 — 135
- 8:22–30 — 135
- 8:23 — 134
- 8:26 — 131–32, 143–44
- 8:26–30 — 135
- 18:3 — 91
- 26:11 — 185
- 30:18–19 — 137
- 33:15 — 137–8

Isaiah
- 2:3 — 72
- 6:1–6 — 175
- 9:6 — 129
- 13:11 — 235
- 26:6 — 179
- 37:1–38 — 105
- 40:28 — 127
- 41:13 — 127
- 41:17 — 147
- 41:20 — 147
- 44:6 — 156
- 45:21 — 156
- 48:12 — 156
- 53:4 — 74
- 65:17 — 179
- 66:12 — 155

Jeremiah
- 4:22 — 274
- 16:12 — 144
- 17:5 — 118
- 17:9 — 144, 160
- 23:24 — 148
- 25:9 — 144
- 30:12 — 144
- 40:18 — 144

Ezekiel
- 1:5–14 — 175
- 1:22–28 — 175
- 3:22 — 147

Daniel
- 2:21 — 73
- 5:6 — 154
- 7:18 — 179

Zechariah
- 14:20 — 221

Malachi
- 3:6 — 90, 156

Deuterocanon

Wisdom of Solomon
- 1:7 — 148

Baruch
- 3:23 — 130–31, 139, 140
- 3:32 — 131–34, 138
- 3:33 — 131
- 3:32–36 — 156
- 3:32–38 — 127, 131, 135
- 3:36 — 157
- 3:38 — 144, 157–58

Pseudepigraphal Works

Assumption of Moses
- 1:6 — 132
- 1:14 — 132–33
- 2–3 (Tromp, "The Lost Ending," Quotations) — 146–47

Odes of Solomon
- 12:15 — 123

Sibylline Oracles
- 3.332–338 — 278

Scriptural Passages Index

New Testament

Matthew
1:16	160
3:11	176
5:5	179
6:25	175
7:7	141
8:17	74
9:1–8	104
9:18–36	104
10:21	95
11:27	141, 277
12:42	138
13:31–32	139
14:13–21	103
14:22–33	104
15:32–39	103
18:17	88
19:3–9	183
19:6	190
24:4–5	91
25:31–46	163
27:38	219
28:19	56–57, 163, 197

Mark
1:4	161
2:1–2	104
2:27	136
4:26–27	175
4:30–32	139
5:21–34	104
6:31–44	103
6:45–52	104
8:1–9	103
10:1–9	183
10:9	190
13:6	91
13:12	95
14:18–21	91
15:27	219

Luke
1:2	160
1:26–38	160
1:35	105
1:52–53	73
2:52	161
5:17–26	104
8:40–56	104
9:12–17	103
10:22	141, 277
11:31	138
12:22	175
12:56	150
16:18	183
21:18	91
23:32–33	219
24:39	162

John
1:1	89, 117, 142
1:1–3	128
1:3	89, 124, 126, 137, 147
1:18	143, 159
1:29	177
2:19–22	162
3:16	89
4:24	149
4:38	174
6:1–14	103
6:16–21	104
7:37–39	156
8:12	174
8:42	155
8:44	178, 254
9:35–38	129
10:15	90
10:30	90, 124, 155
11	227
11:1–46	103
12:24	162
14:6	174
14:9	90
14:11	90, 155
17:24	134
19:18	219
20:27	142

Acts		3:27	176
1:3–11	162	6:11	283
2:5	99		
2:9	99	Ephesians	
2:9–11	98	3:5	155
5:3	148	4:3	87
9:15	129, 138	4:9	162
9:16	250	5:11–13	75
10:42	163	5:25–27	270
18:9	88	6:11	75
18:9–10	250		
22:22	265	Philippians	
23:11	250	2:7	143
23:12–35	250	2:8	177
24:3	56	2:10	153
		3:20–21	178
Romans			
1:3	160	Colossians	
3:6	137	1:15	90
5:14	162	1:16	90
8:9	149	1:26	155
8:21	176		
9:5	139, 160	1 Timothy	
16:17	88	1:7	56
16:22	283	2:4	228
		2:11–12	229
1 Corinthians		2:15	159
2:2	119–20	3:6–7	180
4:20	119	3:16	56, 159
8:6	90	4:1	91
12:4–6	149	5:19	257
12:6	149	6:16	123
12:11	149	6:19	178
12:12–13	203		
12:26	87	2 Timothy	
15:23	178	2:17	91
16:21	283	3:5	254
		4:1	163
2 Corinthians			
2:10	151	Titus	
3:17	149	1:14	91
6:14–15	89	2:13	179
Galatians		Hebrews	
1:1	56	1:3	90, 129

2:10	90
2:16	160
4:12	151
4:12–13	139
4:13	151
10:1–8	177
10:12	162
13:4	189
13:8	90

1 Peter
4:6	162

2 Peter
2:22	185
3:13	179

1 John
1:1	72
2:23	154, 157
5:6	148
5:10	148

2 John
10–11	92

Jude
9–10	132

Revelation
4	175
20:11–15	163
21:1	179

People and Places Index

Abraham, 99, 154, 160, 232
Acacius of Constantinople, 21
Acesius, 173–74
Achaia, 61, 98, 169, 210
Achillas of Alexandria, 85, 249
Adonis, 69
Adriatic Sea, 169
Aelia Capitolina. See *Jerusalem*
Aetius of Lydia, 256
Africa, 38, 170, 206, 223. *See also* Egypt, Ethiopia, Libya, Numidia, Mauretania
    Roman province, 170, 210
Aigai, 69, 233
Aksum. *See* Ethiopia
Alexander, first bishop of Constantinople, 32, 99, 110, 170–71, 210, 231, 256, 296
    hagiographic life of Metrophanes and Alexander, 32, 36, 39–40
Alexander III of Macedon (the Great), 65, 165
Alexander of Alexandria, 27, 38, 86–97, 115, 167, 169, 191–95, 209, 239, 246–50, 256, 292, 296
Alexander of Thessaloniki, 169, 210
Alexander the Great. *See* Alexander III of Macedon
Alexandria, 15, 17–18, 20–21, 27, 35, 80–81, 85–86, 92–93, 110, 115, 167, 171, 182, 191–95, 201–3, 209, 226, 239–40, 245–49, 251–54, 256, 262, 264, 266–69, 271, 276, 278, 287, 288, 292, 296
Allectus, 62
Amasya, 76

Ammianus Marcellinus, 224
Amphion of Nicomedia, 190, 241
Anastasius I, emperor, 21
Ancyra, Council of, 184
Antioch on the Orontes, 15–17, 19, 122, 130, 166, 168, 171, 182, 188, 210, 254–59, 296
    Councils at, 27–28, 94, 96, 196, 259
Aphaca, 69, 233
Aphrodite, 69, 215–16, 233, 275
Apollo, 233
Arabia, 98, 168, 209
Ares, 275
Arius, xi, 8–9, 11–12, 14, 22, 26–27, 29, 43, 50, 53–57, 72, 80, 84–89, 92–95, 110, 112–13, 115–16, 118–19, 121, 123, 144–45, 149, 151–52, 154, 157, 164, 166, 169, 183, 190–93, 196, 200–202, 211–14, 216, 238–48, 252, 256, 258–59, 262, 266–67, 271–72, 274–82, 284, 287, 291, 293, 297
Armenia, 168, 210
Arrian, 65
Arsenius, 263–265
Asclepas of Gaza, 263
Asclepius, 69, 233
Asia (Minor), 78, 98, 168–69, 171, 210, 278
Assyria, 105
Athanasius (the Great), 12, 14, 27–28, 37–38, 41, 43, 54, 79–80, 87, 92, 99, 104, 110, 115–16, 125, 130, 152, 166–67, 173, 192, 195–97, 201, 203, 209, 226, 245–256, 258–271, 273, 276, 277, 283, 289, 292, 296–97

Aurelian, 169
Baalbek. *See* Heliopolis
Bacchus, 216
Bacurius, *dux limitis Palaestinae*, 231
Bartholomew, apostle, 223
Basil of Caesarea, 23, 144
Basiliscus, emperor, 5–7, 9, 20–21, 55
Beirut, 80, 87
Belial, 89
Bithynia, 4–7, 9, 54–55, 82, 97, 165, 190
Britain, 62, 167
Byzantium, 82, 98, 170. *See also* Constantinople
Caecilian of Carthage, 94, 170, 210
Caesarea Cappadocia. *See* Leontius of Cappadocian Caesarea
Caesarea Palaestina. *See* Palestinian Caesarea
Calabria, 169, 210
Cappadocia, 70, 126, 147, 168, 210, 256
   Cappadocian fathers 23
Cappadocian Caesarea. *See* Leontius of Cappadocian Caesarea
Carausius, 62
Caria, 168, 210
Carthage. *See* Caecilian of Carthage
Cassiodorus, 42
Caucasus. *See* Iberia (Caucasus)
Celts, 61
Chalcedon, 19, 82, 110, 266
   Council of, ix–xi, 4–7, 12–26, 29, 41, 55, 57, 143, 171, 220
Chrestus of Nicaea, 190–91, 241
Christ. *See* Jesus
Chrysopolis, 82
Cilicia, 69, 98, 168, 206, 210, 233, 266
Coele Syria, 168, 210
Colluthus, presbyter of Alexandria, 92
Constans I, 84
Constantia, sister of Constantine I, 68, 75, 222, 238–241, 244, 292, 297
Constantine I (the Great), ix–xi, 7–12, 14, 26–29, 31–33, 39–42, 45–46, 50, 53, 55, 57–64, 66–70, 73–85, 93–113, 163–66, 168–73, 176, 185, 188, 193,

Constantine I (cont.)
   200–208, 211–223, 231–38, 240–41, 243–48, 250–55, 260–62, 266–70, 273–79, 282–93, 295–98, 302
Constantine II, 84
Constantinople, 12, 15–21, 32, 42–43, 93, 98–99, 110, 169–71, 210, 223, 231, 244, 246, 252, 254–56, 258, 267–68, 271, 295–96, 302
   Council of, 21, 23, 72, 122, 145
Constantius I Chlorus, 8, 10, 31, 58–59, 61–62, 64, 208, 219, 222
Constantius II, 84, 226, 238, 250, 297
Cordoba. *See* Hosius of Cordoba
Corybants, 216
Councils. *See* Ancyra, Antioch, Chalcedon, Constantinople, Ephesus, Nicaea, Serdica, Tyre
Crispus, son of Constantine, 77–78, 83–84
Cybele, 119, 216
Cyclades, 98, 171, 210
Cyprus. *See* Spyridon
Cyril of Alexandria, 15–21, 35
Cyril of Jerusalem, 64, 220, 299
Cyzicus, 1, 6–7, 9, 13, 54, 168, 210, 299. *See also* Gelasius of Cyzicus
Dacia, 169, 210
Dalmatius of Cyzicus, 6, 9, 13, 29–30, 50, 53–54
Daniel the Stylite, 21
Dardania, 169, 210
David, king of Israel, 119, 132, 139, 147, 156, 160, 179, 244, 250, 255
Decius, emperor, 173–74
devil. *See* Satan
Diocletian, 59, 61, 69, 113, 170
Diogenes Laertius, 65
Dionysius, consular, 261, 263
Dionysius, pseudographer, 175
Dionysius of Alexandria 239
Dioscorus of Alexandria, 18
Diospontus, 168, 210
Domnus of Antioch, 19
Donatus of Casae Nigrae, 170, 183

Dracilian, vice praetorian prefect, 217–18
Edesius, 223–26, 292
Egypt, 20, 43, 89, 94, 98, 110, 113, 167, 173, 182, 191–95, 206, 209, 224, 240, 251, 260, 263, 264, 271, 283. *See also* Alexandria
Elamites, 99
Ephesus, 42, 110
   Council of, xi, 6, 9, 14–17, 21, 42, 54–55
   Second Council of, 18–19
Epiphanius, 18, 23, 116, 144, 183
Epirotes, 98
Ethiopia, 9, 12, 167, 223–226
Eulalius of Antioch, 258
Eupsychius of Tyana, 126–29, 256
Europa (region), 61, 79, 169, 210
Europe (continent), 98, 237
Eusebius of Caesarea, 9–10, 14, 26–35, 37, 50, 54, 58–61, 66–69, 72–85, 93, 97–101, 104, 116, 125, 130–45, 151, 166–68, 171–72, 176, 182–83, 195–201, 203, 205, 207–9, 212–18, 223, 232–37, 239, 254, 256, 258–61, 284, 289, 292, 298–99
Eusebius of Nicomedia, 87–92, 109–10, 118, 166–67, 169, 190–91, 193, 241–47, 251–52, 254–59, 263, 267, 271, 274, 283–89, 292, 297
Eusebius Pamphili. *See* Eusebius of Caesarea
Eustathius of Antioch, 94, 122–23, 130, 166–68, 210, 245, 254–59, 296
Eutocius, presbyter, 10, 239–41, 297
   as unnamed Arian presbyter, 244–46, 254–55, 292
Eutyches, 6, 15–22, 24–25, 55, 57, 120, 143, 239
   followers of, 5–6, 9, 14–15, 20–22, 30, 55, 120, 159, 239
Eutychians. *See* Eutyches
Eutychius of Smyrna, 168, 210
Euzoeus, 88, 248
Evagrius, 18–21
Ezana, king of Aksum, 224–26

Fabian, bishop of Rome, 174
Felix of Aptunga, 170
Flacillus. *See* Flacitus of Antioch
Flacitus of Antioch, 258
Flavian of Constantinople, 16–19
Franks 62–63
Frumentius, 223–26, 292
Galatia, 168, 170, 210
Galerius, 61, 70, 113
Galla Placidia, 279
Gaul, 62–63, 167, 170, 206, 210
Gelasius of Caesarea, 1–4, 10, 64, 295, 298–99, 302
   reconstructed ecclesiastical history attributed to, 9, 23, 29, 32–37, 39–40, 60–61, 64, 67–68, 78–79, 82–83, 85, 87, 92–94, 98–100, 110–13, 117, 163, 166–67, 190, 212–14, 219–23, 226, 229, 232, 234, 238, 243, 245–47, 249, 252–53, 261–63, 268, 271, 283, 297
"Gelasius of Cyzicus," name formerly given to Anonymous Cyzicenus, 1–4, 301–3
Germans, 62
Georgia. *See* Iberia (Caucasus)
Gregory Nazianzen, 23
Gregory of Nyssa, 23, 116
Gregory the Illuminator, 168
Greece. *See* Achaia, Europa, Hellas
Greeks (Hellenes), 65, 69, 78, 82, 165, 172, 178, 232
Hadrian, 182
Hannah, 250
Hebrews. *See* Jews
Helena, mother of Constantine, 12, 27, 34, 168, 218–22, 232, 240, 292
Heliopolis, 69, 232–33
Hellas, 169, 210
Hellenes. *See* Greeks
Hellespont, 65
Hellespontus, 6–7, 9, 54, 168, 210
Heraclea. *See* Theodorus of Thracian Heraclea
Hilary of Poitiers, 99

People and Places Index

Hispania. *See* Spain
Homer, 275
Hosius of Cordoba, 10–11, 22–23, 41, 93–94, 97–98, 116, 118, 123–25, 167–70, 209, 256, 296
Iamblichus of Chalcis, 65
Iberia (Caucasus), 12, 226–31, 238, 292
Illyria, 61, 169, 210, 258
India, greater, 167–68, 210, 223
India, lesser. *See* Ethiopia
Ionian Sea, 61
Irenaeus, 18
Irene, 114–15
Irenopolis. *See* Narcissus of Neronias
Ischyras, 251–52
Italy, 44, 61, 63, 77, 167, 169, 206, 209, 293
Jerome, 166, 201, 224, 298
Jerusalem, 12, 64, 70, 72, 105, 159–61, 168, 170, 182–83, 209, 214, 216, 218–20, 232, 250, 255–56, 261–62, 266–68, 271, 292–93
Jesus, 17, 19, 25, 56–57, 60, 67, 73–74, 86, 90–91, 95, 103–4, 119–20, 129–30, 160–61, 165, 178–79, 195, 197–98, 205, 209, 220, 229–30
  named as Christ, 15–20, 160, 226–33, *passim*
  named as the Son, 54–57, 116–66, 198–200, *passim*
Jews, 64, 116, 129, 153, 173, 175, 178, 182, 195, 204–6, 249–50, 266
Joannes. *See* John, usurper
John, a presbyter, 9, 14, 29–31, 33, 58
John, usurper, 279
John Chrysostom, 23
John of Antioch, 16–17
John the Baptist, 114, 161
John the Evangelist, 89, 92, 128, 137, 142, 148
John the Persian, 168, 210
Julianus, consul, 165
Julius, bishop of Rome, 169
Justin I, emperor, 5
Justinian I, 261, 296
Lactantius, 62, 66, 70, 113, 236, 278

Laodicea, 169, 210, 256, 289
Lazi, 226–27, 292
Leo, bishop of Rome, 16, 18–19
Leontius of Cappadocian Caesarea, 126–29, 147–58, 168, 170, 210, 256
Libya, 43, 89, 98, 167, 170, 182, 192–95, 206, 209, 237, 278. *See also* Pentapolis
Licinius, 11, 31, 59–61, 68, 70, 74–80, 82–83, 87, 97, 100, 184–85, 213, 222, 238–39, 244
Lucian, 233
Lycopolis. *See* Meletius of Lycopolis
Lydia, 168, 210, 256
Macarius, presbyter of Alexandria, 251–52, 263–64
Macarius of Jerusalem, 159–163, 168, 183, 209, 214, 216–21, 232, 256, 292, 296
Macedonia, 61, 98, 165, 169, 210, 295
Manichaeus, 166
Mamre, 232
Marcian, emperor, 19
Marcianopolis. *See* Pistis of Marcianopolis
Marcion of Sinope, 166
Mark the Deacon, 263
Mareotis, 93, 251–52, 266–67, 271
Marinus of Troas, 168, 210
Maris of Chalcedon, 109–10, 266
Marmarica. *See* Theonas of Marmarica
Mars. *See* Ares
Matthias, apostle 223
Mary, mother of Jesus, 15, 25, 55, 57, 160–61
Mauretania, 170
Maxentius, 11, 30, 34, 60–63, 66–67, 70, 74, 97
Maximian, 59, 61, 113, 219, 222
Maximinus Daia, 11, 31, 34, 60–62, 69–71, 74, 113
Medes, 99
Mediterranean Sea, 169
Meletius of Lycopolis, 93, 191–95, 259, 263
Menophantus of Ephesus, 110

Meropius, 224
Mesopotamia, 98, 168, 210
Metrodorus, 224
Metrophanes of Constantinople, 98–99, 170, 296
hagiographic life of. See Alexander, first bishop of Constantinople
Moesia, 61, 169–70, 210
Narcissus of Neronias, 110, 266
Neronias. See Narcissus of Neronias
Nestorius, 15–16, 18–19, 21
Nicaea, 19, 54, 100, 110, 118, 165, 191, 219, 241–42, 246, 255, 266, 292.
    Council of, ix–xi, 1–3, 5–7, 12–15, 22, 42–46, passim
Novatian, 173–74, 183, 194
Numidia, 170, 210
Nunechius of Laodicea, 169, 210
Origen, 132
Orpheus, 65
Palestine, 98, 178, 209, 218, 231–32, 299. See also Palestinian Caesarea
Palestinian Caesarea, 28, 50, 168, 182, 196, 259. See also Gelasius of Caesarea; Eusebius of Caesarea.
Pamphilus of Caesarea, 78, 83. See also Eusebius of Caesarea
Paphlagonia, 168, 210
Paphnutius, 11, 113, 117, 189–90
Parthians, 99, 223–42
Paterius, governor of Egypt, 283
Patrophilus of Scythopolis, 110, 256, 267
Paul I of Constantinople, 171, 210
Paul of Samosata, 166, 188
Paul the Apostle, 90–91, 129, 138, 143, 149, 154, 159, 175, 178, 250, 265
Paulinus, consul, 165
Paulinus of Tyre, 289
Pentapolis, 167, 182, 192, 209
Persia, 12, 53, 98, 168, 210, 223–24, 231, 233–37, 292, 298
Peter, bishop of Alexandria, 85, 192, 249
Phaedo, 11, 14, 27, 41–44, 85, 118, 121–63, 168, 177, 183, 202, 256, 296
Phoenicia, 87, 98, 168, 209, 232

Phrygia, 98, 119, 169, 210, 216
Philip of Side, 14, 39–40, 61, 78, 82, 85, 100, 118, 238, 243, 245, 283
Photinus, 166
Photius, xi–xii, 1–4, 8, 9–10, 12, 33, 39, 41, 43–44, 60, 171, 239, 291, 295–303
Pistus of Marcianopolis, 170, 210, 272
Plato, 65, 122, 125, 139
Pontus, 76, 98, 168, 210, 226
Porphyry of Tyre, 65, 200–201
Postumus, 62
Protogenes of Serdica, 146–47, 169, 210, 256
Pseudo-Gelasius, name formerly given to Anonymous Cyzicenus, 4
Pseudo-Zachariah, 18–21
Ptolemais (Pentapolis). See Secundus of Ptolemais
Ptolemais (Thebaid), 182
Pythagoras, 65
Python, 233
Rhine, 61, 63
Robber Council. See Ephesus
Roman Empire, 9, 31, 53, 60–62, 83, 104, 168–69, 172, 212, 213, 223–24, 231, 234, 237, 298
Rome, city, 18, 44–45, 58–63, 66–70, 74, 77, 98–99, 116, 139, 167–71, 174, 182, 208–9, 224, 226, 232, 270, 296, 299
Rufinus of Aquileia, 4, 9–10, 14, 23, 25, 27–30, 33–36, 58, 60, 68, 78, 85–86, 88, 110–17, 120, 163, 166–67, 171, 179, 219–20, 223, 226, 228–32, 238–9, 242–43, 248–49, 255, 262–63, 297, 299
Sabellius, 166, 188
Sabinus of Heracleia, 30
Samuel, 250
Sapor. See Shapur II
Saracens, 231
Sarmatians, 61–62, 223
Satan, 57, 86, 89, 132, 146, 148, 178, 180, 202, 207, 213, 254, 274, 281
Sauri. See Sarmatians
Scythia, 61, 98, 169, 210
Secundus of Ptolemais, 88, 110, 193

Serdica, 169, 210
  Council of, 169
Shapur II, 234–37, 254, 292
Side. *See* Philip of Side
Sissinius of Constantinople, 54
Smyrna. *See* Eutychius of Smyrna
Socrates, ancient philosopher, 65
Socrates Scholasticus, 4, 30, 32–34, 36–40, 54, 65, 78, 82–83, 85, 87, 92–94, 98–100, 109–11, 121, 165, 167, 169, 171–73, 189–92, 195–97, 201, 203, 212–14, 222–23, 226–27, 229–30, 232–34, 238–39, 241–43, 245–47, 250–51, 253–57, 260–63, 267–68, 271, 277, 297–98
Sozomen, 30, 64, 100, 167, 169, 172, 190, 223, 229, 233, 242, 246, 253, 256, 259, 263, 297–98
Spain, 62–63, 93, 98, 116, 167, 206, 209
Spyridon, 11, 113–15, 117, 120, 189
Sylvester, bishop of Rome, 98, 296
Syria Coele. *See* Coele Syria
Syria Palaestina, 98, 182, 218, 259, 261
Tertullian, 188
Thebaid, 98, 182, 192, 264
Theodoret of Cyrrhus, 10, 19, 26, 27–29, 33, 34–40, 49, 79–80, 99–100, 109–10, 112, 130, 164, 166, 171–72, 183, 190–92, 195–97, 200, 203, 205, 207–8, 212–14, 216–24, 229, 234–38, 240–43, 245–46, 252–63, 265–67, 283
Theodorus of Thracian Heracleia, 110, 259, 266
Theodorus the Perinthian, 266
Theodosius II, 18–19, 204
Theodotus of Laodicea, 256, 289–290
Theognius of Nicaea, 79–81, 109–10, 118, 209, 190–91, 193, 241–44, 246, 255, 258–59, 266, 271, 274, 283–90, 292
Theonas of Cyzicus, 168, 210
Theonas of Marmarica, 88, 110, 193
Thessaloniki, 82, 88, 169, 210
Thessaly, 61, 169, 210
Thomas, apostle, 223
Thrace, 61, 98, 258–59, 266

Timotheus, presbyter, 263–64
Timothy Aelurus, 20–21
Trajan, 169
Trier, 28
Troas. *See* Marinus of Troas.
Tyana. *See* Eupsychius of Tyana
Tyre, 101, 226, 259–61, 266–68, 271, 289
  Council of, 260–64, 267–69, 271, 293
Ursacius, 266
Valentinian III, 279
Valentinus, 18, 166
Valerian, 236
Venus. *See* Aphrodite
Vicentius, presbyter of Rome, 98–99, 167, 209, 296
Vito, presbyter of Rome, 98–99, 167, 209, 296
Zeno, emperor, 4–6, 20–21, 55, 299
Zosimus, 233

www.ingramcontent.com/pod-product-compliance
Lightning Source LLC
Chambersburg PA
CBHW050856300426
44111CB00010B/1276